A Shared Authority

SUNY Series in Oral and Public History
Michael Frisch, Editor

A Shared Authority

Essays on the Craft and Meaning of Oral and Public History

Michael Frisch

State University of New York Press

Published by
State University of New York Press, Albany

Printed in the United States of America

For information, address State University of New York
Press, State University Plaza, Albany, N.Y., 12246

Library of Congress Cataloging in Publication Data

Frisch, Michael, 1942–
    A shared authority: essays on the craft and meaning of oral and
public history / Michael Frisch.
        p.   cm.–(SUNY series in oral and public history)
    Includes index.
    ISBN 0-7914-01321-4–ISBN 0-7914-0133-2 (pbk.)
    1. Oral history. 2. Public history. I. Title. II. Series.
D16.14.F75 1990
907'.2–dc19   88-37030
                                                                                CIP

10 9 8 7 6 5 4 3 2 1

Contents

Acknowledgments

Any author presenting a retrospective collection of occasional essays must necessarily carry a heavy burden of obligation, considering how many individuals may have been helpful in the development of one or another of the essays, much less in the shaping of the framework that hopefully lends them some collective coherence. When, as in the present case, the collection is relatively wide-ranging and the work surveyed spans some fifteen years, the debt is even more substantial and broadly distributed. Though such an intellectual and personal debt can never quite be repaid, it can be publicly acknowledged, an act that is at once a humbling and a deeply satisfying way to conclude the preparation of a book manuscript.

Thus I hasten to mention here individuals whose imprint is palpable, to me at least, in the pages that follow. Some have influenced the general development of my work, and some have been especially helpful in the focused work of particular essays. I will group my acknowledgments so as to follow the general organization of the book.

Section One is the most general, involving reflections on oral history, collective memory, and American culture and history. It also reaches back the furthest. In this sense the entire collection is grounded in, and my greatest debt is owed to, the primary intellectual community from which these essays all arose: my colleagues in the unique American Studies department at the State University of New York at Buffalo, especially Larry Chisolm, Charlie Keil, Liz Kennedy, Bob Dentan, and former colleagues Ellen Dubois and Lillian Robinson. As I began to explore the nascent field of oral history, I soon encountered a new group of colleagues beyond Buffalo, many of whom remain very central to my current work: these include Ron Grele, Jo Blatti, Don Ritchie, Sandro Portelli, Jackie Hall, John Kuo Wei Tchen, Michael Kline, and Linda Shopes. Most recently, the circle has come back to Buffalo, and I have a very special sense of gratitude to the group of very wonderful graduate students in—at last—my very first oral history seminar, taught this past semester while work on this book was being completed. Still closer to home, I continue to learn an immense amount from folklorist Mia Boynton about how social history, community studies, and public presentation can combine in scholarship that is at once intellectually trenchant, politically meaningful, and sharable with the communities from which it comes. Beyond that, sharing with her the process of watching the diverse pieces of this collection come together with a resonance she detected all along has been perhaps the single greatest pleasure I have had in completing this book.

The more particular debts attaching to each of the essays in this first section are numerous. Chapter One's essay on Studs Terkel drew me into oral history, and it traces to an American Studies project—the important if ephemeral journal *Red Buffalo*—inspired and managed by John Trimbur and Norman Plotkin, among other graduate students at SUNY-Buffalo then. A remarkable visiting colleague from Korea, Kim U Chang, contributed substantially to my essay and to *Red Buffalo*'s collective exploration of oral documents and tradition; he has been a continuing influence on my own thinking about culture and change through the years. And a former colleague in the SUNY-Buffalo History Department, David Hollinger, was also important in helping me see the broader implications of the work I did not then quite realize I was beginning in that early essay on Terkel.

The "Memory of History" essay emerged a few years later, influenced by a wider circle of colleagues and my growing interest in the links between oral history, documentary, and American culture and politics more broadly. I am especially grateful for the many helpful suggestions and critical readings this work received from Sue Benson, Steve Brier, and Roy Rosenzweig on its journey from a draft for the *Radical History Review* to its final appearance in their important collection *Presenting the Past* (Philadelphia, 1986). Many others contributed crucially to whatever insights this essay was able to bring together, including Daniel Walkowitz, Sam Schrager, Marcia Carlisle, and the Nigerian writer Chinweizu, another visiting Buffalo colleague, whose perspective is discussed in the text.

Chapter Three, "American History and the Structures of Collective Memory," was first published only recently, but I have been playing with its data for years while waiting, or so it seems now, for the framework giving my student surveys meaning to emerge out of current cultural discourse. Along the way I have drawn deeply on many discussions about the survey course and our students with History Department colleagues Bob Pope, David Gerber, and recently Mary Sheila McMahon. Others, including Michael Katz, Wilbur Zelinsky, Linda Shopes, Don Ritchie, Paul Thompson, Elizabeth Loftus, David Stricklin, and Jaclyn Jeffrey, have contributed substantially to the essay's approach to memory and culture, the latter two as organizers of a remarkable Baylor University conference on "History and Memory" at which this paper was first presented in its fullest form. In preparing the essay for publication in the *Journal of American History*'s special issue on memory, I was propelled and sustained by editor David Thelen's remarkable energy and imagination, and by his own clear thinking about the concerns that issue has helped place at the forefront of an agenda for American historians. My own essay profited immensely from Susan Armeny's equally formidable, incisive copyediting at the *JAH*.

The second section of this book focuses on some common issues of documentary, though each of the essays has a rather distinct genealogy. The study of unemployment that is the basis for Chapter Four was, as I discuss in the text and headnotes, a collective project by American Studies students and faculty at Buffalo. I am indebted to the entire group that worked so intensely to produce this documentary and to figure out what it meant, especially Dick Blau, Barry White, Patty Devinney, John Guicciardo, and particularly the co-author with whom I reported on the subsequent editing battle with the New York *Times*, Dorothy Larson. Dale Treleven and Ron Grele offered some especially helpful comments and criticisms when I first presented this analysis at the Savannah meeting of the Oral History Association.

My current project involving interviews with ex-steelworkers, the basis for the discussion and examples of editing that comprise Chapter Five, owes everything to the collaborator with whom I am so deeply privileged to be working, documentary photographer Milton Rogovin—an inspiration in every personal, political, artistic, and intellectual sense. Others who have helped in a variety of ways to give this project focus and depth include Ramsay Liem, Alex Keyssar, Peter Lunenfeld, and Patricia Kozma.

Chapter Six is an outgrowth of my association with the Long Bow Group in its spectacular ongoing project documenting life in the People's Republic of China, work I have been honored to share as an oral history consultant—in effect, an accessory "China non-expert" hopefully complementing a group of advisors imposingly grounded both in Chinese experience and expertise. The essay thus rests on the work and insights of Carma Hinton, Richard Gordon, Dan Sipe, Kathy Kline, David Carnochan, and Marilyn Young. Others who have been central in helping me refine the critical perspective and cultural analysis developed in the essay include Jo Blatti, Roger and Alison Des Forges, and several friends and students from the People's Republic of China—Xiao Ma, Qiming Ran, Lin Kei Mei, and Nini Yang.

My critique of *Vietnam: A Television Documentary* in Chapter Seven is an outgrowth of most of the previous chapters in the book, turning their collective insights to a very specific critical problem. As such, it draws on suggestions from many of the individuals already mentioned. But in particular, discussions with Ivan Jaksic, Sandro Portelli, Bret Eynon, Larry Chisolm, and Bill Graebner have been important in refining the focus and analysis of this piece.

As I discuss in the Introduction, the final section of this book considers aspects of public history and programming. In these essays, my academic background and scholarship in urban history finally began to come together with the newer interests in oral history and documentary. If the combination is at all synergistic, this owes a great deal to the stimulation of another group of colleagues thus brought within the circle of this book's focus, and thereby able to contribute as much as they have to whatever synthesis I have been able to achieve.

Chapter Eight is a bridge piece between my oral history work and broader issues of public programming. It emerged out of a series of workshops and presentations culminating in the National Federation of State Humanities Councils paper presented here; it has also informed my continuing work in public humanities. In all this, I have valued suggestions and criticisms offered along the way by Steve Weiland, David Brumberg, Marjory Lightman, and Gary Ostrower, and I am especially appreciative of my current opportunity to put some of these ideas into practice through the work of the New York Council for the Humanities, in conjunction with colleagues there who include Jay Kaplan, Elizabeth Janeway, and Jack Tchen.

The invitation that led to Chapter Nine offered me the singular opportunity to re-visit my earliest scholarship, a study of Springfield, Massachusetts, and I had the very special pleasure of discovering this to be not quite as irrelevant to current concerns as I might have thought twenty-year-old work would be. A consequent pleasure came in realizing how much some of my oldest friends and influences, academic and personal, remain important in my thinking: these include the late Robert A. Lively, Stephan Thernstrom, and two very precious Springfield friends, Harriette Michaels and the late Herbert Michaels.

I applied some of Chapter Nine's ideas to a somewhat different context in the next essay, dealing with the genre of urban history coffee-table books. I am grateful to Wendell Tripp for suggesting and skillfully editing this essay for its original publication in *New York History*. The work drew, additionally, on my more recent involvement in urban history exhibits and public programming, especially through the Buffalo and Erie County Historical Society, where I have appreciated the chance to work with a number of inspiring scholar/practitioners from whom I have learned a great deal: G. Rollie Adams, Bill Siener, Betsy Cromley, Tom Leary, and Scott Eberle.

Jo Blatti's imaginative Past Meets Present conference, which became an important book under the same title, (Washington, D.C., 1987), was the origin and context for Chapter Eleven's reflections on Ellis Island. These owe a great deal to the creativity and clarity Jo has brought to contemporary thinking about public history presentation, as well as to more particular discussions about audience with Daniel Walkowitz, Robert Weible, and especially the co-author of this piece, National Park Service historian Dwight Pitcaithley.

Chapter Twelve engages issues about social science and quantification central to the historiography of urban history scholarship. Nobody was more surprised than I to discover how germane these were to public-historical questions, and vice versa. The two came together while I served as a research professor at Theodore Hershberg's remarkable Philadelphia Social History Project, supported by funds from the National Endowment for the Humanities which I acknowledge very gratefully. I owe a very deep, long-term debt to Ted for helping me see the links between social science, public policy, and history, and for helping put scholarship at the service of a new kind of community dialogue about past and present. All this took form in the Philadelphia's Moving Past project, an adventure shared with Cindy Little, Nancy Moses, and Henry Williams, and the resulting essay is as much a result of their creativity, wisdom, and determination as was the exhibit and program we sent rolling through the streets of Philadelphia. I am also especially grateful to John Bodnar and Paul Mattingly for their incisive critical commentaries when an earlier version of this paper was presented at a meeting of the Social Science History Association.

Chapter Thirteen is an appropriate final essay in every sense except its unfortunate number, in that it most completely summarizes the range of concerns about applied history, cultural memory, and interpretive authority developed throughout the collection. The essay was first suggested by Roy Rosenzweig and Warren Leon, who then criticized, shaped, and edited it with great care and skill for inclusion in their important new book, *History Museums in the United States: A Critical Assessment* (Urbana, 1989). I am additionally obligated to a growing circle of colleagues who have helped me to think about museums, public presentation in general, historical programming in particular, and the role of audience, in both broadly cultural and precisely applied ways. These include Linda Shopes, John Alviti, and Sally Yerkovitz, who helped shape the material discussed in this essay, as well as Jesse Lemisch, James Henretta, and Mike Wallace, with whom I have fruitfully discussed these issues more generally. Finally, my current work with the New York Chinatown History Project—soon to become a new museum of a very different and special kind—has both grown from and continues to shape my own critical writing about the issues of concern in this book, which therefore owes a great deal to the remarkable group of people at the heart of that enterprise: Dorothy Rony, Charles Lai, Fay Chew, and especially Jack Tchen.

Having implicated all these friends and colleagues, I now hasten to provide the ritual closing absolution as well, by noting that all responsibility for untaken advice and for the mistakes, misjudgments, and misapprehensions these essays surely contain remains solely mine.

Permissions

Most of the chapters in this book have appeared in whole or part as noted below, in versions only modestly revised for publication now except as explicitly mentioned. I am pleased to record here my grateful appreciation to the designated publishers, co-authors, and copyright holders for permission to reproduce this material here.

Chapter 1. Oral History and Hard Times

Originally published under the same title, in *Red Buffalo: A Journal of American Studies* I/2-3 (1972) (Buffalo: Department of American Studies, SUNY-Buffalo). Reprinted in *Oral History Review* 1979. Copyright 1979, Oral History Association.

Chapter 2. The Memory of History

Originally published under same title in Susan Benson, Stephen Brier, and Roy Rosenzweig, eds., *Presenting the Past: Essays on History and the Public* (Philadelphia: Temple University Press, 1986). Copyright 1986, MARHO [Mid-Atlantic Radical Historians Organization] and Temple University Press.

Chapter 3. American History and the Structures of Collective Memory

Originally published, under the same title, in *Journal of American History* 75/4 (March 1989). Copyright 1989, *Journal of American History*. Illustration from *New York Times Magazine* November 17, 1985, including photograph by Jeanne Strongin. Text copyright 1985, *New York Times*; photograph copyright 1985, Jeanne Strongin.

Chapter 4. Oral History and the Presentation of Working-Class Consciousness: The New York Times v. the Buffalo Unemployed

Co-authored with Dorothy Larson Watts and originally published, under the same title, in *International Journal of Oral History* I/2 (1980). Copyright 1980, Meckler Corporation, Westport, Connecticut. Documents originally published in "Down and Out In America," *New York Times Magazine* February 9, 1975. Copyright 1975, SUNY-Buffalo Department of American Studies. Reprinted here with the additional permission of Dorothy Larson.

Chapter 5. Preparing Interview Transcripts for Documentary Publication: A Line-by-Line Illustration of the Editing Process

"Dick Hughes: A Portrait in Steel" originally published under the same title in *Social Research* 54/2 (Summer 1987), 179-199. Copyright 1987, New School for Social Research, New York City.

Chapter 6. Presenting and Receiving Oral History across Cultural Space: A Note on Responses of Chinese Students to the Documentary Trilogy One Village in China

A brief version of this essay originally published as "Responses of Chinese Students" in "Media Symposium," *Oral History Review* 15/2 (Fall, 1987). Copyright 1988, Oral History Association.

Chapter 7. Oral History, Documentary, and the Mystification of Power: A Critique of Vietnam: A Television History

A capsule version of this essay originally published as "Oral History, Documentary, and the Mystification of Power: A Case Study Critique of Public Methodology," *International Journal of Oral History*, VI/2 (1985). Copyright 1985, Meckler Corporation, Westport, Connecticut.

Chapter 8. Quality in History Programs: From Celebration to Exploration of Values

Originally published under same title in *What Portion in the World: New Essays on Public Uses of the Humanities* (Minneapolis: National Federation of State Humanities Councils, 1982.) Copyright 1982, National Federation of State Humanities Councils, Washington, D.C.

Chapter 9. Town into City: A Reconsideration on the Occasion of Springfield's 350th Anniversary, 1636-1986

Originally published under same title in *Springfield, 1636-1986* (Springfield, Mass: Institute for Massachusetts Studies and Springfield Library and Museums Association, 1987). Copyright 1987, Springfield Library and Museums Association.

Chapter 10. "Get the Picture?": A Review Essay

Originally published under same title in *New York History* 69 (April, 1988). Copyright 1988, New York State Historical Association.

Chapter 11. Audience Expectations as Resource and Challenge: Ellis Island as a Case Study

Co-authored with Dwight Pitcaithley, and originally published, under same title, in Jo Blatti, ed., *Past Meets Present: Essays about Historic Interpretation and Public Audiences*, (Washington: Smithsonian Institution Press, 1987). Copyright 1987, New York Council for the Humanities. Reprinted here with the additional permission of Dwight Pitcaithley.

Chapter 13. The Presentation of Urban History in Big City Museums

Originally published under same title in Warren Leon and Roy Rosenzweig, eds., *History Museums in the United States: A Critical Assessment* (Urbana: University of Illinois Press, 1989). Copyright 1989, University of Illinois Press.

Introduction

This book presents a collection of essays through which I have been developing some ideas about oral history and what has come to be called public history. Although much of this work is relatively recent, the first of the essays was drafted more than fifteen years ago and a number of others mark the distance between then and now in regular steps. Virtually all of the essays, moreover, originated as "occasional" pieces—written for a specific purpose or audience, often in the form of critical reflections on particular historical works, whether book, film, magazine article, or exhibition.

While it may be interesting that a reasonably focused set of concerns has emerged through so many discrete projects spread over so many years, the decision to present a collection of these pieces requires some explanation. After all, book reviews, conference papers, public addresses, and summary reports on teaching, historical programming, documentary editing, and visits to museums might fairly seem more like shavings on the workbench of scholarship, means to the end of a finished product useful for thoughtful reflection on issues of broad significance, rather than the base for such reflection themselves.

In this instance, however, I think a strong case can be made for the proposition that more may be learned from studying the process than from a focus on the position to which it has brought us. For one thing, the central issues in oral and public history are confronted first and most deeply in practical application, whether in conducting and transcribing interviews, organizing a collection, preparing an exhibit or documentary, or drafting historical script or text that seeks explicitly to engage a general audience. Although an emergent theory of oral history certainly exists, and the beginnings of the same in public history, the ideas involved are grounded in practice—virtually everyone who has had much to say about them draws on substantial practical experience and concrete examples. Because the applied level is where most newcomers encounter complexity, and because this is also where the insights of the experienced actually come from, there is something to be said for focussing discussion in concrete particulars.

By itself, however, this argument could lead as well to an instructional handbook or manual, of which there are already many, filled with satisfyingly practical examples. And if oral history or public history and presentation involved only skills to be imparted, then such manuals for novices written by the experienced would be sufficient. What has interested me from the start, however, is the way these approaches raise important issues of culture, communication, and politics—not only in the material they engage, but in the very processes of engagement, in the altered relationship between historian and "source," between scholarship and public discourse, and between dominant cultural forms, assumptions, and institutions and the alternatives that practitioners of these methods so often hope to empower.

Such issues, too, are best examined in particular examples rather than in general, not so much because they require concreteness as such as because they require precise location in cultural space and historical time. Academic discourse has its own internal dynamic, but this cannot explain very much about why oral and public history have become at once uncritically popular in some circles and hotly controversial in others, nor about the more particular issues and concerns that have become the focus of theoretical debate or the cutting edge of practice. These matters all demand a frame of vision that can encompass developments in the field, in the broader political atmosphere, and in the institutional culture of research and communication—all of which have been in dramatic independent motion over time, yet also find themselves intertwined in an increasingly complex public debate about the state of American culture. It seems to me that this context makes a grounded and yet broadly reflective discussion of oral and public history all the more important, especially since choices in presentation, say, or in editing and interpreting interview texts, turn out in practice to be anything but narrowly technical matters resolvable through a guidebook's definition or prescription.

Presenting a series of concrete case studies may thus be a good way to penetrate to what is most interesting in oral and public history, and it is arguably the best way to permit readers to explore what is found there—to sense how issues have come to the surface through engagements with particular problems in particular settings at particular points in a broader, surrounding cultural and political discourse. What might otherwise be a disadvantage in a collection—certain inevitable overlap as ideas, themes, and even sections of text developed in one setting find themselves pressed into useful service elsewhere—thus can serve as a connective thread, revealing the linking of one theme or problem to another, often in a very different area of concern.

Accordingly, this book is organized around both the process of development and emerging themes. It presents a series of occasional essays and case studies, many previously published and most of these re-presented here in their original form, although others have been expanded, generally to unfold evidence or context more explicitly than the initial publication permitted. Some are published for the first time here. I hope that this assemblage of disparate pieces will prove meaningful as a collectively coherent statement of related ideas and concerns, and as a kind of intellectual history of how these unfolded in practice, which is to say how this unfolding reveals the forces at work on the environment within which oral and public history have been developing.

All of this, of course, is unavoidably presumptuous—it presumes that my experiences and responses have been in some way expressive of broader cultural transformations, or at least offer vantages for discussing these, and that the ideas I have come to develop express something important about oral and public history. Each reader can assess these presumptions without assistance, and I happily leave the burden of defending them to the essays. However, considering that the collection is premised both on a response over time and on the thematic concerns emerging from that process, it may be useful here, by way of a more subjective introduction, for me to discuss the way I came to write these pieces and to comment briefly on the issues that run through them.

My interest in oral history traces to a kind of academic schizophrenia which it has taken me a long time to transcend. I emerged from graduate school in the late 1960s as a newly minted "urban historian"; my dissertation/first book and most of my scholarship over the next few years was focused on the nineteenth century, and although I tried in some of my courses to engage the concerns of the then-current "urban crisis," by and large my research and teaching remained focused on history, and history approached in professionally conventional ways.

By the early 1970s, however, I had begun teaching at SUNY-Buffalo, a campus very much involved in, if not almost consumed by, the academic and political ferment of the era. The newly expanded university was a hothouse of intellectual energy, tended by a young faculty streaming in from all over the country in response to the opportunity to build new institutional and programmatic approaches to education and social change. I found myself very much caught up in this ferment, although for better or worse, probably the latter, my situation permitted me to experiment with minimal risk—I was based in a very solid and professionally established history department where I practiced my urban history, while I became increasingly more involved in a unique and controversial American Studies program, recently established at the uni-

versity, which became one of the campus's main sources of academic innovation and community involvement.

All of my early work in and on oral history grew out of collective projects
in this American Studies program. The first was a journal we produced that
was one of the first compilations of essays on the broader political, cultural,
and cross-cultural implications of oral history. Soon after, as a result of the
journal, we received a commission to prepare an oral-history documentary on
unemployment for the *New York Times Magazine*. Somehow, largely because
of the ethos of the program and its near-renegade status in the rapidly cooling
hothouse of the mid- and late 1970s, I tended for quite a while to view this
work as being removed from my academic concerns in history—it seemed an
alternative enterprise, more political work than professional. In this sense,
my initial involvement was resonant with an approach to oral history that saw
the method as a challenge to all the assumptions of conventional scholarship,
a way for a new kind of history from the bottom up and from the outside in to
challenge the established organization of knowledge and power and the politics that rested on it.

At the time, I sensed something was wrong with this formulation, and
much of the writing in my early essays seems, in retrospect, an attempt to
wrestle with just what this might be. This makes it all the more curious to me,
now, that it took me so long to realize that the dichotomy itself was the
problem—the notion that the questions raised were "outside" the discourse of
history and could not be engaged, or advanced and refined, from within it.
Even more faulty, I came to see, was the kind of split intellectual identity into
which I had fallen: as I was drawn more and more into work on oral history,
and through that to work on historical documentary and then historical exhibition, I began to realize that this split was as unnecessary as it was limiting.

This could happen, in large part, because indeed the worlds of historical
and political discourse had been coming together: the 1960s and 1970s challenges from without became an impressive body of substantive new research
that has transformed scholarship profoundly. This new scholarship, especially
in social history, has arguably become the dominant intellectual reality of our
time, defining the critical landscape even where, far from being in control, it
remains controversial and even problematic. Discussion about history more
broadly—about method, topical focus, interpretation, and contemporary
relevance—has become oriented around many of the concerns that only a few
years earlier had made outsiders of younger proponents involved in the more
challenging forms of oral and public history, such as using local and labor
history for organizing, for instance, and exploring the power of oral-history-
based documentary. These sensibilities also had much to do with the recently
ascendant interdisciplinary developments that continue to enrich historical
scholarship. The influences of a broadly defined cultural anthropology and

of more recent literary theories, for instance, make studying cultural history at once more cosmopolitan and more capable of dealing with dimensions of class, race, ethnicity, and gender, the invisibility of which had been correctly held to be among the more profound and distorting limitations in conventional scholarship.

True, a case can be made that all this represents less the success of a challenge to a dominant intellectual culture than its digestion and cooptation. While my purpose here is not to engage this recently fashionable argument, I can note two important considerations indicating its superficiality, both relevant to the developments I have been tracing.

One is the degree to which the evolving sophistication and critical content of historical discourse has flowed in both directions: developments in scholarship and theory have permitted oral and public history to grow substantially in recent years, especially in their capacity to unearth and communicate more complex meanings in the materials with which they deal. Recent work in linguistics and literary analysis, for instance, as well as in folkloristics and fieldwork theory, has explored the processes by which the meanings of broadly defined cultural "texts" are formed, treating this not as inherent or static, but rather alive and often contested—created and modified through an interactive dialogue in many dimensions of communication. Such approaches are quite resonant with ideas that had long been central, if often narrowly grounded in methodology, in discussions of oral history interviewing. Suddenly, these discussions have been energized with new sophistication and broad new dimensions of application, culturally and politically. The challenge and relevance of oral history, clearly, has been anything but diminished or denatured by its increasing proximity to a very turbulent mainstream.

Second, and more basic, is the astonishing degree to which developments in the professional study of history have been at the center in recent years of an increasingly acrimonious political storm about American culture in the broad sense—the writing and teaching of social history, together with new approaches to community history and involvement, have been held accountable for everything from a decline of patriotism and an epidemic of cultural illiteracy to a toxic moral relativism supposedly contaminating education and political discourse alike. This near-hysterical counterattack from the right hardly signals a threat co-opted—rather, it supports the conclusion that both the new academic scholarship and the challenges from the bottom up continue to exercise a substantial and from that viewpoint a threatening power.

My own work, to complete the sketch, has mirrored and in many ways been propelled by these developments. What had once seemed almost an extracurricular interest in oral history moved much closer to the center of my teaching and research. I found it increasingly possible, especially as I began to deal more with the public presentation of history, to bring together previously disparate intellectual and broadly political concerns about history, culture, and change; each interest developed new sharpness and focus through the combination. And in the most recent of this book's essays, it has been especially satisfying for me to be able to return to urban history, examining both the larger politics bearing on the choices we face in public presentation, and the way in which recent urban scholarship, even of the most abstruse variety, can enrich the possibilities of an open-ended public encounter with the complex history of urban structure and change.

In this sense, then, the sequence of one author's essays may be useful as a way to suggest and trace some of the broader processes at work on a generation of historians and in the evolving relation of scholarship to public discourse in our culture. But such historiographical continuity would not in itself be enough to justify the collection if some substantive themes were not also emerging through it, in the body of the essays collectively. And indeed, over the years, my reflections on oral and public history increasingly focused on a constellation of ideas that served especially well at linking the problem at hand to the broader interpretive context surrounding it. Gradually, I came to see that these all had something to do with a concept that has given this collection its title: the notion that what is most compelling about oral and public history is a capacity to redefine and redistribute intellectual authority, so that this might be shared more broadly in historical research and communication rather than continuing to serve as an instrument of power and hierarchy. Perhaps the best way to introduce this concept is to discuss what seems to me to be its embodiment in, and as a link between, three distinct dimensions of practice— dimensions that, in turn, provide the organizing framework for the collection.

Early in my work in oral history, I became fascinated with the questions this method raises about authorship. Who, really, is the author of an oral history, whether this be a single interview or an edited book-length narrative? Is it the historian posing questions and editing the results, or the "subject," whose words are the heart of the consequent texts? And if, as I came to argue, we need to understand the ways in which authorship is shared, what does this mean for understanding how interviews can actually be a source of "H"istory, as distinct from historical data or raw material—history, that is, as a synthetic reconstruction that necessarily involves story, frame, analysis, and interpretation, however implicit? What is the relation between interviewer and subject in the generating of such histories—who is responsible for them and where is interpretive authority located? How are we to understand interpretations that are, essentially, collaboratively produced in an interview, whether the relationship is one of cooperation or tension? How can this collaboration be represented, and how, more commonly, is it usually mystified and obscured, and to what effect?

It became a major focus of my work to examine these matters closely, considering authorship and the complex sources of historical interpretation in a variety of oral-historical and documentary contexts. And in the process, I have increasingly been struck by how closely issues of authorship and interpretive authority are linked—a link manifest in the words themselves: I was tempted to title the book *A Shared Author-ity*, but decided, on wise counsel, that this might seem confusing, precious, or both. Nevertheless, the concept implied by that hyphen is important: not only has it remained central to my work in oral history, but it provided a crucial bridge as well to the broader concerns I encountered in public historical practice, especially as I began to connect this to my own work in urban history.

In public history, approaches to related issues of authority—scholarly and intellectual authority—define much of the landscape. At one pole, much of the energy in this new field involves relatively transparent attempts to create, legitimize, colonize, credentialize, and protect new professional public and private sector jobs for historians at a time of decreasing academic opportunity. Such efforts simply claim new arenas in which the exercises of scholarly authority may be mounted; much attention is given to the new methods and public relationships this necessarily involves, but there is here little place for reconsidering the scope and legitimacy of that authority itself—indeed, the pressures are for precisely the reverse.

At the other pole, new forms of public history have waged a kind of guerilla war against this notion of professional scholarly authority: the promise of community history, of people's video, of labor theater, of many applications of oral history, has been empowerment—returning to particular communities or generating from within them the authority to explore and interpret their own experience, experience traditionally invisible in formal history because of predictable assumptions about who and what matters, interpretations more actively ignored or resisted by academic scholarship by virtue of their political content and implications.

In the journey described above, I find I have been increasingly drawn to approaches that resist each of these poles, or rather, that seek to find a synthesis between them in public historical processes. The hegemony of scholarly authority indeed must be challenged and often qualified, but not by rejecting the insights of scholarship by definition, if only because such an approach vastly underestimates the power of new ideas to challenge deeply entrenched assumptions so often internalized in conventional, popularly grounded categories. Similarly, the power of populist self-empowerment through public history can be as easily and romantically exaggerated; there is something offensively patronizing in the notion that ordinary people and communities have little capacity for communicating with and incorporating approaches to their history originating outside their own immediate experience and knowledge.

I have found in the notion of a shared or sharable authority a promising approach to resolving some of these dilemmas. The essays on public presentation explore ways in which scholars and designers need better to respect, understand, invoke, and involve the very real authority their audiences bring to a museum exhibit, a popular history book, or a public program. Although grounded in culture and experience rather than academic expertise, this authority can become central to an exhibit's capacity to provide a meaningful engagement with history—to what should be not only a distribution of knowledge from those who have it to those who do not, but a more profound sharing of knowledges, an implicit and sometimes explicit dialogue from very different vantages about the shape, meaning, and implications of history.

Not only might this dialogue from different bases of authority more regularly inform the process of participation in design and development, but it might more deeply characterize the experience of finished products themselves. If oral historians need to understand that their method involves much more than the extraction of knowledge from human history mines, public historians need to realize that their method can do much more than merely redistribute such knowledge. It can, rather, promote a more democratized and widely shared historical consciousness, consequently encouraging broader participation in debates about history, debates that will be informed by a more deeply representative range of experiences, perspectives, and values.

All of this matters, finally, because these reflections about history take place in, and should have meaning for, the present—a present in which, quite suddenly, the matter of what people do or do not know about history has become the object of furious contemporary argument. Without denying many legitimate concerns about the adequacy of modern education, I think many other things clearly are fueling this hot debate, foremost among them a host of resentments about the social and political changes of the last three decades and a fear that while these may no longer challenge the power of established institutions, as they seemed to in the 1960s, they have in some deeper and actually more threatening way been eroding the binding values and symbols of American culture.

The issue in recent jeremiads, this is to say, is to a substantial degree one of cultural authority, and the extent to which historical understanding in particular—the teaching of history and the academic exploration of history—has come to seem a threat, even *the* threat to the authority of traditional political culture, rather than the reinforcement these critics hold it to be the central function of both education and scholarship to offer.

This reading of the cultural literacy debate has helped me, finally, to understand better the political meanings in the oral and public historical issues with which I have been concerned. It is one thing to talk about sharing authorship and sharing interpretive authority, as if this were simply a matter of more wisely and sensitively cooperating in our historical dealings across gulfs of expertise and training, much less class and position—as if it were only, as in *Cool Hand Luke,* "a problem in communication." But, of course, if the issues matter, they must involve more than this, in which case we can not expect cultural authority to be shared very willingly by those who exercise it, rendering the sharing of other forms of authority increasingly problematic.

A final dimension of concern in the essays in this book thus involves cultural politics, especially as embodied in the problem of collective memory and memory's relation to history. Memory is living history, the remembered past that exists in the present. In one sense, it is a force that can be tapped, unleashed, and mobilized through oral and public history to stand as an alternative to imposed orthodoxy and officially sanctioned versions of historical reality; it is a route to a broadly distributed authority for making new sense of the past in the present. But in another way, memory is a deeply cultural artifact, manipulated in a host of direct and indirect ways, especially in an age of mass-mediation, to reproduce culturally appropriate attitudes and behaviors. It can thus stand as a prop of cultural power and authority, unless challenged in a variety of ways, of which aggressive historical inquiry and public presentation is certainly one. From this angle, it is history, not memory, that can provide the basis for shared reimagination of how the past connects to the present, and the possibilities this vantage suggests for the future.

These concerns about the dynamics and shareability of cultural power, then, complicate the task of thinking clearly about oral and public history, and what they have to contribute to the process of not only interpreting our world, but also changing it—the authority for which is even more in need of sharing. But at least this helps to locate the challenge in a real space and time, rather than pretending that a broadened public discourse about history is simply a matter of methodology, technique, or translation. Accordingly, I hope that this collection of essays, by wrestling with resonant issues in a rather wide variety of contexts, will help not only to delineate some of the extensive practical choices we face in developing work in these areas, but to explore as well how much it matters, in cultural and political terms, which choices we make.

The essays are organized into sections, with selections roughly chronological within each; each section has introductory headnotes, grouped together, giving full background particulars on its essays, and discussing as well their developmental relation to each other and to the themes they hold in common. The groupings focus on the various dimensions of shared and not-so-shared authority I have been discussing, an approach that permits a certain topical focus while also encouraging the exploration of connections between the modes of historical practice being considered.

The first section offers an overview, in several senses. For one, it focuses on the problem of history, memory, and cultural authority, providing a broader thematic grounding for the more particular case studies that follow. For another, it touches the several modes of practice that run through the collection—one essay deals with oral history, one considers several forms of public history, especially film, and the third deals with neither oral nor public history as usually defined, concentrating instead on the surrounding problem of cultural memory as grounded in some unique materials that come out of my experience as a teacher of the survey course in American history—something much closer to public dialogue, in fact, than to scholarly discourse. Finally, the section ranges from the very first essay I wrote in the area, the review of Studs Terkel's *Hard Times*, to the one on teaching, which is the most recently completed, although its materials and ideas have been under development throughout the fifteen years covered by the collection as a whole.

The second section turns to a much more focused engagement: the essays all involve authorship and shared interpretive authority in the treatment of oral history, particularly as used in historical documentary. It also includes the most "hands-on" pieces in the collection, bringing abstract issues down to the ground of concrete editorial practice and precise decisions about the meaning that oral-historical texts contain. Because several of these pieces allow me the opportunity to analyze, sometimes quite critically, the editing that other people have done, I thought it fair and hopefully useful to present as well an extensive example of my own practice: the point here is that the usually somewhat mystical process of documentary editing needs as much prosaic ventilation as can be provided and that the reflective essays will make more sense in the presence of open-ended documentary examples that readers can explore without much mediating commentary.

The third section concentrates on the sharing of scholarly authority. Its first three essays range widely in form and focus, but all consider the relevance of scholarship to public dialogue and the relationship of scholarship to other forms of experiential authority, whether in particular public programs or in works of popular history. In the final three essays, these notions are applied to the specific context of historical exhibition, with concern for the ways in which interpretive authority can be shared even with very broad audiences wandering through a casually visited museum or site. The last two essays make a personally satisfying conclusion, returning as they do to the urban history with which I had begun, but dealing with this in such a different light and to such a different effect as to confirm my sense that the journey summarized in this book has had direction and cumulative meaning. Hopefully, the collection that follows will convey something similar to readers.

Part I

Memory, History, and Cultural Authority

Headnotes

The Introduction above has, in some detail, located the contents and thematic focus of each section's essays within the broader argument of the book. The prefatory notes in the sections, therefore, can serve a narrower and more informal end: they discuss the background, origin, and publishing history of the section's individual essays. Rather than having such information precede individual selections, I have grouped these headnotes by section, in order to suggest the broader processes of which the individual essays, responding to very specific assignments or experiences, are particular examples. So that the notes may also smoothly read as a narrative, detailed citations, acknowledgments, and republication permissions, as appropriate, will be found in a separate section covering all the essays in the volume.

The first essay in this collection was also my first encounter with some of the issues raised by oral history. As noted in the Introduction, it originated in a collective project in the American Studies Program at SUNY-Buffalo, in the early 1970s. A group of our ambitious graduate students had secured what seemed like secure start-up funds (these turned out to be wrap-up funds as well) for a journal of cultural studies, each issue of which was to have a specific theme or focus that would individually and in sum come to express the critical, cross-cultural approach then under development in our program. The counter-cultural founders somewhat playfully called the journal *Red Buffalo*— a defiantly nonacademic name that was also deliberately ambiguous, suggesting both a left political orientation and an interest in Native American perspectives on culture, history, and environment. Both dimensions were prominent in the program, the latter in a then-nascent Native American Studies component whose work, in fact, provided the basis for the first thematic issue of *Red Buffalo*.

1

For the second issue, the editorial collective decided on oral history. The method was already central to the department's work, there being considerable interest in oral history's capacity to generate alternative visions of American history and culture and to serve as a source for change, especially from the perspective of minorities and women. At the same time, there was also considerable interest, including but not limited to the Native Americans, in the role of oral tradition in traditional cultures as a source of stability and resistance to change imposed from the outside, or from the top down.

The implicit tension between oral history as a source of change and oral tradition as a source of resistance to change did not go unnoticed in the editing of the collection, which grew into a book-length double issue. Beginning to work through this tension provided much of what was instructive in the experience, and what is energetic and interesting in the results. Indeed, we discovered unsuspected complexity even in the notion of oral history as a liberating vision "from the bottom up." The editors had commissioned a friend in the Midwest to write a long introduction to the volume, but when it arrived they found themselves in profound disagreement with what seemed his romantic assumption that the "voice of the people" would in and of itself be a radical force for liberation. We ended up publishing two introductions—the submitted text and an opposing one by the editors. Although this debate was joined in the somewhat arcane language of left theory of consciousness, the issues involved were, in fact, anything but parochial, and struggling with them brought us all to a new appreciation of the complexity of oral history documents as cultural artifacts. My own essay's reading of *Hard Times* emerges from this context, and may usefully be read against it.

Published in 1972, the entire *Red Buffalo* oral history issue received gratifying notice, a sign of how inadequately a burgeoning interest in oral history nationwide had been met by focused critical reflection. The work even developed a kind of underground mystique, largely because occasional citations referred a growing number of readers curious about oral history to a mysterious-sounding journal people had neither heard of nor knew where to find. In any event, my own essay ascended from the underground when it was republished in the then-annual *Oral History Review*, journal of the Oral History Association, in 1979. It is reprinted here, as it was then, in its original form.

The second essay, initially drafted in 1979-80, deals with some of the same issues in a much broader frame, both in terms of the documents considered and the patterns in American history and culture to which they are seen as relevant. This work also had a somewhat unusual origin, as noted in the essay's footnotes: in 1979, the unconventional SUNY-Buffalo law school had, for its annual Mitchell Lectures, invited not some jurist or legal scholar, but rather the eminent documentary filmmaker Marcel Ophuls, who was to come not for the usual formal speech, but rather for a week's residence during which his complex films would be screened and he would be available for ongoing discussions with students and faculty. I was asked to join a panel discussion focused on his remarkable film about the meaning of Nuremberg in history, *The Memory of Justice*.

The remarks prepared for that occasion grew into this essay, which concerns the particular problem of the "memory" of Vietnam and the larger relationship between memory and history, in an American culture in which this relationship is, I argue, especially problematic. The essay was developed in this extended form for a 1981 issue of the *Radical History Review* focused on public history, and it was slightly revised when that volume, much expanded, appeared as *Presenting the Past*, a 1986 Temple University Press book edited by Susan Porter Benson, Stephen Brier, and Roy Rosenzweig that is the most comprehensive and critical exploration yet available of the many dimensions of public history.

The final essay in the section has perhaps the most unusual background and is certainly the most curious in the context of this book. It is based on responses my students have made over the last decade to a kind of free-association quiz designed to reveal the "image" of American history they bring into my survey-course classroom. I have been working over this material for quite a while now, first as a kind of pedagogic gimmick and then, as the data became more compelling, as a way of teasing out some broader curiosities in the results. The exercise has ended up turning centrally on the role of history and memory in popular culture and public discourse.

I first wrote up some of the results as a conference paper for the 1983 annual meeting of the American Studies Association in Philadelphia—a session on "civil religion" needed another paper, and this proved a helpful framework for thinking about the pantheon of heroes and heroines that had been revealed in my students' quiz responses. Several years later, with increasingly striking data accumulating almost every semester in the interim, I received a call for papers for the 1987 Sixth International Oral History Conference held at Oxford University around the theme of "Myth and Collective Memory." Both theme and occasion enticed me to push the analysis another notch, because my material addressed these concerns quite naturally.

Finally, as I began preparing the still-unpublished paper for this book, the explosion of the national debate about cultural illiteracy, education, and the future of American culture (what William Greider, in a review mentioned in the footnotes, calls the "Bloom and Doom" School) helped me see at last what this essay was really all about, and how it could engage concerns far beyond the classroom context. The wider debate also increased the willingness of others to take this unusual material seriously, I'm glad to say: a chance to present the work to a remarkable interdisciplinary conference in 1988 joining historians and psychologists who study memory, sponsored by Baylor University's Institute for Oral History, accelerated the crystallization process. The current version of the essay is only slightly modified from the one delivered there. And finally, at more or less the same time, the completed essay was polished and updated for its appearance in the Spring, 1989 issue of the *Journal of American History*, a thematic issue focused on History and Memory. These connections encourage me in the belief that I was not being self-indulgent to think that such an idiosyncratic exercise might help to frame and engage some of the issues raised in my other essays on oral and public history, and so fit well in this collection.

Chapter 1

Oral History and *Hard Times*:
A Review Essay

Studs Terkel's book, *Hard Times*, is subtitled *An Oral History of the Great Depression*, and it offers a good base for exploring a number of problems inherent in doing, reading, and thinking about oral history, and for understanding why these problems matter. It is, perhaps, appropriate to the topic to begin with some comments about this paper's own genesis and history.

Hard Times is a massive compilation of more than 150 self-portraits of American lives—culled from hundreds more—centered on the experience of the 1930s. The interviews were conducted, edited, and arranged by Studs Terkel, the remarkable Chicago radio personality whose special gift for getting all sorts of people to talk about themselves was so profoundly demonstrated in *Division Street: America*. The people of *Hard Times* range widely, from New Deal officials and famous businessmen and artists to anonymous farmers, workers, and plain people. Terkel also includes a number of interviews with young people who can, of course, only talk about the Depression in terms of what they have read or been told, and who therefore enable us to see the book's topic in terms of received memory as well as given. To read through the enormous range of personality and experience presented in the book is to encounter, in a sort of multimedia exposure, the depth and drama of life in the Depression. As has virtually every other reader, I found it moving, poignant, intense, human, and instructive.

Shortly after a first reading, I noticed that the cover of my paperback edition said, in a blurb from *Newsweek*, "It will resurrect your faith in all of us to read this book." The inside front cover, quoting *Saturday Review*, called the book "A huge anthem in praise of the American Spirit." These intrigued me considerably, because I found the book more depressing than anything else in its overall implications. It had all the moving force of life, I felt, which is why it could so profoundly suggest the Depression's destructive impact on the lives people lived, the personalities that emerged, and on the abilities individuals retained to understand what was happening to them. Rather than "resurrecting my faith in all of us," the book seemed to show why Americans find it so hard to examine their culture and institutions critically, even when massive breakdowns make such examination imperative. And it seemed an anthem in praise of the American Spirit only in the sense of showing the tremendous self-preservative power of a threatened culture, as revealed in and through people whose experiences posed fundamental threats to the society's premises. Perhaps I should not have been surprised at the book's inspiring such different readings, but the contrast suggested that something more was at work than simply a difference of politics or perspective. I went back to the book, and to the full reviews, in order to see whether they contained more fundamental questions, questions about what oral history has to teach and about how, as a particular form of history, it can be read or misread.

The text of reviews in *Time*, *Newsweek*, *Saturday Review*, the *New Yorker*, the *Nation*, and the *New York Review of Books* indicates the paperback blurbs were not unrepresentative. With only two exceptions, which I address shortly, the critics saw the vitality and struggle and life so apparent in the interviews as emblematic of America itself; they located the book's inspirational quality in the "startling decency" of its people, and the capacity of their comments to connect us with deep cultural sources of redemptive, transcending energy. In the *New Yorker*, for example, L. E. Sissman calls *Hard Times* "a folk-song composed by American voices to celebrate and commemorate the 1930's," a song which has its center in "a sense of solidarity in adversity, a willingness to reach out to others, an ability to see others not as households of accreted possessions but as naked human beings. In the birth of that paradoxical nation was the rebirth of some elemental historical principles: truth, justice, and equality."

Beyond the repeated litany of inspiration, one is struck by how the reviewers so inspired seem to share a particular notion of the nature of the book, almost apart from its contents and meaning. In the first place, they treat the interviews as reflecting a distant and discrete historical phenomenon, as being literally evidential of the 1930s, with the critic's job being the provision of a contrastive, contemporary perspective. This explains why the particular atmosphere of 1970 figures so centrally in the reviews. The fragment from Henry Resnick's piece in the *Saturday Review*, quoted earlier, reads in full: "Americans have little reason to be proud of their country these days, but in *Hard Times* Studs Terkel has given us what amounts to a huge anthem in praise of the American Spirit. [It has] an almost mythic quality." Faced with "the hopelessness and squalor of contemporary life," he said, we need the book to "put us back in touch with our elemental humanity." The sources of this need are suggested by the way the critics generally understood Terkel's conversations with young people. Rather than taking these as illustrating the complex process of historical memory and generational transfer, they saw them only as revealing the character of the young people themselves. Writing in a year of protest, of Kent State and Cambodia, Geoffrey Wolf in *Newsweek* thus discovered the "startling decency" of Terkel's people in relation to the arrogance and insensitivity he reads in contemporary youth, and he observed acidly that "memory is long, but curiosity is not."

There are other senses in which the critical comments imply a common view of *Hard Times* and, by extension, oral history. It is revealing, for example, to observe that critics so concerned with the relevance of the book for the present generally ignore the fact that the interviews were conducted only recently; the people who spoke to Terkel so movingly of the past were also trying to live in and understand the 1960s. Thus the basic historicality of the interviews—the degree to which they involve historical statements rather than, or in addition to, historical evidence—was barely alluded to in the reviews being considered. In fact, rather than exploring the oral testimonies as forms of history the tendency was to perceive them as something of a counterhistorical way of understanding the past. The critics described the book in terms of literature rather than history, comparing it frequently to Oscar Lewis and Truman Capote. Resnick's article even saw Terkel as challenging the hegemony of history as a form of knowledge, predicting that "dedication to the truth as fact will be supported by more and more historians as the fundamentals of historiography encounter increasing threats in the form of books like *Hard Times.*"

The critics, this suggests, understood the book as history mainly in the sense of telling it "like it was." "As history the book may be weak on the why," observed *Time*, "but it can hardly be matched by any scholarly work in giving a sense of what it was like at that time." Thus oral history enables us to see history, according to this view, as more or less direct and unmediated experience, rather than as the abstracted and ordered rendering of objective historical intelligence.

Two reviews in the batch did not share this notion of oral history, and significantly, these were the only two that did not find the book a confirmation and celebration of the American spirit and character. In the *New Yorker*, Murray Kempton focused on the variable relation people could have to their own experience in the past—"who noticed what was happening and who didn't" —and what has happened to this sense over time. Exploring the gap between what was felt and what was said in the interview, he sought to locate the controlling level of experience where many levels exist simultaneously and are selectively remembered. He concluded that the Depression "did not teach us what it should have . . . there is a gaiety in these recollections which ought to have been more transfiguring yet wasn't," and he tried to explore why. Nelson Algren, writing in *The Nation*, looked even more closely at the speakers themselves, rather than at the content of their recollections, and concluded that "the author has provided us with a definitive report on the psychological recoil of a generation that suffered a failure of nerve."

The contrast among the reviews confirmed for me the notion that reading oral history depends, more than in most historical writing, on the deeper assumptions one has about the nature of the evidence and the form. Because most of the critics seem at least partially to have misconstrued *Hard Times* owing to an uncritical approach to the book's method, it appeared that one good way to get more deeply into the book might be to look at its historical nature, rather than its content per se. Therefore, I propose to use *Hard Times* as a way of demonstrating the need for a more self-conscious and reflective sense of the nature of oral history, what it has to teach, and what questions the reader is obligated to bring to it. That this perspective leads to a more critically analytic view of cultural processes than does one which sees oral history as direct experience is, I hope to show, far from coincidental.

The discussion so far would reduce to a simple truism were it not for a compelling paradox: oral history is of such self-evident importance and interest that it has proven difficult for people to take it very seriously. By this I mean that those interested in history, culture, and politics have responded so intuitively to recent work in oral history that they have not generally stopped to think about what it is, on levels beyond the obvious, that makes it so worth pursuing. In part, this is because proponents of oral history, particularly in America, are somewhat a prisoner of its own methodological past.

In quasi-formal terms, American oral history came into its own through Allan Nevins's project at Columbia University, the main focus of which was on political and diplomatic history, and the main work of which was the "debriefing" of the Great Men before they passed on. Its nature was explicitly archival, informational, and elitist. This work has profoundly shaped recent interest in oral history, although in a largely negative and reactive way: critics saw the focus on great decisionmakers as a part of the traditional bias toward the articulate and powerful, and calls for history "from the bottom up" found a swift focus in oral history, a form that seemed to fit the object of transcending evidential biases that sustained the elitist perspective. However, while the bottom-up approach seems to promise generically different insights for oral history—by exploring, for example, common shared experiences in preference to individualized and unique actions—these have not yet generated a really clear sense of any special nature and role for oral history. To the extent that oral history has produced such a sense, it has come in work on traditional and folk societies and centers on a view of oral tradition as a distinct type of historical thinking and transference. But in Western society, where culture is so penetrated by literacy, communication, and self-consciousness as to make such notions of oral tradition of dubious application, oral history has not gone much beyond the traditional focus of historical work.

Accordingly, most of us have casually assumed that oral history does one of two things, or perhaps both. First, it functions as a source of historical information and insights, to be used, in traditional ways, in the formulation of historical generalizations and narratives. In this sense, the oral method and the interest in the inarticulate do swing the flashlight of history into a significant, much neglected, and previously unknowable corner of the attic, but they still assume a more traditional sense of the object and nature of explanation. On the other hand, oral history can be understood as a way of bypassing historical interpretation itself, avoiding all the attendant elitist and contextual dangers. It seems to provide a way to communicate with the past more directly, to be presented with a somehow purer image of direct experience.

The prevailing choices can thus be concisely understood as that of "more history" or, in that special sense, "no history." It is risky to associate these leanings with particular positions of other spectrums: Allan Nevins and Staughton Lynd, for example, share the sense of the informational and archival purposes of oral history, while, as we have just seen, conservative journalists are just as likely to take the "pure experience" position as are radicals who might more usually be expected to endorse it as a way of demystifying and reclaiming from historians the experience of the people. In any event, "more" or "no" history seem to represent the poles between which the common notion of oral history hangs in a state of vagueness. Having said this, I wish to return to *Hard Times*, because in spite of its friendly critics, I think it can be seen as outlining a way to transcend these categories, and a way to discover the role for oral history in modern society.

Studs Terkel suggests this in the book's first sentence. "This is a memory book, rather than one of hard fact and precise statistic," he writes. In prefatory notes, he muses more personally on this theme: the book is "about Time as well as a time," he says: "heroes and dragons of a long-gone day were old men, some vigorous, some weary, when I last saw them. Some have died." And in the introduction he quotes Steinbeck's Pa Joad as saying "He's tellin' the truth, awright. The truth for him. He wasn't makin' nothin' up." Adds Terkel, referring to the people of *Hard Times*, "in their rememberings are their truths." From the start, then, Terkel distances the book from the kinds of oral history discussed so far. Were we searching either for information or a pure sense of how it "really" was, both the intense subjectivity of his form and the thirty-year lag would disqualify the interviews from being taken seriously.

But Terkel is clearly not apologizing; rather, he is suggesting that these factors are the strength and uniqueness of the book, in that they force us to look at what the interviews actually represent, rather than at what they can not claim to be. In these terms, the question of memory—personal and historical, individual, and generational—moves to center stage as the object, not merely the method, of oral history. The questions that emerge can be thought of in the following general forms, focused on process and change: What happens to experience on the way to becoming memory? What happens to experience on the way to becoming history? As an era of intense collective experience recedes into the past, what is the relationship of memory to historical generalization? These questions, so basic to thinking about how culture and individuality interact over time, are the sort of questions that oral history is peculiarly, perhaps uniquely, able to penetrate.

The best way to show this is to indicate how many different things are going on in the book, how many different methods the interviews suggest for studying how experience, memory, and history act on lives over time. In somewhat schematic form, the interviews with young people can represent one end of the spectrum of possibilities: here, the Depression takes the form of pure and abstracted memory, wildly subjective and selective. An interview with Christopher Lasch holds down the other end, for he speaks as the abstracted voice of professional history, generalizing with calm confidence and cool breadth about the painful experience bubbling through the surrounding pages. Pure memory, then, with all its faults, and pure history, with all its limitations. All the other interviews lie somewhere between, and accordingly require the most careful reading.

To this end, I suggest three questions that can help in exploring the complexity of the interviews. What sort of person is speaking? What sort of thing is he or she talking about? What sort of statements about it are being made? The range of possible answers to each of these can serve as axes for mapping the territory between the poles, for sensing the possible combinations in which people relate and integrate the dimensions of past and present experience.

Who is speaking? Intuitively, most of us are primarily sensitive to the social class or status of the speaker, particularly if our interest is in oral history's ability to work from the bottom up. Perhaps more important, however, is the way the speaker functioned historically, in relation to the overall experience with which the book is concerned. Some of Terkel's people speak of private and anonymous lives, historical in their generality rather than their particularity. Others, however, were more precisely "actors" in historically visible forums, and their subjectivity thus has important public and self-conscious dimensions. Generally, this spectrum of private and public experience and subjectivity parallels the spectrum of power and position, but with important exceptions: rich people who lived quite privately and unselfconsciously; labor organizers, workingmen, and a remarkable revivalist preacher whose proletarian experience is rooted to a major extent in a public dimension well beyond their own subjectivity.

What is being talked about? Responses can be crudely sorted out according to the way they deal with things actually experienced as opposed to things observed at some remove, or experienced in only the most general terms. What this implies is a more complicated spectrum of particularity and generality, ranging from detailed anecdotal reporting of personal incidents, to the abstracted discussion of general conditions and experiences. In these terms, the interviews show no categorical relationship to the social nature of the speakers—powerful politicians are as likely to give a heavily anecdotal account as are barely literate workers to generalize freely about "how it was" at some time, and vice versa. Interviews with two psychiatrists show in a different way what this concern means. One looks back and discusses his practice, his problems, his professional activity, and his personal perspective as seen through his work. The other discusses the psychic patterns he found himself facing in his patients and generalizes about their significance. Both interviews offer insights into the men and the Depression, yet they are quite different examples of the "evidence" oral history can produce, and they need to be understood, qualified, and digested in different ways.

What are they saying about it? This has to do with the sorts of statements people make; it seems to me the most problematic and yet the most crucial category. At what distance, in what ways, for what reasons, and in what patterns do people generalize, explain, and interpret experience? What cultural and historical categories do individuals use to help understand and present a view of experience? How are we to understand the variable weave of pure recall and reflective synthesis—historical statements as well as historical information—that characterize almost all of the interviews? All these may sound like very abstract matters, but together with the other questions I think they form the core of Terkel's "memory book," and lie close to the source of its enormous energy. By showing people trying to make sense of their lives at a variety of points in time and in a variety of ways, by opening this individual process to view, the oral history reveals patterns and choices that, taken together, begin to define the reinforcing and screening apparatus of the general culture, and the ways in which it encourages us to digest experience.

The perspective afforded by the questions I have suggested helps clarify the substantive lessons of the book, and Terkel notes some of these explicitly. (It is again significant to note that his own clues were apparently uninteresting to critics who had little sensitivity to the complexity of his method.) Despite the systemic and general nature of the Depression—more precisely because of it, of course—people tended to view their problems in atomized, alienating ways. Shame, a sense of personal failure, unavoidable obsession with personal concerns, paralytic insecurity in several dimensions—all these are repeatedly described as the predominant personal responses. Translated somewhat, this can be understood as the perception of collective, historical experience in the form of idiosyncratic personal experience, with all the attendant psychic scarring, searing memory, and sense of crushing responsibility. Anyone who has wondered why the Depression crisis did not produce more focused critiques of American capitalism and culture, more sustained efforts to see fundamental structural change, will find more evidence in the interior of these testimonies than in any other source I know. By seeing people turn history into biographical memory, general into particular, we see how they tried to retain deeper validation of their life and society, and how they deferred the deeper cultural judgment implied by the Depression crisis.

The interviews also show these dynamics remaining central to the way the people live with their history over time. The further the generalizations are located from the crisis itself—people reflecting about it, rather than remembering how they thought about it themselves—the greater the tendency to present the past experience in a variety of romanticized modes. Having never been well-connected with the history, memory continues to function as a creator of distance, not merely as an expression of it. The interviews with youth show this most directly, for their hazy sense of the Depression owes much to what their parents have not remembered and have not told them. But far more than fading memory is involved here. As many of the young people say, and as most of the interviews confirm, current realities have affected the transferal process crucially, just as they influenced the views of the journalists discussed earlier. Contemporary pressures and sensitivities encourage people to screen their memories in a selective, protective, and above all didactic fashion. Sometimes this comes across as a moving tribute to the pain of living, sometimes as a desperate weapon in what has been called "the shootout at generation gap." But whatever their tone, and whatever their limits as history in traditional terms, these responses are fascinating in what they reveal about historical memory patterns as cultural documents themselves.

Contemporary contexts, in this sense, operate as a sort of rearguard attack on the structure of memory, and the needs of validation begin to work in a way paradoxically inverse to their effects on the understanding of initial experience. Failure forced people to reduce general experiences to personal terms, the intense pain thereby sheltering them from deeper, more profoundly threatening historical truths; survival, however, seems to encourage them to elevate personal and biographical generalization into historical terms, at once a self-validating message and a culturally validating legacy for the next generation. The "real" history has thus been doubly filtered by time and subsequent experience before it reaches Terkel's tape recorder, and the contradictions of the culture are thus doubly masked.

These comments just begin to suggest ways in which the interviews can be studied for insights into cultural and historical processes. The crucial point is the centrality of the dimension these questions locate, to the understanding of oral history, particularly in a self-conscious advanced society. Rather than the "more history" or the "no history" discussed earlier, this approach promises unique insights that are profoundly historical in a somewhat special sense. By studying how experience, memory, and history become combined in and digested by people who are the bearers of their own history and that of their culture, oral history opens up a powerful perspective; it encourages us to stand somewhat outside of cultural forms in order to observe their workings. Thus it permits us to track the elusive beasts of consciousness and culture in a way impossible to do within, and this, I think, is at the heart of the variant readings of *Hard Times* with which this chapter began.

To develop this critical perspective, to look for significance on this level of oral history, is to argue that the medium of the retrospective biography is in some ways its message. But only implicitly. Perhaps the greatest danger in modern historical studies is the fascination with new methodology, which makes exciting new forms of evidence seem to exhibit self-evident and unequivocal significance. More careful work in most areas, however, quickly shows that the questions to be asked are by no means obvious, the uses of the materials by no means self-evident, and the results to be obtained by no means necessarily meaningful. What matters, rather, are the insights and questions that the historian brings. The same is just beginning to be realized about oral history. Although it is so tempting to take historical testimony to be history itself, a tendency reinforced by the discomfort intellectuals feel at being intellectuals, the very documents of oral history really suggest a very different lesson. To the extent that *Hard Times* is any example, the interviews are nearly unanimous in showing the selective, synthetic, and generalizing nature of historical memory itself. And far from being restricted to the historian's study, these capacities are shown to be not only present, but central in the way we all order our experience and understand the meaning of our lives. There seems to be no reason why, in order to decipher the meaning of memory, historians should feel uncomfortable about applying the same reflective, generalizing intelligence to the documents of oral history.

Chapter 2

The Memory of History

The last few years have seen an exponential increase in the number of people involved in what is coming to be called *public history*. Often publicly funded, they have been working on historical documentaries, oral histories, archival and bibliographic projects, neighborhood studies and exhibits, policy-related historical researches in business and government, and so on. This has led to a substantial flood of new kinds of historical products, generally meant for various public audiences rather than the usual circle of professional academic specialists.

As both a participant in and observer of this phenomenon over the past few years, I have become concerned by the relatively casual way in which the public history impulse has been discussed. Simply put, far more attention has been paid to the "how" than to the "why" of public history. The latter question has frequently been met through formulaic appeals to unexceptionable goals, such as encouraging a wider sharing of knowledge and a broader participation in the process of history-making; giving an empowering sense of their own history to groups denied this by the form, dissemination, and structural biases of conventional scholarship; and providing business or government with a sense of the recent past usable in complex policy analyses. But these all have the somewhat hollow ring of justification, begging what ought to be prior questions about the very nature of historical sensitivity and consciousness in American society today, and about how, why, and whether this ought to be, needs to be, and can be altered, and if so to what specific ends. These questions have been finessed in a great many public history efforts, including, sometimes especially, those developed in the interest of facilitating progressive social change. Whether top-down or bottom-up, most of the energy in public history has been directed toward what could be called the "supply side" dynamics of the presumably unbalanced market for historical intelligence.

The supply-side reference is only partially facetious, in that efforts to supply more and better public history will be no more likely than Reaganomics to redress the inequities and distortions in our public culture, unless they manage to address as well some fundamental paradoxes in the way Americans —in all their dominant and not-so-dominant cultures—have managed variously to invoke, revoke, and generally shrink from provoking a serious reckoning with their past.

To put the matter this way—to view the capacity to engage and make use of history as at once structured, variable, and problematic—is to suggest the centrality of the relationship between history and the process of memory, individual and collective. What matters is not so much the history that is placed before us, but rather what we are able to remember and what role that knowledge plays in our lives. I argue here that the relationship between history and memory is peculiarly and perhaps uniquely fractured in contemporary American life and that repairing it needs to be a major goal of a public history concerned with enhancing our ability to imagine and create a different future through a reuse of the past. To see why this is so requires some exploration of the problem of historical consciousness itself, an expedition that may help remove public history from the closed, neoclassical circle of supply and demand.[1]

Let me begin this excursion with two stories that are at first glance opposite, but on closer examination make the same point. The first involves a student who forgot who won and who lost the war in Vietnam. This happened in a seminar several years ago. The class had read a good portion of Frances Fitzgerald's *Fire in the Lake.* They came in eager to discuss the book's chilling dissection of America's almost purposeful ethnocentrism, as this had contributed to the devastation of Vietnam. None was more stirred than one who expressed her particular outrage at the cynicism with which American military and diplomatic personnel manipulated a succession of South Vietnamese governments. "That's just outrageous," she exclaimed. "Does that *still* go on there? Is our ambassador *still* giving them orders like that?"

A stunned silence fell over the classroom; you did not then have to be older than twenty or twenty-five to remember vividly the war's end in 1975. Somebody gently pointed out that the United States no longer had an ambassador there, that, in fact, we had no real influence at all, given that the North Vietnamese and the National Liberation Front had won and taken over. The student was quite embarrassed. Of course she knew that, and almost immediately she began to recall and display for the class a series of media images, as if to confirm her knowledge—the helicopter on the roof, the ambassador with the plastic-wrapped flag (an image transposed in memory from the fall of Cambodia), and so on. In the more serious discussion that followed, she noted that although she had followed the war closely while it was going on, she had scarcely thought about it since the day it ended. She felt compelled to point out that she really did know the history—it was just that her sense of it had become remote, inaccessible, and ultimately garbled. The lapse, she insisted, was only one of memory.

The second story comes from a 1977 television documentary by Bill Moyers, a powerful study of the CIA's secret war against Fidel Castro, which focused particularly on what had happened to the Cuban-exile terrorists trained, financed, encouraged, and then suddenly abandoned by the CIA. The program included a long interview with a former high-ranking CIA official who had played a key policy role in these activities. With a liberal's sense of disbelief, Moyers asked him how it ever could have happened—the cloak and dagger Mafia connection, the comic-opera beard powder operation, and the quite uncomical assassination plots. How could it all conceivably be justified under any construction of U. S. policy, given our presumed values and beliefs?

Interestingly, the official—no Gordon Liddy, he—did not attempt in the slightest to offer any such justification. He nodded all through Moyers's litany of horrors, and then replied, in effect (I have no transcript at hand), "Well, it can't be justified or defended. But," he added, shaking his head sagely, "you've got to see it in the context of the period. People back then just had a thing about communism. They were willing to do anything. It was just, you know, the spirit of the times." This, from an official whose agency had plotted to overthrow Salvador Allende only a few years previous, an agency (and a government) whose subsequent and ongoing response to what it presumes to be communism (especially in Latin America) demonstrates how little it has changed or learned from the darkest days of the 1950s.

These are, then, opposite stories. In one the subject forgets; in the other he remembers well, setting his recollections in supposedly helpful historical perspective. But somehow the result is the same: in each, the past is severed from the present almost entirely, sealed in a kind of protective wrapping, either of forgetfulness or artificial distance. All this is hardly exceptional, of course. The most casual reflection locates these two anecdotes within a broad pattern that can be found from popular culture to professional scholarship, a pattern wherein selective amnesia and artificial distance can combine to render even last month's history a two-dimensional caricature. The result, far from coincidentally, is a present that seems to float in time—unencumbered, unconstrained, and uninstructed by any active sense of how it came to be.

These stories from several years back suggest some of the dilemmas public history needs to be confronting now. Indeed, the problem of the way the Vietnam War is coming to be remembered, and understood as history, is an especially important if extreme example worth closer examination here. If so much that is threatening about this recent history can be blocked out now, with the evidence all around us and the experience still painfully fresh, can we expect people to relate to challenging but fragile visions of a more complex past, resurrected and presented by imaginative public history projects? Will they not be ignored, absorbed, deflected, or denatured even more easily, and at precisely the point where they threaten to make a real difference in contemporary life? If public history is to avoid this fate, we need to understand more clearly the processes of denial and disengagement, processes which the current "digestion" of the Vietnam War show to be well-advanced politically, culturally, and intellectually.

In the political arena, for instance, where major conflicts in a democratic society are presumably engaged, the war and its roots were never legitimately discussable. At first, these concerns were out of bounds because the war was still going on. Then they were out of bounds because the war had ended and needed to be "put behind us." Neither the war nor the entire complex of historical questions it begged about the relation of the United States to the forces of change in the Third World were directly engaged in any of the five or six presidential campaigns of this era, or in the ones immediately following. They had to be forced to the surface by an extraordinary, extra-institutional mass movement and faded from view once its immediate objective was achieved. The subsequent invention of the "Post-Vietnam Syndrome" and, more recently, the posing for Central America of the question "Another Vietnam?"—a question at once imprecise and overly literal—show some of the consequences of this depoliticization of experience for both left and right.[2]

Mass-mediated popular culture offers other insights into how complex historical experience is processed for acceptable public remembering. Films such as *The Deerhunter* and *Apocalypse Now* said almost nothing about the real history and impact of the war. But they have an enormous amount to teach, in all their pretentious posturing, about the way we have been encouraged to "deal with" such traumatic collective experience. Each film is willfully and explicitly antihistorical; in a context where the forces of history virtually scream to be noticed, solitary individuals are the heroic focus, men kept deliberately isolated from that history, apparently so they can stand as metaphors for the human condition or some other abstraction the filmmakers imagined might be obscured by contact with the real world.

The means of denial in the world of scholarship are different, but already they have begun to exercise the same cauterizing, distancing influence. What the politicians ignore and the media abstract, the academics have begun to obliterate. A fine example of this is *America in Vietnam* by political scientist Guenter Lewy, a book whose questions and answers—much less the generally positive and respectful reception accorded them—say a great deal about the process of academic digestion.[3]

Lewy's book attempts to strip the war of all those pesky moral, political, and emotional questions that so complicate the study of history. In effect, the book tries to recapture within the narrow bounds of policy models and bureaucratic/military analysis a debate that began, so long ago, with the discovery of the fatal descriptive, predictive, and moral limitations of these bounds. The result, accordingly, is to return us to where we were in 1965. We are offered as sober historical conclusions what were, in fact, that era's question-begging clichés: the armies of South Vietnam performed poorly because of deficient leadership, for example; and, Americans misjudged the nature of a civil war. These are now intoned in the dispassionate voice of social science, with hardly a "why?" or a "so what?" question in sight. Vietnam remembered, in such hands, is a Vietnam without those insights into change and history that extraordinary intensity had forced to the surface and, it was once hoped, left permanently deposited for needed reflection. When all that is excluded as incompatible with the demands of cool, objective scholarship, history becomes as comfortable a shield for Lewy as it was for that retired CIA man helping Bill Moyers see things in such a mature, historical perspective.

Recent documentary efforts to deal with Vietnam's passage into the historical dimension have been no more successful in preventing a momentarily glimpsed reality from slipping back behind a curtain of amnesia, or from receding into a blurry distance. I am thinking of perhaps the most important public historical effort in recent years, and certainly the most elaborate and expensive, the thirteen-segment *Vietnam: A Television History* produced in 1985 by public television station WGBH in Boston.

Most critics have had mixed reactions to the series: some of its features and episodes have been held powerful and striking, some have seemed to most observers wholly inadequate to the complexities under examination. The consensus is that the series has depoliticized the war and portrayed it as a "tragedy" without winners or losers. In ways that are discussed below, much of this depoliticization is rooted in the project's public-historical methodology. But surely there is a deeper dimension to the process of "digestion," which has tended to make Vietnam, as it settles into historical memory, a vague symbol now drained of much of the more precise political and cultural content that once stood at the center of America's conflict over the war. In 1985, the hollow media blitz "remembering" the fall of Saigon ten years after only reinforces this point.

Indeed, the Vietnam example, however extreme, is neither isolated nor even special. To the extent our public culture is characterized by a broad and seemingly willful disengagement from the past, it becomes crucial for public historians in particular to inquire into the sources of this phenomenon. If these are not clearly understood it is hard to see how public history can have even a chance of reaching the ambitious goals toward which it has been directed.

The problem has several dimensions, all of them at least partially relevant to a satisfactory explanation of our uncertain relation to our own history.

For a start, the dilemma of historical consciousness has featured centrally in old, sweeping debates about American "capital C" Culture. Conservatives have generally bemoaned our weak sense of historical interconnectedness, finding Americans insensitive to the presence of the past in their lives and institutions, and disrespectful of the constraints fortuitously conferred by experience. Liberals have celebrated these same traits as sources of the energy needed to escape the dead hand of the past. Both, of course, are describing America in similar terms: a liberal culture born free of a connection with a slowly unfolding past, and hence free, or condemned, to create a culture based on a foundation of dreams about individual freedom, rights, and opportunities, dreams presumably made tangible through pragmatic institutional improvisation.

All of this is not irrelevant to the problem at hand, but such cultural explanations are at once too absolute and too solipsistic to tell us very much. A wry comment by a Nigerian friend is particularly apropos in this regard. "What's so mysterious?" he observed. "Why bother with history, when you're rich and powerful? All it can do is tell you how you climbed to the top, which is a story it is probably best not to examine too closely. No, you don't need history. What you need is something more like a pretty carpet that can be rolled out on ceremonial occasions to cover all those bloodstains on the stairs. And in fact that's what you usually get from your historians." Then he went on more solemnly: "For the rest of us, it's a lot different. We don't have the luxury of ignoring history. History is a giant stone that lies on top of us; for us, history is something we have to struggle to get out from under." To say that most of American history has been seen through the eyes of the powerful is a familiar criticism, but we rarely acknowledge, as my friend suggests, how profoundly power, privilege, and freedom from historical constraint have conditioned our basic relation to the past.[4]

For all its insight, however, this structural dimension is an insufficient explanation for our sense of history, if only because the freedom has always been relative, the privilege contested at home and abroad, and the image of power accordingly somewhat deceptive. All this suggests that beyond cultural generalities and structural attributes lies a third dimension, one that might be called functional, which is responsive to the particular demands of historical conflict and struggle. Far from being merely cosmetic and aesthetic, the impulse to cover those bloodstains has been historically intentional—a deliberate if not necessarily conscious part of the process by which a not-so-solidly established power is maintained and shored up.

This helps to explain why the detachment from history seems now to be widening, when America displays a superficial political consensus seemingly premised on an almost total denial of Third World challenges—especially now in Central America—to both the economic pillars and the ideological mystifications sustaining its power. Whatever its part in rationalizing and sustaining the expansion of this power, a self-serving history has been stretched vulnerably thin, like Napoleon's army, by its very success.

Given the difficulty of explaining now the reality of defeat, or at least the necessity of retreat, through the conventional manipulations of history, the major response has been to fall back on a more simple and desperate denial of memory, and hence responsibility. Shortly after Angola became independent, I recall seeing an African leader on *Meet the Press*. After enduring much indignant badgering about the new government's "tilt" toward the Soviets, he finally replied that after twenty years of Soviet support for the Popular Movement for the Liberation of Angola (MPLA), and twenty years of American loyalty to Portugese colonialism, the Angolan posture should hardly need to be explained to Americans, and it certainly did not need to be justified. In this respect, more recently, the cynicism of the self-righteous American response to post-Somoza Nicaragua is virtually total. When the sky is dark with chickens coming back to the American roost, it would seem that the last line of defense is to slam the door of memory. It is, of course, a gravely dangerous response; the United States in such circumstances is a pitiful but far from helpless giant, whose recklessness is only increased by an amnesia offering dubious refuge from the consequences of our own past acts.

These considerations bring us back to the initial problem—the limits of a simplistic, supply-side approach to public history, and the need to see both its potential and its limitations as rooted in the more broadly problematic nature of historical consciousness in our culture. I have been suggesting that one way to approach this is to deal more frontally with the complex matter of historical memory.

Memory has always proven difficult for historians to confront, committed as they are to notions of objectivity beyond the definitive subjectivity of individual and collective recall. Usually, the evidence of memory is considered as an information source to be confirmed by scholarship, or, alternatively, as a way of getting a kind of impressionistic gestalt beyond accountable testing. Both understandings miss the dimension I am getting at here—the process of historical memory itself as a subject for study, one capable of saying a great deal about how the past does or does not figure in our lives and what this in turn tells us about both history and ourselves.

. The point is perhaps made clearer by noticing a linguistic curiosity: in English, we have no verb that readily corresponds to the noun *history*. We can talk about doing history, or studying it, or reading and writing and teaching it, but there is no way to express concisely the activity of rendering the past comprehensible. With the phenomenon of memory, of course, this is not the case at all. Indeed, the relationship is virtually reversed: the noun, memory, simply cannot exist without presuming the active verb, *to remember*.

Involved as well, by definition, is the leap across time from the then of happening to the now of recall. For all the dilemmas of subjectivity, then, the evidence of memory is indispensable for observing precisely the relationships and the process I am arguing we need to understand better.

A number of tools and methods aid our getting at this, of which oral history is certainly the most important. This is because it is unique in being a method that creates its own documents, documents that are by definition explicit dialogues about memory, with the speaker necessarily triangulated between past experiences and the present context of remembering. Unfortunately, oral history has become one of the best examples of the uncritical rush to the supply side, especially given the ease of entry and the assumed demand for its products. This has been particularly true of many self-consciously radical oral historians, who have tended to assume that once the people can be put in touch with their own history, the hegemonic dominant culture will be undermined and false consciousness dispelled.

The matter is hardly this simple, of course, as I remember learning at one symposium featuring remembrances of 1930s organizing at its most violent and militant: the radical historians present heard in the tapes evidence of pervasive class conflict and a call to militance based on labor's proud heritage of struggle. But many of the trade unionists present came away with a very different message: remembrance of the "bad old days" of strikes and conflict, they tended to say, made them appreciate how much progress—as measured by their current no-strike contracts, grievance arbitration, and pension benefits—they had made since the 1930s. Significantly, the program offered no opportunity for collectively discussing, contrasting, and evaluating these different ways of recalling the past and connecting it to the present, which might have made for an important public historical event. Instead, the oral history was simply presented for consumption, as if its meaning was self-evident.[5] A similar casualness often characterizes the use of oral historical evidence in documentary. In *Vietnam: A Television History*, for instance, it is the presentational strategy rather than the explicit interpretation that generates the effect noted above, the deflecting and defusing of political content in the history being presented to the public. Two attributes in particular illustrate this process.

The first is the tendency for interview subjects to be differentiated in terms of the type of statement the editors have chosen to include, and for this differentiation to follow closely lines of class and power. Thus, peasants, ground soldiers, and random individuals tend to be quoted as to personal experience, direct observations, and recalled feelings. The higher or more important the position of the subject, however, the more likely he or she is to be seen offering historical judgments of a broader nature, sweeping evaluations of what an event meant, what caused it, or what the public felt. This correlation of interpretive power and social class position is neither coincidental nor without effect.

The second attribute involves the near exclusive reliance of *Vietnam* on the recorded remembrances of those who "were there." This "pure" oral history strategy becomes especially problematic when the topic is a political or military decision or event, because those who "were there" tend to be, at best, prisoners of the framework we seek to place in perspective and, at worst, self-serving apologists for their own past actions. Many of the deepest problems of the documentary are rooted in this decision to grant "experience" sole interpretive authority, as if there were no other independent sources of knowledge useful for assessing historical truth. In combination, these two attributes make it virtually impossible for the documentary to place the past operations of power in critical perspective, because both non-privileged reflection and informed but noncomplicit sources of knowledge are excluded, in effect, by oral-historical definition.[6]

Of course, many examples of more careful uses of oral history exist, and I am encouraged that many of the oral-historical efforts that have had the widest impact and public visibility are those that have engaged the dialogue between past and present most explicitly, or at least have given it a central place in the presentation of the historical information itself. These include books such as *Hard Times, All God's Dangers,* and *Brass Valley,* for instance, or films such as *Union Maids, The Good Fight,* and *Seeing Red.*[7]

Making memory the focus of critical attention in using oral history is a good bit harder than it sounds, however, regardless of the intentions or sensitivity of the historian, because audience response is itself such a complicating factor. Audiences used to regarding their history from a safe distance often resist attempts at closing the gap, especially when that process collapses comfortable assumptions as well. I have written elsewhere about the way the critical reception of Studs Terkel's *Hard Times* embodies this problem. The book was so casually understood as a romantic evocation of "the way it was" that critics and presumably many readers managed to avoid its starker evidence about the Depression's role in people's memories and contemporary consciousness, evidence suggested by the dialogue between past and present that Terkel intended to be the focus of his pointedly labelled "memory book."[8] But a better and more current example would be the reception, here and abroad, of Marcel Ophuls's documentary films, a body of work that has tried with singular explicitness to force its audience into a confrontation not only with the past, but with what has been done to and with the memory of that past.

If readers could evade the most challenging aspects of the interviews in *Hard Times* by gathering the book up in an affectionate, emotional embrace, they have frequently accomplished the same end in regard to Ophuls's disturbing films by the opposite response. The films generated angry and shrill controversy, with the documentary methodology becoming so central to the debate that many overlooked completely the complex struggle with history that Ophuls had placed before them. *The Sorrow and the Pity* has been more controversial in France than in the United States, because its issues of occupation, domestic collaboration, and resistance are reasonably remote from recent American experience. It will accordingly be easier to illustrate my point by reference to the film that touches American values, presumptions, and concerns more directly, Ophuls's Nuremberg documentary, *The Memory of Justice*.

The film is not really a study of the trials themselves, although powerful use is made of documentary footage and vivid reminiscence. Instead, the central focus in every respect is Ophuls's exhaustive examination—more than four and one-half hours' worth—of how the issues at Nuremberg appear, some thirty years later, to participants, observers, and later-born heirs to the history of the Nazi era. The film's title, then, expresses its subject quite precisely. Ophuls's context is the moral dilemma involved in the collision of unimaginable atrocity with the necessary but insufficient authority of law and morality, as represented by Nuremberg. But his deeper concern is with the way these dilemmas have figured in people's lives as the atrocities and trials have faded into the past, and whether they have made a difference in the way we make our way through our own present.

To get at this dimension, Ophuls pushes the documentary method far beyond conventional bounds. He includes a great deal of interview and documentary material that is not about Nuremberg at all, paying particular attention to the American experience in Vietnam and to the terrorism employed by the French in their struggle to hold Algeria. Sometimes this is included to set the necessary context for individual memoirs, because so many of the principals, such as Telford Taylor, went on to have a major part in later controversies, which have been informed by and are resonant with Nuremberg. But generally, the contemporary exploration of these other themes is to a broader point.

Ophuls wants to examine, I think, whether and how the memory of Nuremberg explicitly affects our response to issues of war crimes and moral responsibility when they are raised today, and whether and how our way of framing and engaging such issues reveals the more implicit traces of the Nuremberg era. Even more, the non-Nuremberg portions of the film have the effect of dissolving the inevitable moral distance from which outsiders observe Germans confronting their Nazi past. The painful scenes of suburban Americans trying to avoid dealing with the immorality of our bombing in Vietnam are, in this sense, both a dramatic and an historical counterpoise to the famous scene of plump, pink, prosperous German youngsters lolling in the nude by an elegant sauna, agonizing over the degree of their responsibility for the Holocaust.

In many quarters, all this has not been well received, which is to say not well perceived. The film was savagely attacked by many American critics, particularly but not limited to the self-appointed Jewish guardians of the Holocaust clustered around *Commentary* magazine. Harold Rosenberg's long, vicious polemic in *The New York Review of Books* was the most elaborate of these, and bears special relevance to our discussion because of how fundamentally it, like many of the others, misunderstood the role of memory in the film.[9]

Basically, such critics accused Ophuls of denying the evil of Nazism by presuming to compare it to other instances of supposed war crimes. The film, says Rosenberg, ends up in "a near-nihilistic bog, in which no one is guilty because all are guilty, and no one is qualified morally to judge." The focus on Vietnam was held a special abomination by these critics, who seemed to feel it presented them with an intolerable choice: either Ophuls wants us to think the Nazis were no worse than us, or he believes that we are no better than they. In either case, Rosenberg condemned the analogy as the foulest ahistorical and antihistorical distortion.

In truth, the film makes no analogy. It is not the objective reality of Vietnam and the Nazi death camps that the flim compares. Rather, it seeks the reverberation of the Nuremberg issues in a later history that, thankfully, cannot replicate them in scale or meaning, but to which they are unfortunately not irrelevant, either. Rosenberg and many opponents of the film argue that any such attempt to use these reference points in our own time is to undercut the horrific exceptionalism of the Nazis. It is as if they want to preserve it as an example of ultimate evil, a moral yardstick that, like the Bureau of Standards's platinum foot, should be kept hermetically locked away in a vault and never actually employed to gauge the real world.

Such resistance to comparison and resonance occasionally may serve the ends of pure scholarship, although even this seems to me a curious notion. But clearly such an approach is totally alien to the processes of historical memory if these are to mean anything in public life. The truths of history and memory are in this sense distinct. Although obviously our memories ought best to be informed by as much good history as we can produce, the Ophuls film helps to focus on what I think must lie at the heart of their role in a public history that will matter—a fundamental commitment to the importance of that verb at the heart of memory, making it something alive and active as we confront our own world. Through the use of historical documents and current interviews, the film creates a process that actually forces us to actively remember the past in the fullest and most difficult sense of the word. This, it seems to me, is a considerable advance over the general tendency of public history to produce images of the past for our more passive consumption.

This contrast has rarely been more important than now, although for the reasons touched on earlier we are unlikely to appreciate it without the help of the most powerful examples the best public history can provide. It is easier to say this, of course, and easier to underscore the importance of appreciating historical memory as a problematic dimension of our culture, than it is to define how public history specifically ought to engage the problem. Rather than offering any inevitably facile prescriptions in this regard, it might be better to close by pointing to a quality we might seek, one almost palpably evident in Ophuls's films and in the other works mentioned.

Here a final bit of word play, suggested by the debate about *The Memory of Justice*, may help. On reading Harold Rosenberg's malicious attack on the film, it struck me that the critique was ignorant in a special sense of the word, one recalling the active verb near to *its* base. Rosenberg was ignorant not in what he did not know, but in what he chose or was driven to ignore in the film. I suspect a good deal of historical ignorance involves this active dimension: *ignore-ance* might he a better way to write it. At the same time, the word that comes to mind when reflecting on the Ophuls's film and similar work is intelligence. *The Memory of Justice* is an intelligent film not because of what it knows or says, but because of the care, depth, insight, and sensitivity with which it reflects on and explores a profound problem. It reminds us that intelligence is most fundamentally a quality of vision and spirit.

This is a somewhat alien notion in American public life, where intelligence has come to be something to be produced by schools, marketed by business, and thoroughly commodified in a way that requires no reading of Marx to understand. When events in Iran—the Shah's fall and later the taking of the hostages—caught the United States by surprise, officials immediately identified the cause as a failure in intelligence gathering, as if acorns of insight lie about in the forests of foreign policy, needing only to be scooped up. Intelligence gathering was also faulted after the serial car-bombings of U. S. facilities in Lebanon, and, more grandly, following the fall of China in 1949, Cuba in 1958, Vietnam in 1975, and Nicaragua in 1979. If this suggests a pattern, so does the characteristic response: more money and power so the CIA can gather, cultivate, produce, or generate more and better intelligence. The metaphors range from the primitive hunting and gathering to the elegantly postindustrial, but they are always economic, with intelligence pictured as a much sought-after good in mysteriously short supply.

Public historians, I believe, must avoid this trap and not treat historical intelligence as a commodity whose supply they seek to replenish, whether by bringing down illuminating fire from elite heights or by gathering gold in mineshafts dug from the bottom up. Whether one is talking about the history of a war or the memories of old residents in a crumbling ethnic neighborhood, what we need are works that will search out the sources and consequences of our active ignore-ance. We need projects that will involve people in exploring what it means to remember, and what to do with memories to make them active and alive, as opposed to mere objects of collection. To the extent this is done, we will be seizing an opportunity not nearly so accessible to conventional academic historical scholarship, whatever its virtues: the opportunity to help liberate for that active remembering all the intelligence, in the way I am using the word, of a people long kept separated from the sense of their own past.

Chapter 3

American History and the Structures of Collective Memory: A Modest Exercise in Empirical Iconography

For more than a decade now, I have been accumulating some fascinating data on the images of American history that my students have carried around in their heads before entering my classroom. The term *data* may be misleadingly scientific, and I am not even sure my hunting and gathering process deserves to be called research, since it began playfully, intended as little more than a tonic to fortify student recruits setting out on their uncertain trek across the arid reaches of the standard survey course. Increasingly, however, I have come to sense that there may be some broader meaning, or at least interest, in the picture gradually emerging from this experimentation.

That sense has been recently sharpened by loud alarums—the very lively debate about American education's role in the ominously accelerating historical amnesia reportedly afflicting high school and college students. As it happens, my modest experiments in what can be called empirical iconography, conducted well before that debate emerged, address its concerns quite directly, providing a certain reassurance in the face of the jeremiads while raising some disturbing questions of a rather different sort.

Let me begin with some brief frame-setting observations about the problem at hand. I will then turn to a straightforward unfolding of my quasi-scientific data combined with some unlicensed flights of exegetical excess. I will conclude by returning to the contemporary debate about American education and historical memory, in order to see how different it may appear after our excursion into the realm of the collective historical subconscious, or at least that portion of it embodied in the responses of over one thousand students at the State University of New York at Buffalo (SUNY-Buffalo) over the past decade.

As a general matter, discussions of historical memory have not been very clear about the relation of individual-level processes—what and how we

remember, whether about our own or more broadly historical experience—
and the processes of collective memory, those broader patterns through which
culture may shape the parameters, structure, and even the content of our
sense of history. My impression is that the two levels of discussion have
remained relatively separate, the former engaging more those concerned with
psychology, education, language, and to an extent oral history, the latter of
interest to cultural historians.

The current debate about history, culture, and education in American
life has brought these differing aspects of memory together, since it focuses
on what individuals know about history, how they come to know (or not know)
it, and what this says about our collective culture, in terms of both cause and
broader effect. I will presume a certain familiarity with the recently discovered
crisis of cultural illiteracy, which seems to have struck a genuine chord of some
kind. Sermons by the prophets Allan Bloom and E.D. Hirsch, Jr., have been
improbable best sellers for many months, and there has been widespread discussion of documents such as *A Nation at Risk*, the report of the National
Commission on Excellence in Education, and *American Memory: A Report on
the Humanities in the Nation's Public Schools*, by Lynne V. Cheney, the chairman of the National Endowment for the Humanities. These all have worked
their way into newsweekly cover stories and extensive television news reports. A
recent sensation, Diane Ravitch and Chester E. Finn, Jr.'s *What Do Our Seventeen-Year-Olds Know?*, has seemed to offer the hard epidemiological evidence
on which the declaration of a cultural health emergency has been based.[1]

This literature is far from uniform, but for present purposes it is possible
to identify at least three linked propositions sounded consistently in all these
works and others in the same vein. The first, already noted, is that our students and young adults are woefully ignorant of the most basic orienting
facts of history, particularly our own American history, much less its larger
meanings, with the result that the strings of a shared cultural memory have
been cut. The second proposition is that this severing of memory is a direct
consequence of a failure of education, of the diminished place of history
education in the curriculum at every level, and of a deterioration in the pedagogy by which we teach whatever history has managed to survive. The final
proposition, a derivative of the first two, is that unless a drastic change in the
quantity and quality of the teaching of history occurs, the only issue will be
whether we collapse from internal disintegration before we are overwhelmed
by economic and political threats from without. Indeed, the most apocalyptic
critics mirror the homophobic Right in its view of Acquired Immune Deficiency Syndrome (AIDS), seeing the amnesia epidemic as at once a threat to
our survival and a kind of divine judgment on a culture gone wrong.

All three propositions involve history and memory, and all turn out, on
close examination, to be something short of self-evident, at least in the sense

in which they are usually advanced. The last mentioned, of course, is so dependent on a particular ideological world view as to be beyond the critical discussion appropriate in this forum. The first two, however, can be stated in objective form and are amenable to both internal and external test.

The evidence I present here is offered in this empirical spirit. As for the first, root proposition, my data challenge the amnesiac conclusion itself, quite directly. While my tables can lay little claim to scientific validity, in at least one respect they address the central question more squarely than most of the well-funded research on which the current debate rests. Ravitch and Finn's title notwithstanding, the major survey work has pursued a kind of inversion of Howard Baker's famous Watergate query: what don't the students know and since when haven't they known it? But to answer such questions, even assuming the validity of the dubious survey instrument, is not necessarily to discover the other side of the coin, to see and understand what they *do* know.[2] My somewhat whimsical investigation may have stumbled on some very different results, however inadvertently, because it began as an attempt to map that very terrain, to explore an interior historical landscape exactly as presented by students.

In fact, the expedition has revealed an environment so strikingly uniform as to cast a significant shadow over the remaining proposition—that pedagogy and curriculum are critical variables in the structuring of American memory. My evidence suggests that our students' historical memory may not, in fact, be shaped so much by their education or lack of it as by collective cultural mechanisms and structures we need to understand better. In that sense, the research bears quite directly on a central focus of recent cultural studies, the concept of "civil religion." Those studies argue the existence in American culture of a set of shared beliefs, myths, "meaning systems," and historical images forming an essentially religious structure, and inquire into the content, origins, and functions of the complex, both as a general cultural concept and in terms of its particular American meaning.[3]

Because so much prior discussion has relied on literary, rather than empirical, evidence of the very existence, much less shared acceptance, of such core cultural beliefs, my data may help advance the inquiry. Cultural analysis, in turn, has much to contribute to our understanding of the broader relation of history to memory. Unless we can bring those two far-from-identical concepts together in a clearly demarcated arena, we will have difficulty penetrating an increasingly strident public discourse in which they are being pressed into the service of some not-so-hidden agendas. But if the debate is approached with careful curiosity and with the conceptual tools commonly found in our scholarly workshops, it may be possible to get closer to the core of legitimate concern in it. Even more, I believe this may be one of the rare instances where the benefits flow both ways—where the heat of a particular polemic can generate light sufficient to illuminate some of the issues.

A Pedagogic Experiment

Let me describe my classroom laboratory. More than a decade ago, I was first assigned to take my turn conducting the first semester of our standard year-long American history survey course, from the beginning through the Civil War. As one who had been teaching the relatively exotic specialty of urban and social history, I realized that this would be an initiation in which I would have to teach materials that most of my students had previously encountered, in what I presumed to be high school versions that were parochial at best and grossly distorted at the expected worst. With all the arrogance of a beginner, I expected my major task to be the clearing of a forest of facts, names, dates, and conventional concepts in order to build, out of the logs of American experience, a city of insight and understanding.

As a way to survey the wilderness before me, I began the very first class with a spot quiz: I asked the students to take out blank paper and to write down, without undue reflection, the first ten names that popped into their heads in response to the prompt "American history from its beginning through the end of the Civil War." Assuming that the lists would be predictably presidential, starting with George Washington, after the students had finished I asked that the experiment be repeated, but this time excluding presidents, generals, statesmen, or other figures in official public life. I hoped that the two lists in combination would be a reasonable approximation of the image of American history brought into the class. The quiz was anonymous, I assured them, simply a way to obtain, via free association, a kind of collective portrait of our starting point. My intention was to fashion, out of the collated answers, an opening lecture contrasting this high school image to the university-level alternative we would develop during the semester.

The results were in some ways quite surprising, which encouraged me to repeat the quizzes each time I taught the course. I have now run eight such surveys, between 1975 and 1988, involving more than 1,000 students in groups ranging from forty to 270. That is a sufficiently substantial base, I think, to justify taking a close look at the results.

Tables 3.1A and 3.1B present two representative tallies for the first question, one from 1984 and the other from my current class in the Fall 1988 semester. The parenthetic figures are the number of students mentioning each name. (About ninety-five took the quiz in 1984 and 220 in 1988.) I should note that the free association mechanism worked dramatically. Many students listed only five or six names and then froze, their minds blank, although they realized on seeing the lists later that they "knew" virtually every name anybody had mentioned. It is, of course, the difference between those names recognized and those immediately leaping to mind that students of culture, with backing from the psychologists, may find most interesting. The

Table 3.1A
Responses to Question One: 1984

Question One: Write down the first ten names that you think of in response to the prompt, "American History from its beginning through the end of the Civil War."

Rank	Name	Frequency	Rank	Name	Frequency
1	G. Washington	83	21	T. Paine	5
2	A. Lincoln	76	22	J. Davis	4
3	T. Jefferson	70	23	N. Hale	4
4	B. Franklin	52	24	J. Monroe	4
5	R. E. Lee	37	25	B. Arnold	3
6	U. S. Grant	31	26	J. Cabot	3
7	J. Adams	30	27	C. Cornwallis	3
8	C. Columbus	22	28	G. A. Custer	3
9	P. Revere	22	29	George III	3
10	J. Hancock	16	30	Lafayette	3
11	J. Smith	10	31	F. Magellan	3
12	A. Jackson	9	32	S. Adams	2
13	J. Q. Adams	7	33	D. Boone	2
14	J. W. Booth	7	34	A. Burr	2
15	A. Hamilton	7	35	H. Clay	2
16	B. Ross	7	36	T. Edison	2
17	P. Henry	6	37	F. S. Key	2
18	J. Madison	6	38	D. Madison	2
19	A. Jackson	5	39	Pocahontas	2
20	Lewis & Clark	5	40	H. Tubman	2

phenomenon also helps compensate for a methodological deficiency: In a more serious analysis, it would be important to analyze the order of mention as well as the frequency, but as that was beyond my statistical resources, I sought an approximation by limiting the time available and by encouraging students to stop when their minds began to go blank, rather than to fill up all ten places through more deliberate concentration.

The first tables are unsurprising, an array of mostly political and military figures crystallizing around the major defining events of United States history, the Revolution and the Civil War. There is little here to suggest anything other than the dutiful, civic-focused high school history courses whose residue I had expected to find. But as we shall see, the other results cast the lists in a somewhat different light.

Table 3.1C presents an eight-time comparison of answers to this question. The lists are of unequal length because of frequent ties, and because each survey rank orders all those names receiving at least three to six mentions, depending on the size of the class—wherever it falls ordinally, the last name marks a dropping-off point; all those below it received only relatively isolated mentions.

Table 3.1B
Responses to Question One: 1988

Question One: Write down the first ten names that you think of in response to the prompt, "American History from its beginning through the end of the Civil War."

Rank	Name	Frequency	Rank	Name	Frequency
1	G. Washington	197	22	H. Tubman	8
2	A. Lincoln	192	23	George III	7
3	T. Jefferson	140	24	F. S. Key	7
4	B. Franklin	102	25	T. Edison	6
5	J. Adams	78	26	P. Henry	6
6	U. S. Grant	70	27	J. P. Jones	6
7	R. E. Lee	64	28	J. Q. Adams	5
8	A. Jackson	58	29	Lafayette	5
9	C. Columbus	49	30	W. T. Sherman	5
10	J. Hancock	37	31	A. Burr	4
11	J. Madison	25	32	F. Douglass	4
12	P. Revere	25	33	T. J. Jackson	4
13	A. Hamilton	22	34	A. Johnson	4
14	T. Paine	19	35	W. Penn	4
15	B. Ross	17	36	H. B. Stowe	4
16	G. A. Custer	11	37	D. Boone	3
17	J. Smith	11	38	C. Cornwallis	3
18	B. Arnold	9	39	S. Douglas	3
19	J. W. Booth	9	40	N. Hale	3
20	J. Monroe	9	41	Lewis & Clark	3
21	S. Adams	8	42	D. Madison	3
			43	M. Standish	3

The results confirm the initial impression of any one year, but the uniformity is quite striking. Considering first the "top ten" of each list, we find six names appearing every year (George Washington, Thomas Jefferson, Abraham Lincoln, Ulysses S. Grant, John Adams, and Benjamin Franklin). As charted in Table 3.1D, four other names rank in the top ten in five of the eight years: Robert E. Lee, Paul Revere, John Hancock, and Andrew Jackson.

All told, only fourteen different names appear in the eighty slots (ten each year for eight years) at the top of the lists. To be in social-scientific fashion, I have calculated measures of the diversity and consensus on these lists (see Table 3.1E). The maximum number of possible top ten names (eighty) minus the minimum possible (ten) yields a maximum "spread" of seventy. Subtracting from the actual total number of names in the eighty slots (fourteen) that same minimum (ten) yields an actual spread of four. To provide a standardized base for comparison, dividing actual spread by the potential maximum yields an index on a scale where 0.00 represents total lack of diversity (the same ten names each year) and 1.00 represents total diversity (no

Table 3.1C
Question One: Eight Samples

Question One: Write down the first ten names that you think of in response to the prompt, "American history from its beginning through the end of the Civil War."

1975	1976	1978	1982	1983	1984	1985	1988
1. G. Washington	1. G. Washington	1. G. Washington	1. G. Washington	1. G. Washington	1. G. Washington	1. G. Washington	1. G. Washington
2. T. Jefferson	2. T. Jefferson	2. T. Jefferson	2. A. Lincoln	2. A. Lincoln	2. A. Lincoln	2. A. Lincoln	2. A. Lincoln
3. A. Lincoln	3. A. Lincoln	3. A. Lincoln	3. T. Jefferson	3. T. Jefferson	3. T. Jefferson	3. T. Jefferson	3. T. Jefferson
4. U. S. Grant	4. B. Franklin	4. B. Franklin	4. B. Franklin	4. B. Franklin	4. B. Franklin	4. J. Adams	4. B. Franklin
5. R. E. Lee	5. J. Adams	5. U. S. Grant	5. J. Adams	5. U. S. Grant	5. R. E. Lee	5. B. Franklin	5. J. Adams
6. J. Adams	6. U. S. Grant	6. R. E. Lee	6. U. S. Grant	6. R. E. Lee	6. U. S. Grant	6. U. S. Grant	6. U. S. Grant
7. B. Franklin	7. P. Revere	7. J. Adams	7. A. Jackson	7. J. Adams	7. J. Adams	7. P. Revere	7. R. E. Lee
8. J. Madison	8. J. Hancock	8. A. Jackson	8. J. Hancock	8. J. Hancock	8. C. Columbus	8. R. E. Lee	8. A. Jackson
9. A. Hamilton	9. A. Jackson	9. C. Columbus	9. R. E. Lee	9. P. Revere	9. P. Revere	9. A. Jackson	9. C. Columbus
10. J. Smith	10. A. Hamilton	10. P. Revere	10. P. Revere	10. A. Jackson	10. J. Hancock	10. J. Hancock	10. J. Hancock
11. C. Columbus	11. R. E. Lee	11. J. Hancock	11. J. Madison	11. C. Columbus	11. J. Smith	11. C. Columbus	11. J. Madison
12. B. Ross	12. B. Ross	12. J. Smith	12. C. Columbus	12. J. Madison	12. A. Jackson	12. A. Hamilton	12. P. Revere
13. P. Revere	13. P. Henry	13. George III	13. G. A. Custer	13. A. Hamilton	13. J. Q. Adams	13. J. Madison	13. A. Hamilton
	14. J. Madison	14. J. Madison	14. T. Paine	14. J. Monroe	14. J. W. Booth	14. J. Smith	14. B. Ross
	15. C. Columbus	15. B. Arnold	15. A. Hamilton	15. J. P. Jones	15. A. Hamilton	15. J. Q. Adams	15. G. A. Custer
				16. G. A. Custer	16. B. Ross	16. George III	16. J. Smith
				17. P. Henry	17. P. Henry	17. J. Monroe	17. B. Arnold
					18. J. Madison	18. B. Ross	18. J. W. Booth
						19. J. W. Booth	19. J. Monroe

Table 3.1D
Question One: Eight Sample Summary

Question One: Write down the first ten names that you think of in response to the prompt, "American history from its beginning through the end of the Civil War."

		Rank in Year:								Years on List
	Name	*1975*	*1976*	*1978*	*1982*	*1983*	*1984*	*1985*	*1988*	
1	G. Washington	1	1	1	1	1	1	1	1	8
2	A. Lincoln	3	3	3	2	2	2	2	2	8
3	T. Jefferson	2	2	2	3	3	3	3	3	8
4	B. Franklin	7	4	4	4	4	4	5	4	8
5	U. S. Grant	4	6	5	6	5	6	6	6	8
6	J. Adams	6	5	7	5	7	7	4	5	8
7	R. E. Lee	5	11	6	9	6	5	8	7	8
8	P. Revere	13	7	10	10	9	9	7	12	8
9	C. Columbus	11	15	9	12	11	8	11	9	8
10	J. Madison	8	14	14	11	12	18	13	11	8
11	A. Jackson		9	8	7	10	12	9	8	7
12	J. Hancock		8	11	8	8	10	10	10	7
13	A. Hamilton	9	10		15	13	15	12	13	7
14	J. Smith	10		12			11	14	17	5
15	B. Ross	12	12				16	18	15	5
16	G. A. Custer				13	16			16	3
17	P. Henry		13			17	17			3
18	J. Monroe					14		17	20	3
19	J. W. Booth						14	19	19	3
20	T. Paine				14				14	2
21	J. Q. Adams						13	15		2
22	George III			13				16		2
23	B. Arnold			15					18	2
24	J. P. Jones						15			1

names appearing on more than one year's list). This I will declare, only slightly tongue-in-cheek, to be the Diversity Index: for question one's top ten, it is a minuscule 0.057.

The Consensus Index is less complex—those names appearing *every* year in the top ten as a percentage of all names appearing *any* year in the top ten: 42.9 percent. Perhaps more indicative is the Five Plus Consensus Index: 71.4 percent of the names that ever appeared in the top ten did so in five or more of the eight years surveyed.

Moving from the top ten to consider the full lists, we find slots for 132 names, but only twenty-four different ones appearing, resulting in a Diversity Index of 0.036—*lower* than that for the top ten. This is an important indication that the degree of diversity does not increase as one proceeds down the list. Of the twenty-four names, ten (41.7 percent) appear every year and fif-

Table 3.1E
Eight Sample Analysis

Question One		Top Ten	Total List
A	Total Names	14	24
B	Maximum Possible Names	80	132
C	Minimum Possible Names	10	20
D	Maximum Possible Spread (B-C)	70	112
E	Actual Spread (A-C)	4	4
F	Diversity Index (E/D)	0.057	0.036
G	Names on List All Eight Years	6	10
H	Eight-Year Consensus Index (G/A)	42.9%	41.7%
I	Names on List Five Years or More	10	15
J	Five-Plus Consensus Index (I/A)	71.4%	62.5%
K	Consensus Decay Index [(J.1-J.2)/J.1		0.125

teen (62.5 percent) in five of the eight years. Both Diversity Index and the Consensus Index, then, suggest that the overall similarity of the lists is hardly accounted for by the very famous names at the top but spreads relatively evenly through the full range of names my students list year after year.

Perhaps the most culturally revealing characteristic of the lists is their near-exclusive political and military cast, focused on epochal events. In class discussion, we have frequently noted the kinds of people missing from the survey: religious figures, for instance, or artists, philosophers, or scientists. It is hard to imagine a similar poll in England or Italy or China or Chile being quite so relentlessly political, public, and heroic. That narrow focus certainly seemed to say something about American culture, but it is not inconsistent with my original expectation that what I was measuring was the result of high school history curricula focused on our civic traditions and formal institutions. The dramatic uniformity from year to year, however, suggested something else—perhaps an unexpected level of indoctrination, or a deeper set of cultural structures at work on the collective imagination of students year after year.

The results of the second set of surveys offer some powerful evidence for the latter hypothesis and some provocative suggestions as to the content and meaning of those cultural structures. The most recent surveys are presented in Tables 3.2A and 3.2B, a compendium of near-legendary characters whom most Americans encounter in grade school, if anywhere on the educational spectrum; more generally, the figures on the list are the stuff of popular culture rather than school curricula.

I must admit that the first time I encountered such results, I was quite surprised. Indeed, the students were surprised and a little embarrassed themselves: again, they all claimed to "know" something about the more sophisticated names mentioned even once. Yet it seemed clear that when confronting the blank page, many of them had reached back beyond their recent experience and listed figures imaginatively encountered a good bit earlier, or outside of school altogether.

Table 3.2A
Responses to Question Two: 1984

Question Two: Write down the first ten names that you think of, excluding presidents, generals, statesmen, etc., in response to the prompt, "American history from its beginning through the end of the Civil War."

Rank	Name	Frequency	Rank	Name	Frequency
1	B. Ross	37	19	A. G. Bell	3
2	P. Revere	25	20	G. W. Carver	3
3	H. Tubman	15	21	F. Douglass	3
4	Lewis & Clark	14	22	J. Hancock	3
5	J. W. Booth	11	23	W. Penn	3
6	D. Madison	10	24	M. Standish	3
7	J. Smith	10	25	M. Washington	3
8	F. S. Key	8	26	S. B. Anthony	2
9	Pocahontas	8	27	C. Attucks	2
10	H. B. Stowe	7	28	A. Burr	2
11	D. Boone	6	29	D. Crockett	2
12	T. Edison	6	30	N. Hale	2
13	B. Franklin	6	31	C. McCormick	2
14	R. Fulton	6	32	F. Nightingale	2
15	B. Arnold	5	33	T. Paine	2
16	C. Barton	5	34	M. Pitcher	2
17	J. Brown	5	35	Sacajawea	2
18	J. P. Jones	4	36	W. Scott	2

This impression is confirmed, to put it mildly, by comparing the answers to this second survey in the eight different years (see Table 3.2C). The lists are so consistent in character, and even in individual composition, as to suggest that they stem from something beyond the high school classroom. They suggest, as a closer examination can illustrate, that the free association method was opening to view evidence of a very particular cultural imprinting independent of whatever degree of sophistication the students had encountered in high school. To explore the nature and content of that particularity, we need to examine this ad hoc pantheon more closely.

At first glance, it is the uniformity that is the most striking. In fact, given the absence of the focusing presence of Lincoln, Washington, and Jefferson, the similarity of the lists is really astonishing. To repeat the previous analysis, we find here that only twenty different names appear in the top ten for the

Table 3.2B
Responses to Question Two: 1988

Question Two: Write down the first ten names that you think of, excluding presidents, generals, statesmen, etc., in response to the prompt, "American history from its beginning through the end of the Civil War."

Rank	Name	Frequency	Rank	Name	Frequency
1	B. Franklin	124	21	M. Washington	9
2	B. Ross	74	22	Pocahontas	8
3	Columbus	63	23	E. Whitney	8
4	P. Revere	63	24	P. Henry	7
5	J. Hancock	33	25	G. W. Carver	6
6	H. Tubman	33	26	M. Standish	6
7	Lewis & Clark	25	27	D. Madison	5
8	T. Edison	17	28	F. Nightingale	5
9	J. W. Booth	16	29	N. Turner	5
10	F. S. Key	15	30	A. G. Bell	4
11	T. Paine	13	31	J. Brown	4
12	S. B. Anthony	12	32	A. Burr	4
13	N. Hale	12	33	D. Crockett	4
14	A. Hamilton	12	34	George III	4
15	J. Smith	12	35	J. P. Jones	4
16	F. Douglass	10	36	S. Clemens	3
17	H. B. Stowe	10	37	J. Jay	3
18	B. Arnold	9	38	Dred Scott	3
19	D. Boone	9	39	M. Twain	3
20	W. Penn	9	40	Uncle Tom	3

eight years, out of the eighty possible, for a Diversity Index of 0.14—not as low as for question one, but still strikingly diminutive (see Table 3.2D).

Two of the top ten are the same in all eight years: Betsy Ross, the apocryphal creator of the first American flag, and Paul Revere, the horsebacked bearer of the message of the Revolution. Another six rank in this grouping in at least five of the seven years: Christopher Columbus; John Smith, the leader of the first successful colonial settlement in Virginia; Eli Whitney, inventor of both interchangeable parts and the cotton gin and hence a symbol of the rise of both northern industrial and southern slave societies; Meriwether Lewis and William Clark, explorers of the American West who are counted as one— they have become almost a fused individual in the memories of students, always listed together as "Lewis and Clark" or, more than once, Lewis N. Clark; the frontiersman Daniel Boone; and Harriet Tubman, the heroic escaped slave who returned to lead others to freedom, whose presence is the one sign that a century-old pantheon has begun to respond to the recent recognition of blacks as agents of change, not merely objects of misfortune, in American history.

Considering the entire list in a total of 168 possibilities, only forty-six different names are listed, and of them seventeen appear in at least five of the eight years and five appear every year. Our Diversity Index for question two's

Table 3.2C
Question Two: Eight Samples

Question Two: Write down the first ten names that you think of, excluding presidents, generals, statesmen, etc., in response to the prompt, "American history from its beginning through the end of the Civil War."

	1975	1976	1978	1982	1983	1984	1985	1988
1.	B. Ross	B. Ross	B. Ross	B. Ross	B. Ross	B. Ross	B. Ross	B. Franklin
2.	P. Revere	P. Revere	E. Whitney	P. Revere	P. Revere	P. Revere	P. Revere	B. Ross
3.	C. Columbus	C. Columbus	D. Boone	J. Smith	Lewis & Clark	H. Tubman	H. Tubman	C. Columbus
4.	J. Smith	E. Whitney	P. Revere	T. Edison	J. Smith	Lewis & Clark	C. Columbus	P. Revere
5.	Pocahontas	T. Paine	Pocahontas	E. Whitney	T. Edison	J. W. Booth	F. S. Key	J. Hancock
6.	B. Arnold	H. Tubman	C. Columbus	D. Crockett	J. W. Booth	D. Madison	J. Smith	H. Tubman
7.	Lewis & Clark	J. Smith	Lewis & Clark	C. Columbus	H. Tubman	J. Smith	Pocahontas	Lewis & Clark
8.	D. Boone	Lewis & Clark	J. Smith	H. Tubman	E. Whitney	F. S. Key	Lewis & Clark	T. Edison
9.	E. Whitney	B. Arnold	R. Fulton	D. Boone	D. Boone	Pocahontas	E. Whitney	J. W. Booth
10.	D. Crockett	D. Boone	T. Edison	F. S. Key	T. Paine	H. B. Stowe	B. Franklin	F. S. Key
11.	F. S. Key	Pocahontas	A. Hutchinson	N. Turner	Pocahontas	D. Boone	J. W. Booth	T. Paine
12.	T. Paine	F. S. Key	D. Crockett	F. Nightingale	M. Washington	T. Edison	T. Paine	S. B. Anthony
13.	J. P. Jones	J. Brown	F. Douglass	T. Paine	C. Columbus	B. Franklin	M. Washington	N. Hale
14.	N. Hawthorne	J. P. Jones	C. McCormick	J. W. Booth	B. Arnold	R. Fulton	C. Attucks	J. Smith
15.	H. B. Stowe	Lafayette	N. Hawthorne	P. De Leon	A. Burr	B. Arnold	J. Brown	F. Douglass
16.	R. Williams	J. W. Booth	H. Tubman	Sitting Bull	F. Douglass	C. Barton	G. W. Carver	H. B. Stowe
17.	M. Standish	D. Crockett	H. B. Stowe	M. Washington	Sitting Bull	J. Brown	S. B. Anthony	B. Arnold
18.	G. W. Carver	R. Fulton	V. Balboa	E. Allen	J. Hancock	J. P. Jones	D. Boone	D. Boone
19.		G. W. Carver	G. W. Carver	G. W. Carver	F. S. Key	A. G. Bell	N. Hale	W. Penn
20.					G. W. Carver	G. W. Carver	P. Henry	M. Washington
21.						F. Douglass	M. Pitcher	Pocahontas
22.						J. Hancock	M. Standish	E. Whitney
23.						W. Penn	H. B. Stowe	P. Henry
24.						M. Standish		G. W. Carver
25.						M. Washington		M. Standish

Table 3.2D
Question Two: Eight Sample Summary

Question Two: Write down the first ten names that you think of, excluding presidents, generals, statesmen, etc., in response to the prompt, "American history from its beginning through the end of the Civil War."

	Name	Rank in Year: 1975	1976	1978	1982	1983	1984	1985	1988	Years on List
1	B. Ross	1	1	1	1	1	1	1	2	8
2	P. Revere	2	2	4	2	2	2	2	4	8
3	J. Smith	4	7	8	3	4	7	6	14	8
4	D. Boone	8	10	3	9	9	11	18	18	8
5	G. W. Carver	18	19	19	19	20	20	16	24	8
6	C. Columbus	3	3	6	7	13		4	3	7
7	Lewis & Clark	7	8	7		3	4	8	7	7
8	H. Tubman		6	16	8	7	3	3	6	7
9	E. Whitney	9	4	2	5	8		9	22	7
10	Pocahontas	5	11	5		11	9	7	21	7
11	F. S. Key	11	12		10	19	8	5	10	7
12	J. W. Booth		16		14	6	5	11	9	6
13	T. Paine	12	5		13	10		12	11	6
14	T. Edison			10	4	5	12		8	5
15	B. Arnold	6	9			14	15		17	5
16	H. B. Stowe	15		17			10	23	16	5
17	M. Washington				17	12	25	13	20	5
18	R. Fulton		18	9			14			4
19	D. Crockett	10	17	12	6					4
20	F. Douglass			13		16	21		15	4
21	M. Standish	17					24	22	25	4
22	B. Franklin						13	10	1	3
23	J. Hancock					18	22		5	3
24	J. P. Jones	13	14				18			3
25	J. Brown		13				17	15		3
26	S. B. Anthony							17	12	2
27	N. Hawthorne	14		15						2
28	N. Hale							19	13	2
29	Sitting Bull				16	17				2
30	W. Penn						23		19	2
31	P. Henry							20	23	2
32	J. Madison						6			1
33	A. Hutchinson		11							1
34	N. Turner				11					1
35	F. Nightingale				12					1
36	C. McCormick			14						1
37	C. Attucks							14		1
38	P. De Leon				15					1
39	A. Burr					15				1
40	Lafayette		15							1
41	R. Williams	16								1
42	C. Barton						16			1
43	E. Allen				18					1
44	V. Balboa			18						1
45	A. G. Bell						19			1
46	M. Pitcher							21		1

full list is thus 0.15, inconsequentially higher than the 0.14 for the list's top ten (see Table 3.2E). The Diversity and Consensus Indexes for question two are, of course, considerably lower than for the canonical list of question one, but that is unsurprising since the second question prompts responses constrained by the familiar political pantheon. In fact, it is remarkable that the indexes are as low as they are, given the infinite range of possible responses. It is especially significant that the diversity and consensus in the top ten list for question two do not alter very much when the full range of responses is considered: indeed, by at least one measure (which in a last fit of social science I will call the Consensus Decay Index, or CDI) more consistency is found between the top ten and the full list on question two (a CDI of 0.076) than on question one (a CDI of 0.125, nearly 65 percent higher). That is to say, on question two there is a slower increase than on question one in the variation encountered as we move away from the most popular images at the top. This means there is actually more consistency in the images students have offered over the years in response to the second question.

Table 3.2E

Eight Sample Analysis

Question Two		Top Ten	Total List
A	Total Names	20	46
B	Maximum Possible Names	80	168
C	Minimum Possible Names	10	25
D	Maximum Possible Spread (B-C)	70	143
E	Actual Spread (A-C)	10	21
F	Diversity Index (E/D)	0.14	0.15
G	Names on List All Eight Years	2	5
H	Eight-Year Consensus Index (G/A)	10.0%	10.9%
I	Names on List Five Years or More	8	17
J	Five-Plus Consensus Index (I/A)	40.0%	37.0%
K	Consensus Decay Index [(J.1-J.2)/J.1]		0.076

It is hard to know how much we can generalize from the uniformity of these lists or how much interpretive weight they can bear. Perhaps all this is merely an artifact of my western New York sample, or the curriculum of New York State's primary and secondary schools; I would be the first to concede that a similar survey in Waco, Texas, for example, would produce a somewhat different list. But I believe regional variation would be far less than might be expected, and that the consistency of the lists—arguably closer to the heart of their significance than the precise content—might well be as striking. I think the free association producing the lists is tapping a very particular kind of cultural memory, one whose hold is general rather than a product of particular associations. For instance, the most famous local citizen in national life—Millard Fillmore, a lamentable president but a great Buffalonian, whose name inescapably graces city streets, districts, and public institutions—has not made the list even once. Beyond that, Buffalo is a heavily ethnic city, and many of our students come from a highly self-conscious Polish-American community; a parade is held in honor of Casimir Pulaski every year and his name is certainly well known to such students. Yet he has rarely been mentioned on any list *at all*, nor do the tallies suggest much imprint of any other ethnic identification.

Additional positive and empirical support for my claim of generality is found in one carefully controlled replication of the survey in another locale. After learning of my experiment and discussing it in correspondence, the cultural geographer Wilbur Zelinsky tried it on a large group of his own students at the Pennsylvania State University—an institution not terribly far from Buffalo, but not in an identical culture area either, and one whose students are shaped by a different precollege curriculum. Even with the accumulating weight of my own evidence, we were both astounded by the results in Pennsylvania: on questions one and two alike, thirteen of the top fifteen names were identical to those on my Buffalo surveys, appearing in nearly identical rank order, headed once again by the unsinkable Betsy Ross. The tiny differences in the lists almost disappeared in the fuller list of twenty or so: William Penn turns out to be the only figure who holds a very different place in the Pennsylvania rankings. Zelinsky's lists even reproduce some of the peculiarities of mine, such as the curiously misplaced presence of George Washington Carver and Thomas Edison, who belong in a different time period, and the Americanization of Florence Nightingale, who belongs on another continent.

In addition, Zelinsky added one methodological flourish whose products bear usefully on the broader issues I raised earlier: he asked his students to note whether they had ever taken a college American history course before (roughly 30 percent had, and 70 percent had not). Given the cultural importance many attach to exposure to history courses in the curriculum, it is interesting to ask what changes when Zelinsky's responses are tallied under these headings.

The answer is absolutely nothing; the lists compiled by both groups of students are virtually identical in composition and even rank order. Some individual names obtain slightly higher support from students exposed to college history courses (Samuel Adams and Jefferson Davis on question one, Davy Crockett and John Wilkes Booth on question two) while others gain proportionally more of their votes from students without that background (George Washington Carver and William Penn). But the breakdown of support for most of the names shows only the most modest divergence from the breakdown of the class as a whole. There is a final poetic justice in the fact that the one figure on question two at absolute dead center, listed in absolutely identical proportions by history and non-history students alike, is none other than Betsy Ross. Whatever students may or may not have learned in college history courses (and, as I shall argue, high school history courses) seems to have little to do with the images drawn forth by this exercise.[4]

A Patterned Pantheon

Having mollified the gods of empiricism, let us turn to the task of explaining in broader cultural terms the patterns we have uncovered. Each list profiles a strikingly consistent pantheon of generally received and recalled cultural heroes, legends, and near-mythic figures. Quite apparently, I am examining here evidence of cultural transmission, perhaps as mediated through the primary schools and popular culture. Accordingly, my introductory lecture has had less to do with the high-school curricula I had expected to engage in battle than with what I came to pose, for the students, as a kind of anthropological question: "If all you knew about American culture was what you could deduce from this list, what would you know?"

Thus viewed as a cultural artifact, the profile offered in each list is anything but random. Rather, it stands as a dramatic elaboration of what Catherine L. Albanese has termed the "presumption of newness" at the core of the American myth.[5] Indeed, what we see here is a broadening of that theme into an ongoing fixation on creation myths of origin and innovation.

In this, myth must be understood as the driving force behind history: John Smith and Pocahontas were real, of course, but manifestly it is the mythic scene in which the "love" of the Indian "princess" saves the explorer from a "savage" death that accounts for the high-ranking presence of both figures in the imagination of my students. Such a mythic framework reaches out to the explorers, from Columbus to the Siamese-twins Lewis and Clark, who define the nation by "beginning" its history, their "discovery" of space really a beginning of America's historical time, again and again. It includes both the revolutionary progenitors and the practical inventors like Whitney who are remembered as initiators of America's distinctive epoch of technological time.

It is interesting, in this regard, to note the place of the inventor Edison in fourteenth place on the question two summary tally, near the top, and the place of the black botanist Carver, who brings up the rear almost every time and who is the only figure *never* to appear in the top ten who *always* ranks on the overall list. (On Zelinksy's poll, he is the single figure most disproportionately listed by students who had not taken history courses.)

As figures from the late nineteenth and early twentieth centuries, both Edison and Carver represent an overriding of the instructions to focus on an earlier time period. It hardly seems coincidental, given contemporary anxiety about ungraspable technological change and uncontrollable corporate organization on a worldwide scale, that the *only* regularly repeated chronological "mistakes" are these comfortable symbols of practical genius and human-scale progress.

And for a white society shuttling between racial guilt and fear, the symbol of Carver has always offered an additional all-too-convenient balm. The myth of the patient experimenter, the "credit to his race" who discovered manifold new uses for the lowly peanut, has long obscured the reality of a man whose acquiescence in the racism of the early twentieth-century United States stands in dramatic contrast to the resistance offered by black leaders like W.E.B. DuBois and even Booker T. Washington. One wonders if this posture may have contributed more than his modest scientific accomplishments to Carver's not-quite-natural selection for immortality in the evolution of American memory.

There is also something beyond coincidence in the recurrence of John Wilkes Booth and Benedict Arnold, who represent for an innocent nation the serpent-traitors whose evil also sets history in motion—necessary preludes to the transcendent triumph of good. As these observations suggest, the list is not only composed of quasi-mythic figures: as a collective portrait, it has a kind of mythic structure and completeness itself, a character confirmed by its re-creation year after year in nearly identical terms.

But the most compelling indication of this character is the nearly unshakable hold of Betsy Ross on the first place position—she tops the list in seven of the eight classes, and her decline to second place this past semester is actually the exception that proves the rule. My graduate assistant notes that I seem to have omitted the "statesmen" prompt from the list of those to be excluded on question two's list, thus accounting for Franklin's triumph and John Hancock's uncharacteristically high rank on question two. (Always a fixture on question one, in other years both were usually omitted from the second list by students given the intended exclusionary prompt.) In any event, Betsy Ross' position at the top is truly phenomenal, a record that cries out for explanation as it has occasioned a good deal of discussion in my classes each year. Even given everything said so far, it is still not immediately apparent why this *particular* mythic figure has been discovered so much more frequently than others by the searching beam of free association memory.

Part of the explanation may lie in a kind of psychological/feminist interpretation generated by one class discussion. Perhaps the command to produce names of those not in positions of public power led the genderized imaginations of students through the following sequence: Non-public means domestic and private; domestic and private means women; women means Betsy Ross. I think there may be something to this, although it still begs a number of questions. The framework of civil religion and comparative mythology provides some additional insights however, and all combined may serve to make the Betsy Ross hegemony less mystical and more instructive.

The flag, of course, is the primary symbol of what is distinctive about the United States. It represents the core of our nationality—that political identity declared and constituted in the epochal revolutionary experience whose artifactual yet genuine religious content Albanese has documented so powerfully. As Marshall Smelser has written, the flag "has assumed a moral value transcending the mundane purposes of national identification. As a tribal totem, it satisfies the real and almost universal hunger for a public symbol of spiritual kinship above and invulnerable to the contentions and changes of politics—and for which no other totem is available to the United States."[6] If that is true, there is nice logic to Betsy Ross' preeminent place in a structure of creation myth figures and heroic progenitors; she represents the most inclusive symbol of national identity, an identity perhaps more fragile and in need of shoring up than other national identities because of its uniquely political character.

The Ross hegemony also helps to bring the presidential list of question one within the interpretation developed here, for its figures are also more powerful as symbols of political cohesion and identity than as historical figures per se. Indeed, Washington himself "absorbed and unified the elements from the classical and Christian past, becoming for Americans, a divine man."[7] Beyond helping us to respect, and thereby understand, a sometimes ludicrous apotheosis that began even in Washington's lifetime, Albanese's discussion provides a context for some final reflections on the essentially religious meaning of Betsy Ross's place in this collective portrait.

Albanese documents how the revolutionary sons made themselves into Founding Fathers, with Washington the *primus inter pares*, the spiritually literal Father of the Nation. She also shows how his spiritual meaning came to obscure his real existence: his wife, Martha, faded from legendary image and relatively speaking from our memories, because "kindred as was the soul of the father of his country to his wife, it had proved to be far more closely interfused with the structures of meaning and value of his countrymen. Washington . . . had become a grand collective representative, a tribal totem." And in the process, fictive and symbolic kin came to replace his real family in popular imagination: thus the common celebration of the marquis de Lafayette as the "beloved and adopted son."[8]

Albanese could go no further with the myth, but evidence of the symbolic role of Betsy Ross allows us to complete the picture. To this end, it is important to note that the Betsy Ross story is a product of a late nineteenth-century style of religio-mythic craftsmanship. The actual Betsy Ross had, demonstrably, no role whatsoever in the actual creation of any actual first flag. But more important, her story itself played no part in revolutionary-era tradition or mythmaking even at its most instrumental. In fact, the flag story emerged only a century later in Philadelphia, when her descendants sought to create a tourist attraction around the time of the centennial exposition. The reasons for the emergence of the tale were thus prosaic, not to say mercenary; but as Albanese reminds us, however intentional and instrumental, such self-consciousness does not exclude deeper levels of cultural meaning and expression.[9]

It is hard to avoid the speculation that the latter-day invention of the mythic Betsy Ross—and her immediate public enshrinement—came as a kind of needed supplement to the revolutionary myth, a final step in the humanocentric articulation of essentially religious beliefs and experiences. If George is the Father of the Country—of the nation, of all the American sons and daughters—then surely Betsy Ross exists symbolically as the Mother, who gives birth to our collective symbol.

One can go further. If Washington is, indeed, a surrogate for God the Father, the meaning of Betsy Ross is unmistakable: she stands for the Blessed Virgin Mary in the iconography of our civil religion. A plain woman is visited by a distant god, and commanded to be the vehicle, through their collaboration, of a divine creation. And indeed, in the classroom pageants enacted by generations of American schoolchildren over the past century, that is exactly what we see: Washington calls on the humble seamstress Betsy Ross in her tiny home and asks her if she will make the nation's flag, to his design. And Betsy promptly brings forth—from her lap!—the flag, the nation itself, and the promise of freedom and natural rights for all mankind.

There is a final note of confirmation for this hypothesis in the rather after-the-fact addition of Betsy Ross to our national mythology. For the cult of the Virgin Mother was itself a rather late development in Christian theology, a medieval elaboration of an undeveloped dimension of the Gospels, a statement, perhaps, that for a fully satisfying religious symbolism, Sons and Fathers were not quite enough. If I seem to overinterpret what are, after all, trite relics from grade-school primers, then I ask you to remember Albanese's caution that the contrivance or superficiality of mythmaking does not necessarily deny, and may even tend to confirm, its deeper cultural functions.

Collective Memory and Cultural Literacy

That observation provides a pivot on which to return to our initial questions—the relevance of this exploration in historical trivia for the august debates on history and education that loom so large in contemporary discussion.

On one level, my results can be read as a confirmation of the diagnosis that something is seriously wrong. If college students cannot come up with lists showing more depth and grasp than these; if college courses—as Zelinsky's

The certificate records a contribution to the "Endowment Fund for the preservation of the Historic House in which the First Flag of the United States of America was made." Wreath-encircled representations of Betsy Ross's house and grave flank a painting (enlarged below). Behind it the sun rises; on its beams rides an American eagle, clutching arrows and the E Pluribus Unum streamer.

This reproduction of *Birth of Our Nation's Flag* appears on the elaborate certificate of membership (above) that the American Flag House and Betsy Ross Memorial Association issued to Charlotte Kromm in 1919. The certificate has sobering relevance to the politics of past and present cultural literacy campaigns: Kromm, a German American, may have taken out membership less to advance historic preservation than to affirm the loyalty of German Americans, much impugned during World War I. *Certificate courtesy of Donald A. Ritchie.*

This advertisement, appearing widely in American magazines in 1986, represents a visual pun on the historical imagery captured in *Birth of Our Nation's Flag* (page 48). It conveys advertisers' confidence that readers recognize and understand cultural icons, jeremaids on cultural illiteracy from on high notwithstanding.

data suggest, or even high school courses, as the overall survey demonstrates—have so little impact, then surely we are in some kind of trouble. The almost childish character of the revealed pantheon seems quite consistent with the diagnosis that we are producing generations for whom a meaningful national history in even some of its richness and complexity is not an accessible resource. And as such, the survey can only reinforce the resonance many history teachers must feel when they encounter the documented ignorance that so exercises former Secretary of Education William J. Bennett, Diane Ravitch, Lynne Cheney, et al. Everyone who teaches history must have his or her own horror story that seems to confirm the ominous collapse of rope bridges across the generation gap.[10]

As I have argued, however, the surveys are more interesting when taken as evidence of what students do know, rather than what they do not. If the results say little one way or the other about how much history the students surveyed may actually know, they are evidence that cultural imagery seems to be reproduced in our young people with startling consistency and regularity. And this conclusion casts something of a shadow over the current jeremiads, whose core concerns, I would argue, are at bottom more fundamentally cultural and political than educational. This point is worth at least brief examination by way of conclusion.

The sermons being preached in this crusade are difficult to deal with as texts, because they slide so fluidly along a spectrum of analysis ranging from the high-minded and humanistic to the crudely political and instrumental. At the former end, we find the calls for exposure to the complexity of historical studies, for the cultivation of the critical mind, and for provision of the basic orientation to the real world and its history that citizens need to understand the present and make intelligent choices in the future. It is hard to see how anyone could fail to be shocked by the documented effects on students of an almost willful indifference to the value of historical consciousness and training, and the effects on teachers, especially in the secondary schools, of decades of overemphasis on pseudoprofessional training programs and methods at the expense of subject and substance.

It is a different matter when those unexceptionable themes are given a more particular emphasis: that students need not just more of history, but rather more of "our" national history. To a degree, the argument still holds: citizenship in a democracy requires the critical skills that such training should provide, and a certain core familiarity with the history and geography of one's country is arguably essential to knowing what the society is all about. But in most formulations, the educational critique is sufficiently expansive to suggest a different animus behind it: the problem is that our students are spending too much time on "them"—the rest of the world, global and comparative studies, and so forth—rather than on the "us" at home. And to the extent they do study "us," it is the wrong us—too much emphasis on social history, people outside ruling elites, minorities, and women, rather than on the political and military core of national tradition.

That emphasis is held to be problematic, both symptom and cause of a fragmentation of national unity, cohesion, and will in the face of grave political, economic, and military threats from without, and even from within. Virtually every one of the core documents slips into this mood sooner rather than later, after the appropriate genuflections at the altar of humanism and the critical spirit. The issue is put starkly in terms of American competitiveness, the Cold War, and the danger of ethnic and linguistic pluralism run rampant.

I haven't the space to demonstrate this point by citing chapter and verse from the new scriptures, so let me offer a single picture, instead. This lead page from a 1985 *New York Times Magazine* article by Ravitch touches every base. The headline announces the problem in its most generalized form—the "Decline and Fall of Teaching History." The sub-head slides into the Americanization of the cultural literacy problem, masking the shift of focus with syntax that raises concern about plain old literacy at the *Times*: "An ignorance or indifference about studying our past has become cause for concern." And finally, there is the picture, suspended between the two: a teacher leads a small group discussion in a global studies course that is, elsewhere in the article, an object of ridicule. Manifestly, the picture is intended to illustrate both "decline and fall" and "ignorance and indifference." Yet the class seems lively and intense; the lesson plan on the blackboard behind the teacher carries the outline for what could be a satisfying history lecture in any college course. What, then, is the picture doing here? Could it have anything to do with the fact that the teacher is black, the students black and perhaps Hispanic, and the planned lesson a discussion of Russia in the years just before the 1917 Revolution?[11]

I submit that the page captures perfectly the tension between the explicit text, couched in broadly acceptable abstract terms about history, and the deeply political subtext of the current educational crusade. Beneath the huffing and puffing about historical studies lies a fear not dissimilar to that propelling the "Americanization" efforts that so dominated education and politics in the United States in the early years of the twentieth century, fueled by a terror of immigrant cultures and concern for the future of the Anglo-Saxon race and heritage. It is fascinating how often, in the current litany, those educational efforts are taken to represent a kind of golden age to which we should return.

If all this has a quaint ring so soon after the Statue of Liberty centennial, the explicit cold war fixation strikes a much more ominous tone: Secretary Bennett has grounded his own critique of the schools, for example, on the proposition that they have embraced the doctrine of, in Jeane Kirkpatrick's term, "moral equivalence," willfully offering education "designed to prevent

DECLINE AND FALL OF TEACHING HISTORY

An ignorance or indifference about studying our past has become cause for concern.

By Diane Ravitch

FUTURISTIC NOVELS WITH A BLEAK vision of the prospects for the free individual characteristically portray a society in which history — knowledge of the past — has been systematically eliminated. In Aldous Huxley's "Brave New World," the regime successfully waged a "campaign against the Past" by banning the teaching of history, closing museums and destroying historical monuments.

If knowledge of the past is in fact relevant to our ability to understand the present and to exercise freedom of mind — as totalitarian societies, both real and fictional, acknowledge by stringently controlling what may be studied or published — then there is cause for concern about many Americans' sense of history. The threat to our knowledge of the past comes, however, not from government censorship but from indifference and ignorance. The erosion of historical understanding seems especially pronounced among the generation under 35, those schooled during the period of

Craig Bannister teaches a course called "global studies" at Flushing High School in Queens.

sharp declines in basic skills. While achievement in reading and mathematics is regularly tested by national and state educational agencies, the condition of historical knowledge is far more difficult to measure and the attempt is seldom made.

During the past generation, the amount of time devoted to historical studies in American public schools has steadily decreased. About 25 years ago, most public high-school youths studied one year of world history and one of American history, but today, most study only one year of ours. In contrast, the state schools of many other Western nations require the subject to be studied almost every year. In France, for example, all students, not just the college-bound, follow a carefully sequenced program of history, civics and geography every year from the seventh grade through the 12th grade.

Does it matter if Americans are ignorant of their past? Does it matter if the general public knows little of the individuals, the events and the movements that shaped our nation? The fundamental premise of our democratic form of government is that political power derives from the informed consent of the people. Informed consent requires a citizenry that is rational and knowledgeable. If our system is to remain free and democratic, citizens should know not only how to

Diane Ravitch is a historian of education at Teachers College, Columbia University, and the author of "The Troubled Crusade: American Education, 1945-1980" and "The Schools We Deserve."

New York Times Magazine, November 17, 1985, p. 50
Courtesy Jeanne Strongin © 1987 and
The New York Times Company © 1985

future generations of American intellectuals from telling the difference between the U.S. and the U.S.S.R."[12]

In such formulations, educational reform has been given a highly ideological definition: the point of education is not individual but national; the object of improvement in training in history is the production of obedient, patriotic citizens who share a set of presumptions about the United States, its people, economy, and relation to the other nations of the world. The argument has travelled a long way from its humanistic origins, arriving at a point where education and indoctrination—cultural and political—seem almost indistinguishable.

Indeed, in one of the more remarkable documents in the current literature, they *are* indistinguishable. Sidney Hook's 1984 lecture "Education in Defense of a Free Society" is a kind of *Ur-text* of the cultural literacy movement, outlining a set of themes that reappear again and again, less baldly, in the writings and speeches of Bennett, Ravitch, Cheney, and others. To Hook the issue is "whether we possess the basic social cohesion and solidarity today to survive the challenge to our society . . . posed by the global expansion of Communism"; the role of the schools—primary and secondary especially—is to generate sufficient loyalty through what he freely acknowledges is an embrace of propaganda and indoctrination (critical thought comes later, he says). In the final analysis, "no institutional changes of themselves will develop that bond of community we need to sustain our nation in times of crisis without a prolonged schooling in the history of our free society, its martyrology, and its national tradition."[13]

Hook's explicit reference to martyrology, tradition, and the need for cultural indoctrination in the primary and secondary schools brings us back to Betsy Ross and the tables of data I have been discussing here. According to Hook, Bennett, Cheney, Ravitch, and others in what William Greider has called the "Bloom and Doom" school, we are in trouble on every front: the crisis of historical amnesia, the decline of formal studies in history, and the deterioration of critical thinking are taken to be linked to a presumed corrosion of national spirit and will, evidenced in a declining respect for and awareness of the binding symbols of national tradition at the most basic levels. For such critics, there is no contradiction in calling for both patriotic indoctrination under the umbrella of a culturally binding nationalism, and intellectually challenging studies in history. The assumption is that a shared cultural memory and historical consciousness ought to be close to the same thing, or at least linked in some developmental or cumulative sense.[14]

The evidence I have presented suggests that this philosophically dubious proposition is also without foundation empirically. Whatever the deeper knowledge and grasp of history among my students, there is no indication in the data that the chords of cultural memory, in terms of the hold of national historical symbols, have weakened in the slightest. In fact, the consistency and extraordinary uniformity in the images offered up by these students indicates that the president, Secretary Bennett, and their followers have little cause for concern: the structure of myth and heroes, martyrs and mothers, is firmly in place.

This does not mean there is no crisis in the teaching of history, no deficiency in the historical consciousness with which our young people perceive the swiftly changing world around them. It does suggest, however, that frantic injections of cultural symbolism are not needed and almost certainly will not be the solution to the epidemic; if anything, the lesson is that indoctrination and education need to be more effectively decoupled, not conflated. For students who already hold lists of heroes deep in their imaginations need a sense that history is populated by three-dimensional human beings, the famous as well as the forgotten, who live in and act on a real world that is always changing.

In the tension between such a vision and the grade-school pantheon students dutifully remember for my surveys each year, there is a suggestion of what most history teachers in the trenches already know: that alienated students cannot be bullied into attention or retention; that authoritarian cultural intimidation is likely to be met by a further and more rapid retreat; and that there may well be, in that alienation itself, statements about the claims of the present on the past worth our respect, attention, and response. I have concluded in my own teaching that the evidently massive, uniform subsurface reefs of cultural memory are, in this sense, part of the problem, not resources for a solution.

As such, however, those structures merit immense respect from pedagogic navigators. They tell us a great deal about our culture, its resources, and its often problematic hold on the imagination of students—and on citizens as well, to judge from the power in the 1988 presidential campaign of some of the very icons discussed in this essay. My ongoing experiment in the survey course has convinced me that we need to realize what we are up against, in the classroom and in political life more broadly. We must understand the depth of the cultural symbolism our students and fellow citizens carry inside them long before entering our classrooms, if ever they do. Appreciating the powerful grip of collective cultural memory becomes a necessary first step if we are to help our students to understand the real people and processes of history, to locate its reality in their lives, and to discover the power and uses of historical imagination in the present.

Part II

Interpretive Authority in Oral History

Headnotes

This section's essays focus on oral history, and in particular on the uses of oral history in documentary. My concern is with what oral historical documents can mean as statements about history rather than just as sources of information or reports on experience. This dimension can be explored by examining how such documents are treated by editors and perceived by audiences when incorporated in a documentary context. In this sense, the section develops some of the implications of the collection's subtitle, examining the relationship between craft and meaning in oral history. The essays include, to one degree or another, general discussion of documentary, criticism of particular works, exploration of the selective uses of oral texts in documentary construction, and examination of actual oral transcript editing decisions.

The first essay is a blow-by-blow account of the battle our American Studies program at SUNY-Buffalo had with the *New York Times Magazine* over the final editing of the commissioned documentary on unemployment published in 1975. Belated discovery of the disputed "out-takes," included here as an appendix to the essay, made possible an analysis of the *Times'* editing patterns that, we felt, revealed how class can mediate the understanding of what oral documents contain, much less what they mean.

The essay developing this analysis was cowritten by me and Dorothy Larson (Watts), then a graduate student in the program; it was published in 1980 in one of the first issues of the *International Journal of Oral History* founded and then edited by Ronald Grele. Its reappearance here gives me a chance to note an additional dimension to our battle with the *Times*, which ended up on the essay's own cutting room floor: a dispute over whether the piece could appear under a collective byline. We spent much time seeking a way to convey our sense that authorship was shared with the interviewees as well; when all proposals to this end were rejected by the paper, we agreed to a collective attribution to the American Studies Program as author; this was seen as a proxy for the larger community of the speakers, and as an appropriate recognition that the work of planning and editing the article had been a fully collective process, as detailed in the text of the essay here. At the last minute, however, the *Times* insisted that this was "impossible," and that my own name (I had served as the chief contact person) would have to be listed as the author.

We are able to avoid this, but only by threatening to withdraw the article the week before its February 9, 1975, publication. The dispute suggests the broader reach of some of the questions begged by the text editing examined in the essay; recounting it now allows me to underscore how much virtually every point in the analysis Larson and I prepared emerged from a collective effort by some twenty-five students and faculty involved in the preparation of the documentary, as well as many of the subjects who joined us in refining its focus and in discussing it, after publication, in public forums at schools and libraries in the community.

The next selection stems from a work in progress and allows a closer yet more open-ended examination of the editing process. Here, having taken my licks at the *New York Times*, I open my own editing processes to scrutiny—readers are invited to compare a tightly edited, published interview transcript with the complete raw transcript from which it was carved and assembled. The interview with Dick Hughes first appeared in a 1987 special issue of the journal *Social Research* edited by Alexander Keyssar, focusing on unemployment; it is part of a larger project I am developing with photographer Milton Rogovin, to be published by Cornell University Press, in 1990, under the title *Portraits in Steel*.

For presentation here, I have included a brief preceding commentary in which I advance the notion that a relatively aggressive, even manipulative approach to the "actual" text may be the best way to faithfully convey its real meaning and essence. But by and large, the editing is offered without much mediation: the two texts are presented with each line in one keyed to its location in the other, so that readers can see exactly how the edited version was constructed. Almost all oral history editors work in a kind of black box, and I am aware of very few instances where the actual mechanics of transcription, condensation, deletion, and rearrangement have been very thoroughly opened to view. I await with some interest, and not a little trepidation, responses to the craftsmanship shared with readers here.

The section closes with two critical commentaries based on very successfully realized documentary projects. The first involves Carma Hinton and Richard Gordon's trilogy of films on Long Bow Village, nationally broadcast in 1987 by PBS television as *One Village in China*. This is a project I know from the inside, having served as an oral history consultant in its design and editing, hut the commentary here actually offers a different perspective: it stems from my having been in a position to observe one of the first showings of the films to an audience including large numbers of students from the People's Republic of China. Their responses were overwhelming, complex, and surprising, in ways that add a challenging cross-cultural dimension to the interpretation of oral history documentary.

This piece was originally drafted as a brief addition to a special symposium on the Long Bow Village films that constituted the Media and Public History section of the *Oral History Review* in its Fall 1987 issue. The essay has been expanded for republication here, mostly to cover descriptive material about the films originally addressed by the other contributors to that symposium.

The final essay in the section is an appreciative but still critical assessment of the use of oral history in the widely noted PBS television series *Vietnam: A Television History*. This series had an enormous impact and will continue to be influential through use in school and community programs, in conjunction with book spin-offs and related supplementary materials. It also has been quite controversial, although I have been struck with how infrequently debate focuses on its use of oral history as such, despite the fact that this is the central, even the defining, mode of historical exposition and documentation in the construction of the series.

The essay seeks to redress this by focusing on the kind of statements chosen for inclusion, rather than on their particular political analysis or content. The method echoes some of the issues concerns explored in the *New York Times* piece and even earlier, in the review of *Hard Times* reprinted in Part One. But here, a far broader range of subjects and material is involved, and so the points can be pursued much farther.

The essay was first drafted as a brief conference presentation for the 1985 Fifth International Oral History Conference, held in Barcelona, Spain, on the theme of "Power and Society," where a crowded platform only permitted me the space to outline the argument. It was subsequently published in this form in a 1985 issue of the *International Journal of Oral History*, but for inclusion in this collection it has been substantially revised, expanded, and documented with excerpts from the actual program transcripts.

Chapter 4

Oral History and the Presentation of
Class Consciousness:
The *New York Times* v. The Buffalo Unemployed*

This article departs from the usual academic form, in ways appropriate to the promise and complexity of oral history. Our concern is with the process by which oral history materials become public historical documents. We explore some aspects of the process generating a particular oral-historical work, and we do this by presenting an informal memoir of our own experience, a memoir similar, in its mix of detail, subjective recall, and reflection, to the kind of information usually produced by the oral history method.

We are aware of the perils involved in being both subjects of and commentators upon the experiences we describe, and so we stick as closely as possible to the narrative of our story, being sure to include as generous an appendix of documents as space permits so that readers may evaluate our impressions, insights, and hunches on their merits. But we expect that an oral history audience will appreciate without apology this attempt to get at precisely those dimensions of a complex historical experience ordinarily invisible in the documentary record. Oral historians are also, by definition, committed to the proposition that larger themes can be studied in and through the particulars of idiosyncratic reminiscences, and it is in this spirit that we presume to interest readers in our story. We offer it, in fact, as a kind of case study illuminating two general issues central to oral history as a method, each of which we found ourselves engaging in a particular form. It might be helpful at the start to say a few words about these, because they not only came out of our experience but have also framed the way in which we will present it here.

The first general problem is the relation between oral history as data, as the collecting and archiving of memory, and oral History—capital H—as intel-

---

*This chapter has been co-authored with Dorothy Larson.

ligible, communicated knowledge derived wholly or partially from that data. Information alone is not History in any other dimension of historical research, and there is no reason to make tape recording an exception. The question then, as the cassettes pile up on archive shelves and the transcribers pump their pedals, is what happens to oral history beyond the tape—how is it to be used and how is it to become, or be incorporated in, History?

For us, this general question took a quite particular form: communication in the form of a documentary, composed entirely of oral interview excerpts, and a documentary intended for a general public audience, rather than a scholarly one. What happens when transcripts become a public product, not simply material incorporated in a broader work? And what happens in the process of selecting, editing, and ordering, when, to the claims of substantive merit and validity, must be added the demands of dramatic form and effective public communication? As will be clear, our research was not strictly historical in that we were documenting, through interviews, contemporary experiences and attitudes. But we came to feel that in defining our task and its difficulties this mattered less than the more general problem of how to reduce a mountain of interview material to a documentary format. In this sense, our experience should be relevant to all those working with such problems, even if their materials are more directly rooted in history than were ours.

This leads to our second major concern: understanding what, if anything, is unique about oral historical method and the evidence it produces. If the challenge of leaping beyond the tape, of actually *doing* something with collected interviews, was explicit in our project from the start, the necessity of wrestling with this second concern became apparent only gradually, through a painful process: it was only in the face of almost unresolvable differences about the content of our documentary that we came to see how the conflict really stemmed from divergent understandings of what oral history reveals, and how it is to be read.

Here too, the general problem of interpretation appeared in a particular form: whether oral interviews can be studied for what might be called their social subtext as well as their explicit content. That is, in presenting themselves to an interviewer, do subjects express more about their general social identity and consciousness than is apparent on the surface of the narrative, and if so, how is this to be retained when material is being edited? This becomes especially important not so much when one is interested in reconstructing the details of a particular situation, as in much elite interviewing, but rather when the main concern is illuminating a broader social context through the prism of individual experience.

In modern society, the question of the social ground of personal experience, and the way individuals embody and express this, is the problem of class and class consciousness—its nature and sources, how it is articulated in thought and action, its relation to culture, politics, ethnicity, and so on. Does the evidence of oral history have anything to offer this inquiry? Increasingly, the sense among many of us who work with it is yes—and not only because of the working-class orientation of many bottom-up interviewing projects.

What seems far more important than this is how the *particular* nature of the oral historical method affects the nature of the evidence produced, and how this becomes a generator of insights into social complexity. For the root, defining fact—curiously mystified in so many discussions—is that oral historical material is produced in an interview situation, one in which the subject is triangulated between the interviewer and the experience being discussed. No matter how controlled the schedule of questions, the information is produced in a dialogue between individuals, each with a social position and identity, engaging in a conversation that exists at a necessary remove, in time or social space, from the experience being discussed. This is, of course, a fundamentally different relationship than usually exists between historians and the mute and frozen documents of the past; it has generally been discussed as an obstacle to objectivity surmountable through care and precision.

Far less generally understood is the degree to which this represents an opportunity to study memory, the process by which the past is received, digested, and actively related to the present, and an opportunity to see how a broader class consciousness is expressed in the ways people communicate that memory or experience in the social context of an interview. In fact, it could be argued that the question of class consciousness is not simply another issue for oral historians to think about, devising appropriate questions and tools; rather, it is an indispensable tool for exploring the nature of that methodology, precisely because it lies so close to the heart of the interview situation that defines oral history as distinct form of inquiry. To struggle with it is to struggle with the question of how oral history can produce broad insights and intelligence beyond the surface of a transcript or the facts of a narrative.

Our two major concerns come together at this point. The problem of the historicality and the social subtext of an interview is engaged less in conducting it than in reading, editing, and presenting it as a part of a larger work. In the experience we now relate, this was the hidden reef on which the first process—moving from data to public communications—ran aground. We would like to show how this happened, and to reflect on what it tells us about the uses of oral history today.

In 1974-75, SUNY-Buffalo's American Studies Program was commissioned by the *New York Times Magazine* to prepare an oral documentary, in the manner of Studs Terkel, on the subject of unemployment in Buffalo, New York. This was eventually published as the magazine's cover story on February 9, 1975. What we will relate in some detail is a series of conflicts that developed between our group and the *Times* in the final stage of editing, conflicts about the basic content and composition of the article. To the *Times*, the issue was simple: the article had to be cut by a few hundred words. But for us, disputes about particular editorial choices crystallized differences that had been implicit almost from the start of the project. This is because we found, and will try to illustrate here, that the material suggested for excision by the *Times* was the material in which people interviewed expressed most directly a larger social and class consciousness.

Such a purge was hardly the conscious intention of the *Times*; surely its editors were sincere in claiming that their only concern was "journalistic" effectiveness. Nor were our differences with them political in the usual sense—in fact, if anything, they insisted that their intention was to produce a more "radical" vision than we felt the interviews supported in their fuller form. But in struggling to restore what we knew to be the heart of the material— although it took us a while to grasp why this was so or what that heart meant— we discovered that the differences were profound, involving explicitly the presentation, and implicitly the existence of working-class consciousness in the material we had collected. We want to suggest that it is far from coincidental that this issue took the form of judgments about the editing of documents generated by the oral-historical method.

The early stages of the story can be briefly related. The *Times* commissioned the article at a time when the rising unemployment rate was just beginning to be recognized as a front-page problem. The magazine editors wanted a Terkelesque bottom-up perspective, using Buffalo—then "boasting" the highest unemployment rate in New York State and one of the highest in the nation—as a case study. When Terkel himself declined, our group was invited to design and submit an article.

From the start, we were under severe deadline pressure, which permitted us the dubious but real luxury of having no time to worry much about method or technique. We assembled a larger group of faculty and students, improvised some quick training sessions, fanned out to conduct as many interviews as we could, developed ways of mapping our progress, redirecting our efforts as needed, and moved from tapes to transcripts to various proposed edits, going back and forth between the larger group and a smaller editorial committee. Finally, we produced a documentary article that we felt reflected accurately what we had heard in the more than eighty interviews conducted and in the many hundreds of pages of transcripts they generated.

The evolution of this process could be an instructive article in its own right, but for the topic at hand a number of points about it are particularly important. In the preparation process, we did not focus at all on consciousness as such. Rather, we sought to cast as wide a net as we could in every dimension, and see what we learned about people's experience of and opinions about unemployment. Our approach was, however, guided by a number of critical concerns and assumptions. First, we were anxious not to be trapped by a literal, narrow definition of unemployment and whose experience was relevant to it. Thus we made sure to interview men and women of all ages and backgrounds, not only the male factory workers of conventional imagery. And we tried to gauge the impact of unemployment as a more general crisis in work, family life, and society. We therefore interviewed not only those actually laid off regular jobs, but also the underemployed and the unemployable, whether too old, too young, too unskilled, or too overskilled for existing labor markets. We interviewed as well family members affected by the unemployment of others, officials and civil servants dealing with the problem, and so on.

Second, with regard to the ultimate public presentation of the piece, we were concerned that the article's local focus might overly particularize Buffalo's situation, giving rise less to understanding of a complex problem than to a new wave of jokes and negative imagery, reassuring readers elsewhere how fortunate they were not to be living in Buffalo. This concern was hard to build into the research design, but from the start we were concerned about the way we would handle it in the editing and presentation: it became known to us as the "Sunday brunch problem," in the sense that the magazine article would be a failure if all it did was to present the suffering of Buffalo's people as an object for the detached sympathy of distant, privileged readers—serving it up, so to speak, with the Sunday morning paper and pastry of a sophisticated national audience.

As the work progressed, both of these concerns evaporated. The first proved easy to deal with through the breadth and depth of the selections we made for the article. The second concern proved more or less ungrounded—the people interviewed showed no fear of being exploited, by us or the *Times*, and neither did they dwell on Buffalo and its particular problems. Rather, they had a lot to say about unemployment in both personal and general terms, and seemed glad that someone was finally asking them what they knew about it. In fact, they rather welcomed the opportunity to talk to the audience for whom the interviewer was a proxy. Perhaps we could say that they saw themselves as guests sitting at that Sunday brunch table, not as the bagels or coffee cake, a point to which we will return shortly.

The article we submitted to the *Times* had four sections, each introduced by a short paragraph or two of background that we provided. The first section of interviews reflected the breadth of the problem; the second explored Buffalo's particular economic situation and its general setting; the third presented more extensive segments where people discussed the meaning of unemployment in their lives; the fourth offered excerpts in which people reflected on why things were as they were, and what, if anything, could be done about it. This sequence, and the selection and editing of the passages in each section, reflected our assessment of the substance, tone, and drift of the interviews taken as a whole. Although the voices on our tapes were as diverse as the speakers' backgrounds, and although almost every chord was struck at some point or other, our intensive study of the tapes and transcripts showed that people tended to move from personal, localized experience to more general observations; that they spoke in reflective and analytic modes far more often than in emotive ones; that they addressed their audience directly and even didactically, explaining their experiences and what they had concluded from them. All this we tried to capture in our editing and arrangement, a point that should also be held aside, for the moment, with the bagels and coffee cake, for it becomes central to the story at a later stage.

Until this time, our dealings with the *Times* had revealed no differences of purpose or approach. The magazine had fully endorsed our early outline, and immediately accepted the submitted piece for publication. We then entered into the revision and production stage where variant understandings of the piece began to emerge. Only gradually were we able to distinguish routine editorial differences from more fundamental ones, and so it is worth examining the process in some detail. Our experience can be organized in three major stages.

Round One

The first suggested revisions seemed to us quite reasonable; as we had been immersed in the research and editing for so long, and so intensely, we welcomed an outside perspective. The *Times* editors felt that the structure was overly elaborate and academic, and that we needed more explicit, locating discussion about Buffalo to counter the generalized tone of many excerpts. They were not sure they liked the blend of working-class and upper-middle-class voices that we had included, advising more exclusive a focus on working people. In fact, they asked us to submit some additional interviews from the working-class out-takes; more hard-hitting testimonies about unemployment from which they could choose.

We gladly complied. Many in our group, worried that the elite newspaper would undercut the implied politics of a bottom-up focus, were reassured by this request for more proletarian testimony, and we quickly submitted the new interviews. We also reorganized the original submission: now it began with a consolidated introductory section putting all of our own comments in one place, set off from the interviews, in order to reduce the academic presence and to allow our subjects to occupy the center of attention in what was, after all, their article. Excerpted interviews were now presented in three broad sections— one more Buffalo-specific, one expanding the image of unemployment and exploring its personal dimensions, and the final section, as before, stressing the reflective and analytic voice we had found so distinctive in our research.

We felt our second submission was a distinct improvement, due in part to the suggestion from the *Times*. We were therefore not overly alarmed when, upon receiving it, the editors told us that although we had met the word limit they specified, the piece might still have to be reduced. We awaited this next round of editing, confident that the piece could remain faithful to our subject and our research even if truncated.

Round Two

Shortly after receiving the second version, the *Times* informed us that they wanted to eliminate entirely the thematic sectional organization of the interviews. They argued that the various levels and dimensions would come through clearly enough in a montage format. We were unsure of this, but we could not argue strongly against the notion that the words of the people, rather than our intervening structure, should carry the burden of communication. The clinching argument was the *Times*'s point that their regular format would be fatal to any other mode of presentation because the article was being led by two or three full pages up front, with the rest of the piece marching in single columns through the jungle of high-fashion lingerie advertisements in the back of the magazine. To entice readers to finish the article, they argued compellingly, we would have to capture interest on those opening pages with our most effective material, whatever its place in a thematic arrangement.

The editors wanted to lead with the Rosie Washington interview. (All interviews referred to in the following discussion will be found, in alphabetical order by subject, in an appendix at the end of this chapter, pp. 71-80.) Although this is perhaps the most moving and dramatic—and longest—of our interviews, the choice made us uneasy; we felt it important in our editing to have the more emotive material set in context, for this is how it had emerged out of far denser and more complex interview transcripts. Beginning with such volatile material might create a misleading sense of the overall article, obscuring as well the complexity of Washington's interview itself.

Our uneasiness increased when we received the *Times*'s full rearrangement. The order was not the problem—we conceded that the strong lead and the mixed montage were effective and probably appropriate. However, several of the substitutions and omissions made concerned us.

The contrast between working-class and middle-class voices was almost entirely eliminated. We had felt that the contrast underscored, rather than diluted, the working-class focus of the piece, as much through the vivid differences in language as anything else. Without that contrast, a certain social dimension in the interviews was diminished. This is illustrated by the omission of the brief but representative excerpts from the Ed Hausner and Gerald Kelly segments.

But the issues here were hardly major, nor was the impact on the article very substantial. They would have been less bothersome were it not for some other ominous hints in the *Times*'s suggested arrangement: they wanted to insert all of the new interviews we had sent them, at the expense of several others—well beyond the few nonworking-class excerpts we included. At this point, virtually all the proposed cuts came from what had been, in our revised thematic framework, the first and third sections—where people such as Della Love and Stanley Lewandowski discussed and analyzed the Buffalo situation or reflected generally on the meaning of their personal and social situations. But the second section—which tended to emphasize, more descriptively, the personal "impact" of unemployment—was untouched. Then, too, three of the four new working-class interviews accepted by the *Times* were relatively more personal and emotive, and relatively less socially grounded, than the working-class interviews now proposed for omission. This emerging pattern seemed confirmed by a request for an expansion of the Lewis Hawkins interview, the angriest one we had, a segment close to a *lumpen* cry of pain and a call to violence, quite unrepresentative of the bulk of our collection. Nevertheless, none of these seemed insurmountable differences, and we were reassured by their inclusion of the fourth new interview—"Steelworker"—one that in its control of detail and reflective focus lay close to what we thought to be the heart of the piece. As it happened, however, this was the exception that proved the rule, so far as the emerging contrast between our understanding and that of the magazine's editors.

Round Three

While we mulled these changes, the *Times* informed us that the article needed further editing in order to fit the magazine, but we would be able to retain all the interviews. As the publication deadline approached, the article had been typeset. If, upon inspecting the proof sheets, we had no objections to the final editing, and they saw no reason to expect any, the article could then move directly to layout and publication.

The excitement of seeing our scrawled-over typescript set into the clean columns of actual print diffused our editorial apprehensions. But not for long—on a first full reading of the new version, the tone of the article seemed strange and unfamiliar. Reading more closely, we discovered why: the new cuts were far from simply occasional prunings. In one interview after another, crucial sections, often quite extensive, had been excised, in ways that substantially altered the meaning of the words that remained.

Comparing proofs to draft, we began to see a pattern in the *Times*'s editorial judgments, a pattern not only responsible for the article's new complexion, but one that threw into sudden perspective the magazine's earlier responses to the material, from the initial call for more hard hitting working-class interviews to be presented in an almost random montage, to the removal of the middle-class viewpoint, to the justified fascination with Rosie Washington and the not-so-justified fascination with Lewis Hawkins. We offer both versions in the appendix to allow readers to determine what patterns they detect in the excisions documented there. But hopefully the following reading is more than an idiosyncratic interpretation of the process, in that it is informed by our familiarity with the full range of material and by the insights into the nature of the editorial process obtained in the long struggle to edit miles of tape and pounds of transcript into a meaningful public representation.

We detected at least three distinct dimensions to the *Times*'s implicit selection criteria. First, in their search for unnecessary verbiage they tended to settle on passages where people, having made a point or expressed a feeling, went on to explain, support, elaborate, justify, or apply the point. However necessary this might have been editorially, the effect was to undercut or even eliminate the authority with which people spoke, making their statements seem arbitrary and ungrounded, exclamations rather than the products of conscious reflection. This can be seen across class lines, as evidenced by the Fred Koester interview or the "Job Counselor" segment. It becomes more problematic in the working-class interviews, of which the Della Love and especially the "Steelworker" excisions—the heart of the interview we had been so reassured to see them accept—are the best examples.

Second, is the *Times*'s indifference to the self-reflective quality of many of the statements, those passages where the speaker is self-consciously looking at him or herself, often locating that self in a social and class context, implicitly or explicitly. We had been struck by the prevalence of the self-reflective mode in the transcripts, and by its importance for the understanding of what people had to say. The *Times*, however, while approving and, in fact, encouraging personal statements, seemed to find more reflective self-consciousness to be a kind of unnecessary personal static, interfering with the "real" transmission, and they cut such passages wherever possible. The Bill Phillips and Frank Martinez interviews are good illustrations of this, the latter in particular: this had seemed to us one of the most revealing of all the interviews we had conducted, which is why we included relatively more of it and placed it very carefully near the end, so as to maximize its capacity to draw the article's themes together. The *Times*' editing, however, removed almost all of the self-consciousness that makes it a moving expression, one filled with complex social comment. In confronting the gutting of the Martinez interview, we finally began to understand that differences with the *Times* did not trace solely to our journalistic *naivete*, or to matters of taste, but implied rather a fundamentally different sense of what the people had to say, and what it was important for the article to allow them to say.

Finally, the *Times* editing seeemed to select for omission those passages suggesting that the text had, in fact, been generated in a direct dialogue; this, too, they tended to see as extraneous to the text-as-statement. By paring the quotes in the interest of economy, we felt the editors had excised or drastically suppressed the definition and expression of personal style, the mode of self-presentation to the interviewer that can embody the complexity of personal identity and social relations in a word or phrase. Such expression, we had found in the transcripts, occurred most often where the interview was most conversational, where the subject addressed the interviewer directly. Because we were not working in a dialogue format, we tried to capture this sense of style and personal dialogue in our editing, as the most economical way of suggesting the texture and social subtext of long, complex interviews.

In this sense, for instance, we had thought the insistent pride and the redundant irony of the Chester Midder selection anything but superfluous; similarly important to us, but not to the *Times*, was the embarrassment that surrounds but does not obstruct Frank Martinez' discussing with a college-educated interviewer his own study of current economics, or Della Love's unembarrassed analysis of Buffalo's decline and potential resurrection, the confident advice of experience offered without any confidence that it is going to be heeded or appreciated. The *Times*, the reader will recall, had earlier sought to eliminate this interview entirely, as well as Stanley Lewandowski's resurrecting of Dr. Townsend's economic prescription, another interview that evokes a sense of communication across substantial social and experiential space. Now, the overall editing made it clearer to us that in its search for the essential minimum in each interview, the *Times*, uninterested in the process that had generated the "statements," was in effect flattening to the point of elimination the sense that people were speaking to anyone in particular, much less across a class line clearly sensed and occasionally articulated. Where we saw such references as providing a crucial context, the *Times* saw superfluous asides distracting attention from the basic story each person had to tell.

We hasten to acknowledge that each editing decision does not necessarily support the weight of these interpretations; together, however, the excisions do suggest the patterns we detected. Sculpture, someone once said, is the art of removal, a statue being simply the residue of myriad small decisions about what to take away from a block of stone. This well describes the editing of oral transcripts for documentary use. What the *Times* sought to remove revealed a very different vision of the meaning enclosed in the block of material we had collected: their sculpting would have resulted in the core being emotion and exclamation rather than the reflection and intelligent discussion we found so central in the evidence; it would have emphasized the revelation of experience rather than its instrumental, even didactic communication;

and it would have tended to sever that experience from the social and class context with which it had been invested by our subjects, implicitly or explicitly.

This vision seemed to us unacceptable. Fortunately, given how deeply our group felt about this, the *Times* grumblingly accepted our immediate demand to the right of editorship, as long as we managed to meet the word limit they were forced to specify. In fact, they were more puzzled than provoked, claiming to detect, sincerely, we believe, no differences between our ultimate selections and theirs. The final editing then proceeded without incident, although not without hard choices. We restored as much as we could of what seemed absolutely crucial; we cut one or two interviews entirely; and we proved able to find passages that could be cut because the points they had to make were, at least, expressed to some extent or other elsewhere in the article. We were far from satisfied with what this did to a number of interviews, and the appendix gives some sense of how much important material still had to be sacrificed. But having earlier become somewhat steeled to this inherent frustration in editing, and accepting the compromises inherent in our particular magazine format, our group felt that the integrity of the editing had been restored and the larger meaning of the collected material successfully captured in the article.

Lest it seem to readers—as it did to the *Times*—that we were making oral historical mountains out of routine journalistic molehills, a curious coda to our story helps clarify the substantial gulf in sensibility involved, showing as well how this bears directly on the question of the relation between oral history and the exploration of class consciousness.

As finally published, our article bore the title "Down and Out In America." This should seem strange given our argument to this point—nothing we have said about the material or our struggles over its editing suggests that our portrait was of the "down and out." The excerpts in the appendix, it will be readily seen, hardly support this image. It should not be surprising, therefore, to learn that the title was the original contribution of the *Times*. After tolerating our editorial idiosyncrasies, they announced impatiently that titles were, as an aspect of layout and production, under their sole control. They rejected our best title, "America Not Working," at once a play on the words themselves and a reference to the then-current and widely discussed *Working* by Studs Terkel, to whom our efforts owed so much. Admittedly not a perfect title, it had the minor virtue of being consistent with the content of the article. But even after the editorial history just related, we were still a bit staggered by the inappropriateness of the *Times*'s creation. It had been crafted, so we were told, by the editor-in-chief, Max Frankel, himself, and was, therefore, unquestionable. The copy editor replied to our protestations by pointing out the reference to George Orwell's *Down and Out in Paris and London* as a compensating virtue, apparently indifferent to the fact that this portrait of *lumpen* outcasts was a curious referent indeed for a study supposedly concerned with the way working-class people perceived the problems they faced as integral members of a troubled community in a troubled society.

The *Times's* fascination with this title crystallized, to us, the values we had sensed in the editors' treatment of the documents. For all of the professed concern in commissioning the article, the *Times* seemed comfortable viewing the working class only at a safe moral distance, which their editorial judgments tended consistently to exaggerate. Those who are down and out, to put it simply, do not sit at the breakfast table of those who are up and in. It does not seem unfair to suggest that the *Times* sought to offer its readers stimulating fare, not uninvited guests. While the magazine editors were quite willing to serve up the pain and suffering of the working class, they were less inclined to open their pages to the ideas, values, reflection, advice, and social consciousness of these people. Nor were they interested in sharing the right to interpret this experience. Tell us what happened and what you feel, the message seemed to be, and our readers will worry about what it means and how to think about it. It is not inconsistent with this spirit to note that the *Times* had been sincerely proud of its intention to include the working class in its magazine. It was the content of that concern that proved problematic, a paradox best summed up in perhaps the single most distressing moment in our relationship with the *Times*, when in the midst of an editorial wrangle the copy editor claimed that the real problem was our inability to provide angrier material. "Can't you give us more stuff," he said, "where, you know, they say how the system's fucking them over?"

The system, indeed. We hope it is not indelicate to suggest that one might learn more about the "system" by studying closely what the *Times* tended to see and not see in these oral historical materials. Surely it is not coincidental that they were drawn to the pain of the working class but not to its subjectivity and consciousness. Nor is it insignificant that they edited our documents so that authority, judgment, and historical self-consciousness tended to remain in the hands of those already controlling the culture, and its mediation through journalism, literature, and history.

More is involved here than merely throwing brickbats at the *Times*, an easy target, after all. We think there are positive lessons in our story, lessons we began to discover with some surprise, and to understand only gradually. These involve editing as a general matter, but they are especially relevant to those concerned with the study of class, and the special place in this inquiry that oral history is often presumed to have. As we suggested initially, our struggle, in the sense, was not really with the *Times*, but with the larger problem of understanding how class consciousness can be found in oral history—lower case "h"—and how as historians and editors we can help it to become visible as we move from the tape to the public table—Sunday brunch or otherwise.

The three dimensions described—the self-reflective voice, the social grounding and location of that voice, and the self-conscious engagement of an implied or presumptive audience—seem to be a good starting point in such a search. As oral historians, we must be sensitive to these dimensions, however implicit they may be in the tone, stance, and voice of a speaker, or however hidden they may be in the interstices of a conversation. We have to explore the power of this methodology itself, one that is unique in its essential dialogic nature, in its bridging of the historical past and the temporal present, and most fundamentally in its capacity to generate the very documents it then wishes to study.

The lessons can be put in another, more sober way. Nothing is inherent in the oral historical process that guarantees that its documents will be sensitively understood, much less used to create a version of history accurately informed by their unique perspective. The crucial issue is not import, but authority. Those truly interested in a history from the bottom up, those who feel the limits of the historical reality defined by the powerful, must understand that presuming to "allow" the "inarticulate" to speak is not enough. We must listen, and we must share the responsibility for historical explication and judgment. We must use our skills, our resources, and our privileges to insure that others hear what is being said by those who have always been articulate, but not usually attended to. Only in this way can the arrogance of the powerful be confronted by the truth of another reality, by those history-makers whose consciousness provides the record of that reality and the measure of its challenging power.

Interviews

Space does not permit the simple reprinting of the entire article on which this essay is based, "Down and Out in America," an Oral Documentary by Members of the American Studies Program, SUNY-Buffalo, *New York Times Magazine,* February 9, 1975. We have, however, tried to include in this appendix enough material to give readers a sense of the way that article read, as well as illustrations of the editorial out-takes discussed in the essay. Our decision to place all the "evidence" for our argument here in the appendix, rather than in the text, is deliberate, and, we hope, consistent with the points we are making about the integrity of oral historical material. By handling it in this way, we intend to offer readers a greater chance to react to the material directly, rather than through our argumentative mediation. This also permits the words of our subjects—already heavily edited from the original transcript—to remain as close as possible to the context that informs their meaning, both within the interview and as they appeared as part of the final article.

The interview excerpts are arranged alphabetically by subject for ease of reference while reading the preceding essay. Several different kinds of material are included, however, that are important to distinguish for those reading this appendix separately as a way of approximating the original article.

Some of the interviews are reprinted exactly as they appeared in the eventual article. Of these, some were part of our original submission, and some were part of the second group, submitted at the request of the *New York Times Magazine* staff as discussed in the text. Together, these represent approximately 50 percent of the final text of the article. Other excerpts represent interviews submitted to the *Times,* but eliminated by the editors in the final revision. Finally, we have included a number of illustrations from the galleys, whose inclusion were greatly debated during the final round of editing decisions.

The editorial illustrations are presented in the following manner: *Italicized passages* represent material the *Times* excised in preparing the proofs, but which we aware able to restore in our editing. *[Italicized passages in brackets]* represent passages cut by the *Times* that we were unable to restore due to the word limit.

At the time of publication, our group prepared reprints of this article, under our copyright, for distribution to community groups in Buffalo and to individuals requesting them. A number of these reprints are still available, and interested readers may obtain free copies by writing to the Coordinator, American Studies Program, SUNY-Buffalo, Buffalo, New York 14260.

1. Ed Hausner: Farmer, interviewed while selling vegetables from his truck at the Broadway Market. (Interview cut by the *Times.* Cf. interview with Kelly, for contrast, as discussed in text.)

> It ain't the way it used to be, for sure. Yeah, they're leaving, like birds migrating south. Sealtest is closing, Hewitt-Robbins, we got a number of customers who work there, they closed it down. All your feed mills in the last few years have been going out of business. Agway is out of here. Wayne Mills is out of here, Farina, Allied Mills, all stuff that used to be in Buffalo, they're all gone.

2. Lewis Hawkins: Concrete finisher, twenty-eight; in the unemployment line. (Interview submitted in the second batch and selected for inclusion by the *Times.*)

> There's going to be a lot of stealing, a lot of mugging and everything … People are going to get tired, tired of coming down here and standing in line. And when they finally get unemployment, a person who, say, only gets $45 or $50 a week might have three or four children; before a man's going to see his children and his family go hungry, it seems he's going to go out there and do something.

3. Florian (Pete) Horvath: Wire cutter, fifty-five, unemployed since 1972 when GTE Sylvania closed its Buffalo plant; he had been with Sylvania for thirty-one years. (Interview published as submitted.)

> Whenever they had visitors, they always took them right in our department. They were so proud of that. Big Wheels would come in, and people from different parts of the country. Even foreigners. They would take them in and show them that machinery. Even the school kids: they had a tour like that, too, for the kids. I used to get a kick out of that. They'd all mill around you, and then you explain to them what's going on. The guy that brought them in there, he'd shut up, because to him it's a machine; he didn't know a thing about it, so he let me talk. . . .
>
> I was laid off just before they closed the plant. I had a feeling, anyway, like one guy said, "This place is going down." They had been threatening us for years that they would move, especially after they moved TV production out of Buffalo in 1952, to the plant in Batavia. That's on the way to Rochester. Now just before they finally closed down here, they were also threatening the people *there*. They talked the people into taking a pay cut in Batavia. But when they were taking the cut, we were getting our raise. Just before we got the news of our pay raise, we had an idea they were moving out, 'cause they were getting rid of a lot of odds and ends, like desks and cabinets and all sorts of things.
>
> I think another reason why they closed up—all these people, including myself, were getting up in our years. It seemed like just about every other week there was someone who was retiring, and as far as the company was concerned, that was running into a little bit of money. This group that was retiring about the same time they closed up were all the ones that started in the thirties, from way back in Colonial Radio days, even ahead of me . . . I feel as though we got the short end of the stick, let's put it that way.

4. Job Counselor, New York State Employment Service. (Illustrates editorial out-takes.)

> I'm a Pollyanna, there's no getting around it. I gravitate to what looks like hope, and I do believe there is hope. *The thing I want to stress is this: even though there are 10 percent unemployed, there are 90 percent that ARE employed, so somebody is flourishing. And even if a plant holding firm, someone is resigning, somebody is dying.* [*They're not completely lowering their work force by attrition.*] *Openings are there.* No matter what the unemployment rate, there are still some businesses that are flourishing. And identifying those is part of the job. And that's why I say to the job-seeker, "Beat all the bushes. Go to the private agencies; read the want ads; talk to your neighbor, for Pete's sakes— lookit, nothing drops in your lap anymore. The idea is to pursue and pursue."

5. Gerald E. Kelly: Executive Vice President, Greater Buffalo Development Foundation. (Entire interview cut by *Times*.)

Interviewer: What is your view of the national economic picture?

I just have to get a bit philosophical on that, and say, everybody has that problem. I really don't have time to worry about that. I'm involved in very specific things in Buffalo, and to the extent I sit back and worry about the big picture nationally, I'll get so depressed I'll lose all my energy and won't be able to work on the specific projects I'm trying to work on. I think it's bad. I think the economy's in trouble. But I can't do anything about it. And so I try not to burden my feelings with that problem, and I try to get involved with the things I can have some influence over.

6. Fred Koester: President, United Rubber Workers of America, Local 188. More than 500 members of this local were laid off when Hewitt-Robbins, a Litton Industries subsidiary, was closed last May in the midst of a strike. Litton held the union responsible; many observers felt this was a pretext for Litton's liquidating what it took to be an unfavorable position. (Illustrates editorial out-takes.)

I tried to run this union just like a family. And with the company, everybody's happy, picnics and the whole bit. There was a time when I knew everybody in the plant. But then Litton came in, in 1965, they loaded the plant with salaried workers; these out-of-towners would be walking around there and we couldn't even find out what their jobs were. . . .

Most people knew that Litton is a holding company. They get in; they make a buck; they get out. [*I don't think it's fair. I don't think it's right to the community. You're not only talking about 750 jobs. Add their families, warehouses, and other interests all over the country, there's truckers involved, there's railroads involved, people getting cut back all over. Now, when you're talking 750 jobs, you might be talking 10,000 people before you're done.*]

7. Stanley Lewandowski: Retired steelworker and former president of United Steelworkers Local 2603. (Interview initially excised by *Times* and restored in its entirety in our final editing.)

To start off at the starting point, you have to come back to Dr. Townsend. [Francis Everett Townsend, 1867-1960, author, in the 1930s, of the Townsend Pension Plan.]He's an old-timer. He originated a kind of social security. Hey, they called him a nut. I was amazed; I used to think he was the greatest man out, I really did. Laugh all you want, they said that Social Security would never work. So look, I think we ought to look at his proposal again. You give everybody $200 a month in money that becomes worthless at the end of the month, so you got to spend it. But the thing is, when you're on a guaranteed national income or something, you can't have Rockefeller, and Hughes, and Del Webb. Because they'll have the money eventually, they'll take it away from you. To keep it, you'll have to distribute it evenly, and break it off every month. You want to save? You're a miser? You just lost some. Dr. Townsend. I don't know, maybe you need somebody that's a so-called nut like that to come up with some solutions.

8. Della Love: Does part-time house cleaning to supplement her pension, sixty-five. (Interview excised completely by *Times*, restored at our insistence and subject to further editing as illustrated.)

Interviewer: What's the problem with Buffalo? What do you think could help the city?

It's something about the people. They got the wrong type people for the wrong type job to make Buffalo come up. Buffalo could be number one, it could be done. If they put the right type people in, they'd see how Buffalo would bloom. *You have to spend to make, that's all there is to it. In Buffalo, it seems like they don't want to put out money, they just want to hold money, and they're just killing it. If we could put our money in something good, why we could get something out of it. But we got to put it in first.* [*They're going to have to do something, people can only go hungry but so long. I don't know what the cause is, but it's something other to think about. I'm telling you.*] It looks like people, we pull against each other so much now. We're not like we used to be: more together. We're divided, and it looks like all we care for is: if I live, I don't care what becomes of you. [*But we can't be like that. Until we get together we're gonna be this way, and further apart, in worser shape. That's true in Buffalo. You could come out of that, though, but you're not going to bloom overnight; when you're into something so deep, you got to gradually work your way out of it.*] But I feel like if we had the right kind of leadership, and all, we could come on out. But we ain't got it, no kind of way.

9. Frank Martinez: Auto worker at Chevrolet's Tonawanda complex, in the metal-casting plant; his wife teaches at a nursery school. They have four children, ages seven to fourteen. (Interview illustrates editorial differences with *Times*.)

Myself, I'm practically in a state of financial bankruptcy. As of two years ago, when wage and price controls went into effect, since that time [my wife] Sally and I have withdrawn a sizable amount from our savings, and see no conceivable way we're going to put it back. ...

Last week, we had a layoff, they laid off a number of men; there were twenty-two in our department, the maintenance department, and three men from our shop, two sheet-metal workers and one apprentice-trainee. What the foreman said is, he had no idea there was a layoff at all, and he controls a lot of men. He thought if anyone should know about a layoff it would be him, but he wasn't expecting it. In fact, our department, which is short-handed, he thought they'd be hiring, and instead they laid off. They just sent the word out, with a list of names to lay off these people. Corporations have their way of operating. I have heard this is a big corporation and conglomerate scheme; in other words, they have made their profit, they can afford to give the workingman the business: let him take a vacation, they could care less.

It looks hopeless, unless somebody really takes hold of the whole situation, reverses the trend, or at least stabilizes it. This is something I've recently read into, and it seemed to be the general thinking when Nixon got into office that we were going to have a lot of unemployment, because the philosophy is, to take the money out of the working people and put it back into the hands of the rich and the corporations. Of course, this is a surefire way to do it. If a man is unemployed, and he doesn't have any money to live on, he's going to draw on any savings he has until it's finally gone. You do this to 100,000 Americans, multiply it by $11,000 apiece, and you are talking about a lot of money. [*Of course, I've done a lot of reading on this subject, but that means nothing because I'm not an expert.*] *A lot of the experts say that unemployment is necessary.* [*The economists I've read say that 13 percent is necessary to stabilize the economy, but it will only work with a number of things, systems from government, and so forth and so on. That the government has been striving too hard to keep unemployment down by excess spending.*] *Some of the people I work with, we discuss these things, we really don't know what it's about because we're not intellectuals. Most fellas just throw up their arms in the air, curse, and walk away, saying, "I've heard enough, I don't want to talk about it anymore." It seems as though they feel hopeless, there's nothin' they can do. They're just a cog in the wheel, the wheel's going to turn, the cog's going to go to the other side, and that's the way the working fellas that I work with feel.*

   10. Chester Midder: Baker, forty-eight, in line at the unemployment office. (Illustrates editorial differences with *Times*.)

I worked at Loblaw's Supermarkets four and a half years. I'm a baker—bread rolls, pies, cakes, according to what the desk calls for. I'm a mixer, too. I worked upstairs in the mixing part. Local 16 for the National Bakers Union. Can't do nothing else. I never did no construction work; even the construction workers are out.

Interviewer: What are you going to do now?

Get me a brick. Any time I see a meat market, break it in and get me some food. By the rock, sweetie; I don't have the money to buy nothing with.

[Laughs.] Nah, I wouldn't do that. I don't work in that department, no, 'cause I'm healthy. I'm used to working; I worked all my life.

Now I could work at a lot of places, at some small bakery, but they won't pay me my due. They want to give me $1.95. See, I'm a mixer and a baker; I was making $4.95 an hour, and I'm not going to make all that bread and stuff for those people and they're gonna give me $1.95. Up at Loblaw's, the lowest man would get $3.95 and he was only pushing a broom on the floor.

Interviewer: Why did they close the place where you worked?

Big business, you know, big business, big business, you know, chains. Loblaw's chain was in Canada. They open this one, they close that one. Man been there thirty years, they gave us a bonus pay, you know, you take the superintendents, they go with the company, but the workers out the door. *And they didn't give us a party. You'd think about all them meats and that kind of stuff. They didn't give us a turkey, or a chicken, or nothing. [Why this is it: the superintendent says, "Nice working with you." But then they go to the warehouse, they go to different stores. But the workers, the man who was. doing the things, they didn't get nothing. If you're a superintendent, they take you right along with them. If you're a worker, they don't give a damn if you've been working there twenty years. If you're not a superintendent or a foreman, you're not in the club.]*

   11. Bruce Nowak: Autoworker at Ford, twenty-two. (This interview, excised by the *Times*, was restored at our insistence.)

Well, I guess I'm a laborer. I don't know what you call it, automation-tender. I'm working a welding gun. I go all over, but mostly I've been working on the pan line, lately, for the Grenada, the new car. I feel like a robot.

Interviewer: What will happen if you're laid off?

I'll stay laid off. Well, like if it's starting to get close, then I'll start looking. Last time, I was at the bottom of the list, and you know I was one of the last to be called back but now there are 500 guys under me. So I'll get laid off, but I don't think it would be for too long. To me it doesn't matter. I'll work in my house and everything. I'm remodeling my cellar, right now, and paneling.) [Nowak was laid off soon after the interview.]

   12. Charles (Bill) Phillips: Bethlehem Steel worker, Fifty-eight. (Illustrates editorial differences.)

Well, I marvel, I have to marvel at the Establishment, because they can make a person believe they are at fault for not working. *Now I don't know whether it is the mentality of the general population or what it is. Me, I'm nothing, a mere cipher, that's what I call myself. But I don't buy the establishment package. This is it—you have your one pull at the brass ring, and you can't do it without money in this society, you can't do it without a job.* The young person who goes out, they're the hardest hit. For one thing, they've swallowed everything they've been taught. Then they go out and can't get the jobs. And yet they blame themselves. Just as everybody in my day blamed themselves, except me. I say, "You don't blame me, Buddy, it's the system—the jobs aren't there." *That's the part that makes me angry, because anyone with a little bit of common sense can see that there aren't the jobs, and there never were enough jobs.*

13. Steelworker: Recently laid off at Bethlehem Steel, where he had worked for two years; still active at the plant in a rank-and-file caucus trying to organize workers against what is seen as a company-dominated union; twenty-five. (Interview selected by the *Times* out of the second set of submissions, but then subject to extensive editing by the *Times*, as discussed in text.)

[*I work in a BOF open-hearth department, and I'd say there's probably been 150 layoffs in the last two weeks, and there's probably another 1,500 around the plant. And this Friday there'll be more because the open hearths are going down. At capacity, the whole plant runs about 21,000; in the last six months, it came down to fifteen and I imagine soon it's going to be running down around ten. It's the highest percentage laid off since 1971, when there was a major shut-down. The company got in a major tax dispute with the city of Lackawanna then, threatening to, you know, shut down the plant if Lackawanna didn't give them a major tax break. Naturally the city, which is practically owned by the steel plant, had no choice. If Bethlehem pulled out there goes most of the jobs.*]

What's happened recently with the layoffs where I work is that there is a stipulation in the new contract of last August saying that if the plants have to cut down and people are laid off due to a shortage of raw materials, like coal, then it alleviates the company's obligation to pay SUB pay. (SUB pay is the money paid by the company as a supplement to unemployment benefits, to bring the laid-off workers pay up to about 95 percent of normal. The duration of SUB pay depends on seniority—eds.) At this point, it's pretty obvious the economy's down, that construction's down that auto's down, so what they've done is to create the facade that the plant has to cut down because of the lack of coal and the coal strike. [*It works out perfectly for them. And this layoff came conveniently two weeks before Christmas pay, and we generally have about a $200 bonus Christmas week and a $100 bonus New Year's week. By being laid off now, we lose both of them.*]

Theoretically, if a union was a union, and really worked as a fighting body representing the working people, it would fight back against this. But the

United Steelworkers of America, in most cases the only response we've drawn from them is that you've got to look at the company's side of things. And with the no-strike clause we have right now, it's an illegal wildcat if we try to pull people off from inside ourselves. The union has sold us out so badly that there is nowhere to go.

[*Our group, we put ourselves together on a loosely knit basis. Right before we got sent out we talked to workers around the plant, and brought litera-ture to show it wasn't the miners on strike that caused our layoffs, that the miners aren't even making as much as the steelworkers and WE can't make it on what we earn now, so they deserve anything they can get. It's the companies giving them less, and fighting to maintain, you know, (laughs) total control over people, and make more money at any cost, and create these divisions at the same time.*]

14. Rosie Washington: Unemployed and on welfare, 27, she lives in the small apartment she shares with her daughter, 6, and another woman, from which they are about to be evicted. (Unchanged by the *Times*, although differ-ences concerning placement, and their significance, are discussed in the text.)

You look in the paper, see all these jobs in Cheektowaga, Williamsville, no way to get to them, bus don't even go that way. You go up and go looking for a job; the jobs they send you to, 50 percent of the time there's not a job anyway. "Well, we're not hiring now, but we'll take your application." Then they send you out to jobs that they know you're either underqualified for or overqualified for, I was an administrative assistant at a community center; I've been an employment coach on a federal program, then a counselor. I've done all this, and I really like it. But my biggest problem is that I don't have that piece of paper that says I'm qualified, so now, well, I went to the restaurants, hotels, plants. I've said I never wanted to work in any plant. I wish I could get a plant job now—I have applications in at Bethlehem, Chevy, Ford. You can't get any answers, you can't get any services, just sit around and wait, just to be told to come back and go through it again. Honest to God.

And the welfare system. Isn't that a design, a design to fail? They give you just enough money so you don't starve to death, so you're always hungry. They don't give you enough to live on, just to exist. You know, I think these clerks, they look at me as an imposition on their paychecks. They're paying for me: "If it wasn't for her I might have a nickel or a dime more." But you know, they want us here. They always got to have somebody on the bottom so they know they're closer to the top. A crummy welfare recipient chewing up their tax dollar, you dig it? With me here, I can make you feel better. . . .

I'm tired, I really am. I have a child, and she's part of me. She sees me doing nothing, never going out to work, depressed, worried, sometimes crying. I mean, I try. I try to play with her. When I have some money, we even go out together. We can't afford the movies, but I take her to Henry's and buy her a hamburger. I do love her. I do care, but with all the pressure, sometimes I can't even talk to her—you know. She comes home: "Hi, Mommy." "Hi, how was school today?" "Fine." She wants to play, but I can't. I think it's going to affect her emotionally. I went to school with her and the teacher said. "She's a good, bright child, but she's so sad. Why?" I said, "Because that's all we got in our home. Sadness. No hope, no future.

And this country thinks it's so damn great. It's NOT. It's hard to believe, but I really feel we're going to have a revolution, because this government ain't doing it, not to say any other kind is better. What I'd like to know is, what am I supposed to do with my life? I had my goals, but no means to make them. I'm just at the breaking point. And when I break, what am I going to do? You're just never right for anything. At first you're too young; then you don't have experience. By the time you're thirty-five or forty years, you're too old. So all through your life you were never right for anything. You know, it's everything—job and experience; no experience, no job. To get a job you gotta have money, you gotta have a job to get money. So it's just a vicious circle of nothing. And you're all locked up in this thing, crossed in it all your life. One circle that leads nowhere. That makes you pretty angry. Angry isn't even the word for it. I don't even KNOW how to describe that feeling.

Chapter 5

Preparing Interview Transcripts for Documentary Publication: A Line-by-Line Illustration of the Editing Process

Doing something *with* oral history materials, beyond collecting and cataloging them, necessarily involves substantial editorial intervention. The most elemental transcription and even indexing requires a range of important decisions about how the spoken material is to be represented, and how complex content is to be summarized or categorized. To use oral history extracts in research, especially in combination with other forms of evidence and documentation, is to confront additional questions of context, selection, representativeness, and verification. The incorporation of substantial interview material in documentary works, especially those intended for broad public audiences, turns even more centrally still on editorial decisions about what is to be included and how it is to be arranged and presented.

Given this importance, it is surprising—or perhaps not so surprising—that the process of editing transcripts for publication is shrouded in considerable mystery. A rich literature surrounds transcription, of course, but most of it is focused on the transfer of sound onto paper for archival purposes, rather than the editorial issues involved in refining these transcripts into a meaningful and publicly communicable form. Anthropologists and linguists have worked hard at devising elaborate and compelling systems of notation and arrangement by which the texture and cultural meaning of speech patterns can survive in printed form. But this approach presumes a self-conscious focus on the oral discourse as such, as a cultural expression and an object of study and research; the approach is distinct from what I take to be the more casual way in which oral historical materials are usually engaged by those of us who confront the problem of digesting a long and complex interview transcript into a meaningful, readable, form that can be incorporated in historical documentary.

I am concerned with this more ordinary process here, for it is almost never made visible as such. Readers are inspired to try oral history through the work of Studs Terkel, say, only to discover that their choppy interview transcripts bear little relation to the powerful, flowing narratives in his documentary books. Because little indication is found of how those narratives were produced—what the raw interviews were like and how they were edited—and because most manuals, guides, and oral history courses focus on intake rather than output, providing little help at such an editorial juncture, the novice is left with a file full of raw transcripts, feeling overwhelmed, inadequate, or simply unsure of how to make use of the materials he or she has collected. This, I have found, is especially true when there is a documentary project at hand for which research has been completed and for which refined and focused transcript excerpts are needed. Major editorial choices are confronted—but it is as if making them involved some arcane artisanal skill whose mysteries experienced craftsmen and women never reveal in public, and which the novice must wrestle with alone.

This is an unsatisfactory state of affairs for many reasons. It constricts access to important skills and mystifies a fascinating process. By removing editorial principles and practices from discussion and scrutiny, it begs important questions of accountability—questions that ultimately cast a shadow over the integrity of the very documentaries produced in these curtained editorial workshops. And perhaps most important of all, the absence of straightforward discussion of editing obscures some fascinating dimensions through which the editing process amplifies and thus helps us to engage more fully the complexities that make oral historical documents so unique and important.

This essay represents an attempt to part the curtain somewhat. I present a full source transcript of an interview from a current project of mine and a much briefer edited version of that same interview as prepared for a specific publication purpose. The two will be presented, with each line numbered and with the two versions keyed to each other—that is, the full transcript indicates which passages were selected for the edited version and where they are located in it, while the edited version indicates where, in the full transcript, each line came from. Readers can thus see how this editor, at least, went about moving from raw material to finished product. Although I hope it does not need saying, I must state directly that in opening these texts to scrutiny, I am hardly presuming either the interview or the editing to be exemplary in any sense. I do believe that becoming more self-conscious about the issues implicit in editing can help each practitioner engage and resolve these challenges in ways appropriate to his or her own interests and needs, and I hope that moving from the abstract level to a very concrete example can serve readers in this way.

In considering how to present the material, I have been tempted to annotate the transcripts as well—to discuss in detail this or that choice in placement, selection, or rearrangement. But if editing is a craft that needs to be opened to view, perhaps such textual analysis is not the point: I suspect it is better simply to follow the artisanal model—to open my workshop, to lay out both the finished product and raw material on the bench, and to leave visitors alone to discover exactly what was done to move from one to the other, evaluating this for themselves and drawing whatever lessons seem appropriate, without my kibitzing defensively over their shoulders.

This being said, however, the exercise will work better if, by way of preface, I at least make explicit some of the general understandings I have brought to editing and to this text and editing project in particular. These will serve to make my editing choices examinable less as technical expressions than as the way in which one editor grappled, however intuitively, with some of the broader challenges of editing oral documentary texts. Very briefly, then, I will comment on the value of specifying the particular nature of these challenges, on the approach to editing that seems to me the most appropriate response to them, and on the context of the particular interview material.

Oral History and Documentary

Preparing material for a historical documentary is fundamentally different than simply recording and preparing material *as* a historical document. For one thing, the documentary use implies an end or focus, the necessity of having the material fit within and contribute to the exposition or illustration of some kind of thematic framework. This requires shape, focus, and movement, which is rarely explicit and controlling in the inevitably more open-ended documents at hand, but must rather be brought to them.

In addition, to work on documentaries is to make the audience a far more explicit dimension of consideration than in scholarly writing: a film, radio script, exhibit, or magazine documentary text must not simply express historical content and ideas, it must also communicate this material—and communicate it to specifically imagined audiences who encounter the materials in forms and under conditions that directly affect the meaning that can be communicated. Thus, preparing material for documentary use involves considerable attention to how the material will actually "work," how editorial choices will bear on its effectiveness in advancing the purposes at hand.

The use of oral historical materials adds at least two further dimensions of complexity to this process. Unlike documents that simply come to us *from* the past, whether they are film clips or letters or reports, interview materials are unique in themselves being documents *about* the past—reflections more than simple reminiscences, in which the interpretation of a past reality is not only something the audience brings to the document, but to some degree is implicit in the document itself. This makes the insertion of relevant interview excerpts into the larger (and not always resonant) interpretive structure of a documentary a complex matter. And such considerations bear as well on editorial choices for documents that will themselves carry the full burden of documentary communication, rather than being components in a broader mosaic. In all these instances, good work requires a broad sensitivity to the levels of meaning and commentary oral history interview documents contain.

Finally, to use oral history in documentary in most cases involves an act of translation as well as selection and presentational shaping. Radio shows, films, and television documentary, of course, edit audio tapes, videos, and films of actual interviews for inclusion in documentary, but this is still a small percentage of the oral history finding its way into documentary use. This is fortunate, because we would miss much of the content, historical value, and meaning in any extensive interview were we limited only to what is articulated in specific "sound bites." The ability to edit fuller interview transcripts for use in texts thus opens up wider and historically more significant documentary possibilities. But this begs important questions, because to work with texts in a transcript is to encounter them in a form once-removed from the original; to edit and prepare them for presentation, whether in print, in exhibit scripts, in stage use, or in other forms of documentary re-creation, removes them still further. Editing for presentation thus requires careful attention not only to the initial transcription, but to a whole range of concerns bearing on how an excerpt or condensation or thematic focusing of diffuse material can retain its faithfulness to the original on the one hand, communicate to the audience on the other, and do not only either but both, in the world of the third hand—translated from the sound and flow of the actual interview document into a very different medium of communication.

Fidelity, Translation, and the Social Context of Transcription

Together, these considerations have led me to a position that may seem at first paradoxical: the integrity of a transcript is best protected, in documentary use, by an aggressive editorial approach that does not shrink from substantial manipulation of the text. One must respect the original enough to come to know it deeply, and this knowledge must be the benchmark for measuring the validity of any digest, excerpt, or editing. But on this basis, one must also be able to abandon the pretense of literal reproduction, in order to craft the document into a form that will answer to the needs of successful presentation and communication. This hypothesis can best be defended by discussing some of its specific implications in practice.

First and most obviously, an editor must digest essential material, a process that is more complex than mere compression, the removing of extraneous matter or filler. For if a subject addresses a certain theme or event at several points in a long interview or narrative, it will not necessarily represent this expression to string the excerpts together like beads. A thought or remembrance or description that an informant knows clearly and well may be expressed in bits and pieces, as things are encountered in the flow of an interview. Conversation and talk have their own structure and logic, of course, the study of which is one reason why it is imperative to preserve and accurately transcribe the actual full interview. But in documentaries with other ends in mind, there is neither the time nor the necessity to reproduce this complexity. Indeed, the responsibility is very much the reverse: if it is clear from the full context that the informant has said something coherent, then I believe the bits and pieces can be assembled, and even reassembled, to represent that thought or information accurately for a condensed excerpt or in a digested narrative.

Translation from sound to print begs other questions of what constitutes fidelity to the material. Some might say that every dropped "g" or nonstandard vocalization should be represented in print, and that editing must strive to preserve accents, dialect, and so forth. Generally, I find this approach another species of misplaced literalism—such transcription may have its place for some kinds of language study, but it is ultimately counterproductive for editing concerned with content and communication: speech that sounds articulate and coherent to the ear tends to read, when too-literally transcribed in print, like inarticulate stage mumbling; such transcription becomes an obstacle to hearing what the person in the interview is trying to say, much less an obstacle to obtaining a sense of that very texture and feel of voice and character the approach presumes to capture. For most documentary purposes, I believe it is far better to edit in close-to-standard transcription: character, culture, and voice come across via the overall syntax, flow, and word usage of transcribed spoken language, rather than through the attempt to recreate sound itself.

The same can be said for the editorial handling of hesitations and catches, and those sounds or phrases speakers use to fill the pauses in speech—"uh," "you know," and the like. To transcribe each pause or false start or tic would make an otherwise clear tape absolutely unreadable on paper, inevitably suggesting to readers an inarticulateness anything but characteristic of the speaker-as-heard. On the other hand, to eliminate them all arbitrarily might risk a distortion of a different kind. In the final analysis, rules cannot substitute for judgment in such matters. When one knows an interview intimately, it is possible to sense how many "you knows" are needed in print to give the feel of a speaker's rhythm and style without distorting how their voice "reads," or to know when a nonstandard locution is worth preserving because to "fix" it would deviate unacceptably from the texture of the original, as with the term *gonna*, rather than *going to*: I usually decide to keep "So I said, I'm gonna tell you something ..." while *not* writing "So I said, keep doin' that and ... ."

Such judgments take on a final dimension of complexity, which can only be touched on in these brief remarks, when we understand the problem of translation and communication in a social and political context. I am thinking specifically of that substantial proportion of oral history that documents speakers and experience "from the bottom up."

There is a class and cultural dimension to the communication of such testimonies, in terms of who is speaking to whom, that renders both literal transcription and passive editing especially problematic. This is because, in our society, every newspaper and magazine contains statements of people of position or power, statements routinely printed with correct syntax and spelling; interviews are selectively edited so that articles or reports always contain coherent statements; readers are similarly used to autobiographical prose in which the established or well-known talk about themselves and their lives in regular words, flowing sentences, and shaped paragraphs.

In this context, to encounter the narratives of common people or the working class only in the somewhat torturous prose of "faithful" transcription ("So I wuz jes', uh, y'know, talkin' t' the foreman, uh, when, y'know ...") is to magnify precisely the class distance it is one of the promises of oral history to narrow. Similarly, to be limited to the exact sequence and linkages with which such an informant's story emerges in an interview is to deny such speakers the privilege of communicating their fuller experience or understanding as they know it, and indeed as they spoke it, broadly understood—a privilege enjoyed by the powerful who are almost never encountered in such rough form, even though they drop as many g's, utter as many uh's, and would seem as inarticulate as anyone else were their discursive interviews or rambling thoughts presented as literally expressed.

The *Portraits in Steel* Project

All these concerns inform the approach I have taken to editing, in both general and specific ways that should be visible in the editing decisions and choices that readers can examine in the transcripts below. It is also important to know something of the broader project itself, however, because this has a great deal to do with my strategy in conducting the interviews and editing the transcripts.

The interview with Dick Hughes presented here was conducted as part of a collaborative documentary project with the noted photographer Milton

Rogovin. Almost ten years ago, Rogovin produced an important travelling exhibition entitled *Working People*, based on the deceptively simple theme of paired portraits—the same individuals pictured on the job, and at home. Most of these workers were in iron, steel, and related industries in and around Buffalo. The portraits had been taken just before Buffalo's heavy industry tumbled into the catastrophic collapse announced by the shutdown of the huge Bethlehem Steel complex, which at its peak had employed more than 19,000 workers. The Bethlehem shutdown was soon followed, in the Buffalo area, by that of Republic Steel and other facilities. Together with similar changes elsewhere in the once-strong Great Lakes heartland of American heavy industry, the plant closings in Western New York signalled a change of immense proportion in America's economy and in the lives of its working people. Rogovin's celebratory portraits, taken between 1975 and 1978, inadvertently documented a home life and work life on the verge of a historical transformation.

Over the last several years, I have been asking many of these same people to speak with me about their work, homes, families, and communities. Rogovin and I are currently completing a book, *Portraits in Steel*, linking these interviews to his photographs—the original set supplemented by recently taken updates. By combining photographic and oral-historical portraiture, we hope to document a contemporary crisis in a way that transcends the problem/victim focus of contemporary journalism, permitting the people at the center of these epochal changes to share their experience and perspective.

Beyond what all this implies for my general approach to the interview, more particular implications are inherent in the collaboration with this remarkable photographer. Rogovin's approach is special in that his portraits—almost all of them full-faced, self-posed presentations directly to the camera—seem "given" by the subjects rather than "taken" by the photographer. In the interviews, I have sought to collect the tape-equivalent of this quality, by working for broad oral-historical portraits shaped less by a specific interrogative agenda than by the self-presentation of the subjects. To this end, it has proven exceptionally helpful to structure the interviews around responses to the photographs themselves.

I generally have begun by asking the subject to describe what i going on in Rogovin's "work" photograph, a request which in almost every instance has been met by detailed and spirited descriptions of work processes, tools and skills, shopfloor life and stories, and individual work history. We then have moved to discussion of the plant-closing crisis and the subject's thoughts about the more general changes in steel and industrial America. The interviews have then usually shifted to the "home" photograph, and discussion of personal and family history, community life, and the particular experiences in the immediate aftermath of the steel shutdowns, and in the longer period of adjustment and change that followed. The interview with Dick Hughes, which lasted about ninety minutes, follows this pattern—or rather, it helped to set it, because it was one of the first done in the project and I was more or less feeling my way toward a style and approach as well as getting used to the subject matter and the subjects. Subsequent interviews have been similar, with some shorter and more focused, and others, some running as long as seven hours in several sessions, getting more deeply into family history and broader social analysis.

Although intended for inclusion in *Portraits in Steel*, the edited version of the Dick Hughes interview printed here was prepared for a slightly different audience and purpose: a special issue of the academic journal *Social Research* (54/2, Summer 1987) focused on unemployment, for which special editor Alexander Keyssar thought this worker testimony would be especially appropriate. This focus, not to mention the journal's space limitations, forced me to omit large sections on union activity, shopfloor life, and home and leisure. I hope to incorporate some of this material in the longer version being prepared for *Portraits in Steel*, but space here is still at a premium, and thus the present demonstration omits these fully-deleted portions from the rough transcript as well—my aim is to document the process of close editing and composition, not wholesale excision. I have, however, retained on the rough transcript line numbers keyed to the full transcript, indicating where major excisions were made, so that readers can still sense the proportion of the full document and locate edited passages accurately within it.

Having at least sketched some of the general principles involved in my editing, and having provided some introduction to the specific example here, I am now ready to leave my workshop to the visitors, with all the materials laid out for examination. I suggest that the edited transcript be read first straight through, before examining the rough draft to determine the way it was put together. Or perhaps one could start by reading the rough cut in its entirety; the choice is the reader's. Like any artisan thus inviting visitors to examine his work on their own, I can't seem to avoid edging out of the shop somewhat nervously, and with a final caveat: I do not claim that the chair taken apart on the table is the best chair ever made—it is not even the best chair *I* have ever made. But if the reader is interested in the way chairs are made, or in actually making one, then it may prove helpful to study the process close up and step-by-step.

The edited transcript, sequentially line numbered in italics in the right column, will be found on pp. 89-103. The source transcript, sequentially numbered in Roman type in the left column, will be found on pp. 104-146.

Dick Hughes: A Portrait in Steel
[Edited Transcript]

Source	Edit	
1, 3	*1*	MF: Well, we can start with the work you were doing,
3	*2*	or ....
4	*3*	DH: Well, I could say the last four years since being
5	*4*	out at Shenango, the most I made, for money, was
6	*5*	about $4,000 a year, just working minimum wage jobs,
7-8	*6*	security jobs, nobody wants you, you know, just can't
8, 11-12	*7*	find a job. Other jobs would pop up, being with the
12-13	*8*	economy so bad as far as mechanics' jobs, they just
13-14	*9*	want to pay you minimum wage. Carpenter's job, I
15	*10*	think I worked for what, five bucks an hour, they just
16, 26	*11*	want to work you to death, work you six days a week
26-27	*12*	and ten hours a day, and pay you forty hours no mat-
27, 16-17	*13*	ter what you did. And knowing that you're hurting,
17-18	*14*	and that they can take advantage of this, you don't
18-19	*15*	have no choice, you just have to either work the way
19-20	*16*	they want you to, or take a walk—they pick somebody
20-21	*17*	else up that's in the same boat. That's about it.
30, 34	*18*	MF: Well tell you what, I'd be interested in first get-
34-35, 36	*19*	ting a sense of what you were doing before, and then
36-37, 44	*20*	we can talk about what's happened since. So, let me
45-46	*21*	just start by asking if you could talk about the picture
46-47	*22*	Milton took of you on the job, and tell me what you
47-48	*23*	were doing—what's going on, what kind of work you
49	*24*	did at Shenango, and ....
50	*25*	DH: OK. What Shenango consisted of, we were mak-
51	*26*	ing ingot molds for the steel mills. What an ingot mold
52-53	*27*	was, was to hold the steel until it cooled, and they
53-54	*28*	would re-use the ingot mold and keep just getting cast-
54	*29*	ings out of it.
135	*30*	MF: And what, exactly what part of the process is that
136	*31*	picture getting, you're just sitting on a ....
137	*32*	DH: Oh, that's the finished product, that's the prod-
138	*33*	uct before it goes into the railroad car to the customer.
143-144	*34*	What we did here, what my job was, was to chip out
144, 146	*35*	the excess iron in there, grind it, smooth it, clean all
146-147	*36*	the excess sand off, and it went to one other guy, and
147-148	*37*	he painted it, and into the railroad car.

Source	Edit	
[added]	38	MF: And then it goes to the steel mill?
448	39	DH: Right. Because when the blast furnace was going,
449-450	40	you have to have someplace to put the steel, so that's
450, 433	41	what the purpose of the ingot mold was. So what they
433-434	42	would do, is, pour the ingot mold, wait for it to cool a
434-435	43	little bit, then you put it in a tank, bump it out, and
435-436	44	then that block of steel would just sit in the yard and
436-437	45	they'd just go back get another one, pour it, and—and
437-438	46	all that steel would sit, and when they wanted to bring
438-439	47	it into the rolling mills, they would bring it in, heat it,
439-440	48	they would get the blast heat and get it real soft, and
440-441	49	they'd start sectioning it off, they would chop it, and
441-442	50	that piece would just keep rolling down to the size
443-444	51	they'd want, whatever tubing they wanted to make, or
444	52	sheet metal, whatever they wanted.
298	53	MF: What other kinds of specialties did your place
299	54	have, so someone looking at the picture would have
300	55	some sense of what goes on.
301, 304-305	56	DH: Well, actually there's three main departments.
301	57	There's also the casting department, which casts the
302	58	molds that you see in the picture, and the stage before
303	59	that is the ram department, where they ram the sand,
304, 310	60	to make the mold, that goes in the oven. They put the
310-311	61	sand in, ram it, finish it with a blackening, which was
311-312	62	wet, which would dry to a hard finished product.
63-64	63	The thing what happened was, the continuous cast
64-65	64	came in to the steel mills, you know, trying to keep
65-66	65	the steel flowing, keep it going, and stamping every-
66-67	66	thing out the way they wanted it. So they didn't need
67-68	67	no ingot molds, so they wouldn't have to go around
68-70	68	buying ingot molds, so that became an expensive oper-
70-71	69	ation, and that's what knocked us out of business.
76-77	70	MF: The plants here didn't completely go over to con-
77-78	71	tinuous casting, did they? I mean, they still use the . . . .
79-81	72	DH: They still use ingot molds, yeah. Continuous cast
81-82	73	you got to have temperature going exact all the time,
83-84	74	temperature in the whole place got to be exact to keep
84-85	75	it going. Now they're finding out that it's pretty expen-
85, 527	76	sive, in fact. We heard of continuous cast and every-

Source	Edit	
528-529	*77*	thing, but we figured, well, that'll just be for small
529-530	*78*	products. We figured for big products there's no way
530-531, 534	*79*	that they'd be able to keep, to heat these buildings at
531, 534-535	*80*	an exact temperature, it wouldn't be feasible. The mold
535-536	*81*	business would stay in business forever, all we would
537-539	*82*	lose is the small products. I mean, the steel mills
541, 540	*83*	would be OK if they weren't getting the flood of the
540	*84*	foreign steel.
192	*85*	MF: How long did you work there?
193-194	*86*	DH: Ohhhhh [ironic]—eighteen years. Eighteen years
195	*87*	and I didn't get nothing.
196-197	*88*	MF: Yeah, I want to talk about *that*. But first, the eight-
197, 209	*89*	een years—was this the kind of shop that tended to
210	*90*	have a really stable work force, that people had been
211	*91*	there ten, fifteen years, twenty years?
212	*92*	DH: Yeah. A lot of guys came up from Pennsylvania,
213-214	*93*	and they had, oh, anywhere between ten and twenty
214-215	*94*	years. You know, they told us because we're from up
214-216	*95*	here in New York, they'd say, well, if you get ten years,
216-217	*96*	you got it knocked, nothing will happen to you, just
217-218	*97*	ride it right out, and retire and have a good pension.
218	*98*	Which it didn't turn out that way.
220	*99*	MF: Was it pretty steady during most of those eight-
220-221	*100*	een years?
222-223, 225	*101*	DH: Well, I was never laid off. Never laid off. They
225-226	*102*	were working six, seven days a week, a good business.
230-231	*103*	As long as they're making cars and, you know, pouring
231-232	*104*	steel, there's no problem, you just keep making molds.
187-188	*105*	It falls right back to the automobile. They made the
188-190	*106*	steel and supplied the automobile places, they'd stamp
190-191	*107*	'em out and everything, so it all leads right back to
191	*108*	that, the car. But it's the foreign competition.
330-332	*109*	MF: How aware were people of where the company
335-336, 332	*110*	was, where the steel industry was? Or was it just sort
333	*111*	of assumed that this would go on pretty steady . . . ?
338-339	*112*	DH: Well, I'd say about four or five years, just before
339-341	*113*	they closed, like we were selling molds to Canada, too,
341-342	*114*	and they were getting molds from England, and they

Source	Edit	
342-344	*115*	were trying to make a comparison, you know, how the
344-345	*116*	mold would stand up under the castings of the steel
345-346	*117*	being poured in them. And the English molds were
346-347	*118*	only getting like abut ten castings, where our molds,
347-349	*119*	they would get about 105, 110. And then the guys
349-350	*120*	started talking about, well, jeez, you know, if it's over-
350-351	*121*	seas they're trying to make molds to be competitive
351-352	*122*	with ours, but we found out they were only getting
352-353	*123*	about ten heats out of them, we'd say, well, there's
353-354	*124*	nothing to be concerned about.
359	*125*	MF: How come there was such a difference in quality,
360-361	*126*	was it the nature of the materials, or the skill, or what?
362	*127*	DH: What it was, was the temperature and the amount
363	*128*	of iron and steel that you mix in to make the iron.
364-365	*129*	What they were doing was making a softer ingot mold,
365-366	*130*	they were just burning the heck out of the mold, they
366-367	*131*	were just cracking them, they just wanted to get the
367-368	*132*	heat out of 'em. Where our molds, you know, it was
368-370	*133*	more like a secret, you get the exact part in the lab,
370-371	*134*	how much steel, how much iron mixed into it, and
371-372	*135*	what the heat should be at.
386	*136*	MF: Is that something you can tell on the floor, when
387	*137*	you're chipping on one of these things?
389-390	*138*	DH: Oh, yeah. Hey, if there's too much steel in it, it
390-392	*139*	just breaks your chisel. It just comes to a halt and just
392-393	*140*	sits there and vibrates—it don't move, it's like a dia-
393, 396	*141*	mond. What it is, is it's too hard, there's no give in the
396, 394-395	*142*	mold. So when they get a casting out of it in the steel
395	*143*	mill, the chances are it'll break open, it may kill
395, 397	*144*	somebody—you'll just pour it, and if some guy's there
398	*145*	in the steel mill, chances are that mold'll open up and
399	*146*	crack, and the steel'll come flying out.
937, 944-945	*147*	MF: So mostly during those years, you liked your job,
937-939	*148*	you felt pretty good about being a steelworker?
946-947	*149*	DH: Yeah, I enjoyed the company and the work. Like I
947-938	*150*	say, you couldn't go in there all the time happy,
948-949	*151*	because you're working in the steel mill foundry, and
949-950	*152*	it's dirty and filthy and hot and freezing during the

Source	Edit	
950, 952	*153*	winter, but I went there every day for eighteen years,
952	*154*	except for the six days I missed.
544-545	*155*	MF: Was the union strong in your plant?
546	*156*	DH: Well, it was—it was too strong, yeah, that's what
547	*157*	puts us out of business.
547	*158*	MF: Really, how so?
548-549	*159*	DH: Oh, they just wanted too much, you know, push-
549-550	*160*	ing too much, they didn't want to bend, they didn't
550-551	*161*	want to give up nothing, they didn't believe in no
551,554	*162*	changes. It was a case of playing it the rough guy, you
555-556	*163*	know—your father did it, he gave up a lot, and he had
556-557	*164*	to buckle down in Pennsylvania and Ohio, and he went
557-558	*165*	through the hard times, and they made the unions,
558-559	*166*	and you know, we don't want to hear no sad stories
560-561	*167*	from the company, they're just pulling our leg, and,
561-562	*168*	you know, why give up what your father struggled for,
562-563	*169*	you just keep going forward, keep pushing, get every-
564-566	*170*	thing you can. The unions, they didn't want to really
566-567	*171*	sit down and hear the story—company says, Hey, for-
568	*172*	eign import's killing us, we're going in the red, we
568-569	*173*	need concessions, breaks, we gotta be competitive—
569-570	*174*	there was no trust.
818-819	*175*	MF: Was that a real division, these guys who'd come
820	*176*	through the struggles of the '30s, '40s, had one way of
820-821	*177*	looking at things?
822-823	*178*	DH: Yeah. They'd remember how, when they'd started
823, 824, 830	*179*	the unions, they'd get beat up by the cops. The older
830-831	*180*	guys down there really went through heck, you'd hear
831	*181*	the stories about what they went through, get hit in
832-833	*182*	the head with billy clubs by the local police and every-
833-835	*183*	thing, when they were starting off. You worked down
835-836	*184*	there, there was no union, and you walked out the
836-837	*185*	door sick, and that was your job, too, they had fifteen
837	*186*	guys waiting.
838	*187*	MF: That must—it puts you in a funny position, be-
839	*188*	cause you don't want to say that organizing was wrong,
839	*189*	I mean ....
840-841, 843	*190*	DH: It was the *right* thing, it was the right thing. The
843-844	*191*	union would protect you and keep your seniority, other-

Source	Edit
844-845	192
845-846	193
846-847	194
847, 890	195
891, 898	196
898-899	197
899-901	198
901-904	199
904-905	200
905-907	201

wise the plant wouldn't have to pay you no benefits, no retirement, you know, kick you around. But then the union got too powerful, they didn't know when to stop. I mean, I'm still a union man. I think union is right in a lot of points. You know, you have certain protection plans, through the union—that's where the union should draw their line, not try to operate the company. I mean, if the company says, you want to take a cut in pay, then come up front and say, give us good cause, show us your books, show us something.

Source	Edit
913-9914	202
914-916	203
916, 601-603	204
603-604	205
604-605, 614	206
614-615	207
615-616	208
616, 618	209
619	210
619, 622-623	211
623-624	212
624-625	213
627	214
628-629	215
629-630	216
631, 633	217
633-634	218
635, 637	219
637-638	220
638-639	221
639-640	222

But the union didn't do that—the union just showed strength all the way to the end, and they just died with it. You just get the attitude, you don't give up nothing and you don't want to listen to the company's side. Which was bad, 'cause they were hurting. They wanted them to take a cut in their incentive and every-thing—not hourly pay, but just the incentive, it was more like bonus money. We were out of work for so long, I think there was thirty guys working in the plant, and we were out in the street, see, so when us younger guys said, well, let's hold a special meeting—you know, we were still talking to the company, I was talking to this guy, he said, Jeez, we'd like to have you guys all back to work, this plant up here would be the number two plant, if the guys would take a cut in pay, in incen-tive, and why don't you guys vote on it. We went back to the union, said, We'll hold a special union meeting, we want to vote on this and get back to work. So, we went up to the union hall, told them what we wanted, to get back to work, and the thirty older guys that were working say: Well, you guys ain't allowed to vote!

Source	Edit
640	223

MF: Why was that?

Source	Edit
640-641	224
641-644	225
645-646	226
646, 656	227
656-657	228
657-658	229
658-659	230

DH: You have to work five consecutive weeks in a year. They said, you guys don't have no say in it. They said: [abruptly] "We're not giving up nothing . . . . You guys don't have no word in it." So now everybody's out, the union's all done away with. And like I say, we seen the guys, now, some of the union guys, [mock, dreamily] "Oh, I thought the company was bulling,

Source	Edit	
659-660	*231*	huh, well, that's the way it is." Instead of saying they
660-661	*232*	were wrong—"Well, that's the way it is."
957-958	*233*	MF: When did it go down for good?
959-960	*234*	DH: Eighty . . . two, August of '82, they definitely closed
960, 963-964	*235*	the plant. And, as I say, I had eighteen years, so I didn't
964, 963	*236*	catch the pension; twenty and you get the pension. I
1019-1020	*327*	was shut down, I didn't draw nothing. Nothing for
1020, 1022	*238*	nothing. Just got unemployment till that ran out, no
1022-1023, 1011	*239*	food stamps, no gas assistance, no nothing. When
1011-1012	*240*	you're shot down, you're owing so much, and then
1012-1013	*241*	when you need some assistance from the government,
1013-1014	*242*	they tell you, you own too much, you got this, you got
1014-1015	*243*	that, you got to sell it before we can do anything for
1015-1017	*244*	you, that's about hardest part. They tell you sell your
1018	*245*	houses—'cause I own two houses—sell your house and
1019, 1020	*246*	we'll give you some assistance. It's just more or less—
1029-1030	*247*	you know, if you work eighteen years or fifteen years
1030-1031	*248*	someplace, you gotta show something for it. And what
1031-1032	*249*	the government's saying, that you should have worked
1032-1033	*250*	eighteen, fifteen, twenty years and showed nothing!
1034-1035	*251*	Then we'll give you something. That don't make sense—
1035-1036	*252*	you gotta show something. What they're saying is, you
1036-1037	*253*	should have drank all your money up . . . .
1040-1041	*254*	It gets you. I know a couple of guys that are collecting
1041-1042	*255*	welfare. OK, when I went down to try to get some assis-
1042-1043	*256*	tance, them guys were collecting welfare, and their
1043-1044	*257*	rent payment was three hundred something dollars a
1044-1045	*258*	month, and I told them, my house payment's only two
1045-1046	*259*	twenty-five, but we can't help you cause you own two
1046-1047	*260*	houses—it don't make sense! You're gonna get three
1047-1048	*261*	hundred something dollars here, four hundred, pay
1048-1049	*262*	the gas, pay the electric—and all I'm asking is for two
1049-1050	*263*	twenty five, but you say, can't do that, we'd rather pay
1050-1052	*264*	the four hundred something than pay the two twenty-
1052-1053	*265*	five, the difference is I own this, and that person rents.
1053-1055	*266*	You know, that don't make sense. If I sold this place,
1055-1056	*267*	stuck the money someplace, ran down and rented an
1056-1057	*268*	apartment for four hundred dollars and wasn't work-
1057	*269*	ing, they would pay!

Source	Edit	
1068	270	Well, when [my wife] Nancy was at work, I had a hear-
1069-1070	271	ing down in East Aurora about food stamps. They did
1070-1071	272	all the bookwork, then I went in, and there was a
1072-1073	273	Cuban sitting there, couldn't even speak English. I
1073-1074	274	went in, asked the guy, I said, Well, how did I make
1074-1075	275	out? He says, Uh, we turned you down. I said, Why?
1075-1076	276	Well, you know, you're wife's working. I said, So? Well,
1076-1077	277	can't give you nothing. Well, before I leave, I says, The
1077-1078	278	guy out there, he's a Cuban, right? He says, Yeah. I
1080-1081	279	said, How'd he make out, did he get it? He said, Oh
1081-1082	280	yeah, he got it. So I said, That's nice, he gets it, he's
1082-1083	281	not a citizen or nothing and I've been working since I
1083-1084	282	was seven years old, and I get nothing. Well, I feel
1084	283	sorry for you, he says, you know, his hands are tied,
1085	284	he's got to go by what rules the state and local govern-
1086	285	ment gives him.
1088-1089	286	MF: It's an interesting kind of angle on being left with
1089-1091	287	nothing after eighteen years—I mean, because you'd
1091-1092	288	done a lot, you had something—and yet you can't use
1093, 1102	289	that something to help rebuild yourself. And the point
1102-1103	290	of that, like unemployment, ought to be to help you
1103-1104	291	through till you can really get something else going.
1104, 1112	292	DH: Yeah, keep you going. Well, with the unemploy-
1112-1113	293	ment they got a deadline—twenty-six weeks. It's not
1114	294	that the people are taking this hundred and twenty-
1115-1116	295	five dollars, whatever it is, now—they're not taking the
1116-1117	296	money and putting it away, they're using that to sur-
1117-1118	297	vive. So, it's keeping the economy going, even though
1118-1119	298	it's a little bit. That guy's spending a hundred twenty-
1119-1120	299	five dollars every week, buying food or paying his gas
1120-1121	300	and electric—it's keeping something going, the whole
1121, 1136	301	economy ain't stopping. You're gonna have your little
1136-1137	302	cheats, no matter what you do, but a majority of the
1138-1139	303	people are really benefitting through the federal gov-
1139-1140	304	ernment, state, or your local government assets—you
1140	305	know, they're trying to use it the right way.
1142	306	MF: You mention these two houses, where were you
1142-1143	307	living during most of the time that you were working
1143-1144	308	there, were you living in South Buffalo, or were you
1144-1145	309	living out here? [Hughes's home is in Colden, New

Source	Edit	
–	*310*	York, a country town in the hills to the south of Buf-
–	*311*	falo and Lackawanna.]
1146	*312*	DH: No, thirteen years out here, a couple of years up
1147	*313*	on top of the hill in Boston [New York], that just about
1147-1148	*314*	covered it—we lived with my mother-in-law about for
1148	*315*	a year.
1149	*316*	MF: The second house is, then, around here too?
1150	*317*	DH: Right behind us, on the same land.
1151	*318*	MF: And you rent that out, do you?
1152	*319*	DH: Yeah, I rent that out.
1295-1298	*320*	MF: Living in the country here is real different, was
1298-1299	*321*	that a goal of yours to get a place out here, or did that
1299	*322*	just sort of happen?
1300-1301	*323*	DH: Well, you know, if you're taking care of somebody
1301-1302	*324*	else's family, which was my father's family, when you
1302-1303	*325*	get married you really have got to make that commit-
1303-1304	*326*	ment to leave the nest.
1313-1314	*327*	MF: How'd you choose out here—there are a lot of
1315	*328*	places to get away to.
1316	*329*	DH: Well, you see the hills out there? That's your
1319-1320	*330*	answer. I just like looking at the hills.
1321	*331*	MF: You don't like cities either? Did you really want
1322	*332*	kind of a small town, when you thought about what
1323	*333*	kind of place you wanted to have your kids in?
1325	*334*	DH: Yeah, a small town area, such as this, a town that
1326	*335*	never really is going to grow. This town will stay like
1327, 1334	*336*	this for years and years. There's no subdivision or
1334-1335	*337*	nothing like that. It's mostly old families that were
1335-1336	*338*	here—all interbreeded and that. Their mothers were
1336-1337	*339*	here. Most of them are rich, well-off people. You have
1337-1338	*340*	a lot of doctors out here, lawyers. There are the hid-
1338-1339	*341*	den parts of the hills that really have nice places.
1339-1340, 1343	*342*	They're more or less looking for the same thing. Most
1344-1345	*343*	of the people are nice. You know, every town you have
1345-1346	*344*	so many bad people. If you live in a small town, you
1346	*345*	got less bad people, I guess.

Source	Edit	
1363-1364	*346*	MF: So has the community been supportive when
1364-1365	*347*	you've gone through rough times like this, do you
1365-1366	*348*	think it's been easier in a place like here than it would
1366-1367	*349*	be someplace else?
1368	*350*	DH: I think it would be easier on ourselves if we were
1369	*351*	in Buffalo, we'd be close by when—you know, you can
1370	*352*	look for a job you don't have to drive the distance.
1371-1372	*353*	That part would be better. But as far as helping—how
1372, 1374-1375	*354*	much can you really help, it's not that some guy'd come
1375-1376	*355*	up and just offer you a job or just give you money.
1378-1379, 1389	*356*	MF: You said a lot of the people are wealthier. Does
1384-1385	*357*	that make it hard—do people look at you like, oh,
1385-1386	*358*	there's so and so, and he's going to have trouble pay-
1386	*359*	ing his bills?
1389	*360*	DH: Some of them do, some of them don't. Only a
1390-1391	*361*	couple, I'd say a handful that know—neighbor, the girls
1392-1394	*362*	up front, the guy in the post office, a couple of guys in
1394-1395	*363*	the gas station. But, no, 90 percent of them don't
1395	*364*	know that you're going through hard times, having
1395	*365*	to struggle ....
1396	*366*	MF: Do you have this place pretty well paid off now,
1397	*367*	you must be close to it?
1398	*368*	DH: Oh, $15,000, I think it was, fifteen something.
1399	*369*	But the only thing is, you can't do repairs now. You
1400	*370*	can't do the things you want to do because it costs
1401	*371*	money, you just can't go out and buy stuff and do
1402-1403	*372*	what I want to do. Now I got the time, but no money
1404	*373*	to do repairs.
1154-1155	*374*	MF: Are you from out here, both grow up around here?
1156	*375*	DH: I'm originally from the First Ward of Buffalo. And
1157	*376*	I used to shine shoes when I was a little kid up there,
1158	*377*	worked, and from there we moved to Orchard Park.
1162, 1165	*378*	We come from a big family, a big South Buffalo Irish
1165-1168	*379*	family. So we had to work all the time, since I went to
1167-1168	*380*	school from eight to eleven, then I had to go to the
1168-1169	*381*	greenhouse, so I only had three hours ....
1276	*382*	MF: You finish school?

Source	Edit	
1277	*383*	DH: Nope. I quit my junior year. That was strictly
1278-1279	*384*	because I had to work all the time. That just drove me
1279-1280	*385*	nuts, I was helping to support my father's family.
1264	*386*	MF: When you were growing up there, was steel one of
1265-1266	*287*	the things you thought about going into? You can't be
1266-1267	*388*	too far from steel when you grow up in South Buffalo.
1268-1269	*389*	DH: Who, me? The steel mills? No, I was thinking
1269-1270	*390*	about being in the Mafia. [laughs] Being a crook!
1270	*391*	[laughs]
1271	*392*	MF: [laughs] And they didn't have any openings for
1272	*393*	you?
1272	*394*	DH: They didn't have no openings.
1272-1273	*395*	MF: Oh, I hear they're recruiting all the time!
1274	*396*	DH: [laughs] No, I never really thought about it. It
1275	*397*	never entered my mind.
[added]	*398*	MF: So how did you get started at Shenango?
1249, 1252	*399*	DH: Well, Nancy's brothers worked there. Most of her
1252-1253	*400*	family works in the steel business. Down at Ohio Tool,
1253-1254	*401*	family, and uncles there, most of them went into steel.
1254-1255	*402*	You heard the same thing from them—you know, when
1255-1256	*403*	they started off they got their heads pounded in, went
1257, 1260	*404*	through the hard times. It's like getting a part of your
1260-1261	*405*	stomach cut off, if the plant closes. You know, if the
1261-1262	*406*	plant just says you're on layoff, there's always a chance
1262-1263	*407*	you're going to go back. But when it shuts down,
1263	*408*	closed . . . whew.
1421	*409*	MF: Did you go into a kind of tailspin after you got
1422	*410*	laid off, or sort of a crisis period?
1413-1414	*411*	DH: Well, I was bad, oh, I was bad. I think if I didn't
1415	*412*	have accepted the Lord and everything, and being laid
1416	*413*	off one year, or hearing the news that Shenango was
1417	*414*	going to close, I probably would have robbed some-
1418-1419	*415*	one, just kept robbing off the rich—you know, being
1419-1420	*416*	mad because they're the ones that have control of it.
1410-1412	*417*	MF: This religious conversion, how did that happen—
1410-1412	*418*	was it right after the layoff?

Source	Edit	
1424	419	DH: No, it came—you know, there was no definite
1425	420	thing that Shenango was going to close. We were on a
1426-1427	421	layoff, and kept thinking we were going to get called
1427-1428	422	back, and I was collecting unemployment and some
1428-1429	423	SUB pay, and so—I was working up in East Aurora,
1429-1430	424	working in this Antique Barn, there was a Christian
1430-1431	425	family, and they kept telling me about the Lord, and I
1431-1432	426	says, Get out of here! Wacky, don't want to hear that
1432-1433	427	stuff. They'd play music, and I'd go turn it on rock 'n
1433-1434	428	roll or country and western, and they'd turn it back.
1434-1435	429	And then, all of a sudden they bought me a Bible.
1435-1437	430	What's this? Take it home and read it. All right, brought
1439-1439	431	it home, I wouldn't read it. And then it kept going on
1442-1443	432	and on for a couple of weeks, and before you know it I
1443-1444	433	started going in there and I started turning on the
1444-1445	434	Christian music, and humming it. So it kept going
1447-1448	435	on, they kept talking more about the Lord, every day
1448-1449	436	and every day and every day, and it just happened.
1450	437	One day, it happened, outside.
1461	438	MF: You were brought up Catholic?
1462-1463	439	DH: I was brought up ... nothing. Protestant, yeah,
1463-1464	440	but I didn't believe in nothing. No God. I just believed
1464-1465	441	that you make as much money as you can, you live as
1465-1467	442	good as you can, and you die. I just didn't believe in
1468, 1535	443	nothing. Then I just changed around, you know, read-
1535-1536	444	ing the Bible the right way, accepting the Lord, and
1536-1538	445	knowing that Jesus died for them, the only way to
1538-1539	446	Heaven is through Jesus Christ. I was really shocked
1539, 1543	447	that after I got affiliated with the Church there, these
1543-1544	448	new guys I know, they said that 95 percent of the
1544-1545	449	Church is Roman Catholic, they said Roman Catho-
1545-1546	450	lics. I said, "Wow, that's really something. Boy, if they
1546-1547	451	can do that ... !" It's hard, you know, to get the Catho-
1547-1549	452	lics to see the right way, to get them rolling the right
1549-1551	453	way. You know, to convert a Catholic is hard. Here they
1552-1553	454	sit and listen to Latin, they don't understand Latin,
1553-1554	455	they believe in the Virgin Mary, and it's nice to believe
1554-1555	456	in it, but they worship her! Not to worship Jesus Christ,
1555-1556	457	just knowing Jesus Christ is something different,
1557	458	knowing that through the Son you will go to Heaven.

Source	Edit	
1469	*459*	MF: What kind of difference—how has it made a
1470	*460*	difference?
1471	*461*	DH: Oh, it made a big difference. Kept me out of jail!
1472, 1476-1477	*462*	[Laughs.] No, it made a big difference—now I don't
1477, 1482	*463*	think about stealing. We got Bible study, and we help
1482-1484	*464*	an alcoholic, he lived here. You got to struggle through
1484-1485	*465*	hard times, and helping somebody out, you got him
1485, 1490	*466*	on his feet, going in the right direction. Just help
1490-1491	*467*	somebody else and take some of the pressure away.
1492-1493	*468*	The last four years the gas company just started com-
1493-1494	*469*	ing out with fantastic gas bills, shortage of gas in your
1495-1496	*470*	car and your taxes are skyrocketing, it just seems like—
1497-1498	*471*	somebody, they started the bandwagon with the can-
1498-1499	*472*	ning jars, the canning lids, the shortage, and it just
1499-1500	*473*	started from there, everybody making up the short-
1500-1501	*474*	age, to get rich, and before you know it we're running
1501-1502	*475*	out of natural gas, we're running out of oil, we're run-
1502-1503	*476*	ning out of everything.
1503-1504	*477*	And just everybody got on the bandwagon—just when
1504-1505	*478*	the country needed help, all those businesses jumped
1505-1506	*479*	in and made it worse. Instead of saying, let's lock our
1506-1507	*480*	horns together and get out of this crisis. They all just
1507-1508	*481*	jumped in, and the telephone company, everybody—it
1508-1509	*482*	seems like they want to take every dollar they could
1509-1510	*483*	take from you, they just use that word, there's a short-
1510-1511	*484*	age, instead of saying, OK, we're all Americans, let's
1516-1517	*485*	show that we can all pitch in and help each other, rich
1517-1518	*486*	businessman can hand out a little bit where it ain't
1518-1519	*487*	going to hurt him and use it as a tax write-off, and
1519-1520	*488*	everybody can help each other and we could all get
1520-1521	*489*	back on our feet. Because if people don't have money
1521-1522	*490*	to spend, the economy's only going to get worse.
1558	*491*	MF: How does this all relate to these other pictures
1562	*492*	Milton took at your home? I see cars, I see Elvis, and I
1563-1564	*493*	see, in the other picture, who is it we got there, Buddy
1564-1565	*494*	Holly? And these dolls. So I'm curious about the dolls,
1566, 1576	*495*	and the music, about Elvis. When Elvis died, was that
1577-1578	*496*	something that you were involved with?
1591-1592	*497*	DH: Yeah, yeah it hurt. It hurt more to find out that
1593, 1596	*498*	he was on drugs, and he wasted himself. At first when

Source	Edit	
1596-1597	499	he died, you know, they tried to keep it hush-hush,
1597-1599	500	and I says, it's a waste that he killed himself, he's so
1599-1600	501	rich and he made his life so miserable, by being so
1600-1601	502	protective of himself, instead of going out in public
1601-1602	503	and associating, he just grew too big.
1605-1606	504	MF: What's your theory about why his music was pow-
1606-1607	505	erful for so many people?
1608	506	DH: Oh, it was from the heart, the soul. Soul music,
1609-1610	507	the blues mix. Yeah, he wasn't like a white man sing-
1610-1611	508	ing colored music. He just ... he was a country boy,
1612-1613	509	he wanted things to happen, he was young, and he
1613-1614	510	loved his mother and father. He didn't want to go out
1614-1615	511	where the big wheels were, he didn't want to go to
1615-1616	512	Hollywood—but he wanted the money and everything,
1616-1618	513	he knew he was going that way. He come in with the
1618-1619	514	sideburns, changed things around. I think it was a
1620-1621	515	good thing to call him, you know, the King of Rock 'n
1620-1621	516	Roll, because he did break it wide open for everybody.
1639-1640	517	MF: Now what about the dolls, it's quite an impressive
1640-1641	518	collection. Are these old dolls, or any kind of dolls?
1642	519	DH: No, those are mostly newer ones. Madame Alex-
1643-1644	520	ander's Collectibles. This is what rich people buy their
1644-1645	521	kids to play with. She come over from Germany, her
1646-1648	522	father was a doll doctor, and he died and she took
1648-1650	523	over, and she's a real old woman now. What she does
1650-1652, 1655	524	is, make them for the richer kids. But she'll just make
1655-1656	525	so many and there ain't no more, and you send in
1656-1657	526	your order, whoever, first come first serve. And if the
1657-1658	527	stores wants more, there is no more, that's it.
1679	528	MF: Did you used to have a few of these Corvettes,
1680-1681	529	that you'd bought up and then worked on the engines?
1690, 1682-1683	530	DH: Yeah, but they're gone. I sold those, I got one car
1683-1684	531	left that's a '58 Chevy, plan on selling that. So most of
1684-1685	532	the rest is gone, just to pay the taxes. Like now, I got
1685-1686	533	to by the fifteenth of this month, I got to come up
1686-1687	534	with a thousand and ten dollars to pay the school tax,
1687-1688	535	that I don't have. So I don't know what's going to hap-
1688	536	pen there.

Source	Edit	
1689	*537*	MF: What do you do when you're not working these
1690	*538*	days?
1691	*539*	DH: Not a heck of a lot! You know, really—just worry-
1692	*540*	ing, thinking, get the pen out and figure out how
1693	*541*	you're going to make it, and writing down figures after
1694	*542*	figures, hoping everything turns out right. And I go
1695	*543*	back, worked at the racetrack, being a guard, mini-
1696, 1703	*544*	mum wage, it's not a heck of a lot. The thing is that
1704	*545*	you do work, when you get into construction, they
1706	*546*	throw that salary stuff at you: we'll put you on salary,
1707	*547*	but we'll work you sixty hours a week. Just take com-
1708	*548*	plete advantage of you—they really know you're hurt-
1709-1710	*549*	ing, and they can get everything they want out of you.
1712-1713	*550*	MF: Do you have any long-range hopes, if the econ-
1713-1714	*551*	omy starts picking up, where things might....
1715	*552*	DH: Well, I'm just hoping that they don't destroy all
1716-1717	*553*	our steel mills, in case we really need them. Because
1717-1718	*554*	you're dependent on foreign oil, and they're going to
1717-1718	*555*	lock themselves into dependent on foreign steel, and
1719-1720	*556*	then you're getting into a crisis. They'll just raise every-
1720-1722	*557*	thing else, they control the world market on steel
1722-1723	*558*	prices, and—well, over here they can just knock us
1723-1724	*569*	0out of the ballpark. I just think if they can keep the
1724	*560*	steel mills going, get 'em back on their feet.
1764	*561*	MF: I bet you must feel good that way back when you
1765-1766	*562*	socked some stuff into a place like this out here. Well,
1766-1767	*563*	like you were saying, if they're not going to give you
1767-1768	*564*	anything after eighteen years, at least you know you've
1768-1769	*565*	got this really beautiful house and land....
1770	*566*	DH: Well, I can sell it to you, Mike! [laughs]

Dick Hughes Interview
[Full Source Transcript]

Source	Edit	
1	*1*	MF: Well, we can start with the stuff that you were
2		just mentioning, or we can backtrack and talk about
3	*1-2*	the work you were doing, or, which would you ....
4	*3*	DH: Well, I could say the last four years since being
5	*4*	out at Shenango, the most I made, for money, was
6	*5*	about $4,000 a year, just working minimum wage jobs,
7	*6*	security, you know, security jobs, nobody wants you,
8	*6-7*	you know, just can't find a job.
9		MF: Yeah, so it's been mostly sort of temporary things
10		that you'd—a little here and a little ....
11	*7*	DH: Yeah, more or less, just that. Other jobs, you
12	*7-8*	know, would pop up, being with the economy so bad,
13	*8-9*	you know, as far as mechanics jobs, they just want to
14	*9*	pay you, you know, minimum wage, carpenter's job, I
15	*10*	think I worked for what, five bucks an hour, they just
16	*11, 13*	want to work you to death, you know, and knowing
17	*13-14*	that you're hurting and that they can take advantage
18	*14-15*	of this, you know, you don't hve no choice or nothing,
19	*15-16*	you just have to, either work the way they want you to,
20	*16-17*	or take a walk—they pick somebody else up that's in
21	*71*	the same boat. That's about it.
22		MF: Yeah. A lot of these have been local here, in the
24		Colden area, or do you still have to ... ?
24		DH: No, in Buffalo, working for a guy in Cheektowaga,
25		and another guy in Eden—same way, you know, he'd
26	*11-12*	work you six days a week and ten hours a day, and pay
27	*12-13*	you forty hours no matter what you did, you know ....
28		MF: And, you know, you say two words and, yeah ....
29		DH: Yeah, you're out on your ear, you know.
30	*18*	MF: Well tell you what, let me—I think that in a way, a
31		lot of this will be more, well sort of say more about it,
32		and put it in context if we go back and—since one of
33		the things we'll be doing is working from the pictures,
34	*18-19*	I'd be kind of interested in first getting a sense of what
35	*19*	you were doing before, and what the iron and steel work

Source	Edit	
36	*19-20*	was about in Shenango, and then we can sort of talk
37	*20*	about what's happened since, and in a way it's the—the
38		whole background is really kind of part of where people
39		are now. One of the things we really want to get across
40		is, everybody knows folks who are unemployed, but they
41		don't really have a sense that, you know, this could be
42		them, or it's just a person who has just as much in their
43		life, as much complexity and has been through a
44	*20*	whole lot of things, rather than just a statistic. So, let
45	*21*	me just start asking, 'cause I don't know that much
46	*21-22*	about it, if you could talk about that picture, and tell
47	*22-23*	me what you were doing—do you remember when Mil-
48	*23*	ton took that, and where you were, and what's going on,
49	*24*	and what kind of work you did at Shenango, and . . . .
50	*25*	DH: OK. What Shenango consisted of, we were mak-
51	*26*	ing ingot molds for the steel mills. What an ingot mold
52	*27*	was, was to hold the steel, you know, until it cooled,
53	*27-28*	and they would re-use the ingot mold and keep just get-
54	*28-29*	ting castings out of it. All we did there was just chip 'em
55		and grind 'em and get 'em ready for the steel mills.
56		MF: Is that all that Shenango did, that's what its main
57		business was?
58		DH: That's what its main business was, yeah, just sup-
59		plying ingot molds for the steel mills.
60		MF: This is a Buffalo Company?
61		DH: No, this is a Pittsburgh outfit, Pittsburgh, Penn-
62		sylvania, and they had three mills, two in Pittsburgh—
63	*63*	uh, two in Pennsylvania, and one in Buffalo. Thing
64	*63-64*	what happened was, the continuous cast came in to
65	*64-65*	the steel mills, you know, trying to keep the steel flow-
66	*65-66*	ing, keep it going, and stamping everything out the
67	*66-67*	way they wanted it, so they didn't need no ingot molds,
68	*67-68*	so they wouldn't have to go around buying ingot
69	*68*	molds, so that [came into a fact (?)], an expensive
70	*68-69*	operation, which they did, that's what knocked us out
71	*69*	of business.
72		MF: And that company's completely gone, now?

Source	Edit
73	
74	
75	
76	70
77	70-71
78	71
79	72
80	
81	72-73
82	73
83	74
84	74-75
85	75-76
86	
87	
88	
89	
90	
91	
92	
93	
94	
95	
96	
97	
98	
99	
100	
101	
102	
103	
104	
105	
106	
107	
108	
109	
110	

DH: No, they've still got, they're working, I think, one turn [term?] down in Pittsburgh, the other plant's closed up, but there's no . . . .

MF: 'Cause, I mean, like the plants here didn't completely go over to continuous casting, did they? I mean, they still use the . . . .

DH: They still use, yeah, they still use ingot molds. I heard that they might go back to it, you know—it's *cheaper*, you know, but . . . . Continuous cast you gotta have temperature going exact all the time, you gotta have, you know, temperature in the whole place gotta be exact to keep it going. Now they're finding out that it's pretty expensive, in fact—gotta be competitive with the foreigners/ MF: So it might end up being/ DH: Yeah, they might end up going back/ MF: It might be one of those kind of improvements that ends up being not such a/ DH: Right, you know . . . .

MF: Like they were saying, in the defense stuff now, they got some of these new weapons systems that are so complicated that, you know, they just don't do what they're supposed to do, they're trying to evaluate, maybe whether they'd be better off just going back to an old M-1 or something like that.

DH: Yeah, see with this, here, they used, they used everything. They used the ingot mold, and when they got thirty, forty castings out of it they broke it up, then they'd get, there's always iron in the steel, so they just broke it up, put the iron in with the steel, so there's actually no waste.

MF: And how were the ingot molds made at Shenango, that's a casting process itself, there.

DH: Yeah, they got molten iron from Hanna Furnace, which is closed now [indistinct phrase]. But they bought all their iron from Hanna. You know, with Republic opening back up, maybe, uh, maybe something will happen out there.

MF: So they were really, like, tied in with all these, it's kind of like a whole interdependent web/ DH: Yeah/

Source	Edit	
111		of these companies. The molten iron, would already
112		be brought over molten from Hanna in, in—how would
113		that be done?
114		DH: Torpedoes. You know, like a train—it's like a train
115		that's like a torpedoe size and/ MF: Right, I've seen
116		pictures of that/ DH: You've seen those? Yeah, you
117		pour the iron in there, and just bring it over and dump
118		it on, and ladle . . . .
119		MF: Where was the Shenango—where is that, in
120		Buffalo?
121		DH: Next to Hanna.
122		MF: Uh-huh, so it didn't have to go very far.
123		DH: No, it's a matter of about a five minute ride on
124		the track.
125		MF: And where's that exactly?/ DH: Next to Hanna
126		Furnace. MF: Yeah, and where's that?/ DH: Furhman/
127		MF: Furhman, Furhman Boulevard, okay. [Wife inter-
128		jects: Tell him I didn't work at Shenango] [laughs]
129		DH: [laughs] [Not quite clear. I may have looked to
130		her for help on the location. . . .]
131		MF: Okay, so—and how many people tended to work
132		at a place like Shenango? This is a small/
133		DH: Yeah, a small outfit, two hundred twenty-five
134		guys.
135	30	MF: And, what, exactly what part of the process is that
136	31	picture getting, you're jus sitting on a . . . .
137	32	DH: Oh, that's the finished product, that's the prod-
138	33	uct before it goes into the railroad car to the customer.
139		MF: And what did you do, in there, in that process,
140		what was your—in a smaller shop like that did people
141		tend to do all sorts of things, or did they have depart-
142		ments like the bigger mills and stuff?
143	34	DH: Well, this was a big department, what we did here,
144	34-35	what my job was, was to chip out the excess iron that
145		was in there, that shouldn't have been in there, and

Source	Edit
146	*35-36*
147	*36-37*
148	*38*

grind it, smooth it, clean all the excess sand off, and it went to one other guy and he painted it, and into the railroad car.

MF: Right. So you'd work with it after it came out of the, the mold/ DH: Yeah, after it cooled off and everything, we would get it.

MF: How long a process is that, from when they pour it till when it's ready to . . . ?

DH: Poured until the finished product, would be about, uh, let's say about a thirty-six hour process for one finished project.

MF: And they would keep—so they didn't make any of their own iron, then, they just had/ DH: No, they just bought their own iron/ MF: Right, the torpedoes came in and the ingots went out the other end, and/ DH: Yes./ MF: and that was pretty much the/ DH: Right, all they did was make the sand and everything.

MF: Is that something that's usually, like, subcontracted out by a mill, or did some of them get involved in making their own, did they/ DH: Yeah/ MF: have their own foundries/

DH: Well, yeah, Shenango did, down there in Pennsylvania, their other two plants had their own, you know iron foundry and melt their own iron and everything. But being up here, and being that their customer was Great Lakes, and Great Lakes was an affiliate of Hanna Furnace, and what they were doing was/ MF: So it was all/ DH: Yeah, actually, they'd make molds for Great Lakes, and they buy the iron off of Hanna, but Great Lakes *owned* Hanna Furnace, so in a way they're/ MF: So it's really like/ DH: It's like a part of the family/

MF: Except that it probably made sense for them to have different companies doing it rather than organize it all under one. What's happened to Great Lakes, they're down too, are they?

DH: Yeah, they're really folded out, there's not much going on, foreign import really killed them.

Source	Edit	
184		MF: Right, that was a steel mill?
185		DH: Yeah, it was like—like U. S. Steel, one of the big,
186		you know—Great Lakes was a very big steel mill. They
187	*105*	mostly, Great Lakes was affiliated with—you know, it
188	*105-106*	falls right back to the automobile, they made the steel
189	*106*	and everything, and supplied the automobile places,
190	*106-107*	they'd stamp 'em out and everything, so it all leads right
191	*107-108*	back to that, the car.
192	*85*	MF: Right. How, how long did you work there?
193	*86*	DH: Ohhhhh [ironic]—eighteen years./ MF: Wow,
194	*86*	that's a long time, that's a lot of years/ DH: Eighteen
195	*87*	years and I didn't get nothing.
196	*88*	MF: Yeah, I want to, I want to talk about *that*. The
197	*88*	eighteen years, in terms of the work itself, you were
198		doing that kind of work, or did you tend to move
199		around?
200		DH: Well, that—right down in that department, I think
201		I worked thirteen years. . . . I worked a little bit in the
202		ram department, and the rest of it was on the labor.
203		MF: What's that, what's the ram . . . .
204		DH: That's where they ram the sand to make the mold,
205		for making the casting for the ingot.
206		MF: And general labor is sort of working around?
207		DH: Well, sweeping up, you know, running a fork lift,
208		and making sure everything's going right.
209	*89*	MF: Was this the kind of shop that people tended to
210	*90*	have a really stable work force, that people had been
211	*91*	there ten, fifteen years, twenty years?
212	*92*	DH: Yeah, because—a lot of guys came up from Penn-
213	*93*	sylvania, and they had, oh, anywhere between ten and
214	*93-94,95*	twenty years. You know, they told us up here, because
215	*94-95*	we're from New York, they'd say, well, you get hired in
216	*95-96*	there, if you get ten years, you got it knocked, noth-
217	*96-97*	ing will happen to you, just ride it out, and retire and
218	*97-98*	have a good pension. Which it didn't turn out that way.

Source	Edit	
219	–	MF: During the time when you were working there, was it pretty steady during most of those eighteen years, or did it tend to/
220	*99-100*	
221	*100*	
222	*101*	DH: Well, I was never laid off./ MF: Never laid off!/ DH: Never laid off./MF: And they're turning out ingots pretty constantly, then all through that/
223	*101*	
224		
225	*101-102*	DH: Yeah they were working six, seven days a week, a good business.
226	*102*	
227		MF: Cause, as you say, the ingots are sort of used up, so that there'd be a continuous/ DH: Yeah, a continuous/ MF: As long as they're pouring steel somewhere/ DH: Yeah, as long as they're making cars. You know, pouring steel, there's no problem, you just keep making molds.
228		
228		
230	*103*	
231	*103-104*	
232	*104*	
233		MF: Yeah, cause I know in a lot of the plants in different corners of industry, that they can get really caught in these whiplashes, I was talking with somebody from Harrison Radiator, and of course they get laid off about three times as much as the auto people, because they just stock up on radiators, or the Trico people, and so on—but something like this, as long as they're going, they're going to need what they've been making.
234		
235		
226		
237		
238		
239		
240		
241		DH: Yeah, as long as they're making cars and selling them, there's no problem.
242		
243		MF: How did you start there, is that something you grew up with, or was it the first job you had, or . . . ?
244		
245		DH: No, uh, actually, my, uh, fourth job. I drove a truck, worked for a meat place. Then my brother-in-law worked there, so I figured, well, there's a lot of overtime, so I'll go over there, got a job, started out on the labor gang. The money was good, the overtime was there, and, you know, it's hot and dirty, but, you know, you talked to the guys there, they'd say, once you get those years then you're gonna have it knocked, so . . . .
246		
247		
248		
249		
250		
251		
252		
253		
254		MF: So you pretty well thought as you were starting in that it looked like a pretty good track.
255		

Source	Edit	
256		DH: Yeah, I figured that I was gonna retire from there,
257		you know.
258		MF: Was it a, kind of happy place to work, people
259		kinda feel like, you know—I'm trying to compare it in
260		my own mind to, when I talk to people from Bethle-
261		hem, you get a sense of the difference between the
262		smaller shops and the giant ones, where there are, it
263		seemed, more . . . .
264		DH: Well, the guys knew each other, more I think than
265		in a bigger plant. They knew each other, you know,
266		but it wasn't happy all the time—the guys were out for
267		that buck, you know, just make as much as you can
268		make, you know, and cheat where you can cheat, you
269		know—say I, I need the overtime, try to get as much
270		overtime as they wanted—but they all knew each other,
271		you know, and the families, it was pretty close.
272		MF: Was there much kind of elbowing around, then,
273		sort of trying to get the foreman to put this person on
274		overtime assignment—did the foreman have control
275		of that kind of thing?
276		DH: Yeah, they had control of the overtime for each
277		department. And they would sneak in, try to become—
278		you know, like you say, rub elbows with the foreman,
279		and say, don't mark my overtime down for two days,
280		and I'll be lower the next time around, and I'll still get
281		an extra day, and you know, stuff like that. There was
282		enough money there that—you know, there was no,
283		some guys wouldn't like it, but there was no—it wasn't
284		that bad that people were going to kill each other over
285		the overtime.
286		MF: Did the work stay pretty much the same during
287		that period, time in terms of how fast they were push-
288		ing you, or things like that?
289		DH: Yeah, it stayed like that, I'd say, pretty close for
290		the eighteen years, it stayed pretty steady, the pro-
290A		duction, you know, was pretty good.
291		MF: And you moved up from the labor thing to this/
292		DH: Chipping Department/ MF: That was a special/

Source	Edit	
293		DH: Special department, yeah, you had to bid into it,
294		and your seniority [... indistinct phrase] and you had
295		to learn the job, and if you learned the job, and then
296		they made you a first chipper, and that was your job,
297		and your seniority [??] from then on.
298	53	MF: What other kinds of specialities did they have,
299	54	what other kind of departments—so people looking at
300	55	the picture would have some sense of what goes on.
301	56-57	DH: Well, the casting department, which casts the
302	58	molds that you see in the picture, and the stage before
303	59	that is the ram department, where they ram the sand,
304	60, 56	to make the mold, that goes in the oven, so actually
305	56	there's three main departments.
306		MF: So they would actually make their own molds/
307		DH: Make the mold there./
308		MF: Put the sand in a shell and then it would sort of
309		get baked?
310	60-61	DH: Put the sand in, ram it, finish it with a blacken-
311	61-62	ing, which was wet, which would go to the mold, would
312	62-63	dry to a hard finished product, and they used two dif-
313		ferent sides—they used the inner, the inner mold, and
314		then the outer mold, they poured it, your iron/
315		MF: And these molds are destroyed when they crack
316		it open to get the thing out?
317		DH: Yeah, the sand's broken out, and then it's re-used
318		again, so there's actually not—no waste, they re-use
319		the sand, pour it back in the hopper, and it goes
320		upstairs, and they use new sand, to blend in with the
321		old sand, pretty much everything is re-used, so there's
322		not really too much waste.
323		MF: So you have the moldmaking at one end and then
324		you're/ DH: the finished product/ MF: Chipping the
325		product at—was there a shipping department or some-
326		thing like that, or it would be ready to go when ... ?
327		DH: Well, then the railroad would come in, the South
328		Buffalo Railroad, they would load the molds on the
329		cars, and weigh them, and then they'd be on their way.

Source	Edit	
330	*109*	MF: How much, how aware when you're doing that
331	*109*	kind of work, were people of where the, sort of, the
332	*109-110*	company was, or was it is more or less that it was just
333	*111*	sort of assumed that this would go on pretty steady?
334		Was there much, did people in the shop kind of get
335	*110*	involved in sort of questions about where the steel
336	*110*	industry was, or the policy of the country, and this
337		and that?
338	*112*	DH: Well, just about, I don't know, I'd say about four
339	*112-113*	or five years, just before they closed, we were getting
340	*113*	a lot of these different outfits, you know, like we were
341	*113-114*	selling molds to Canada, too, and they were getting
342	*114-115*	molds from England, and everything, and they were
343	*115*	more or less trying to make a comparison, you know,
344	*115-116*	how the mold would stand up under the castings of
345	*116-117*	the steel being poured in them and they were only
346	*117-118*	getting, like—English molds were only getting like
347	*118-119*	about ten castings, where our molds, they would get
348	*119*	about a hundred and five, hundred and ten/ MF: Is
349	*119-120*	that because/ DH: And then the guys started talking
350	*120-121*	about, well, jeez, you know, if it's overseas they're trying
351	*121-122*	to make molds to be competitive with ours, you know,
352	*122-123*	but we found out they were only getting about ten
353	*123-124*	heats out of them, we'd say, well, there's nothing to be
354	*124*	concerned about, they can't ....
355		MF: So there was no question that you had the qual-
256		ity here/ DH: Yeah/ MF: and so it made it harder to
357		see that they were sneaking up/ DH: they were sneak-
358		ing up the back door on us.
359	*125*	MF: How come there was such a difference in qual-
360	*126*	ity, was it the nature of the materials, or the skill,
361	*126*	or what?
362	*127*	DH: What it was, was the temperature and the amount
363	*128*	of iron and steel that you mix in to make the iron,
364	*129*	and, uh, what they were doing was making a softer
365	*129-130*	ingot mold, [indistinct phrase], they were just burn-
366	*130-131*	ing the heck out of the mold, they were just cracking
367	*131-132*	them, they just wanted to get the heat out of 'em,
368	*132-133*	where our molds, you know, it was more like, more
369	*133*	like a secret, you know, you get the exact part of the

Source	Edit
370	*133-134*
371	*134-135*
372	*135*

iron in the lab, you know, what you wanted, how much steel, how much iron mixed into it, and what the heat should be at.

| 373 | |
| 374 | |

MF: Right. Now did that get kinda done at Hanna, in other words when that iron came over/

| 375 | |
| 376 | |

DH: At Hanna's lab and Shenango would more or less tell them what they wanted, in the iron.

377	
378	
379	

MF: And so your people—and did you have, you had like—would those be engineers, who would do that, or was that down on the floor?

380	
381	
382	
383	
384	
385	

DH: Yeah, that would be your engineers, and they would want the results sent back from Hanna, make a comparison, and Shenango would dip some of the iron out, and check it, you know, for temperature and everything, and analysis, and if it was no good, you'd send the whole shipment back.

386	*136*
387	*137*
388	

MF: Is that something you can tell on the floor, when you're chipping on one of these things, can you kind of tell/

389	*138*
390	*138-139*
391	*139*
392	*139-140*
393	*140-141*
394	*142*
395	*142-144*
396	*141-142*
397	*144*
398	*145*
399	*146*

DH: Oh, yeah! Hey, you can't . . . if there's too much steel in it, it just breaks your chisel, and you just—you don't move as you're chipping, it just comes to a halt and just sits there and vibrates—it don't move, it's like a diamond. What it is, is it's too hard, it's no good for the mold, so when they get a casting out of it, in the steel mill, the chances are it'll break open—it may kill somebody, it's too hard, there's no give in the mold, chances are you'll just pour it, and if some guy's there in the steel mill, chances are that mold'll open up and crack, and the steel'll come flying out.

400	
401	
402	

MF: And what would happen in a case where you saw that, would you then report that up, or would the guys on the floor have any way to/

403	
404	
405	
406	
407	

DH: Well, you'd just tell the inspectors, you know, the inspector would look at it, and they would check it for—maybe like a spray paint they spray on there to look for hairline cracks, you know, see if it's really that bad, that they wouldn't be able to sell it, you know

Source	Edit

408
409

and if they couldn't sell it they'd just break it up, they wouldn't want to take a chance on it.

410

MF: Did that happen often or did. . . ?

411
412

DH: Oh, I'd say in eighteen years it probably happened maybe twenty times, and that would [?] be a lot.

413
414

MF: But generally, in a department like that, they're kind of like the final check.

415
416
417
418
419
420
421
422
423
424
425
426

DH: Yeah, they got, like three inspectors, they check, and they get the work finished, when they get the check, and report it and paint it, 'cause after they paint it they can't really see too much. So they was more or less checking them, you know, look at the log to make sure everything was—the iron wasn't too soft, the iron wasn't too hard, you know. But most of the casting guys, when the iron came over from Hanna Furnace, they could tell just by looking at it, when it's pouring out of the torpedo going into the ladle, you could see it—it's too white, they'd say, uh-uh, the iron's no good, you gotta be careful.

427
428
429

MF: After the—the ingot goes through a, what's that called, that kind of mill where it sort of knocks it down into/

430
431

DH: Where they block it down and remelt it and shape it and everything?/

432

MF: Yeah, is that what usually would happen with/

433	*41-42*
434	*42-43*
435	*43-44*
436	*44-45*
437	*45-46*
438	*46-47*
439	*47-48*
440	*48-49*
441	*49-50*
442	*50*
443	*50-51*
444	*52*

DH: Yeah, what they would do, is, pour the ingot mold, wait for it to cool a little bit, then you put it in a tank, bump it out, and then that block of steel would just sit, in the yard, and they'd just go back get another one, pour it, and—and all that steel would sit, and when they wanted to bring it into the rolling mills, they would bring it in, heat it, they would get the blast heat on it and get it real soft, and they'd start sectioning it off, they would chop it, and that piece would go to fall down, going through a roll, just keep rolling down to the size they'd want, whatever tubing they wanted to make, or sheet metal, whatever they wanted.

Source	Edit	
445		MF: So the stuff coming out—these ingots could then
446		go through any part of the/
447		DH: Yeah, any stage after that. But they had to have
448	*39*	someplace along when the blast furnace was going,
449	*40*	you're making steel, you have to have someplace to
450	*40*	put it, so that's what the purpose of the ingot mold
451	*41*	was, to pour it, and wait for it to chill, cast it [?], and
452		just set the steel outside.
453		MF: Were there other places in Buffalo doing that,
454		aside from Bethlehem, pretty well . . . .
455		DH: Just Republic and Bethlehem, were the only ones
456		I knew.
457		MF: No, I mean doing the ingots/
458		DH: Ingots—no, just Shenango.
459		MF: So you really had the local market, such as it was.
460		DH: Yeah, the local market, Republic, and like I say,
461		the Canadian outfits, Great Lakes, Stelco. But there
462		was a couple of other outfits, out . . . Michigan, Detroit,
463		a couple mold plants. They were—pretty competitive,
464		but we made a better, a longer-casting, you know, for
465		molds, but, uh, as I say, the [?] business died out and
466		that was it./ MF: The what business died out?/ DH: the
467		automobile business, and that just killed us, and there
468		wasn't enough for Shenango to keep going, so they
469		just gave some of their orders to the other competitors.
470		MF: Right. Did the Europeans end up getting, you
471		know, you were saying at the beginning that they/
472		DH: End up getting into the market? I don't know, I'd
473		like to find out, follow up on that/ MF: Cause obvi-
474		ously, they're still making steel someplace./
475		DH: Yeah, they're still making steel overseas. I can't
476		see how they—I can't see how they can be competi-
477		tive. If they're making an ingot mold over there that's
478		only gets ten heats, then they can sell the steel cheaper
479		over here, I don't know how they do it, it's really . . . I
480		know how they're doing it: the government's paying
481		them, you know, they talk about that up at UB [?], the

Source	Edit
482	
483	
484	
485	

government's assisting them, to make it, you know, to flood the market with a cheaper product,/ MF: So they can ... ?/ DH: to sell in bulk, where our government ain't helping.

486	
487	
488	

MF: Would an ingot that didn't have that quality be a lot cheaper to make, just 'cause of the materials in it, or ... ?

489	
490	
491	
492	
493	

DH: No, it would cost—I think the Europeans would sell it almost the same price as ours, but they're just saying it's gonna be a better mold, you know, it would last, and they just weren't getting the heats out of them, was only getting ten heats out of them.

| 494 | |
| 495 | |

MF: So without some other form, it's—you can't even begin to think how they could keep going like that.

496	
497	
498	
499	
500	
501	
502	
503	
504	

DH: The only way they could be more competitive was just/ MF: cutting the prices?/ DH: to get 150 or 200 heats out of their molds, but—to sell steel over here, you know, at their cheap price, their government's helping them, they're just flooding the market with cheaper steel. ... Just gotta check and see which businessmen are involved, the Americans, which are involved with the overseas steel mills, and that'll show you the picture right there.

| 505 | |
| 506 | |

MF: Yeah, I would think you're right, I mean, a lot of people/

507	
508	
509	

DH: They just think that they're foreign steel mills because they're over in another country, but there's a lot of our businessmen got their hands in over there.

510	
511	
512	
513	

MF: Oh yeah, I don't even know if that means anything anymore, you try to follow the automobile business/ DH: Yeah/ MF: Say what's an American car, what's a Japanese car/

514	
515	
516	
517	
518	

DH: Yeah, that's right, cause the Japs are over here now, and everybody's got their hands into it, and they want to be a part of it, you know, just to keep the people buying cars. Because you don't keep saying, "Well, that's a Japanese truck," you can say, "Well they

Source	Edit
519	
520	

got a plant over in Tennessee now, they got Americans working there, so you might as well buy it."

521	
522	
523	
524	
525	
526	

MF: So, like you were saying, when this started to go in that direction, that was a harder thing to see from the shop floor, because you were making a good quality product, and that seemed to/ DH: have its market stable and you'd been able to ride through all these other recessions and depressions.

527	76
528	77
529	78
530	78-79
531	79-80
532	
533	
534	79-80
535	80-81
536	81
537	82
538	82
539	82
540	83-84
541	83
542	
543	

DH: Yeah, we heard of continuous cast and everything, but we figured, well, that'll just be, you know, for small products, you know, we figured for big products there's no way—there's no way that they'd be able to build these buildings and keep an exact temperature, it would just cost them too much money, what with the gas prices going up, you know, natural gas, to heat these buildings at a certain temperature, it wouldn't be feasible, you know ... the mold business would stay in business forever, you know, all we would lose is the small—because continuous cast would run in a small field, you know, for small products .... Well, it's—the steel mills would go if there was, you know, if they weren't getting the flood of the foreign steel. Then we would be OK. But then again, it breaks down to a lot of things, you know, high wages over here, and stuff like that.

| 544 | 155 |
| 545 | 155 |

MF: What was the—was the union strong in your plant, this was a Steelworker's local?

| 546 | 156 |
| 547 | 157-158 |

DH: Well, it was—it was too strong, yeah, that's what put us out of business./ MF: Really, how so?/

548	159
549	159-160
550	160-161
551	161-162

DH: Oh, they just wanted to check the company books, they wanted too much, you know, pushing too much, they didn't want to bend, they didn't want to give up nothing, they didn't believe in no changes.

| 552 | |
| 553 | |

MF: Was that always the case, or did that tend to develop when things started to ... ?/

554	162
555	162-163
556	163-164

DH: Oh, that was more a case of playing it the rough guy, you know, you know your father did it, he gave up a lot, and he, you know, he had to buckle down in

Source	Edit	
557	*164-165*	Pennsylvania and Ohio, and he went through the
558	*165-166*	hard times, and they made the unions, and you know,
559	*166*	we're not giving up nothing, we don't want to hear
560	*167*	no sad stories from the company, they're just pulling
561	*167-168*	our leg, and, you know why give up what your father
562	*169*	struggled for, you just gotta—you can't give up, you
563	*169*	just keep going forward, keep pushing, get everything
564	*170*	you can, and .... You know, it was more of being a
565	*170*	bully type, the unions, you know, they didn't want to
566	*170-171*	bend, they didn't want to really sit down and hear the
567	*171*	story, you know, company says, Hey, foreign import's
568	*172-173*	killing us, we're going in the red, you know, we need
569	*173-174*	concessions, breaks, we gotta be competitive—there
570	*174*	was no trust.

571   MF: You have your own local at Shenango, is it/
572   DH: Yeah, our own local/ MF: And Hanna's not part
573   of that? DH: No./ MF: So it's a pretty small, what is it
574   about 250—everybody's in the local right?/ DH: Yeah,
575   225 guys in the local.

576   MF: And did they have a history, had there been labor
577   trouble there, any strikes?

578   DH: Yeah, we had one wildcat strike, it only lasted a
579   little while, couple of days, but the company was really
580   disturbed over it. The guy down in Pennsylvania was
581   disturbed over it, distrubed him so bad that he said
582   he'll do everything in his power to close that Buffalo
583   plant./ MF: Hmm!/ DH: Yeah, you know/ MF: So you
584   think that may have/ DH: They—Yeah, cause the union
585   was so cocky and everything .... And they were going
586   to put the electric furnaces in up here, make their
587   own steel, so when they went on that wildcat strike,
588   he was so teed off, he said ....

589   MF: When was—how far back was that?

590   DH: Oh, I think that was in '75, '76./ MF: And that was
591   about what, just wages, or working conditions, or ...?

592   DH: Oh, it was more or less they were trying to fire a
593   couple of guys, and they did fire a couple of guys, and—
594   they just wanted to have control, the company, and the

Source	Edit
595	
596	
597	
598	
599	
600	
601	*204*
602	*204*
603	*201,205*
604	*205-206*
605	*206*
606	
607	
608	
609	
610	
611	
612	
613	
614	*206-207*
615	*207-208*
616	*208-209*
617	
618	*209*
619	*210-211*
620	
621	
622	*211*
623	*211-212*
624	*212-213*
625	*213*
626	
627	*214*
628	*215*
629	*215-216*
630	*216-217*
631	
632	

union just wanted to have, to be in control of the company, the union wanted to do what they wanted to do.

MF: This union went all the way back, then, when Buffalo was organized in the '30's, then, I guess, huh?

DH: Way back to the—you know, when Pittsburgh, the plants down there and the big plants started in Ohio and everything, you know, more or less, you just get the attitude you know, you just talked it over and you don't give up nothing and you don't want to listen to the company's side. Which was bad, you know, 'cause they were hurting.

MF: Did this, was there—I remember the other interview talked about that a bit, when things began to get rough, there was sort of issues about givebacks and stuff like that, the company came to you and, there was something in there, in that transcript.

DH: You mean where the company would give us something back?/ MF: No, no, where they were asking the union to accept pay cuts or/

DH: Yeah, they wanted them to take a cut in their incentive and everything—not hourly pay, but just the incentive, it was more like bonus money, they wanted us./ MF: And this came to a vote or something, you said?

DH: Well we wanted to—we were out of work for so long, I think there was thirty guys working in the plant, and we were out/

MF: So this is already after the big layoffs?

DH: Yeah, we were out in the street, see, so when us younger guys said, well, let's hold a special meeting, get the [in to the?] company—you know, we were still talking to the company, I was talking to the [?] over there, and the company was [indistinct phrase] and everything—he said, jeez, we'd like to have you guys all back to work, you know, this plant up here would be the number two plant, if the guys would take a cut in pay, you know, in incentive and everything, you know, why don't you guys vote on it. We said, well, we'll get back to the union and we'll talk to them, we

Source	Edit
633	*217-218*
634	*218*
635	*219*
636	
637	*219-220*
638	*220-221*
639	*221-222*
640	*222-224*
641	*224-225*
642	*225*
643	
644	*225*
645	*226*
646	*226-227*

went back to the union, said, we'll hold a special union meeting, we want to vote on this and get back to work, the company says they'll have work for us, you know, if we give up the incentive program, or pay part of it. So, we went up to the union hall, told them what we wanted, you know, to get back to work, and the thirty older guys that were working say: Well, you guys ain't allowed to vote .... MF: Why was that?/ DH: You have to work five consecutive weeks in a year .... They said, You guys don't have no say in it. And we said, Yeah, we can go back to work, company's gonna make this their number two work, if you guys give up a, They said: [abruptly] "We're not giving up nothing .... You guys don't have no word in it."

Source	Edit
647	
648	
649	
650	
651	
652	
653	
654	
655	

MF: So according to that kind of—the fine print of the constitution just let all of the people who had a lot at stake, didn't have a chance to vote on it./ DH: Yeah, right, didn't have a chance to say nothing./ MF: I gather it's coming back to haunt them now, because a lot of these places, with those same kind of rules, now/ DH: Yeah, the same guys./ MF: It just destroys the union completely, because nobody has the right to vote, everybody's just out.

Source	Edit
656	*227-228*
657	*228-229*
658	*229-230*
659	*230-231*
660	*231-232*
661	*232*

DH: Everybody's out, the union's all done away with. And the guys, like I say, we seen the guys, now, some of the union guys [mock, dreamily], "Oh, I thought the company was bulling, huh, well, that's the way it is." Instead of saying they were wrong—"Well, that's the way it is."

Source	Edit
...	...
792	
793	

MF: So then they had to lay off some of you, and that's when things started getting ....

Source	Edit
794	
795	
796	
797	
798	

DH: Kept getting bad, and the company kept pleading with 'em, telling them ... and the union more or less, said, you know, we have to see your books. It's just you know ... to tell the company you want to see their books! The company just laughed about that.

Source	Edit
799	
800	

MF: Was this just your local, or was it pretty much the union down in Pennsylvania?

Source	Edit

801
802
803
804
805
806
807
808
809
810
811
812
813
814
815
816
817

DH: No, just the local here. The union down in Pennsylvania, they took a cut—and the plant kept those guys going, they took a cut in pay, because I think they more or less understood, they seen the writing on the wall, the company more or less told them, look, we're going to shut the—they told them first, we're going to shut this plant down, if you guys don't take a cut. Well, what if they took a cut, they kept working. And they gave us the same option, you know, told us, that's the way it is .... MF: And you're more vulnerable up here, cause you're sort of stuck way out/ DH: Yeah, and they just—the union said, no, we're not taking no cut, and that's it. And they said, furthermore we want to see your books and we want to take you to court, so they wanted to go through arbitration and take them to court—that just blew the company's mind, company said, no way, you know.

818   *175*
819   *175*
820   *176-177*
821   *177*

MF: You mention this thing about the older guys, was that a real division, these guys who'd come through the struggles of the thirties, forties, had one way of looking at things?

822   *178*
823   *178-179*
824   *179*

DH: Yeah, they didn't want to bend. They'd remember how, when they'd started the unions, they'd get beat up by the cops, and, you know.

825
826
827
828
929

MF: So many things it's the other way around, you know—I think of the universities, when I was there, it was the old professors, they just had never had any struggles about anything, and the young guys, of course, who were pushing ....

830   *179-180*
831   *180-181*
832   *182*
833   *182-183*
834   *183*
835   *183-184*
836   *184-185*
837   *185-186*

DH: No, the older guys down there really went through heck, you'd hear the stories about what they went through, get hit in the head with billy club/ MF: by the unions?/ DH: No, the local police and everything, when they were starting off. You know ... you worked down there, there was no union, and you got sick—you walked out the door sick, and that was your job, too, they had fifteen guys waiting.

838   *187*
839   *188-189*

MF: That must—it puts you in a funny position, because you don't want to say that's wrong, I mean, it's

Source	Edit
840	*190*
841	*190*
842	

obviously/ DH: It was the *right* thing, it was the right thing, and/ MF: probably better with the union rather than no union, and yet you get in a situation where/

832	*190-191*
844	*191-192*
845	*192-193*
846	*193-194*
847	*194-195*
848	
849	
850	

DH: Yeah, the union would protect you and, you know, keep your seniority, otherwise the plant wouldn't have to pay you no benefits, no retirement, you know, kick you around. But then the union got too powerful, you know, they didn't know when to stop. You know, that's why you gotta have—I guess you have two different kinds of unions./ MF: Yeah./ DH: It's like politics, you know.

851	
852	
853	
854	
855	
856	
857	

MF: Was it more, you think—on the one hand, you have this mind-set, you know, people just have all these memories and so on—or was it a real power push, they really wanted to sort of have their say in the plant. I mean, was there anything in it for them, or—was there any question of corruption in the union, that kind of thing, or was it just really a set of attitudes?

858	
859	
860	
861	
862	
863	
864	
865	
866	
867	
868	

DH: Well, I think it was a little bit of corruption. They were getting, you know, kickbacks on—bend the rules a little bit, throw things out that weren't—you know, that weren't in the bylaws and everything, I think—yeah, I think there was corruption in there too, the company—buckled down and told them that—they were like a little kid, their feelings were hurt, and the union got teed off and said, no, we're not going to bend no rules, we ain't going to do nothing, we're going to take this place over. You know—how can you tell a company that.

| 869 | |
| 870 | |

MF: And you've got a no-strike contract anyway, and all these other things./ DH: Yeah, yeah.

871	
872	
873	
874	
975	
876	
877	
878	
879	

MF: Yeah, somebody was saying, in one of these other talks, that of course steel union was so meshed in with the companies anyway, and it wasn't the '30s anymore, that then when things got rough like this—someone said almost exactly the same thing you did, that it's almost like they tried to go back to that attitude, almost like they wanted to live up to their image, but/ DH: It didn't work./ MF: It didn't work, and the whole thing wasn't set up for that.

Source	Edit
880	
881	
882	
883	
884	
885	
886	
887	
888	
889	
890	*195*
891	*196*
892	
893	
894	
895	
896	
- 897	
898	*196-197*
899	*197-198*
900	*198*
901	*198-199*
902	*199*
903	*199*
904	*199-200*
905	*200-201*
906	*201*
907	*201*
908	
909	
910	
911	
912	
913	*202*
914	*202-203*
915	*203*
916	*203-204*
917	
918	

DH: Right. They more became—just like management, just became a part.

MF: Until that time, did—how did, you as somebody who, and say the guys you worked with—tend to feel kind of indifferent about the union, or did your attitudes change when—I mean, obviously, that would have changed my attitude, if I were you, that vote—did that catch you by surprise, did you feel like betrayed by the union, or was this sort of what you more or less would have expected all along?

DH: No, I'm still a union man, you know, I think union is right, you know, in a lot of points. But you gotta know where to draw the line, you can't overstep your bounds. You start to become a part of the company, like you say, you join up, you become part of the company and you're trying to tell the company, we're going to take this place over, we're not going to bend, you're trying to control the company—it just ain't going to work. You know, you have certain protection plans, through the union—that's where the union should draw their line and end right there./ MF: and not try to operate the company?/ DH: Yeah, not try to operate the company and tell the company, you know—and be that demanding. You know—I mean, if the company says, you want to take a cut in pay, or something like that. Then come up front and say, you know, give us good cause, for you asking for this cut in pay. Show us, you know, would you show us your books, show us something.

MF: Yeah, like the guys at Chrysler, that took the cut in pay, then when the company started turning over millions of dollars, they go back and they say, OK, now we want/ DH: Right, when things go good/ MF: get back on your feet and then we want our share/

DH: Yeah, that would be good that way. But the union didn't do that—the union just showed strength all the way to the end, and they just/ MF: ran it into the ground/ DH: they just died with it, yeah.

MF: Well, especially—it's interesting, you think of a company like that, whatever the company wants, it's

Source	Edit	
919		like right in the middle of—I mean, probably, there's
920		not that much that a company that's that stuck—I
921		mean, you got Hanna here, you got this, you got the
922		mills here, and the iron ore down there, and they're
923		just like one link in that chain, so there's probably a
924		limit to how much they—how much movement, they—
925		room for movement they have, their costs—the iron
026		comes in and it costs whatever it costs, and the steel
927		goes out at that end.
928		DH: Yeah, so there's not much you can give, you know,
929		the union wants something, you got—many times they
930		told the union, well, Hanna Furnace's prices went up,
931		we're paying this much for a ton of iron, we're selling
932		it for this much for a finished product, and you got
933		this many man-hours in to finish this product, you
934		know, we just can't do it, we're not making enough
935		money. And the union would—they just sat down, they
936		didn't want to hear nothing about it.
937	*147-148*	MF: And so, mostly during those years, you felt, pretty
938	*148*	good about being a—would you call yourself a steel-
939	*148*	worker or an ironworker there?
940		DH: I called myself a steelworker. Even though you're
941		dealing with iron, and everything, the major thing is
942		involved with the steel mills, so you might as well be
943	*147*	a steelworker.
944	*147*	MF: And you felt pretty good about the way things
945		were headed—would you say you enjoyed the work?
946	*149*	DH: Yeah, yeah, I enjoyed the company and the work.
947	*149-150*	Like I say, you weren't always—you couldn't go in there
948	*150-151*	all the time happy, because you're working in the steel
949	*151-152*	mill foundry, and it's dirty and filthy and hot and
950	*152-153*	freezing during the winter, but, you know, I went
951	*153-154*	there every day, except for the six days I missed. But,
952		you know—the body didn't have control, you know,
953		that's the weird thing, the body didn't have control of
954		what was going on. You'd have your representative,
955		I'd have to say they get into a clique, and then they'd
056		spoil everything.
957	*233*	MF: So then things went—then the plant went down
958	*233*	in '80, '79 you said, the layoff was?/ DH: '70 the layoff

Source	Edit	
595	*234*	was, yeah/ MF: And then the closing was/ DH: Eighty
560	*234-235*	... two, August of '82, they definitely closed the plant./
061		MF: And as you say, things have been pretty/ [Turn
962		over tape]
963	*235-236*	DH: ... twenty years and you get a pension. And, as I
964	*235-236*	say, I had eighteen, so I didn't catch the pension. And
965		being that the union was so rough with the company,
966		when the union asked, well, how are you going to take
967		care of the guys, you know, you're supposed to have
968		five years and you get a, what's that, we were fighting
969		for—severance pay, you know, how're you going to take
970		care of the guys with severance pay, and the company
971		said, we aren't giving you nothing, you guys are going
972		to have to fight for everything you're going to get, now.
973		You know, if the union would have broke down, we
074		probably would have still been working, and if things
975		didn't work out, I think the company would have just
976		paid us all off, gave us a, you know severance pay and
977		everything, but now, it's through arbitration and every-
978		thing, and we haven't seen nothing yet.
979		MF: So you think that in part because of the/ DH:
980		because of the friction that the union caused/ MF:
981		Because of the friction, they just said, well, screw you
982		and that's going to be the end of it, and, you know,
983		you want to play—you want to fight, we'll fight, and/
984		DH: Yeah, right, you want to fight, we'll fight, and you
985		guys don't have no backing now, because your union's
986		dissolved, your local's done away with, now your best—
987		next step is going to the big steel mills to fight for
988		you, and they're running out of money, they're just
989		about done, more or less. I think if the union would
990		have handled it more appropriate, we would have been
991		paid off.
992		MF: So you ended up with/ DH: Nothing./ MF: Not
993		even severance pay, just a pink slip with two week's
994		notice or something, maybe not even/ DH: [laughs,
995		bitterly] No two weeks—nothing./ MF: Nothing, for
996		eighteen years/ DH: Just—done. Just what you made,
997		and that was it, you know, for eighteen hard years, all
998		out the window ....

Source	Edit	
999		MF: I don't know what that hum is, except, uh, cheap
1000		foreign import [laughs]/ DH: [laughs] No wonder I'm
1001		out of work! [laughs]
1002		MF: And the guys who had their twenty years, they
1003		get a pension?
1004		DH: Yeah, they get their pension and everything, the
1005		only thing they don't get is their Social Security, you
1006		know, on account of what their age is, you know. Oh
1007		yeah, they got guys that are drawing, you know, two
1008		hundred something bucks a week, pension [indistinct]
1009		—which ain't bad, it's enough to survive on.
1010		MF: Yeah, well that's gotta leave you feeling kind of....
1011	*239-240*	DH: Yeah, when you're shot down, you're owing so
1012	*240-241*	much, and then when you need some assistance from
1013	*241-242*	the government, they tell you, you know, you own too
1014	*242-243*	much, you got this, you got that, you got to sell it
1015	*243-244*	before we can do anything for you—that's about the
1016	*244*	hardest part, that's the part you don't understand:
1017	*244*	they tell you, you know, you own too much, sell your
1018	*245*	houses—cause I own two houses—sell your house and
1019	*246, 247*	we'll give you some assistance. I was shut down, and
1020	*237-238*	everything, I didn't draw nothing. Nothing for noth-
1021		ing./ MF: Did you get unemployment, then for ...?/
1022	*238-239*	DH: Just got unemployment till that ran out, no food
1023	*239*	stamps, no gas assistance, no nothing.
1024		MF: It's almost like they say, beyond that, you know,
1025		you've gotta be really be just so far down, that/ DH:
1026		Yeah, you're supposed/ MF: Then they give you only
1027		enough so that you'd stay where you are, and never
1028		really get back on your feet.
1029	*246-247*	DH: It's just more or less—you know, if you work eight-
1030	*247-248*	een years or fifteen years someplace, you gotta show
1031	*248-249*	something for it. And what the government's saying,
1032	*249-250*	that you should have worked eighteen, fifteen, twenty
1033	*250*	years and showed nothing!/ MF: And then we'll give
1034	*251*	you the welfare/ DH: Then we'll give you something.
1035	*251-252*	That don't make sense—you gotta show something.
1036	*252-253*	What they're saying is, you should have drank all your
1037	*253*	money up, and ....

Source	Edit
1038	

MF: Well, that/

| 1039 | |

[Nancy: and rent and electric]

1040	*254*
1041	*254-255*
1042	*255-256*
1043	*256-257*
1044	*257-258*
1045	*258-259*
1046	*259-260*
1047	*260-261*
1048	*261-262*
1049	*262-263*
1050	*263-264*
1051	*264*
1052	*264-265*
1053	*266*
1054	*266*
1055	*266-267*
1056	*267-268*
1057	*268-269*

DH: Rent, and—it gets you, cause I know a couple of guys that are collecting welfare, OK, when I went down to try to get some assistance, them guys were collecting welfare, and their rent payment was three hundred something dollars a month, and all that, and I told them—my house payment's only two twenty-five, but we can't help you cause you own two houses—it don't make sense! You're gonna get three hundred something dollars here, four hundred, pay the gas, pay the electric—and all I'm asking is for two twenty-five, but you say, can't do that, we'd rather pay the four hundred, three hundred something, than pay the two twenty-five, the difference is I own this, and that person rents. You know, that don't make sense, it just—it seems like you're cheating the government. If I sold this place, stuck the money someplace, ran down and rented an apartment for four hundred dollars and wasn't working, they would pay.

| 1058 | |
| 1059 | |

MF: They'd say, great, here's four hundred dollars/
DH: Yeah, here's four hundred bucks, so you can live.

1060	
1061	
1062	
1063	
1064	
1065	
1066	
1067	

MF: It's like you say, the crazy thing is that they're saying—it's not only what they do now, but it's like a judgment on—it's saying, what you should have been doing all those years is NOT saving anything, and not buying anything, and not putting anything away, and then you'd be flat on your back when they cut you off with eighteen years with nothing, and then we'd help you, I don't know, roll over or something.

1068	*270*
1069	*271*
1070	*271-272*
1071	*272*
1072	*273*
1073	*273-274*
1074	*274-275*
1075	*275-276*
1076	*276-277*

DH: Yeah. Well, when Nancy was at work, I had a hearing down in East Aurora about food stamps, I figured, well, I'll try to get some food stamps. So they did all the bookwork, then I went in, and as I walked in, there was a Cuban sitting there, couldn't even speak English, you know, we brought the Cubans over. Went in, asked the guy, I said, Well, how did I make out, he says, Uh, we turned you down. I said [disbelieving] Why? Well, you know, you're wife's working. I said, so? Well, can't give

Source	Edit	
1077	*277-278*	you nothing. Well, before I leave, I says, the guy out
1078	*278*	there, he's a Cuban, right? He says, yeah. He's not a citi-
1079		zen of the United States, or nothing, can't even speak
1080	*279*	English. I said, How'd he make out, did he get it? He
1081	*279-280*	said, Oh yeah, he got it. So I said, That's nice, he gets
1082	*280-281*	it, he's not a citizen or nothing, and I've been working
1083	*281-282*	since I was seven years old, and I get nothing. Well, I
1084	*282-283*	feel sorry for you, he says, you know, his hands are tied,
1085	*284*	he's got to go by what rules the state and local govern-
1086	*285*	ment gives him . . . ./ MF: No, it's crazy . . ./ DH: It's
1087		hard. You know, they got to start changing the rules. . . .
1088	*286*	MF: It's an interesting kind of angle on that whole
1089	*286-287*	thing of being left with nothing after eighteen years, I
1090	*287*	mean, the real point you're making is that because
1091	*287-288*	you'd done a lot—you had something, and yet you can't
1092	*288*	use that something to help rebuild yourself/ DH:
1093	*289*	Right, get back on your feet/ MF: And turn it to your
1094		advantage./ MF: Yeah, it's almost like they want to
1095		punish you more.
1096		DH: Yeah, it seems like the government—the way the
1097		government and the laws are set up, it's like you said,
1098		they just don't—it's against somebody that did well,
1099		you know, that participated in the government and,
1100		you know, you paid your taxes and helped people all
1101		along, through your taxes and working/
1102	*289-290*	MF: And the point of that, like unemployment, ought
1103	*290-291*	to be to help you through till you can really get some-
1104	*291292*	thing else going/ DH: Yeah, keep you going/ MF: Not—
1105		it's almost like, you know, if you had something that's
1106		in motion, like a car, or something, they're saying, no,
1107		you got to come to a complete dead stop before you
1108		can get started again./ DH: Right/ MF: And you're
1109		saying, well, gee, you know, if I could keep rolling,
1110		like anything, keep things moving, you're really keep
1111		it going long enough to . . . ./
1112	*292-293*	DH: Well, like you say, with the unemployment they
1113	*293*	got a deadline twenty-six weeks, you know—it's not
1114	*294*	that the people are taking this hundred and twenty-
1115	*295*	five dollars whatever it is, now, it's gone up a little
1116	*295-296*	bit—they're not taking the money and putting it away,

Source	Edit
1117	296-297
1118	297-298
1119	298-299
1120	299-300
1121	300-301
1122	
1123	
1124	
1125	
1126	

they're using that to survive. So, it's keeping the economy going, even though it's a little bit. You know, that guy's spending a hundred and twenty-five dollars every week, buying food or paying his gas and electric—it's keeping something going, like you say, the whole economy ain't stopping. But then when they try to take the unemployment away from the guy, say Okay, your twenty-six weeks is up, no more unemployment, then the little places are slowly—more people folding out, going back on the unemployment.

Source	Edit
1127	
1128	
1129	
1130	
1131	
1132	
1133	
1134	
1135	

MF: Sure, well, that's why even with the welfare, I mean—the point of that is, it's not just to help that person, it's to—you think about the neighborhood around those steel mills and so forth and/ DH: Yeah, keep everything going/ MF: And hey, you gotta go in and spend something in the seven eleven, and the food stamps, of course, are a big part of that too, cause it keeps those stores—they get accepted [?] for that.

Source	Edit
1136	301-302
1137	302
1138	303
1139	303-304
1140	304-305

DH: Right, you're gonna have your little cheats in every—no matter what you do, but a majority of the people are really benefitting through, you know, the federal government, state, or your local government assets—you know, they're trying to use it the right way.

Source	Edit
1141	
1142	306-307
1143	307-308
1144	308-309
1145	309

MF: You—just tell me a little bit about where you were—you mention these two houses, where were you living during most of the time that you were working there, were you living in South Buffalo, were you living out here?

Source	Edit
1146	312
1147	313-314
1148	314-315

DH: No, thirteen years out here, a couple of years up on top of the hill in Boston, that just about covered it—we lived with my mother-in-law about for a year.

Source	Edit
1149	316

MF: The second house is, then, around here too?

Source	Edit
1150	317

DH: Right behind us, on the same land.

Source	Edit
1151	318

MF: And you rent that out, do you?

Source	Edit
1152	319

DH: Yeah, I rent that out.

Source	Edit
1153	

[MF: (to wife serving cider) Oh, thanks.]

Source	Edit	
1154	*374*	MF: Tell me a little bit about—are you from out here,
1155	*374*	both grow up around here?
1156	*375*	DH: I'm originally from the First Ward of Buffalo. And
1157	*376*	I used to shine shoes when I was a little kid up there,
1158	*377*	worked, and from there we moved to Orchard Park,
1159		went to Orchard Park, then I worked—maybe go to
1160		school a couple of hours a day, and then work in a
1161		greenhouse. And then summertime come, I had to
1162		work on a farm. We come from a big family.
1163		MF: Your family was a big, sort of South Buffalo
1164		family?
1165	*378-379*	DH: Yeah, big South Buffalo Irish family. So we had
1166	*379*	to work all the time, you know, since I went to school,
1167	*380*	in Orchard Park went to school from eight to eleven,
1168	*380-381*	then I had to go to the greenhouse, so I only had
1169	*381*	three hours . . . .
1170		MF: What kind of work did your family do, were they
1171		in iron and steel too?
1172		DH: No, the old man worked for the Goodwill, drive a
1173		truck, now he's a foreman I think . . . . Your part, Nancy
1174		[NH: indistinct]
1175		DH: What's your family in? [stage whisper, to MF:] I'll
1176		ask the question.
1177		NH: My father was in the steel, he worked at Hanna
1178		Furnace; my mother was a cook at school, and I myself
1179		make toys.
1180		MF: Oh, really? These dolls here?
1181		NH: No, Fisher-Price toys.
. . .		. . .
1238		MF: How'd you all meet? DH: [laughs] NH: [laughs]
1139		DH: Going to a drive in. Blind date, going to a drive-in.
1240		Four weeks later we were married.
1241		MF: Wow! DH: Wow! I knew that would blow your
1242		mind. [laughs] MF: Well, sometimes that's the best
1243		way to do it. DH: Yeah. [laughs]

Source	Edit
1244	
1245	
1246	
1247	
1248	

MF: And how long ago was that? DH: Twenty years. It's a long time. MF: So that was before you started working at .... DH: Shenango, yeah. MF: Did her father have anything to do with your being able to get in there, is that/

1249	399
1250	
1251	
1252	399-400
1253	400-401
1254	401-402
1255	402-403
1256	403-404
1257	
1258	
1259	
1260	404-405
1261	405-406
1262	406-407
1263	407-408

DH: No, her brothers worked there. One brother worked there, then after the other brother got out of the Air Force, he worked there, he had seven years in the Air Force. Most of her family works in the steel business. Down at Ohio Tool? Family, and uncles there, most of them went into steel. It was more or less you heard the same thing from them, you know when they started off they got their heads pounded in, went through the hard times, it more or less rubs off at work, you realize and see what's going on, if there's a chance the plant's going to close—it's a part of your life, it's like getting a part of your stomach cut off, if the plant closes. You know, if the plant just says you're on layoff, there's always a chance you're going to go back. But when it shuts down, closed up ... whew.

1264	386
1265	387
1266	387-388
1267	388

MF: When you were growing up there, was that one of the things you thought about going into, cause you can't be too far from steel when you grow up in South Buffalo.

1268	389
1269	389-390
1270	390-391

DH: Who, me? The steel mills and everything? No, I was thinking about being in the Mafia. [laughs] Being a crook! [laughs]

1271	392
1272	393-395
1273	395

MF: [laughs] And they didn't have any openings for you? DH: They didn't have no openings. MF: Oh, I hear they're recruiting all the time!

1274	396
1275	397
1276	382

DH: [laughs] ... No, I never really thought about it. It never entered my mind. MF: You just put one foot in front of the other? DH: Yeah. MF: You finish school?

1277	383
1278	384
1279	384-385
1280	385

DH: Nope. I quit my junior year. That was strictly because I had to work all the time. You know, that just drove me nuts, it was more or less I was helping to support my father's family.

| 1281 | |

MF: You say you had a big family, how many?

Source	Edit	
1282		DH: Eight [to wife], right? NH: Seven boys, one girl.
1283		DH: Seven boys, one girl, I almost forget. MF: She
1284		must have—my mother had five brothers, and she was
1285		the only girl, and she's filled with stories about . . . .
1286		DH: Yeah, it's hard. MF: Well, she said—hard on the
1287		one hand, on the other hand she had a lot of protec-
1288		tion when anybody come buzzing around the house.
1289		DH: [laughs] Sometimes too much protection! Here
1290		your dad was scared to death, what are you doing tak-
1291		ing her out, she's got five brothers watching her.
1292		MF: That's right, you got to be real careful. DH:
1293		[laughs] Careful. MF: Absolutely.
1294		MF: Where did—you said you moved to Orchard Park,
1295	320	how did you get from there to—I mean, living in the
1296	320	country here is real different than DH: Who, me?
1297		MF: Yeah, did you sort of decide you wanted to, I
1298	320-321	mean was that sort of a goal of yours to get a place out
1299	322	here, or did that just sort of happen?
1300	323	DH: Yeah, more or less you learn—you know, if you're
1301	323-324	taking care of somebody else's family, which was my
1302	324-325	father's family, when you get married, more or less,
1303	325-326	you really have got to make that commitment to leave
1304	326	the nest, you know. My other brothers aren't—they sort
1305		of like stick around home, they're divorced now, and I
1306		think it's more that they didn't really leave the nest
1307		and get out on their own. It's more or less you got to
1308		get out there, and get away, and . . . you know, survive,
1309		and do what you're supposed to really be doing.
1310		MF: And so, when you got married was that when you
1311		moved out here to Colden? DH: Yeah, more or less.
1312		NH: [indistinct]
1313	327	MF: How'd you choose out here? Did you—cause you
1314	327	could have gotten away to North Tonawanda, there
1315	328	are a lot of places to get away to.
1316	329	DH: Well, you see the hills out there? MF: Oh yeah,
1317		they're real pretty. DH: I love the hills, I don't like the
1318		flatland, I don't like looking out and—you see flatland
1319	330	and you can't see nothing else. I just like looking at
1320	330	the hills.

Source	Edit
1321	*331*
1322	*332*
1323	*333*
1324	

MF: You don't like cities either? Did you really want kind of a small town, when you thought about what kind of place you wanted to have your kids in, and stuff like that?

1325	*334*
1326	*335*
1327	*336*
1328	
1329	

DH: Yeah, small town area, such as this, a town that never really is going to grow. This town will stay like this for years and years. I think if you buy a house out here now, if you want to build a house I think you have to buy five acres, seven acres of land.

1330	
1331	
1332	
1333	

MF: What kind of town is it, what kind of people are out here, is it old—it must go way back, Colden./ DH: Yeah./ MF: It's not really a suburb, you get a sense it was here before.

1334	*336-337*
1335	*337-338*
1336	*338-339*
1337	*339-340*
1338	*340-341*
1339	*341-342*
1340	*342*

DH: Yeah, there's no subdivision or nothing like that. It's mostly old families that were here—all interbreeded and that. Their mothers were here. Most of them are rich, well-off people. It's a rich town, you have a lot of doctors out here, lawyers. There are the hidden parts of the hills that really have nice places. They're more or less looking for the same thing.

| 1341 | |

MF: Well, you're not far from all the ski . . . .

1342	
1343	*342*
1344	*343*
1345	*343-344*
1346	*344-345*

DH: The ski area is about five minutes up the road, you get a lot of Canadians coming down . . . . But most of the people are nice. You know, you still—every town you have so many bad people. If you live in a small town, you got less bad people, I guess.

1347	
1348	
1349	
1350	
1351	
1352	
1353	

MF: Right. And you—I was wondering, are you sort of accepted as natives here now, or do people still treat you like—eighteen years is a long time, but I mean— you say a lot of these people were sort of born, grew up, and intermarried, and you guys come in from Buffalo—was that an unusual thing then, or were there a number of people . . . ?

1354	
1355	
1356	

DH: Well, they treated us like outsiders, you feel like you weren't really wanted, you know, But we're accepted now.

| 1357 | |

MF: Your daughter went to school here?

Source	Edit
1358	
1359	

DH: Yeah, Springville. MF: That's a regional school ... that way?

1360	
1361	
1362	

DH: That way, yeah, south .... You know, as I say, we accepted the Lord four years ago, are re-born Christians .... It's a lot better.

1363	*346*
1364	*346-347*
1365	*347-348*
1366	*348-349*
1367	*349*

MF: Yeah. So has the community been supportive when you've gone through rough times like this, do you think it's been easier to be going through all this in a place like here than it would be some-place else?

1368	*350*
1369	*351*
1370	*352*
1371	*353*
1372	*353-354*
1373	
1374	*354*
1375	*354-355*
1376	*356*
1377	

DH: I think it would be easier on ourselves if we were in Buffalo, we'd be close by when—you know, you can look for a job you don't have to drive the distance and everything. That part would be better. But as far as helping—how much can you really help, you know, it's not just a section that's doing bad, it's the whole world. You know. There's bad all over. It's not that you can say, well, some guy'd come up and just offer you a job or just give you money. Everybody's struggling, going through hard times.

1378	*356*
1379	
1380	
1381	

MF: Is there a lot of that right around here? You said now a lot of the people are wealthier, and so on, but you're not the only ones around here who are having a rough time, I should think.

| 1382 | |
| 1383 | |

DH: I don't really think there's that many here hav-ing a rough time.

1384	*356-357*
1385	*357-358*
1386	*358-359*

MF: Does that make it hard—do people look at you like, oh, there's so and so, and he's going to have trou-ble paying his bills?

1387	
1388	
1389	*360*
1390	*360-361*
1391	*361-362*
1392	*362-363*
1393	*363*
1394	*363-364*
1395	*364-365*

DH: No, not really, they more or less/ NH: I don't think they know we're having such a rough time/ DH: Some of them do, some of them don't. Only a couple—I'd say a handful that know—neighbor, the girls up front, the guy in the post office, a couple of guys in the gas station. But on the other hand, they're tied, they can't really do too much. But, no, 90 per-cent of them don't know, that you're going through hard times, having to struggle ....

Source	Edit	
1396	*366*	MF: Do you have this place pretty well paid off now,
1397	*367*	you must be close to it?
1398	*368*	DH: Oh, $15,000, I think it was, fifteen something.
1399	*369*	But the only thing is you can't do repairs now. You
1400	*370*	can't do the things you want to do cause it costs
1401	*371*	money, you know, you just can't go out and buy stuff
1402	*372*	and do what I want to do./ NH: You have the time,
1403	*372*	but/ DH: Yeah, now I got the time, but no money, to
1404	*373*	do repairs.
1405		MF: So you can keep up your payments, but not ....
1406		DH: It's hard, when she goes to the hospital now, we
1407		don't know what we'll do. MF: You got some kind of
1408		insurance from work?/ NH: Yeah/ MF: Well, that's
1409		something.
1410	*417*	MF: The religious change, was that something that
1411	*418*	happened suddenly in relation to this, or would you
1412	*418*	say that'd been coming for a long time?
1413	*411*	DH: Oh, no, no [laughs] it wasn't coming. I was bad, I
1414	*411*	was, oh no, I was bad. I don't think—I think if I didn't
1415	*412*	have accepted the Lord and everything, and being laid
1416	*413*	off one year, or hearing the news that Shenango was
1417	*414*	going to close, I probably would have robbed some-
1418	*415*	one, just kept living off the robbing, robbing off the
1419	*415-416*	rich—you know, being mad because they're the ones
1420	*416*	that have control of it, you know.
1421	*409*	MF: Did you go into a kind of tailspin after you got
1422	*410*	laid off like, or sort of a crisis period? This sort of
1423		conversion came shortly after that, or . . . ?
1424	*419*	DH: No, it came—you know, there was no definite
1425	*420*	thing that Shenango was going to close. We were more
1426	*421*	or less on a layoff, and kept thinking we were going to
1427	*421-422*	get called back, and I was collecting unemployment
1428	*422-423*	and some SUB pay, and so—I was working up in East
1429	*423-424*	Aurora, you know, working in this Antique Barn, and
1430	*424-425*	there was a Christian family, and they kept telling me
1431	*425-426*	about the Lord, and I says, Get out of here! Wacky,
1432	*426-427*	don't want to hear that stuff. Then they'd play music.
1433	*427-428*	and I'd go turn it on rock 'n roll or country and

Source	Edit
1434	*428-429*
1435	*429-430*
1436	*430*
1437	
1438	*430-431*
1439	*431*
1440	
1441	
1442	*431-432*
1443	*432-433*
1444	*433-434*
1445	*434*
1446	
1447	*434-435*
1448	*435-436*
1449	*436*
1450	*437*
1451	
1452	
1453	
1454	
1455	
1456	
1457	
1458	
1459	
1460	
1461	*438*
1462	*439*
1463	*439-440*
1464	*440-441*
1465	*441-442*
1466	*442*
1467	*442-443*
1468	*443*
1469	*459*
1470	*460*

western, and they'd turn it back. And then, uh, all of a sudden they bought me a Bible. What's this? Take it home and read it. All right, I'm not going to read this thing, it ain't about about sports or something I'm not going to read it, you know, brought it home, I wouldn't read it [to NH] remember?

NH: You opened it and read what they wrote in it.

DH: Yeah, that was it. Set it down, I wasn't going to do it. And then it kept going on and on for a couple of weeks, and before you know it I started going in there and I started turning on the Christian music, and humming it. And they come in and turned the radio on, and I says, oh no, so I turned it back—cause if they catch me .... So it kept going on, they kept talking more about the Lord, every day and every day and every day, you keep hearing it. And it just happened. One day, it happened, outside. You wouldn't catch me in a church—but I came home and told her, I want to go to church Sunday.

MF: Is there a community here, that you kind of then ....

DH: Go to Orchard Park, Old Gospel Tabernacle.

MF: [to NH] Is this something that you participated in too?

NH: Well, he didn't like me to go to church./ DH: She was always religious./ NH: I was raised that way.

MF: In a Protestant house? [NH nods]/ [To DH] And you were brought up Catholic?

DH: I was brought up ... nothing./ NH: They were Protestant./ DH: Protestant, yeah, but I didn't believe in nothing. No God, you know, I just believed that you make as much money as you can, you live as good as you can, and you die./ MF: The family had been Irish Protestant, then?/ DH: Yeah. And I just didn't believe in nothing. Then I just changed around, and here we are.

MF: What kind of difference—how has it made a difference?

Source	Edit
Source	Edit
1471	461
1472	462
1473	
1474	
1475	
1476	462
1477	462-463
1478	
1479	
1480	
1481	
1482	463-464
1483	464
1484	464-465
1485	465-466
1486	
1487	
1488	
1489	
1490	466-467
1491	467
1492	468
1493	468-469
1494	469
1495	470
1496	470
1497	471
1498	471-472
1499	472-473
1500	473-474
1501	474-475
1502	475-476
1503	476-477
1504	477-478
1505	478-479
1506	479-480
1507	480-481
1508	481-482
1509	482-483

DH: Oh, it made a big difference. Kept me out of jail! [laughs] No, it made a big difference, cause I wasn't—like I say, I would have gave up, just went out and figured society owed me something, and I would have just made judgment, figured out what they owed me, and that's what I would have took. And now I don't do that stuff, I don't steal, I don't think about stealing./ NH: Now he counsels people./ DH: Yeah, counsel people, talk to people, try to help other people.

MF: Do they have a program for that that you could be active in?

DH: Oh yeah, we got Bible study, and we help an alcoholic, he lived here. You got to [indistinct] struggle through hard times, and helping somebody out, you got him on his feet, going in the right direction.

MF: Well that must help you too, cause usually one of the worst things about being in trouble is you feel like you're alone in the world./ DH: Yeah./ MF: You're at the bottom of the pile, and nobody, you know/

DH: Yeah, just help somebody else and take some of the pressure away. But it just seems like the outside is so much pressure, you know. It just seems like the last four years the gas company just started coming out with fantastic gas bills, shortage of gas, and the gas in your car—everything happened in four years, you know, and your taxes are skyrocketing, it just seems like—somebody, they started the bandwagon with the canning jars, or something, the canning lids, the shortage, and it just started going from there, everybody started making up the shortage, to get rich, and before you know it we're running out of natural gas, we're running out of oil, we're running out of everything, and just everybody got on the bandwagon and just—when the country needed help, I think all those businesses just jumped in and made it worse, instead of saying, let's lock our horns together and get out of this crisis. They all just jumped in, and telephone company, everybody wants—it just seems like they want to take every dollar they could take from you, they just

Source	Edit
1510	*483-484*
1511	*484*
1512	

use that word, there's a shortage, instead of saying Okay, we're all Americans, let's stick this thing out and just get back on our feet.

1513	
1514	

MF: Yeah, it's kind of like a higher level of the same problem you had locally that you were talking about.

1515	
1516	*485*
1517	*485-486*
1518	*486-487*
1519	*487-488*
1520	*488-489*
1521	*489-490*
1522	*490*

DH: Yeah, more or less. You know, let's get this thing going and show that we're going through hard times, we can all pitch in and help each other, rich businessman can hand out a little bit where it ain't going to hurt him and use it as a tax write-off, and everybody can help each other and we could all get back on our feet. Because if people don't have money to spend, the economy's only going to get worse.

1523	
1524	
1525	
1526	

MF: Cause you can't do anything for anybody else, aside from .... Well, that's interesting about the counseling stuff. That must be ... so there's that, and the Bible classes, or a study group more?/

1527	
1528	

DH: Bible class, yeah. You know, you help people. There's a lot you can do, you know.

1529	
1530	

MF: Are those a lot of new people, that you didn't know before, or ....

1531	
1532	
1533	
1534	

DH: Yeah, quite a few. About 3,000 of 'em .... They got Christian retreats. Well, most of the church was, the Tabernacle is originally 95 percent Roman Catholics./ MF: Really!/

1535	*443-444*
1536	*444-445*
1537	*445*
1538	*445-446*
1539	*446-447*
1540	
1541	
1542	
1543	*447-448*
1544	*448-449*
1545	*449-450*
1546	*450-451*
1547	*451-452*
1548	*452*

DH: Converted to Christians, you know, reading the Bible the right way, accepting the Lord, and knowing that, you know, Jesus died for them, the only way through Heaven is through Jesus Christ. You know— like I say, I was really shocked that after I got affiliated with the church there, you know, I figured, well, you know, I know the Catholics and everything, what they believe in and everything, and I just—start talking, and start talking, to all these new guys I know, and they said that 95 percent of the church is Roman Catholic, they said Roman Catholics, I said, Wow, that's really something. I said, Boy, if they can do that ... ! It's hard, you know, to get the Catholics to see the right way./ MF: Talk about chipping away at a mold!/

Source	Edit
1549	*452-453*
1550	*453*
1551	*453*
1552	*454*
1553	*454-455*
1554	*455-456*
1555	*456-457*
1556	*457*
1557	*458*
1558	*491*
1559	
1560	
1561	
1562	*492*
1563	*493*
1564	*493-494*
1565	*494*
1566	*495*
1567	
1568	
1569	
1570	
1571	
1572	
1573	
1574	
1575	
1576	*495*
1577	*495-496*
1578	*496*
1579	
1580	
1581	
1582	
1583	
1584	
1585	
1586	
1587	

DH: Yeah, yeah, to get them rolling the right way. I don't know if you're Catholic/ MF: No./ DH: You know, to convert a Catholic is hard. You show them the right way, and here they sit and listen to Latin, they don't understand Latin, they believe in the Virgin Mary, and you know, it's nice to believe in it, but they worship her. Not to worship Jesus Christ, just knowing Jesus Christ is something different, just knowing that through the Son you will go through Heaven.

MF: How does that all relate to .... I was interested in that other picture over there [The Elvis picture], which indicates [DH: laughs] you're a man of many interests, some of which are displayed on the wall here, and I was wondering .... I see cars, I see Elvis, and I see, in the other picture, who is it we got there, is it Buddy Holly? And these dolls. So I'm curious about the dolls, and about Elvis, and ... the sort of the role of that kind of music, is that an old interest of yours, or ...?

DH: Well, we were born in, you know, we were in the era of the '50s, you know, riding around in the cars. I dont' know if you're from that era, Mike/ MF: Oh yeah, pretty much./ DH: Yeah? We sort of hung on that, you know. Most of the music, I'd say 90 percent of the music back in the '50s was pretty good music, there was a message behind it, and it was pretty good. The stuff today is/ MF: Yeah, it's DH: It's hard to take.

MF: Did you sort of keep up with it? And like, when Elvis died, was that something that you were involved with?

DH: When Elvis died [DH & NH: laugh] she freaked out, yeah, she was all broken up, so I had to go out and buy all the Elvis, listen to records, keep it going. But I was into antique cars, you know, Corvettes and stuff, and I had to get something for her to do, you know keep her busy, it wasn't right for me to be doing what I wanted to be doing, and not for her [indistinct], the dolls, or the Elvis records and stuff, keep her going.

Source	Edit	
1588		MF: But you'd been interested in the Elvis stuff too./
1589		DH: Oh, yeah./ MF: You got broken up when he
1590		died, too?
1591	*497*	DH: Yeah, yeah it hurt./ MF: On those things, it's
1592	*497*	hard to explain/ DH: It hurt more, it hurt more to
1593	*498*	find out that he was on drugs, and he wasted him-
1594		self./ MF: Yeah, some of those articles have been
1595		really, really—he was . . . /
1596	*498-499*	DH: Yeah, that's when I felt hurt, at first when he died,
1597	*499-500*	you know, they tried to keep it hush-hush, and I says,
1598	*500*	it's a waste that he, you know, he killed himself, he's
1599	*500-501*	so rich and everything, he made his life so miserable,
1600	*501-502*	by being so protective of himself, instead of going out
1601	*502-503*	in the public and associating and everything else, he
1602	*503*	just grew too big, and he more or less put pressure on
1603		himself, he got into the drugs, and you can't believe
1604		it, eventually. [indistinct]
1605	*504*	MF: How do you, what's your sense of why he's—what's
1606	*504-505*	your theory about why his music was powerful for so
1607	*505*	many people?
1608	*506*	DH: Oh, it was from the heart, the soul. Soul music,
1609	*507*	the blues mix./ NH: He put himself into it./ DH: Yeah,
1610	*507-508*	he wasn't like a white man singing colored music. He
1611	*508*	just . . . he was a country boy, you know, he wasn't . . .
1612	*509*	he was a country boy, he wanted things to happen, he
1613	*509-510*	was young, and he loved his mother and father, he
1614	*510-511*	didn't want to go out where the big wheels were, he
1615	*511-512*	didn't want to go to Hollywood, he didn't want to—but
1616	*512-513*	he wanted the money and everything, he knew he was
1617	*513*	going that way. That's more or less—you know, he
1618	*513-514*	come in with the sideburns, changed things around. I
1619	*514-515*	think it was a good thing to call him, you know, the
1620	*515-516*	king of rock 'n roll, cause he did break it wide open
1621	*516*	for everybody.
1622		MF: Do you listen to a lot of the gospel music and
1623		stuff now?/ DH: Yeah./ MF: And the country and
1624		western? Do you see a lot of him in the country and,
1625		are you involved in the country and western music?/
1626		DH: Yeah, we listen to that a lot./ MF: What is it,

Source	Edit
1627	
1628	
1629	
1630	
1631	
1632	

what's the station . . ./ NH: All I can think of is WYSL/ MF: No, it's up there at the end of the dial, but I always forget, WR . . . K . . . ./ NH: WYRK./ MF: YRK, yeah./ DH: I don't know what they call it, I just turn it on./ MF: Yeah, and you listen to that a lot?/ DH: Yeah, I listen to that quite a bit.

1633	
1634	
1635	

MF: Do you find, I've always had this sense that there's something about that music, even if it's not about religion, which is somehow close to/

1636	
1637	
1638	

DH: Close to home. You get a—you feel a part of it, you know, and there's a message behind it, you know. It's good . . . down home music.

1639	517
1640	517-518
1641	518

MF: Now what about the dolls, tell me a little bit about the—it's quite an impressive collection. Are these old dolls, or any kind of dolls?

1642	519
1643	520
1644	520-521

DH: No, those are mostly newer ones./ NH: Madame Alexander's Collectibles. This is what rich people buy their kids to play with.

1645	521
1646	522
1647	522
1648	522-523
1649	523
1650	523-524
1651	524

DH: Yeah, that's what it was, more or less. She come over from Germany, her father was a doll doctor, he repaired dolls, he just got to making them, and he died and she took over, and she's a real old woman now./ MF: This is Madame Alexander?/ DH: Madame Alexander. What she does is, make them for the richer kids, you know./ MF: Is this somebody around here?

1652	524
1653	
1654	
1655	524-525
1656	525-526
1657	526-527
1658	527

NH: She's in New York City. But she doesn't make too many issues, so many on each doll./ MF: So it's not like Fisher-Price, she's not churning out 1,800. DH: Right, she'll just make so many and there ain't no more, and you send in your order, whoever, first come first serve. And if the stores wants more, or something, there is no more, that's it.

1659	
1660	
1661	
1662	
1663	
1664	

MF: And this is basically—so is your entire collection her stuff, or do you do . . . . NH: Mostly hers, a few odds and ends, but mostly hers./ MF: Do you go to old shops and stuff and look for dolls—is this just like a collection, like people who collect stamps or something like that?/ DH: Yeah, more or less./

Source	Edit	
1665		MF: They're really pretty. Yeah, I saw a doll at some-
1666		one's house the other night that he'd gotten—one of
1667		these things passed down from, I don't know/ DH:
1668		Families/ MF: how many grandmothers back, and it
1669		was really something, it had real leather shoes on it,
1670		really impressive.... That's a nice case, too. How long
1671		have you been doing that for?
1672		DH: Oh, four years. No, maybe five years, because I
1673		was still working at Shenango [to NH] when we bought
1674		... we used to go down to [Erie's?] house, remember,
1675		when I was still working at Shenango. Yeah, probably
1676		about five years.
1677		MF: So a lot's that changed these last four years.
1678		DH: Yeah. Sold most of my cars.
1679	*528*	MF: Did you used to have a few of these—these Cor-
1680	*530,529*	vettes and stuff./ DH: Yeah, they're gone./ MF: You'd
1681	*529*	bought up and then you worked on them, worked on
1682	*529*	the engines and stuff?/ DH: Yeah, I sold those, those
1683	*531*	are gone, I got one car left, that's a '58 Chevy, plan on
1684	*531-532*	selling that. So most of the stuff is gone, just to pay
1685	*532-533*	the taxes, you know. Like now, I got to by the fifteenth
1686	*533-534*	of this month, I got to come up with a thousand and
1687	*534-535*	ten dollars to pay the tax, the school tax, that I don't
1688	*535-536*	have. So I don't know what's going to happen there.
1689	*537*	MF: What do you do when you're not working or wor-
1690	*538*	rying and so on, these days?
1691	*539*	DH: Not a heck of a lot! You know, really—just worry-
1692	*540*	ing, thinking, get the pen out and figure out how
1693	*541*	you're going to make it, and writing down figures after
1694	*542*	figures, hoping everything turns out right, and you
1695	*543*	go back, worked the racetrack, being a guard, mini-
1696	*544*	mum wage and, you know, it's not a heck of a lot./
1697		MF: Which track is that?/ DH: Hamburg racetrack./
1698		MF: So you can pick up just little things, here and
1699		there./ DH: Yeah./ MF: You must have a lot of con-
1700		nections around, you sort of can tend to hear of things
1701		if something comes up?
1702		DH: Oh, my ears are always open, open to sugges-
1703	*544*	tions, to try something. Like I say, Mike, the thing is

Source	Edit
1704	545
1705	
1706	546
1707	547
1708	548
1709	549
1710	549
1711	
1712	550
1713	550-551
1714	551
1715	552
1716	553
1717	553-554
1718	554-555
1719	555-556
1720	556-557
1721	557
1722	557-558
1723	558-559
1724	559-560
1725	
1726	
1727	
1728	
1729	
1730	
1731	
1732	
1733	
1734	
1735	
1736	
1737	
1738	
1739	
1740	
1741	
1742	

that you do work, when you get into construction, they want to pay you the lowest pay they can pay you, and throw that salary stuff at you. We'll put you on salary, but we'll work you sixty hours a week. Just take complete advantage of you, you know—they really know you're hurting, they know you need the money and they can get everything they want out of you. They really take advantage of you.

MF: You see any way—do you have any long-range hopes, if the economy starts picking up, where things might . . . .

DH: Well, I'm just hoping that they don't destroy all our steel mills, over there, in case we really need them. You know, because you're dependent on foreign oil, they're going to lock themselves into dependent on foreign steel, and then you're [going to go through a] crisis. You know, they'll just raise everything else, you know they control the market, the world market on steel prices, and just—well, over here they can just knock us out of the ballpark. I just think if they can keep the steel mills going, get 'em back on their feet.

MF: It really seems crazy to me, because you look at all this stuff now, about the bridges and infrastructure— you know, it's a big word, now, infrastructure. I mean, it's really clear that obviously we still need a lot of steel, they're going to have to rebuild half the damn highway bridges and abutments and everything else in the country, and that's gonna come from someplace.

DH: Yeah, and most of them are buying the Korean steel and everything. It just don't make sense. You know they're American businessmen that own the Korean steel mills./ MF: Really./ DH: The Koreans don't know nothing about steel, before, they've got to be our businessmen over there./ MF: And the Japanese too./ DH: Right./

MF: Yeah, I knew a bit about that situation, what was happening. I spent a year over in Korea a few years back. It's a really interesting country, but really kind of screwed up in lots of ways. And one of the things

Source	Edit

1743 — that happened, was the Japanese were starting to—
1744 — they were having more of an environmental movement
1745 — in Japan, you know, people were beginning to worry
1746 — about the pollution, so they just took everything and
1747 — sent it to Korea, so they're getting that now, but it's no
1748 — more their business than anything else.

1749 — DH: That's what I think hurts us over here, too. The
1750 — pollution and everything they're worrying about, and
1751 — pushing it, it was more of—and closing the places up,
1752 — you know. They just couldn't afford, outfits just couldn't
1753 — afford that.

1754 — MF: Had that been true at all at Shenango, or did
1755 — they go through that pretty . . . ?

1756 — DH: Yeah, they come down there pretty heavy, cracked
1757 — down on them, at Hanna Furnace. There's only so
1758 — much you can do, you know. Car pollution, I think, is
1759 — worse than the steel mills, everbody's concerned about
1760 — the steel mills. You know, it was bad. I agree that they
1761 — cleaned it up quite a bit, they cleaned their act up,
1762 — but the push—to push it to the limit, where they want
1763 — almost, you know 80 percent pure, that's pretty hard.

1764 — *561* — MF: I bet you must feel good that way back when you
1765 — *562* — socked some stuff into a place like this out here. It
1766 — *562-563* — may be a little hard to—well, like you were saying, if
1767 — *563-564* — they're not going to give you anything after eighteen
1768 — *564-565* — years, at least you know you've got something, and
1769 — *565* — this is really beautiful . . . ./

1770 — *566* — DH: Well, I can sell it to you, Mike! [laughs]/ MF:
1771 — [laughs]/ DH: No, we're, we're trying to sell it./ MF:
1772 — Would you then move into the place back there, do
1773 — you rent that out?/ DH: I would want to rent, out here,
1774 — then just go to school, take something up, something
1775 — I figured would be around to last. Computers is a hard
1776 — field, it's just changing so fast that . . . ./

1777 — Daughter: Do you know what the price, how much it
1778 — is to go to school?/ DH: what, college?/ D: For four
1779 — years?/ DH: Here's the man you have to ask, right here,
1780 — how much it costs to go to school?/ D: I [got] the price
1781 — to go to school/ DH: Mike'll tell you./ MF: No, how

Source	Edit
1782	much?/ D: $36,000./ MF: Jeez./ DH: Thirty-six—Does
1783	that sound right?/
1784	MF: Well, to go through—you mean through college
1785	and the whole thing? Yeah—well, college, the private
1786	colleges, now, it's just—I mean, for one person it's just
1787	really crazy. We see a lot of that at, you know at the
1788	state university, now, a lot of kids coming there now
1789	who used to be in all sorts of other schools, and
1790	nobody—I don't know who can afford to go to private
1791	colleges now.
...	...
2062	
END	

Chapter 6

Presenting and Receiving Oral History Across Cultural Space: A Note on Responses of Chinese Students to the Documentary Trilogy *One Village in China*

Oral history has been very much at the methodological center of a wave of highly successful historical documentary films in the United States throughout the last decade—so much so, perhaps, that its particular characteristics as a mode for presenting history to audiences have been easy to take for granted. Attention both positive and negative has generally centered on the oral history in the films as documentation, not communication—on the perspective of the informants chosen for inclusion and the historical material they have to contribute. In discussing such films as *Babies and Banners, Union Maids,* and *The Good Fight,* for instance, criticism has tended to read the broader impact and effect of such material as a function of these documentary choices—who is or is not presented and what they do or do not talk about—rather than as the outcome of presentational choices that bear on a more complex interaction between film and audience.

In this sense, we have been slow to discuss the way films work with and on audiences, and how they are understood or misunderstood and why by particular classes of viewers—a level of commentary almost unavoidable in general nondocumentary film criticism. Not coincidentally, one of the few instances I can recall where the filmic choices made in presenting oral history have been identified by most viewers as of central importance is a dramatic film, an exception that proves the rule: the complex and daring counterpoint, in Warren Beatty's "Hollywood" film *Reds,* between the carefully-framed testimonies of actual "witnesses" and the dramatized recreation of the life of John Reed and the Russian Revolution.

Conversely, in response to Claude Lanzmann's monumental documentary film *Shoah,* surprisingly little exploration has been made of the enormously complex ways in which Lanzmann makes use of the texture, setting, pacing, and even the translation of his interviews about the Holocaust—and this in a film whose nine and one-half hours rest exclusively on oral history. Indeed, *Shoah* is probably unique among historical documentaries in offering no documents at all "from" the past: it exists only in the present, consisting entirely of interviews *about* the past set amidst the camera's languorous meditations on the Holocaust's sites, landscape, and horrific monuments as they exist now. The film focuses almost obsessively on the complexity of memory, on how an unimaginable past might be made real in and to the present; Lanzmann pushes both oral history and his wandering camera eye to the limits of bearability in order to create a reflective space somehow adequate to the enormity of the horrors at hand. And yet, although everyone remarks the absence of the stock concentration camp archival footage, Lanzmann's choices in conducting, editing, framing, and presenting his oral histories have not frequently been seen as central to this unsettling film's intent, impact, and controversial reception by many audiences: instead, argument has swirled around the film's explicit and implicit historical statements— particularly those bearing on the relation of Poles toward the Jewish victims of the Holocaust.

These considerations suggest, not surprisingly, that those concerned with history are better at evaluating film as history than at sensing how history does, doesn't, and might work as film, a general problem that has more specific meaning when oral historical documents and communication are a central focus of presentation. To redress this balance, we need to bring to discussion of documentary oral history the tools and concepts that have recently made media and literary critical theory so intellectually powerful. Much of this theory focuses on the way texts are in essence defined as much in the reading as in the writing, having meaning as a "dialogic" relationship between author and audience. This ought to be especially useful for unravelling the way documentary films "work," and for developing insights into how oral historical materials—themselves complex dialogues between interviewer and subject—function in such settings, how this bears on the presentational choices one faces in using them, and on the effects such choices can have.

Unfortunately, this critical theory has come to seem an intimidatingly arcane art whose practice I am happy to leave to others more versed in its intricacies. In any event, there is perhaps a prior obligation if we are to redirect attention from the historical content to the issues involved in its presentation to an audience: we need to get better at the basic task of describing how filmmakers present and how audiences respond to oral history films, thus documenting an interaction it can then be the goal of theory to read in more complex ways. This essay-note is a brief exercise toward such a modest descriptive end. Although dealing with a very particular historical and cultural setting, and a very specific problem in cross-cultural communication, it does suggest, through this very particularity, how an audience-centered perspective may contribute to a more sophisticated appreciation of the filmic possibilities of oral history.

The Long Bow Films

This comment was originally drafted as an addition to a multiauthor symposium on an important recent documentary trilogy; I supplemented a more general critical discussion by describing a particularly notable screening and its surprising aftermath. Although recapitulating the many interesting issues raised in the symposium is not necessary, I should at least briefly introduce the films it examined before turning to the story of this showing. As televised nationally by the Public Broadcasting Service (PBS) in the fall of 1987 and as subsequently distributed, the trilogy is entitled *One Village in China*. Its three one-hour segments, however, had been initially released as self-standing films, and are, perhaps, best known under their individual titles. The first appeared in 1984: *Small Happiness: Women of a Chinese Village*; the second, *All Under Heaven: Life in a Chinese Village*, in 1985; and the third, *To Taste a Hundred Herbs: Gods, Ancestors, and Medicine in a Chinese Village*, in 1986. Individually and together, the films have received many awards and prizes; the national broadcast was carried by a record number of local stations and the public response was extensive and enthusiastic.[1]

The trilogy offers a portrait of life and history in rural China through its focus on Long Bow, a village 400 miles southwest of Beijing. The view and approach are absolutely unprecedented in a number of respects deserving mention—they bear directly on oral-historical matters to be discussed below.

The films were codirected by Carma Hinton, an American who was born in China in 1949 and lived there until first coming to the United States in 1971, when she first began to develop any competence in English. With her husband, photographer Richard Gordon (himself a frequent visitor to China since 1975 and fluent in Chinese), she returned to Long Bow in the early 1980s for the extensive fieldwork and filming that provided the material for these documentaries. The choice was anything but random: Hinton knew the village well; it had been the focus of her father William Hinton's world-famous portrait of the 1949 Revolution, *Fanshen* (1966), and of the later *Shenfan* (1983), which traces the village through the many phases of post-revolutionary Chinese life, policy, and politics.

The Hinton family occupies an unusual and unique role in modern China: William Hinton's work enjoys continuing respect within the country and its government. During the long years of China's nonrelations with the West, he was one of the few Americans known and trusted by the Chinese, and he played an important role in interpreting to the West the immense complexity of Chinese life and politics at a time when it was hard for anyone, left or right, to cast China in other than one-dimensional stereotypes. His sister Joan had emigrated to China as well after 1949 with her American husband, and raised her children there too. Carma Hinton thus returned to Long Bow as a native-speaking member of a family known and trusted both by villagers and government; there was no need for translators, and no supervision from above. Accordingly, she and Richard Gordon had absolutely unlimited freedom to film and interview as they wished—and to respond to the enormous political changes just beginning in the 1980s: they arrived just as the village's commune system was being dismantled on orders from above. They were thus able to document an epochal change as experienced at the ground level rather than as a symbol of political debate, much as Carma's father, in 1949, had been able to witness and to document the actual process of revolution in Long Bow in day-to-day detail.

Both the background and opportunity have much to do with the kind of films Hinton and Gordon set out to make, and the methods they chose for making them. Consistent with the general tone of much of William Hinton's work, they sought to allow the remarkable complexity of China to speak for itself, especially the rural China that was being overlooked in the rush of Westerners to Beijing, to the Great Wall, and to the familiar cities of package tours, diplomatic display, or business contact. They hoped to transcend the abstractions of political polemic, which had been pretty much exhausted by the Cultural Revolution in any event, in order to present a sense of life in the People's Republic as grounded at once in a real political system unfamiliar to western audiences in its prosaic day-to-day particularity, and in a Chinese culture and tradition remarkably resistant, especially in the countryside, to relatively ephemeral political forces. Each of the films works this tension, though in different ways and to different effects.

Small Happiness focuses on the lives of women in the village, at present and as remembered from pre-Revolutionary China. The contrasts are enormous, as old women tell of bride-sale and foot-binding, but the persistent constrictions of women's role in the present stand as comments on the limited ability of politics to transform culture. And the film is able to ground such observations not in abstractions about "tradition," but in resilient structures in village life and organization that reinforce old practices, such as the "marrying-out" of girls to other villages that make more understandable the preference for boy babies who will remain in the village and family. (The film's title comes from a villager who says that there's nothing bad about having a baby girl—all births are happy events. But "to give birth to a boy is considered a big happiness. To give birth to a girl is a small happiness.")

All Under Heaven is the densest and most complicated of the three because its subject is complex changes in the political and economic organization of the village, especially in the face of the recent demobilization of the commune and the institution of the new "contract" system for farming and production. Here too, the filmmakers are most interested in showing the way people deal with these matters in day-to-day terms that have little to do with formal abstractions. In this film, the element of continuity with an older China is the surviving mandarin tradition of top-down imposition regardless of local circumstances: while some aspects of the new system are clearly welcome, villagers note the irony of being penalized for their perhaps unrepresentative efficiency under the commune: heavy equipment the village had invested in for farming its large collective fields lies rusting as these fields are divided into the small family plots mandated by the new system.

Finally, *To Taste a Hundred Herbs* focuses on Shen Fasheng, the village doctor. He is at once a modern paramedic and a practitioner of acupuncture and traditional herbal medicine with a particular renown for handling psychiatric disorders, treatment powerfully documented in the film. Shen is also a member of the village's substantial Catholic community, which has survived the Revolution but is seen as a familiar but odd minority, treated with bemused condescension by others in the village. Although this is the most genial and least political of the three films, it is perhaps the most powerful in forcing audiences to recognize the inadequacy of whatever fixed categories and expectations one brings to an encounter with rural China. Science and superstition, Western religion and Chinese household gods, family and politics—all are woven almost seamlessly into the fabric of daily life and community, and viewers intent on determining the right political or cultural labels to apply to what they see find themselves thrown back in frustration to reexamine their own assumptions.

Most viewers have found the trilogy powerful and distinctly original. Not only do the films permit a contexted, nonideological examination of communism and tradition in the real life of a village, but in terms of documentary type they manage a rare blend: they combine the best virtues and avoid the characteristic limitations of, on the one hand, ethnographies of culture and tradition generally strong on description but weaker on the analysis of change over time, and of studies of political movements on the other, which usually overemphasize change and conflict to the detriment of deeper cultural continuities.

This success traces in large part to the filmmakers' unique background and resources and their deep knowledge of the Chinese countryside, as well as to the power of Gordon's spectacular photography and David Carnochan's sensitive editing. An additional dimension stems, as well, from a distinct filmic decision to structure the films around sustained oral history: each segment of the trilogy is composed mostly of filmed interviews with villagers who talk about things that matter to them, past and present.

On viewing the films, this all seems so natural that one has to stop to notice how unusual it is. While there is some very impressive photography of live events and happenings in the village and its surroundings—children in the streets, people working in the fields or small factories, a visiting circus, Dr. Shen treating patients, a Catholic service, and so forth—by and large Hinton and Gordon do not focus on documenting the village and village life as such. They do not permit the logic of narration and the sequence of filmed views and episodes to structure the film, as so often is the case in such documentaries, especially of "exotic" contexts, with comments by villagers and participants introduced as a kind of illustration or a reinforcement of a general point.

Here, in fact, the relationship is reversed: the narration is spare, and mainly it stitches together more extensive analysis and commentary that even on complex matters of politics or economics, comes directly from informants in the interview setting. In effect, most of our time in the village is spent not touring, but rather sitting around the courtyard or in the fields, talking with people who speak, to a trusted and known listener, about what they know, what they have seen and experienced, and the way things seem to them. I can testify personally, as an oral history consultant asked to help the producers and directors refine their approach to the conduct and later the editing of the interviews, as to how central and self-conscious this choice of emphasis was from the very beginning through the final completion of the project.

The reliance on formal interview conversation gives the films a remarkable authority and solidity: the issues are complex, and there is no pretense that informants, by definition, have all or even part of the truth. But it is clear that they are sharing their truth with us, as equals, and they help us explore the complexity that any culture will reveal if it is attended to with such guides. In this sense, the triumph of the films is to conflate our categories of familiar and exotic: the people become more and more recognizable in human terms, and this permits the differences in their world and their attitudes to be more deeply appreciated. Both similarities and differences help us to measure ourselves, and our place in the world, in new ways.

Almost every review of each of these films has been laudatory, and although these do not always discuss the use of oral history explicitly, most of them locate the films' uniqueness and power in the dimension noted here: the way the villagers engage us directly through their filmed conversations with Carma Hinton. I think it fair to say that the general audience response in the United States, both in somewhat self-selected theater audiences and in the broader, quite responsive television audience as well, has shared this perception. This certainly is the way I had always thought of the films, as I watched them take shape on the editing deck, and as, together with filmmakers and other China scholar consultants, we discussed specific editing choices and emphases in narration. I thought we had a pretty good idea of the way oral history would work in the films, and the way audiences would respond to it.

Which is why Carma Hinton, advisor Marilyn Young, and I were so surprised when we moderated a showing and discussion of the trilogy to large audiences including (perhaps for the first time) large numbers of viewers from the People's Republic of China. Their very different responses, and the debates these provoked, suggest we need to examine more closely the way oral history "translates" across cultural space. By so doing, in this informal report, I hope as well to make a modest contribution to the dialogue addressed at the start—the need to develop more finely our vocabulary for discussing how the presentation and reception of historical material, particularly oral history statements, functions as part of any film's broader if implicit dialogue with its audience about the history it intends to explore.

A Complex Dialogue

In 1987, the New York Council for the Humanities instituted a program called "Films in the Humanities," under a special grant from the National Endowment for the Humanities (NEH). The program provided for free public showing of a sequence of notable documentary films, each to be followed by a discussion with the audience featuring the filmmaker and a humanities scholar involved in the making of the film. One of the films was *Small Happiness*, and when in scheduling the overall sequence for presentation in Buffalo we learned that Carma Hinton would be able to attend along with Professor Marilyn Young of New York University, we arranged to show the other two Long Bow films the next day, encouraging people to see all three as a group. There was substantial interest and word-of-mouth publicity about the films, and on the first evening, for the formal showing of *Small Happiness*, Hinton and Young were surprised and delighted to see one of the largest audiences the film had attracted in any similar showing—well in excess of 250 people, nearly one-half of whom were evidently a substantial proportion of SUNY-Buffalo's large number of visiting students from the People's Republic.

For these students, the evening was certainly an unusual experience, as it would be for any of us watching a complex documentary portrait of our own country shown to foreigners for whom this was most likely a first in-depth exposure. But sensing this still did not prepare us for the audience response: Hinton and Young had never encountered so many questions and comments expressing, many with considerable emotion, skepticism about the film's picture of China and cynicism about the filmmakers' motives.

Heated argument continued at a reception following the showing, and the debate stretched well into the night. It was, at first, hard to know exactly what was propelling the students' complaints, as these took the form of more general denunciations of the film as inaccurate and one-sided, giving too much credence and voice to ignorant women and their complaints. Because most of the comments came from Chinese men who plainly had found the women in *Small Happiness* provocative and threatening, Hinton and Young at first saw their reaction as predictable, a kind of confirmation of the film's perspective and point about the persistence of traditional roles of men and women in Chinese culture.

The next day, however, discussion after the other two films made the issue seem more complex and mysterious: the criticisms were less biting and emotional, but at the same time more broadly based among a larger number of students, now including women as well as men. In the days that followed, in fact, the Chinese students remained in great ferment, arguing passionately among themselves about the intent and effect of the films. Finally, a number of these students suggested that it would be helpful—indeed, they said, it was almost imperative, so deep was the disturbance—for Chinese and Americans to sit down together and sort through reactions to the films.

We arranged a meeting in response to this urgent request, and some forty people jammed the room at its start, more than one-half of them students from China, with many others joining in later. The talk went on for nearly four hours and could have lasted another ten, it seemed. The flavor is suggested by one Chinese woman who began by nervously announcing "I have seven points I want to discuss," and went on for twenty minutes, talking through objections, before saying, "Now to my second point . . .", upon which she finally was persuaded to yield the floor.

There was no prevalent "Chinese" response, I should say: the students were deeply and passionately divided about the films, and those who either loved the trilogy or hated it did not always do so for similar reasons. Nevertheless, there were some suggestive patterns in their responses to the Long Bow Trilogy's portrait of rural China.

In her contribution to the *Oral History Review* symposium noted earlier, Young discusses a first dimension of response, beyond male chauvinism, which had been evident in the discussion at the filming, particularly after the showings of *All Under Heaven* and *To Taste a Hundred Herbs:* a pervasive embarrassment at peasant life and the poverty of rural China, intimations that there was callousness and even irresponsibility at "exposing" this backwardness to the view of the outside world, and fear that the American response would be a mixture of contempt for the people and misreading of China's progress. But in the crucible of the subsequent extended discussion, other concerns began to appear beneath the surface of such objections. As it happens, these turned on issues that had less to do with China and more to do with deeper disagreements about documentary and oral history. Three particular themes are worth brief notice here.

First and most centrally, those critical of the films raised the issue of "representativeness": all the ways in which this village, these individuals, and the subjects chosen for presentation may not actually be representative of more general patterns of Chinese life. The filmmakers insisted that they did not presume to generalize at all, pointedly titling the trilogy *One Village in China*. But the Chinese critics countered, correctly, I think, that this did not dismiss the question of accountability. A set of images was being presented to huge Western audiences, they argued, and if these were misleading or distorted, the claim of nominalism—just one person speaking, just one village—was not an adequate defense. The filmmakers had to take responsibility for their choices.

Those who liked the films had no trouble defending those choices as such. But it is interesting how, in the process, discussion came to revolve around a central issue in documentary, and indeed in the oral-historical method itself: the catch-22 tension between the insights that can arise only from the depths of an informant's idiosyncratic narrative, and which thereby beg the question of how much can be concluded on the basis of such singular evidence.

A second related concern involved discomfort with the films' reliance on historical and political analyses as offered by the villagers themselves. It became clear only in the fuller discussion that a good deal of the students' embarrassment was grounded in the degree to which the peasants were not only observed and pictured, but were broadly permitted to articulate the film's analysis, and hence its politics.

A confirmation of this came not from the films detractors but from its staunchest defenders—at least some of whom seemed to resist a direct engagement with the complex interviews. One Chinese student, for instance, offered a rapturous appreciation: The films had provided him, an urban person, with his first view of rural China, he exclaimed—the people there were wonderful, "like some primeval tribe," exotic survivors of an ancient world. This is the precise opposite of the reaction of most Western audiences, who are touched by the thoroughly recognizable humanity of the people encountered in the direct conversations filling all three films. The Chinese students critical of the films were, in a sense, closer to this position than to that of their romantic colleague. Rather than being able to comfortably dismiss the peasants as distant and quaint, they sensed the importance of the films' permitting villagers a voice in assessing past, present, and future—and they found this disturbing.

This resistance to having peasants speak "for" a larger situation seemed closely linked to an uneasiness at being unable to identify the films' political "voice." Carma Hinton and Richard Gordon had no official Chinese approval or status, yet they had received some cooperation from the government and had not been criticized. Many of the Chinese students seemed unsettled, especially amidst the volatility of recent Chinese politics, by a text whose pedigree they thus could not clearly read. And for all their fashionable talk of democratizing China, a number of them fell back to the most extreme line of defense: the films should have been presented for official approval in China, and not shown in the West until and unless this approval was received.

This attitude, first understood by many of the Americans present in narrow political terms, actually had deeper roots, a third dimension that became evident when the students offered specific examples of where they thought the films were irresponsible or distorted. Early on, one talked at length about the most dramatic moment in *Small Happiness*, where a grandmother confesses to having many years ago smothered her own baby, whom she could not begin to be able to feed in the crushing poverty of feudal China. The student did not deny that this might have been true—but she faulted the film for having, by including it, implied that the behavior was appropriate. If infanticide is wrong, she went on, it must be clearly identified as such, not hidden behind a more complex message about the nature of pre-1949 poverty.

The argument was vigorously resisted by both Chinese and American students, yet there was something compelling about the critique, which became clearer in a less-charged example late in the discussion. Another student pointed to the image of the young bride dressed in an elaborate traditional wedding costume yet sporting brazenly contemporary sunglasses. For him, it was the epitome of everything wrong in the film. While it made the audience laugh, he said, it made him want to crawl under a rock in shame. And in trying to explain this feeling, he made a point that had been implied in the infanticide discussion and a number of the other complaints: he well understood the image's point about the relation of tradition to change, but he felt that by seemingly celebrating the bride's expression of complexity and cultural confusion, the film abdicated a responsibility to introduce clarity into confusion, meaning into chaos. The purpose of documentary and of art more broadly, he said, was not to passively reflect a paradoxical or ambiguous reality, but rather to introduce moral clarity and truth—which he took to be much the same thing.

This produced another heated flurry of discussion, but the point suggested a profound difference that cut the argument loose from the films and their context, at the same time providing a kind of resolution to the debate. After all, the Long Bow Group had chosen that very same image of the sunglassed bride for its poster advertising *Small Happiness*; the editing and placement of the infanticide confession had been struggled over for months, with everyone aware that this episode's power could either propel or deform the film and its portrait. And I knew, as an advisor to the group, how hard they had worked to have the films present the reality of life in rural China on its own terms, avoiding the easy labels that commentators are so relentlessly eager to attach to China. The one thing that was explicit in editing decisions was the intent to let the villagers themselves unfold the complexity of their world, and their worldviews, without a mediating message declaring the recent economic reforms as good or bad, women as truly liberated under socialism or still culturally enslaved, Dr. Shen as a good doctor or a primitive quack, Catholicism as alien or rooted in Chinese tradition—and to thereby challenge viewers to examine their own categories and assumptions, in dialogue with the villagers.

In the final analysis, then, the trilogy's very success in this intention produced a good bit of the response of its Chinese critics. Their implicit belief in the clarifying and didactic responsibility of documentary art has, of course, a rich heritage with many echoes in the West, reaching beyond Communist propaganda and Socialist Realism to the Confucian roots of traditional Chinese culture, with its stress on the "rectification of names." But it proceeds from a very different set of assumptions about oral history and documentary than those propelling these films.

This suggests differences not to be resolved in an afternoon's discussion. But appreciating their dimension helped us all conclude, I think, that we had in fact actually seen the same films and focused on the same qualities about them however different our responses. In so doing, the discussion confirmed the power of oral history, embodied in films as powerful and as well crafted as the Long Bow Trilogy, *One Village in China*, to force to the surface the most enduring questions of history, politics, art, and communication across cultural space.

In the broader context of this essay, the experience suggests some of what is to be learned from attending more carefully to the way audiences respond to historical films generally, and to the presentation of oral-historical material in particular. The more we respect and understand the complexity of this interaction, the more we can make presentational choices that will enhance the already substantial capacity of documentary film to generate a very special kind of interpretive dialogue with its audience.

Chapter 7

Oral History, Documentary, and the Mystification of Power:
A Critique of *Vietnam: A Television History*

Discussions of oral history tend to focus on the process of the interview or the organizing of oral history projects, which is to say on the nature and generation of this particular kind of historical document. There has been relatively less attention given to issues encountered in the reading and interpretation of such documents, much less to the theory and methodology of presentation—what is actually done *with* oral history, and how its documents appear, are used, and are perceived in publicly shared documentary forms.

As a way of engaging some of these general concerns, this chapter addresses the issues raised by the use of oral historical materials in mass-mediated historical documentary. I will use as a case in point the thirteen-part Public Broadcast System's documentary, *Vietnam: A Television History* recently aired in the United States and throughout Europe, a major attempt to "package" the history (and meaning) of the Vietnam War, and a major document of the current cultural and political moment.

The relatively undeveloped discourse concerning the interpretive uses of oral history is a curiosity worth some attention before turning to the case study. Oral history has been fueled by a diversely grounded impulse to escape the bounds of academic history, to break the bonds of traditionally defined source materials and their implicit biases, to broaden participation in the process of historical interpretation, and to empower the people who actually make social history in their lives and struggles to reappropriate it for their own purposes. The agenda of an oral history movement so grounded and charged suggests as a central concern the exploration of how oral history is actually presented to and engaged by the public in practice.

And yet the power and accessibility of oral history have seemed so compelling and self-evident that there has been relatively little attention paid to the communicative implications of this distinct kind of documentation. To be sure, in recent years, discourse on oral history in general has become more sophisticated, with commentators increasingly focusing on the uniqueness of a form of research that generates its own documents, and on the interview process as a distillation of that complexity, involving the play of memory, personal interaction, consciousness, and politics. Although some of us have tended to work out these ideas by critically examining public as distinct from academic products—books, films, and magazine articles—we have barely begun to focus squarely on issues raised in public presentation and interpretation. For instance, there has been substantial discussion of authorship, the degree to which both subject and historian share "author-ity" for the interpretations an interview carries. But this notion of authority is rarely employed critically in the evaluation of documentary uses of oral history, and it does not seem to have figured much more prominently in the choices governing documentary construction. Oral history as used in documentary has been characterized by a "supply side" tendency: effort has focused on accumulating and displaying, with meaning presumed to be explicit in the edited content rather than more implicitly and problematically carried by the method and forms themselves.

This supply-side emphasis has been reinforced by material factors including the role of major film and documentary funders such as the National Endowment for the Humanities, (NEH) whose funding is generally conditioned on the prominent use of academic "humanists" in the planning, execution, and ultimate public form of documentary projects. This expectation, not inherently inappropriate, has frequently had the unfortunate effect of placing intellectuals in the position of validating the supposedly "raw" material of oral history interviews, and placing them in "perspective." This reinforces the already deeply-rooted, class-based ideology that sees ordinary people as sources of data, rather than as shapers and interpreters of their own experience.

To this emphasis—related to what in academic terms I have called the "More History" approach, reducing oral history to simply another kind of evidence to be pushed through the historian's controlling mill—there is an opposite. This is to view oral historical evidence, because of its immediacy and emotional resonance, as something almost beyond interpretation or accountability, as a direct window on the feelings and, in some senses, on the meaning of past experience. This tendency, which I have called the "Anti-History" approach, produces dramatic editing choices, and makes for vivid documentary, but it is equally problematic: to confer unquestioned authority on direct experience is usually to mystify, rather than bypass, the process of drawing meaning from the stream of history.

Let me now turn to the case study, which will show how these concerns are illuminated by a review of the function and place of oral history in *Vietnam: A Television History.*

Documentary Materials and Strategy

A thirteen-part, thirteen-hour series is difficult to discuss concisely, especially when several production teams in different countries, beyond the core group operating out of WGBH in Boston, Massachusetts, were responsible for particular programs. This explains much of the variance in tone, quality, and politics that critics have been quick to detect in assessing the units of the series. Nevertheless, the project was conceived and realized as a whole, and the overall control of the WGBH producers is evident in the way each episode is structured, documented, and presented. Indeed, the more one focuses on the implicit methodology of interpretive presentation, rather than content, the more the consistency of the episodes becomes apparent.

Each episode is constructed from three primary kinds of material. First are the archival documents, including both newsreel-style footage and contemporaneous file interviews with key personages. Second are the recently-filmed interviews in which individuals look back on the events being considered. For present purposes, these we can call *oral-historical*, although most of the interviews seem to have been occasional, rather than part of a systematic oral-history documentation process. Finally, there is narration, used to set the frame and weave the threads of documentation together.

The style of assemblage is spare and simple: the narration is modest, and the usually substantial segments of documentation carry the burden of moving each episode along, with frequent cuts back and forth among several related interviews, often to highlight contrastive arguments and experiences. Generally, the choice in each program is to make extensive use of a relatively smaller number of "informants" in the interest of coherence, rather than a larger, perhaps more representative group of smaller excerpts requiring greater narratorial intervention and framing. The narrator himself speaks as if at a distance, providing general historical frame and continuity, but not introducing, assessing, or directly commenting on the documentary material. The results seem close to what the producers have claimed to be their intention. In the words of executive producer Richard Ellison:

> No fancy intercut editing, no emotive music, no omniscient narrator. Plainness is in the interests of the philosophical objective, which is to manipulate the viewer as little as possible. The archival film is what it purports to be; sources are identified when necessary; contradictory viewpoints are clearly articulated; conclusions and value judgments are expressed by participants and interview subjects, not by the program makers.[1]

Most critics, of whatever stripe, have had mixed reactions to the *Vietnam* series; some of its features have been held powerful and striking, some have seemed to most observers wholly inadequate to the complexities under examination. In political terms, there is a relative consensus, and not only on the left, that the overall effect of the series has been powerfully to humanize but also to depoliticize the war, to see it as a "tragedy" without winners or losers. And yet the mechanisms of this depoliticization have not been clearly understood.

In general, from whatever vantage, most observers have implicitly accepted the validity of the documentary strategy employed, and criticized supposed failures of realization. They have cited this quote or that, this editing decision or that, this piece of footage or that narration, to support a claim that even within the limits of the form, the producers failed to capture the historical and political essence of their subject, because they are held to have failed to realize, or even betrayed, the methodological intentions quoted above.

It is my impression, however, that the political and formal questions are most closely related, with limits in historical vision a direct consequence of methodology: given the way documentary has been defined and approached, the results trace to intention and successful realization, not to inadvertent lapses, failures of vision, or political biases in the narrow, literal sense. This is especially apparent in the use of the oral-historical materials that form the dramatic and historical core of the series. Attention to the uses and effects of oral historical evidence may thus help us to understand the connection between documentary form and implicit ideological message—and how invisibly this can be forged.

Varieties of Oral History Evidence

The first thing to be noticed is the staggering richness and variety of oral historical documents animating any single episode, much less the series as a whole. For all the ingenuity and imagination of the archival researchers and the footage they have exhumed—usually the heart of an historical documentary—the most exciting and revealing moments here tend to come in the historical interviews, whose variety offers a kind of implicit mapping of the many ways in which oral history can provide otherwise unreachable vantages on the substance and texture of the past.

To start with, excellent use is made of the occasional telling and well-told anecdote from within the halls and chambers of power, long a staple of written memoirs but somehow even more powerful when recorded in an interview's conversation, and when used as a way to provide a density of insight otherwise far too complex for concise presentation in the time-constrained format of an hour's documentary. Consider how long it would take to explicate the themes conveyed by Bill Moyers's description of President Lyndon Johnson after his famous Johns Hopkins speech of 1965, in which the president offered to turn from escalation to join the North Vietnamese in a kind of mammoth Tennessee Valley Authority (TVA) for the Mekong Delta, if only they would abandon the conflict: "He leaned across to an assistant, put his hand on his knee, and said, 'Old Ho can't turn that down, Old Ho can't turn that down.' You see, if Ho Chi Minh had been George Meany, Lyndon Johnson would have had a deal."[2]

Oral history is also good at restoring pivotal moments to life, at helping us imagine the drama of impending decisions and their unimaginable consequences, as distinct from the all-too-familiar monuments these decisions become in the landscape of the historical past tense. Thus, State Department aide Paul Kattenburg describes the moment at which the United States decided to block the elections called for in the 1954 Geneva accords, which almost certainly would have placed Ho Chi Minh at the head of a united Vietnam: [John Foster Dulles] "sat very quietly, we all sat very quietly. I can recall distinctly the clock ticking away on his wall, and his breathing heavily, as he read through the paper, turning to us, the few of us who were there at that meeting, saying [imitates]: 'I don't believe Diem wants to hold elections; I believe we should support him in this.'"[3]

Variants of this approach could as easily be cited—instances in which oral history documents not so much the texture of a moment whose formal history is known, as in these examples, but rather an inner reality very much at odds with the public image of historical events, or a process in which the steps in a complex process, such as the Paris negotiations, can be historically constructed through a mosaic of recollections of actors from every side of the complex conference table.

Some of these forms of evidence are examined below; for now, it suffices to notice that even within the parameters of the study of the history of power—one of the most traditional uses of oral history—there is substantial variety in the insights oral-historical documents contribute, and the roles they play, in the *Vietnam* documentary narratives.

It is, of course, one of the familiar virtues of oral history to remind us that one need not be in the president's office or a key actor in a major event to be a participant in history; the *Vietnam* series repeatedly demonstrates the way the historical record is enriched by our capacity to obtain direct testimonies from an immense variety of actors whose experience, much less whose reflections, would not be accessible through conventional written documents and memoirs—informants on all sides and of all kinds, from villagers to bomber pilots to U.S. footsoldiers to National Liberation Front (NLF) saboteurs to Saigon prostitutes to North Vietnamese doctors and nurses to American prisoners of war (POWs), and more. Interview testimonies range from the direct witnessing of specific historical happenings, to the description of an individual's own particular acts, to suggestion of the broader patterns carried in the

description of everyday activity, to subjective reflection on experience or observation, at the moment and as remembered over time. The cumulative effect
of this testimony is to broaden our sense of who makes history and how, and
what matters in it—by the very complexity of the witness perhaps even more
than by the variety of informants, as the following examples, chosen almost at
random, may serve to suggest:

> So many people died of hunger here in this village. I myself had to bury
> four persons, and we did not have enough wood to make coffins for them. I
> had to wrap the four corpses I buried with hemp cloth. I buried four persons
> in that graveyard over there. In this village more than two hundred fifty per-
> sons died of hunger. I witnessed families in which every member died.[4]

> The Reverend Quang Duch decided to dedicate his body as a torch to
> light the struggle to preserve religious teaching. I saw him step out of his car
> and assume the lotus position. Then a monk stepped forward and helped the
> Reverend pour gasoline on himself. At that moment, a flame engulfed his
> body.... During the ... cremation, everything was burned except for his heart,
> which remained intact. His heart was set on fire two more times, but it still
> did not burn.[5]

> At the end of November I was given the order to attack the Brink's hotel,
> which houses high American officers. All the crimes committed by the Ameri-
> cans were directed from this nerve center. I sat in a nearby cafe to wait for the
> explosion, which occurred at exactly 5:45 on the afternoon of December 24th,
> the anniversary of the founding of the People's Army of Vietnam. Our com-
> manders had ordered us to attack the place when the most Americans were
> there, and it was precisely as we had expected ... the attack succeeded and
> we never were detected.[6]

> Most of our enemy contact at that time was not contact at all, it was
> mines and snipers. Mostly mines .... And here's Joe the rice farmer out in his
> field, he just, he don't even stop, he don't even, it's like he didn't even hear
> the blast. And after a while, you start thinking, well, these people must know
> where these mines are, how come they never step on them? They must be,
> uh, they must be VC [Viet Cong]. And so, over a relatively short period of time
> you begin to treat all the Vietnamese as though they are the enemy.[7]

> I kept hearing this, this friend of mine hollering "Tex, help me, help me."
> So finally ... I just instinctively jumped up out of the bomb crater and ran
> over to help this guy. Just as I got to him ... I felt this thud in my back ... and
> I realized that I'd been shot.... And it's a, you know, all of a sudden I thought—
> how did I get here? I never wanted to be a trained killer, I didn't want to kill
> anybody I didn't know the first thing about, I started thinking, you know, for
> the first time. What the hell is Communism? I couldn't define it and I'm
> laying here and going to die for killing a bunch of people 'cause they happen
> to be Communist![8]

We always knew when they were about to drop their bombs. For example, in the morning, they usually arrived about ten o'clock just after breakfast. Then they took a break, and went back to their bases for lunch. Then they came back to drop their bombs again at about three in the afternoon. Since this was the routine, we tailored our schedule accordingly. We began our surgery at about five in the morning, and took a break at nine or ten. When the bombs didn't fall on time, we felt extremely uncomfortable, wondering why they hadn't fallen yet. This wasn't fear. We simply wanted the bombing to be over with so that we could get back to work.[9]

The people were fleeing, running across the field in front of the airport. The planes came and thought they were Khmer Rouge and bombed them. The bodies were all mixed up ... and the survivors jumped over the corpses. Then there was shelling and everything was aflame. It was already dusk and people could hardly recognize each other. When everyone was gone, the Khmer Rouge came in. The next morning they went into Phnom Penh.[10]

Added to the memoirs quoted earlier, these examples indicate something of the varieties of oral history evidence, both broadly and subtly differentiated, found in *Vietnam*. The voices come from different points on a landscape whose complexity could be mapped by means of latitude lines of nationality and politics (speakers representing pro- and anti-war Americans, NLF, Buddhist, and pro-government South Vietnamese, North Vietnamese, French, and so on) and longitude lines of power and class (from draftee and peasant to president and prime minister). And there is a complex third dimension as well, involving the kind of statements, the level of consciousness and subjectivity, the generality of memory, and the connections drawn between direct experience and broader meaning, between personal and social or political, between past and present.

Given this complexity, there is arguably more insight to be gained by examining the documentary through the frame of such a subtextual organizing grid than by focusing on the explicit historical statements made by the narrator or any particular interviewee. In other words, the greater our sense of the three-dimensional differences among the various pieces of the oral history evidence, the more important it becomes to examine the "how" of their use in the documentaries. Like any mosaic, these films depend for their effect on the selection, juxtaposition, and assembly of the pieces. Consequently, criticism must attend to the techniques of oral-historical construction as something distinct from the oral-historical content as such.

A Wide Repertoire of Techniques

The producers of *Vietnam* climb with remarkable agility around the three-dimensional jungle gym of nationality and politics, social status or level of speaker, and type of statement, selecting and arranging very different kinds of segments from its various locations in such a way as to keep the films refreshingly fluid while expressing narrative and thematic points that lessen the burden on explicit narration. In doing so, the producers' choices fall into some distinct oral-historical patterns that have much to do with the limits and the accomplishments of the films as documentary history. These patterns will be clearer if we first notice the broader repertoire of specific techniques most characteristic of the construction of these documentaries.

The simplest is the juxtaposition of witnesses from very different perspectives on a given event, a remarkable technique because we are hardly used to hearing the voices of our wars' enemies or innocent victims at all, much less as providers of contrastive testimony on particular episodes usually observed only from "our" vantage. Perhaps the most dramatic example of this is the testimony about the destruction of the village of Thuy Bo, in Program Five, "America Takes Charge." Even for readers familiar with the similar reportage in Jonathan Schell's magnificent "The Village of Ben Suc," the war emerges in new horror and depth from the sustained back-and-forth recollections of participants themselves:[11]

> Edward Banks: We ended up going some thirty-six plus hours without food or water, or sleep obviously. And, uh, that is saying a lot when you consider the temperature was around 100 degrees, no water, no food, no rest . . . .
>
> Nguyen Bay: When the Americans came, I was a boy in the fourth grade. I was on my way to school when I heard the Americans were coming. I was very scared and ran back home with my friends. By the time I got there and had hidden my things the Americans were close to the villages. Airplanes were overhead bombing, soldiers were coming, and shells were exploding.
>
> Edward Banks: Somebody had seen some movement in some of the houses, and the next thing we knew we were receiving automatic weapon fire. Lieutenant O'Connor was hit in the left shoulder above the heart . . . . He kept trying to get up, it taking the three of us to keep him on the ground. He kept trying to get up to get to his platoon to deploy and command them, not realizing how seriously he was hurt. The corpsman put a hemostat on the artery to stop the bleeding and, uh, we were successful to get a helicopter to take out Lieutenant O'Connor at the same time as we assaulted the village 200 or 300 meters to the front of us where the fire was coming from.
>
> Jack Hill: We was the first team in, we, we unloaded several rounds. We dropped a couple of grenades in the hootches to get the people out, because to get one Vietnamese out of that hole they won't come. I mean you, we didn't speak perfect Vietnamese so in order to get them out of there you either cranked off a couple of rounds or you dropped your M-26 grenade down there and they get the message and they come on out of there.

Le Thi Ton: When they came to my house, there were ten family members inside, including my fourteen-year-old son.... When they came in, I stood up and greeted them. They laughed when I did that ... they seemed to hate us. They just turned around and threw a grenade into the house. Nine or ten people were blown to pieces. I was the only one who was wounded and survived. My son and everyone else just fell dead. I was wounded and extremely frightened and crawled quickly into a corner of the house. Although the grenade had already exploded, the soldiers fired their guns at the people to make sure that nobody would survive.

Jack Hill: It was mass chaos. Like I say, everybody's running around screaming. We got in the village and asking where the VC were and people in the village saying no VC and like at one end of the village you could hear machine gunfire going off and people screaming, you know, and you know that somebody was either down in one of them holes getting dug out of there or something and, and you, we dropped plenty of hand grenades down in, in booby traps and I mean in holes and stuff to see if we could root them out. And, you go into a hootch and you got, ah, you got tunnels in there and you got old ladies and kids in there running out and, uh, we didn't, uh I didn't shoot any old ladies and kids. I know, I know half the guys in my squad didn't shoot no old ladies and kids because it, it just, there wasn't a fight there.

Nguyen Bay: They came and asked us about the Viet Cong. There were only women and children around then and we didn't know where the VC were. But they shot at us anyway. After they fired at us, they burned down the houses, they burned them down, and then they killed all our farm animals.

Thuong Thi Mai: After they killed the people, they burned down all the houses, so the survivors had no place to live. They burned everything. Even dead children were burned. So I could collect only this much of the remains of three children. It was only a handful of bones.

Nguyen Bay: The soldiers used their guns in a very brutal way. Some of the wounded people went to their beds to lie down .... Then the soldiers shot at their stomachs and their insides splattered all over. Then they smashed people's heads, using the butts of their guns. This terrified everybody who was still alive, the children screaming at the brutality they were seeing. But the soldiers kept on with their questioning. First, they shot our water basin to pieces, then they just opened fire at us, just opened fire continuously at us. I was wounded and fell down. Looking back at that time I have to say that it was so horrible I can't describe it all.

Jack Hill: Like I say, we done a dog-gone job that third day and it wasn't nothing unusual about burning them hootches down and digging them Vietnamese people out of them holes and scattering animals, pigs, and chickens around like we normally done. It's just a normal procedure we do. Especially after three days. Three days of blood and guts and in the, in the mud. Hey, you can't take it. You couldn't take it, and like I said, I can't account for every Marine that was there and what they done at, at that particular time, they done it because they felt that ... that's what they had to do. I can't account for how they acted, you know. Everybody's got their own way, but if he seen it that way, that's the way he seen it. And the way I seen it was ... was ... it was war.

In this staggering example, the witnesses are on opposite sides but report at the same level, in that they are recalling events experienced directly and personally. In other places, the producers add a contrast in the level of the commentators and the kind of recollection they offer. For instance, in Program Seven, "Tet," much of the power of the description of the battle in and for the city of Hue stems from the contrast between closely juxtaposed recollections of horrors experienced by civilian victims of both sides and comments on their broader policy by both American and VC field officers, whose strikingly parallel statements evade responsibility—in the former case for the manifestly general and intentional bombing and destruction of homes and neighborhoods, in the latter for the terroristic rounding up and assassination of supposed "enemies."

In still other instances, the producers effectively juxtapose eyewitness testimony and the distant, characteristically contemptuous, arrogant, or merely detached and self-delusive reflections of major political or military figures. Such settings suggest powerfully the corruption of feeling, tone, content, and language within the discourse of power, and the role of this detachment in propelling and sustaining a conflict with such enormous human costs.

Early on, for example, the dramatic description cited earlier of one of the first Buddhist protest self-immolations is followed by a comment by Madame Nhu, Diem's notorious sister-in-law, that the Buddhists "have barbecued one of their monks," and that "even that barbecuing was done not even with self-sufficient means because they used imported gasoline."[12] Near the end, in Program Ten, "Peace is at Hand," Admiral Thomas Moorer's defense of the infamous 1972 Christmas bombing of Hanoi is set against grim eyewitness testimony by the surviving victims, the contrast confirming what Moorer's halting speech itself reveals—especially in the pauses and hesitations included in a transcription provided by the producers, and hence indicative of the meaning they found in the passage:

> The targets selected in the 1972, ah, Christmas bombing consisted of, entirely of military targets. Ah, for instance, ah, they would, ah ... ah ... consist of, ah, warehouses, ah, command and control stations, ah, missile sites, ammunition storage, communications sites, things of that kind. A, the, ah ... the accusation that we were conducting ah carpet bombing of course is ... ah ... ah, absolutely false. For that matter had we, ah ... conducted carpet bombing, ah ... I think that there wouldn't be a Hanoi today.[13]

As this example suggests, the quality of language itself becomes a kind of independent variable which the producers employ with great care. Beyond techniques of contrast and juxtaposition in fixing our attention on particular episodes or broader situations, they seem alert to the capacities of language contrasts to capture the underlying dynamics of complex historical narrative itself, as in the story at the root of those bombings, the tortuous triangular negotiations on the Paris Treaty between the Americans and the North Vietnamese and then the Americans and the South Vietnamese.

This exposition is carried almost entirely by the principals, whose voices suggest much about the subtext of the problem at that stage, much less the configurations underlying the war more generally. In straightforward affect-less, news-conference prose, Henry Kissinger's aide William Sullivan clings to the claim that the North's stubbornness drove the United States to resume bombing at Christmas, even though everyone else virtually acknowledges that the campaign's aim was to convince the reluctant South to accept the treaty agreed on in October. Kissinger's recollections are more deeply revealing in their characteristically charming, arrogant affect, which seems aimed at covering, in the military sense, the U.S. retreat, and in a more uncharacteristic defensiveness about the bombing itself:

> Le Duc Tho had a tendency to, ah, make the same speech every day, months on end, and, ah, it was sort of like a prayer session at the beginning of a meeting, and, ah, it meant, what it symbolized was that they had all kinds of time, that we were going to have to collapse long before they would even think of yielding. ... Nixon was of the view that something shocking had to be done. That was not my view at the time, but I didn't disagree with it and I went along with it and I think Nixon turned out to be right. ... Publicly, [Le Duc Tho] refused to shake hands with me, and in all the pictures that were taken he never appeared with me. But inside the negotiating room, he moved at tremendous speed and with as much human warmth as he was capable of generating towards a representative of the capitalist system.[14]

The North Vietnamese Vice Foreign Minister, Nguyen Co Thach, focuses his recollections on specific details of the negotiations, although when he speaks of the final denouement, he suggests much of the determination, confidence, and self-righteousness that had carried the North to victory: "After shaking hands, Kissinger told Le Duc Tho that, 'I am very sorry. I could not prevent the decision of the President in bombing North Vietnam on Christmas day.' So Le Duc Tho say that, 'I know who are responsible: all you are responsible. And you are the criminals.'"[15]

And for the South Vietnamese, it is also a quality of language— in this case the ironic, colloquial English spoken by Thieu's chief aide, Hoang Duc Nha—that helps the oral history to convey the humiliation of the client state whose impotence the negotiations exposed, as when Kissinger's October draft treaty was brought to Saigon:

> We say fine, you know, thank you, uh, could we see the text? . . . Of course, they gave us the text in English, and at that time, I thought, I say, if our opposition knew that right at this moment we were discussing the fate of a country in a text in English, boy, you know, it would be so bad that we shouldn't even think about it! So I ask, I say, where is the Vietnamese text? Oh, we forgot, and I say, what do you mean, you forgot? The other side, I know they don't present a text to you in English. You know, between Vietnamese we know each other, you know, there is something called national pride, and you present your own language. They say, "Oh, this is good translation," and "we have our own translators. . . ." And I say, "You mean to tell me an American is, uh, you know, understand Vietnamese better than a Vietnamese? We want to see the Vietnamese text."[16]

This passage suggests a final use of oral history, beyond carrying immediate narrative or expressing broader moral perspectives on the violence of war: the way the producers select and arrange oral history excerpts to help advance a general historical analysis of the war, opening to view themes that move beyond what the narration deals with explicitly, resting them squarely on evidence presented. Two final examples illustrate this technique, one a comment on the origins of the Vietnam conflict and the other on the dynamics, internal and external, of the U.S. defeat.

In Program One, "Roots of a War," many segments testify to the nationalist, rather than Communist, essence of Ho Chi Minh's Vietminh movement, the point being that for the Vietnamese there was nothing ideologically inevitable about conflict with the United States, given our own historical origins in an anticolonial "war of national liberation." The combination of several distinct kinds of witness help reinforce the theme. Thus Archimedes Patti, an OSS [Office of Strategic Services] officer on the scene in 1945, recalls that,

> Two or three days after I met Ho, he asked me to come in and stop in and see him . . . and what he wanted to show me was a draft of the Declaration of Independence that he was going to declare several days later. . . . When it was interpreted to me, I was quite taken aback to hear the words of the American Declaration of Independence. Words about liberty, life and the pursuit of happiness. I just couldn't believe my own ears.[17]

And this is followed by a confirming, touching eyewitness account by Dr. Tran Duy Hung:

> I can say that the most moving moment was when President Ho Chi Minh climbed the steps and the national anthem was sung. . . . Uncle Ho

then read the Declaration of Independence, which was a short document. As he was reading, Uncle Ho stopped and asked, "Compatriots, can you hear me?" This question went into the hearts of everyone there. After a moment of silence, they all yelled, "Yes, we hear you!" And I can say that we did not just yell with our mouths, but with all our hearts, the hearts of over 400,000 persons standing in the square then. After Uncle Ho finished reading the Declaration of Independence, an airplane—a small one—circled over us. We did not know whose plane it was. We thought it was a Vietnamese plane. But when it swooped down over us, we recognized the American flag. The crowd cheered enthusiastically.[18]

Perhaps the most dramatic example of implicit thematizing is in Program Eight, "Vietnamizing the War." At one point, the narrator says, simply, "Every American had his own version of the Vietnam War." But what follows is a series of dramatic testimonies by soldiers which document declining morale, corruption and blackmarketing, the impact of drugs, racial conflict among troops, rising antiwar sentiment, and refusal of orders, extending to attacks on officers and disintegrating discipline in general—a painful but historically crucial pressure behind the Nixon Administration's search for a way out of the war. The experience of Peter Mahoney, the last American soldier quoted in the program, suggests the broader futility and misguidedness of the overall American involvement in Vietnam:

The Vietnamese that we were training were very responsive. They asked questions. They were very interested in, you know, in what was going on, and this, you know, made me feel good because, you know, the standard rap on the South Vietnamese was that they, they just weren't interested, they were lethargic and this particular group seemed like very involved in what was going on. So, it made me feel good. It made me feel as if I was accomplishing something. Ahm. We put them through a six-week training program. At the end of the training program the province ahm chief came down and there was a big graduation ceremony and they all got these colorful neckerchiefs as sort of souvenirs of the whole thing and, you know, it was like this whole sort of media publicity thing about how, you know, these people have been trained and everything. Then it was about a month after the training program was completed and this graduation happened that three NLF cadre came into the vill one night and all twenty-nine of those people's self-defense forces that I trained walked off and joined the NLF taking all their weapons and all their training with them.[19]

A Narrow Range of Choices

We have seen that the several producers of the *Vietnam* programs assembled an enormous variety of oral-historical documents of many different kinds and from all vantages. We have seen that the programs demonstrate, as well, a substantial variety of techniques for arranging and presenting these materials, and for conveying through these arrangements a complex of historical statements, from narrative to analysis. Having thus seen that the repertoire of documentary options is extraordinarily open-ended, we are in a position, finally, to consider how choices in material and construction selectively constrict this range, falling into particular patterns that can be linked to the particular shape and limits of the historical analysis suggested by the documentary as a whole.

It is, of course, impossible to determine cause and effect from a formal reading—to know whether a historical vision controlled the approach to documentary or whether documentary assumptions and aesthetic or journalistic choices, often implicit, rendered some kinds of historical questions and answers appropriate and others unreachable. My hunch is that the latter is probably more descriptive of a product as complex as *Vietnam*, but in any event the distinction may be less important than appreciating how the two dimensions become indistinguishable in the production process, much less in the experience of viewers. With this in mind let us reexamine the series, this time looking for major patterns in the use of oral history.

My own reading suggests that the programs are firmly in the grip of two consistently characteristic approaches. Almost irrespective of the substance carried in the evidence, each has the tendency to deflect and defuse specific political analysis in favor of a more general, vaguely tragic view of the war and the larger issues informing it.

The first is a tendency for subjects to be differentiated in terms of the *type* of historical statements they are presented as making, and for this differentiation to follow closely lines of class and power. Peasants, ground soldiers, and random individuals tend to be quoted as to their personal experience, their direct observations, their feelings. The more powerful or prominent the subject, however, the more likely he or she is to be seen offering historical judgments of a broader nature, sweeping evaluations of what such and such event meant, or what caused it. Both ends of the spectrum are oral history, but they are very different kinds of evidence; the correlation of interpretive "power" and sociopolitical power is hardly accidental or without effect.

At first glance, this seems to be a product of a technique we have already discussed—the producer's fondness for juxtaposing different species of interview material in order to expose the limits of general statements, as in the siege of Hue statements by both American and NLF officers, described earlier. On a grander level, in Program Eight, "Vietnamizing the War," there is a dramatic sequence of such alternations between an interview with William Colby of the Central Intelligence Agency (CIA), who mystifies in broad strategic and historical terms the notorious Phoenix Program of assassination, and U.S. field officers, who describe anecdotally this program's brutal reality.

The stark contradiction between the two discourses might be taken as itself a comment on authority but for the fact that the same rhythm is employed in instances where the anecdotal information seems to confirm, rather than contradict, the generalizations of those in power and authority. In the same program, for instance, aides to President Thieu argue that the North had failed in its objectives and escaped defeat only when the United States inexplicably began to withdraw; this testimony is then seemingly reinforced by soldiers who describe their own bewilderment in the field as the United States posture turned to retreat.

In such instances, and many others that can be cited in virtually every episode, the claims of power are not critically examined in their own terms; they are simply held up against the measure of "experience" and implicitly confirmed or contradicted, usually the former. In Program Eight, for instance, a young woman describes how she was forced into prostitution:

> I answered an ad in the newspaper for a job as a cashier. While I was working there, the woman who owned the establishment bought me a lot of new clothes. . . . I didn't think she was going to deduct these things from my salary. But after a while she began to demand repayment. . . . I don't know where I would get the money. Then she suggested I ought to go with a certain man who would give me money so I could repay my debt to her. . . .[20]

This is followed by Bui Diem, the last South Vietnamese ambassador to the United States, who observes, "Vietnamese are by tradition, ah, very, very respectful to their families, for instance, you see. But by the time these people who get their money the quick way, ah, it if happens that they were scolded by their parents about it, they bypass it very easily, you see."[21]

The rhythm is similar throughout the program—ground-level description of the black market, or experiences in the field, and higher officials placing things in a broader perspective, as when Bui Diem says, "The Vietnamese couldn't think in terms of the Americans intervening in something and not succeeding . . . they couldn't think that the Americans once having committed their troops in Vietnam, having spent so much money in Vietnam could one of these days leave everything behind and all that."[22]

Such usage cuts across lines of content. Interviews and footage from the North Vietnamese/NLF side are strengths of the series, and have been taken as evidence of its "balance" and "objectivity." In oral-historical terms, these indeed follow a similar methodological pattern: in Program Six, "America's Enemy," a NLF cadre explains how "unexploded American bombs and shells were dug up by old people and the kids . . . sawed up in order to get to the gun powder and explosives. Then they produced various kinds of explosive devices themselves. In each village and hamlet we had a workshop for producing these devices."[23]

Then Le Thi Ma, a peasant, remembers the process: "We scraped the powder into two large cauldrons, bigger than this one here. Next we melted the powder down into a thick liquid and poured it into a container like this one, until it was completely full. We then made a detonator and inserted it here. We placed these mines along the routes we knew the tanks were going to take."[24]

Similarly, the program juxtaposes descriptions of the Ho Chi Minh Trail by North Vietnam Premier Pham Van Dong: "The Ho Chi Minh Trail developed day-by-day, becoming a network of roads over which weapons, military supplies, and tens of thousands of soldiers were moved into the South for combat,"[25] and by North Vietnamese Army (NVA) Captain Tran Van Ngo: "I left the North, taking three months to reach the South. On the way, we constantly faced flares, all kinds of bombs and rockets. We couldn't stop for any time along the route until we had reached our resting place. Then we would sleep in hammocks and begin marching at four o'clock the next morning."[26]

These rhythms consistently extend to historical generalizations as such, the level of interpretation rising with the position of the speaker. Thus, at the end of this program, NVA Captain Nguyen Van Nghi's assessment is explicitly grounded in direct experience: "Having fought against the American troops many times I came to the conclusion that they had a lot of bombs and shells, that they were very powerful as far as war materials were concerned. But they did not fight very well at all. They moved very slowly and really were not that mobile."[27] In contrast, Pham Van Dong and General Vo Nguyen Giap, the North Vietnamese defense minister and military commander-in-chief, speak throughout the program in a more sweeping historical voice. Thus, Pham states, "The destruction of the North, with all the efforts and all the barbarity of Imperial America only caused the people to be more resilient and more resolute in their determination to resist and to win."[28] And Giap, whose program-concluding assessment provides the documentary bridge to the next film's focus on the Tet Offensive, states, "They had spread the hostilities over the entire territory of our country. It was absolutely normal and necessary for us to mobilize all our forces, political and military . . . in order to carry on the struggle and to reach final victory."[29]

The role of those without privilege or prominence, however, rarely extends beyond contributing their personal experience for the reflection of others, including the audience. There are a few instances in which such individuals do speak on the broader level, but these are exceptions that prove the rule. Thus American footsoldiers express broader thoughts about the war only in the context of individual experience, as when Charles Sabatier remembers thinking about the nature of communism while lying wounded on the battlefield, quoted earlier, or when in that same Program Five, "America Takes Charge," William Earhart's political statement takes off from autobiography:

> In grade school we learned about the Redcoats, the nasty British soldiers who tried to stifle our freedom in the period of George the Third.... I began increasingly to have the feeling that I was a Redcoat. Uh, and I think it was one of the most staggering realizations of my life.... Somehow, in the space of eight months I'd reached the point from being a volunteer hurrying off to do his duty for his country to seriously contemplating desertion, to just disappearing into the world somewhere.[30]

One of the few unqualified general statements from the bottom up is by an American pilot, Robinson Risner: "We believed that the North Vietnamese who are Communists led by the old atheist dictator Ho Chi Minh wanted to take over the rest of Southeast Asia. In other words his doctrine was the same as Mao Tse Tung's and all the rest of the militant communists. We didn't want this to happen."[31] But by the time of the interview Risner had become one of the more prominent and politically visible spokesmen for the released POWs, and his statement thus confirms rather than contradicts the general pattern of the documentary: A broader perspective seems a natural extrapolation of power, public position, access to information, and privilege. These implicitly confer the license and capacity to make general statements about the nature of a society, about military strategy, a moment in diplomacy, or the character of a movement. Whether for Americans or Vietnamese, the right to historical generalization itself is uncontested and unshared; the message seems to be that ordinary people do not and in some sense cannot venture broader historical reflection and analysis.

Whatever the limits of such a view of human capacity and experience, it might be argued that the documentary need not suffer in historical terms because the circle of privilege and power is surely big enough to bring all relevant perspectives into view, especially if it has widened to include the former enemy, pro- and anti-war activists, and so forth. This claim is problematic, but even were it not, its meaning would be limited by the second oral-historical choice at the core of the producers' strategy, a choice with ominous implications for those who care about the capacity of oral history to provide a special vantage on historical process and experience.

Although it may seem a paradox, the threat lies in the producers' decision to confer on oral history a controlling power over the documentary. Aside from the narrator, with very few exceptions all other comments on the past, whatever their nature, are made by individuals who "were there" in the most immediate, literal sense; a direct, specific role in the actual history is the defining principle of inclusion. No other sources of authority or historical insight are used to test, qualify, probe, or assess the hegemony of actual experience.

Borrowing the old-time radio character Baron Munchausen's stock response to accusations of lying, this can be called the "Vas You Dere, Chollie?"

approach to documentary construction. It works well, in terms of both content and drama, when evoking the experience of being bombed, or fighting in
the jungle. But it is more problematic when the topic of concern is a political
or military decision or event, because those who "were there" tend to be at
best prisoners of the frameworks we seek to place in perspective, and, at
worst, self-serving apologists for their own past actions. Many of the deepest
problems of the documentary stem from the fact that this "experience" is
granted sole interpretive authority.

The process of the American escalation, for instance, is examined almost
exclusively by various Johnson Administration, military, and Congressional
leaders who were directly involved in the decisions—which constricts the range
of analysis by definition, however much the producers strive to "balance" General William Westmoreland's views with those of State Department "moder-
ate" George W. Ball. A related consequence is the profoundly anti-intellectual
notion that a participant's reflections have more authority than those of one
who has researched the events in question after the fact.

Both tendencies are particularly evident in dealing with crucial turning
points, as in Program Four, "LBJ Goes to War." Here, Johnson Administration
officials are the main "informants" for placing in perspective the Gulf of Tonkin
incidents and other landmarks in escalation. Dramatic anecdotes from White
House insiders render the program particularly moving in its picture of LBJ
as a partly tragic, partly pathetic figure whose sentimental, culture-bound
populist liberalism, so effective in mobilizing opinion and political power for
the civil rights bills and the Great Society at home, proved so delusive and
inadequate for reading the reality of Vietnam, bringing himself and his administration down in ruins in the process.

But such sources, however implicitly and inadvertently, lock the narrative into a particular set of assumptions that beg precisely the questions a
retrospective history ought to examine more critically: the result is that there
is no methodological alternative to the "slippery slope" or "quagmire" approach
to the overall Vietnam dilemma, the appeal and limits of which are both equally
apparent in Bill Moyers's poignant and affectionate memoir—the George
Meaney anecdote cited earlier, or the recollection of a beleaguered LBJ's opting
for escalation in the face of the near-collapse of the South Vietnamese politically and militarily in 1965: "and the President says, 'I feel like a hitchhiker
caught in a hailstorm on a Texas highway. I can't run, I can't hide, and I can't
make it stop.' "[23]

It is as if students of the Pentagon Papers or journalists or historians,
over the years, have not learned more about those events than immediate
participants can possibly have experienced, much less remembered and
willingly discussed, and as if we had not, in the process, arrived at any alternative ways of understanding these events. Similar questions are begged when

the "Was You Dere Chollie?" point of oral-historical privilege permits a self-serving Henry Cabot Lodge or Henry Kissinger and his deputy William Sullivan to continue to interpret their own records, serving as the chief American guides to the "real" history of the murder of Diem in the first instance and the Paris negotiations, the Christmas bombing, and the Peace Treaty in the second. South Vietnamese politicians and generals, uncontested by any broader analysis, are the sources of indigenous reflection on the U.S. "betrayal" and responsibility for the subsequent collapse of their armies.

Interpretive Authority and the History of Power

Together, these methodological choices conflate the two problematic and usually contrastive tendencies noted at the start as characteristic of casual approaches to oral history: the uncritical elevation of the historical authority of experience, and the reservation of interpretive power to those seemingly qualified to pass judgment. Thus, in *Vietnam: A Television History*, entry is reserved to those with direct testimony to offer, whether commoner or king, and this is made the base of meaning—the "Anti-History," "Vas You Dere, Chollie?" approach. But the "More History" approach to testimony—placing experience in analytic perspective—is also at the heart of the enterprise. Because interpreters with other bases of authority have been excluded and in the interests of a nonmanipulative tone the narrator has foresworn extensive commentary, most of the explicit interpretation necessarily has to come from those figures of stature who, here as in "real life," hold the power not only to act, but to define the terms in which their actions, past as well as present, have meaning.

I am thus suggesting that the mode of presenting oral-historical material in the documentary makes impossible a genuinely critical assessment of the history of power. However balanced the footage between Americans and North Vietnamese, between generals and foot soldiers, between oppressors and victims, on whatever side, the larger politics cannot really be engaged because nonprivileged sources of reflection and analysis, and privileged but noncomplicit sources of knowledge and perspective, are equally excluded by oral-historical definition.

Such a result need not be the consequence of deliberate intent or explicit bias. In this instance, I suspect it derives from documentary convenience as much as anything else, the search for a simple, modular strategy that could shape the construction of thirteen episodes with vastly different subject matter so that they had a reasonably consistent look, feel, and sound. Given the casual way in which oral history has generally been discussed, and given how infrequently, though it lies at the heart of the overall method, it has figured in the criticism of this widely-discussed documentary, the producers can not be singled out for particular insensitivity to the deeper historical implications of their documentary approach. But the point is that choices have been made, however implicitly—on the wider map of possibilities charted in this essay, particular paths have been etched consistently and deeply enough to end up having a great deal to do with the shape and meaning of the History that results.

This brings us back to the point raised at the start of this paper, the general need for more critical self-consciousness about what oral history is and how it is and might better be used in a full range of public documentary forms. I believe oral history can contribute a substantial counter to officially received history and officially defined policy, by empowering people to generate alternative understandings and approaches. But for this to happen, we will need more critical self-awareness of the method and materials, the choices we face in using them, and how our decisions function as a mode of historical communication to broad audiences. In the absence of such an understanding, *Vietnam: A Television History* suggests that oral history may have the effect, far more readily than generally realized, of reinforcing the power and authority of those its proponents so often imagine it to be challenging.

Part III

A Shared Authority: Scholarship, Audience, and Public Presentation

Headnotes

This section's essays illustrate the thematic convergence discussed in the introduction. In them, I began to extend to public programming, community projects, and exhibition ideas originally developed in the course of working with oral history. The essays also engage, more directly than in the previous sections, the specific issues—and possibilities—raised by the interaction of scholarly authority and wider public involvement in presentations of history.

The section opens with a grouping of three essays that approach these concerns from several vantages. The first originated as one of several invited theme presentations to the 1981 annual meeting of the National Federation of State Humanities Councils. These talks were designed to advance discussion of how public humanities programs could more effectively reach and involve diverse publics while also presenting the best insights of humanistic scholarship. I had become more involved in oral history grantsmanship at the time, as a consultant, mostly unsuccessful grantwriter, and program evaluator; this invitation gave me a chance to consolidate this experience in reflections on the specific challenge of community programming.

To do this, the essay literally redirected themes and text from some of the earlier oral history essays and reviews, using this material to a very different end. Hopefully the value of illustrating this process—a natural one for scholars who often develop bigger ideas through such piecework—balances the modest repetition involved. The essay was published in 1982 by the Federation in a pamphlet collection of these presentations, under the title *What Portion In the World?*

The next essay arose from an invitation of a very different kind. As noted in the introduction, my formal training and earliest published work was in nineteenth century American urban history. My dissertation was a study of the city-building process as illustrated in the history of Springfield, Massachusetts. This was published in Harvard University Press's new urban history series, in 1972, under the title *Town Into City: Springfield, Massachusetts and the Meaning of Community, 1840-1880*. Whatever the academic impact and reputation of this work elsewhere, it was almost guaranteed a certain position in Springfield's heart. When the city prepared to celebrate its 350th birthday in 1986, I was invited to return, along with a number of other writers who had dealt with the city's history, to offer one of a series of anniversary public lectures.

The invitation forced me to wrestle with the personal dichotomy discussed earlier, between urban-historical research scholarship and my more recent involvement in public history. Rather than simply recapitulate a fifteen-year-old book, I tried in this presentation to explore what relevance my own work, and formal academic urban history in general, might have for Springfield in the present—and what, more broadly, public interest in history and academic concerns might have to do with each other. The lecture was published in the locally produced and only locally relevant volume coming out of this celebratory series. But as a record of an approach to public history from the standpoint of scholarship, I think it may have value in this collection even for readers uninterested in my monograph's issues and unfamiliar with the local references.

The third essay in the group reverses the focus, in a sense, by exploring what popular history offers to a scholarly audience used to treating its products—in this case coffee-table picture books—with patronizing condescension. The essay culminates a long series of academic book reviews in which I began to find myself forging insights from oral and public history into tools for criticism of scholarship, finding these insights surprisingly relevant to substantive issues about evidence and interpretation needing greater attention by historians.

I had originally planned to include a garland of some of these smaller book reviews in this collection, as a way of showing how ideas evolve through such practice. Few things seem more ephemeral than short book reviews, yet it is not surprising to discover that many scholars seem to plow some of their most fertile soil under the satisfying yoke of such assignments. Space did not permit this indulgence, however, and I can now concede that perhaps it is best to leave the reviews ephemeral, especially as the themes end up in more concentrated form in larger essays resulting from the process, of which "Get the Picture?", appearing in *New York History* in 1988, is a good example.

The collection concludes with three quite resonant essays dealing with public history, appropriate concluding essays in that the book's theme of shared authority is here developed the most explicitly, yet in a variety of forms. The first deals with public history generally, although in the form of a very specific case study about the relation of site and audience. It is a product of an unusual pathbreaking conference organized by the New York Council for the Humanities in 1984. This event brought together historians, museum directors and staff, designers, and programmers of all sorts to begin to create a discourse about common interests. It featured a unique combination of visits to diverse historic sites and interpretations, small-group discussion about these en route to and from the site, and plenary sessions dealing with common themes and problems. I served, together with National Park Service historian Dwight Pitcaithley, as "expedition leader" for one of the field trips, to Ellis Island in the last days of its pre-renovation status as an interpreted historic ruin. Pitcaithley and I developed our reflections on both tour and discussion as a contribution to the valuable book of conference essays that organizer Jo Blatti edited for the Smithsonian Institution Press in 1987, entitled, as was the event itself, *Past Meets Present.*

This leads to an essay that parallels the movement in the preceding cluster by narrowing the focus to urban history, in order better to engage the relationship between modern scholarship and new possibilities for presentation. Previously unpublished, it was originally drafted for the 1986 annual meeting of the Social Science History Association. For this audience, I explored some of the lessons about the public "translatability" of social-scientific scholarship, lessons I learned when, as an associate at Theodore Hershberg's cliometrically controversial Philadelphia Social History Project, I helped develop a travelling neighborhood history exhibit for the City of Philadelphia's 1982 tercentenary celebration.

These themes echo in the book's final essay, which examines the current state of historical interpretation in a number of major big city history museums. It offers some thoughts on where this dimension of practice seems to be headed, and, as a kind of collection-summary-in-effect, it argues the importance of recasting the relationship between audience and urban scholarship, based on an appreciation of alternative bases of interpretive authority and on the as yet untested possibilities of dialogue between them. This essay was written as the urban history contribution to a new collection of very useful theme or topic-specific essays on the relationship between historians, history, and museums. Organized and edited by Warren Leon and Roy Rosenzweig and titled *History Museums in the United States: A Critical Assessment*, this book was published in 1989 by the University of Illinois Press.

Chapter 8

Quality in History Programs:
From Celebration to Exploration of Values

This title, originally assigned by a conference organizer, not only raises questions, but also suggests a framework in which they may be answered. It suggests that history programs have been deficient to the extent they have focused on parochial celebrations and that quality may be obtained by finding ways to shift the emphasis to a broader humanistic exploration of values. Beneath this formulation is an implicit assumption that such programs involve almost by definition a tension between public and community expectations, on the one hand, and the perspective brought by humanists on the other. There also seems to be a hint in the title—despite the absence of an activating verb—that humanists ought to be more aggressive or less reticent about pushing for such broader exploration and that funding agencies like the state humanities councils ought to be more insistent that proposals transcend the narrowly celebratory.

I am not so sure that this formulation is the most helpful way to get at what are some very real and pressing problems. Accordingly, I begin by first recasting the issue somewhat. Then, I explore, as a specific illustration, some issues and opportunities in a programming area I know well—community-based oral history projects. I hope this discussion supports a more general argument that quality in public history programs is not to be found by regarding the genre itself as inherently problematic and beset by contradictory tensions. Rather, I want to show that public history offers some very special and unique characteristics that need only be more fully appreciated and expressed in order for programming to become a source of value exploration and broader public meaning.

Let me begin, then, by taking a closer look at what is involved in the perceived "quality gap" in contemporary programming. In recent years, public history has sought to extend beyond the limits of conventional academic scholarship in several related dimensions: it has sought a broader audience, a broader sense of what (and whose) history is appropriate for public attention, whether celebratory or exploratory, and it has sought a broader range of participation in the process of actually "doing history"—in collecting, forming, assessing, and articulating a sense of the historical past.

Much of the recent criticism of public history programming has centered, variously, on whether it has gone too far or not far enough in some or all of these directions. Many have faulted programs for giving in to a tempting parochialism and not succeeding in introducing broader humanistic perspective and content. Other critics have charged that the impulse has been worse than parochial, introducing dangerously "presentist" populistic bottom-up orientations that have undercut a more appropriate and elevated discourse about history. In the hands of the Heritage Foundation (which wrote a report attacking the National Endowment for the Humanities (NEH) at the start of the Reagan Administration), such criticisms have transparently political purpose, but the concern must be acknowledged to be a wide one. A roughly parallel critique from the left as well: that public history has been on the verge of succeeding in opening the way to new questions, which is why so many efforts to bring it under more direct professional and/or political control are now evident.

What is interesting about these varied criticisms is the degree to which they share certain assumptions, in particular the belief that an antithesis exists between professional and community roles and interests, and that an alteration must be made in one direction or the other. The politics of public history criticism, that is, often come down to debates about who is framing and executing the program, for what purposes, and for what audiences. These debates, in turn, are often worked out in terms of the appropriate qualifications of designers, the "mix" of participants, the "role" of humanists and community members, and the formats chosen for reaching specified audiences in intended ways.

I am concerned about the temptation to see the issue of quality as derived from, if not quite reducible to, such structural considerations. Any public program must, by definition, embody some resolution of these questions; its dimensions express the relationship between them. But given a structural mix, it is at least arguable that the essential quality of a program may derive as much from the process of the interaction of elements, rather than their relative roles or proportions in the structure of a program. Rather than inquiring about the adequacy of community involvement or the sufficiency of the humanists' contribution, we might do better to take a closer-than-usual look at how the program brings these elements together and the room it allows for their interaction. This may seem only a slight adjustment of perspective, another way of saying the same thing, because obviously structure and process are closely related. In my experience with oral history projects, however, the distinction is important and poorly understood: an overemphasis on formal structure has had much to do with the uneven quality of so many projects. Conversely, a greater sensitivity to process may help to diagnose the problem and provide resources for its resolution at the same time.

Understanding why oral history has been so close to the center of the explosion of public historical activity is easy. As an activity and a program production tool, it is unintimidating and accessible; its products are generally interesting and hardly exclusive in their appeal. It thus contributes readily to the three dimensions mentioned above: the broadening of the audience, of the subject matter and issue of concern, and of the participatory base in history-making. It is helping to refashion our sense of what history is, who does it, under what auspices, and to what end.

Yet oral history projects also stand very close to the center of the controversy about public funding for history programs. They have been singled out for special criticism in the Heritage Foundation report and other attacks. They have offered more than enough ammunition for those seeking to expose seemingly frivolous, poorly planned, make-work projects of little public significance or impact. There is a sense in which these attacks are a backhanded tribute to the way oral history programs have succeeded in challenging, or at least threatening, an established orthodoxy, both professional and community-based. But a fair-minded analysis must conclude that legitimate grounds for concern exist. The very accessibility of oral history has made it too popular for its own good, and often it is approached uncritically and with little preparation, conducted haphazardly, and presented indifferently. Practitioners are concerned that a serious approach has turned into a fad, one that will inevitably raise unrealistic expectations and lead only to disappointment, with an inevitable devaluation of the currency of the overall field. Although my comments are not meant to characterize all or even most publicly funded projects, from a public history vantage it seems safe to conclude that concern about the issue of quality is germane, perhaps urgently so.

Much recent discussion about oral history programs, consequently, has focused on what might be called the issue of quality control. In this, as in the industrial origin of the term, the emphasis has been more on control than on the definition of quality. Project planners, prodded by evaluators and program officers, have given great attention to reinforcing the role of humanist scholars, both to validate the historicity of oral testimony and to help ensure that public presentations contribute to a broader historical vision. Meanwhile, academic humanists themselves have been working to improve the training of oral historians, to develop usable guidelines and criteria for evaluation of community oral history projects, and to institutionalize skills through new degree programs in public history.

These impulses are generally appropriate and often quite constructive, though they fall somewhat short of being self-evidently and universally appro-

priate, as seen in the growing feeling among experienced community historians that "credentialization" may be intended primarily to secure jobs for
academics at the expense of the uncredentialed, or will at least have that
effect. But beyond such problematic aspects, the quality-control impulse is
not so much right or wrong as it is simply beside the point. This is because
the issue of quality in oral history programs has less to do with who is in
control than with how the method is being understood, used, and presented.
And the differences that matter in this regard, it turns out, cannot be located
comfortably along the frequently invoked spectrum that locates nostalgic,
uncritical, and naive amateurs at one end, and value-sensitive academic
humanists at the other. These assertions require some discussion if an alternative landscape is to become accessible.

In a curious sense, oral history has been of such self-evident importance
that few have stopped to think about what it is, beyond the obvious, that
makes it worth pursuing. The term itself is provocative in this respect: it
implies both the raw material for study, and the product of that study in some
intelligible, communicable form. But the relation between the archiving and
collecting of data and the production of history from it has been finessed in
many projects. In some cases it has been ignored entirely with—in community based projects—runaway tape collection the result. This problem occurs
throughout the field on a more professional basis as well, whether the approach
is top-down or bottom-up. Information is not history in any other dimension
of research, and there is no reason to make tape recording an exception. But
while intended public program use underscores the importance of understanding how oral history is to be used, beyond accumulating audiotape cassettes on the library shelves, most oral history projects have dealt with such
issues obliquely, if at all. The prevailing emphasis has been on what can be
termed—only partly in jest—a supply-side approach, more concerned with generating oral history materials than with presenting them critically to some
clearly thought-through public purpose.

To understand why this is the case requires a closer look not at who is doing
the projects under what control, but rather at the underlying assumptions
informing much of this work. From this vantage point, I think it can be said that
most oral historians proceed on the intuitive assumption that oral history does
one of two things, or perhaps both. First, it provides a source of new information
about otherwise inaccessible experience. In this sense, it is seen as a kind of
searchlight throwing a beam of inquiry into an ordinarily unreachable corner of
the attic of history. This presumes that what is discovered in this beam will then
be incorporated into more traditional historical understandings, and evaluated
for validity and significance with and against other kinds of information. The
second approach assumes that conventional historical frameworks are not only
inadequate, but more fundamentally obstructive of deeper understanding. In

this sense, oral history is offered as a way to bypass such obstacles, a short cut to a more direct, emotionally informed sense of "the way it was." What better way, in this view, to touch the "real" history than by communicating with it directly, rather than filtering everything through the usual screen of historical narrative, and pushing it all through the even more relentless and destructive mill of academic analysis? In this view, oral history is a method for obtaining first person experience, and for presenting it with relatively little mediation by the intellectualizing and abstraction of scholarship.

In practice, oral history has tended to shuttle uncomfortably between these two poles, between what could be called the "more history" approach on the one hand, and an "anti-history" sense of the gestalt of the past on the other. These poles suggest quite different approaches to what and how oral history "means," and consequently to how it should be used in public programs. Moreover, these conceptual positions vastly complicate the issue of "quality," for they tend to have no necessary correlation with the structural issues I have mentioned—the role of academic humanists, the relation to particular audiences, and so on. For example, it is true that professional historians are often "written in" to oral history projects in order to validate the quality of the testimony collected and presented. Nevertheless, this structural role frequently has little critical impact because it reinforces assumptions already in place: many such projects are parochial precisely because they are, from an amateur standpoint, the "more history" orientation. In fact, they frequently are simply mirroring conventional history by chronicling community leaders, events, and contributions, thereby generating the very celebratory problems that a more professional orientation is expected to resolve.

Similarly, academic humanists themselves have often taken the lead in stressing the "anti-history" approach, especially with regard to the presentation of oral historical materials, seeking to upset conventional notions through the powerful images oral documents can convey. But this has sometimes made the problems only worse: humanists withhold the critical contributions they might make out of a desire to avoid imposing interpretation on people's experience. In some instances, the reticence is less straightforward, leading to suspicions that material is being manipulated and shaped to a given end, then presented in a form that offers little room for historical reflection, appearing simply to be a vision grounded directly in oral testimony.

If I am correct that deeper divisions about the nature and purpose of oral history underlie debates about "quality" and undercut structural reforms seeking such quality, then perhaps a clearer understanding of what the oral method can do may be helpful in clearing a path to more satisfactory programming. My own work and a good deal of program evaluation suggests that many of the qualitative dilemmas of program design and public presentation can be substantially diminished by a fuller appreciation of the processes of oral history and their public implications.

On this close examination, it is readily apparent that the main value of oral history is neither in the "more history" nor "anti-history" styles. The former requires substantial validation and contextualizing, easy enough in scholarship but a real obstacle to public presentation; the second can hardly be taken very seriously as an approach to the immediacy of the past, because testimony recorded years after the fact can hardly be evidence of how experience felt at the time, or what people thought about it then, in the sense often claimed.

But these weaknesses are, in fact, oral history's strengths. Invert these disadvantages, and oral history emerges a powerful tool for discovering, exploring, and evaluating the nature of the process of historical memory—how people make sense of their past, how they connect individual experience and its social context, how the past becomes part of the present, and how people use it to interpret their lives and the world around them. In an infrequently noted preface to *Hard Times*, author Studs Terkel observed that the collection was really "a memory book, rather than one of hard facts and precise statistics." He quoted Steinbeck's Pa Joad, who said of another character: "He's telling the truth, awright. The truth for him. He wasn't makin' nothin' up." As Terkel suggests, memory is the key to the meaning and uses of oral history, not merely its imperfect means. It forces us to look at what interviews actually represent.

Oral history is unique in that it creates its own documents, documents that are by definition explicit dialogues about the past, with the "subject" necessarily triangulated between past experience and the present context of remembering. The centrality of the process, I believe, offers some important resource for public presentation and community-based programming. In the first place, it leads to a more mutually reinforcing relationship between historian and "subjects." Historians have generally been uncomfortable with memory, committed as they are to notions of objectivity and truth beyond the subjectivity of individual and collective recall. Yet, to the extent that these same historians frequently bemoan their isolation from public discourse, it may be useful to reflect on the power of shared memory to repair precisely this relationship and give it energy. History, Staughton Lynd observed, is simply people remembering things, a point made even clearer by noticing a linguistic curiosity: in English, we have no verb that corresponds to the noun history. We can talk about doing history, reading it, writing it, or studying it, but there is no way to express concisely the activity and process of rendering the past comprehensible. With the phenomenon of memory, this is not the case at all: in fact, the relationship is virtually reversed in that the noun memory cannot exist without presuming the active verb, to remember. Involved as well, also by definition, is the leap across time from the "then" of happening to the "now" of recall.

It is this kind of "active-ity," I think, that we often have in mind when we seek to design programs that are relevant and explore wider historical and not-so-historical values. In oral history, this quality emerges from the nature of the central process, and the forging of a connection between past and present is made by those on both sides of the tape recorder. Yet, the engagement between the truths of history and the truths of memory is only implicit in the process of oral history; for its meaning to be more fully developed requires a self-conscious commitment by all concerned to explore the meaning of experience and its connection to people's lives in the present.

Making informed reflection on memory the focus of oral history programming, as it is the heart of the methodology itself, turns out to be a good bit harder than it sounds and not simply for technical reasons. Audiences, lay and professional, used to perceiving history from a safe distance, often resist attempts at closing the gap, especially when that process collapses comfortable assumptions as well. Nevertheless, I am increasingly persuaded that such a focus holds an important key to the elusive quality we seek, precisely because of its ability to reduce the ground between humanists and community people without obliterating the distinction between their perspectives and without denying particular value to each. It provides, in short, an appropriate meeting ground for the common exploration of the meaning of historical experience. It recognizes that humanists have a crucial responsibility to provide perspective and questions helpful in this exploration process, but it also acknowledges that memory itself has much to teach and that its vantage point is a valuable one for more general reflection. It leads to a genuine sharing, not only of historical experience, but of the "author-ity" for its interpretation.

These considerations suggest some criteria for assessing public history programs based on oral history. My sense is that the greatest need is for projects that take seriously the task of involving people in exploring what it means to remember, and what to do with memories to make them active and alive, as opposed to mere objects of collection and classification. The vulnerability of oral history will only be increased, and quality further undermined, by continuing to focus, as so many projects do, on the generation of overly general images of the past presented without serious reflection or discussion. It will not be helped by continuing to rely on professional humanists to validate and certify and interpret the experience of oral history informants.

Recently, I attended an ambitious labor history symposium that brought together academics, trade unionists, and community people. The symposium featured the presentation, both in person and on videotape, of oral history interviews concerning the militant strikes that organized steel workers in the 1930s, amidst great conflict and violence. It was a wonderful presentation, which the audience seem to follow intently and with great enjoyment. It was not clear until one overheard comments in the lobby, however, that people had seen it very differently: many of the academics heard in the tapes evidence of the pervasiveness of class conflict and a call to militance inspired by labor's heritage of struggle. But the trade-unionists seemed to come away with a very different message: recalling the "bad old days," they said, made them appreciate the distance between then and now, as measured by their current no-strike contracts, grievance procedures, and pension benefits. But the interviews had not focused on such messages in either sense, and the program offered no opportunity or framework for discussing, contrasting, and evaluating the connection of this particular past to the present. However vivid the testimony, and however professionally conducted, the history was simply offered for immediate consumption. The program ended where it should have begun.

My remarks have focused here on oral history programming, but I think the implications are broader. To focus on the process of interaction, and the distribution of interpretive authority more broadly among program participants, may be relevant in other areas as well. I have been involved, for instance, in designing a community-based public history program for the City of Philadelphia's 300th birthday celebration. Much of this will involve what might seem to be the opposite pole from oral history: computer-generated, social-scientific data developed by the Philadelphia Social History Project. Yet in some ways our approach is similar to what I have been describing here: we want to distribute the resources and some of the skills through which people can be empowered to recreate for themselves a detailed portrait of their neighborhood and its people over time, and, on this basis, come to discuss the history of their neighborhood in relation to their current concerns as citizens. The focus is neither on teaching lessons about the past nor trying to "evoke" it: rather, the program features the process of active discovery, in order to liberate the imagination process, informed as well by all the experience, knowledge, and perspective that people bring to the event.

This leads to a more general observation. My own experience in public history convinces me that the crisis of quality is real and must be addressed. Yet, we need to appreciate and understand the extent to which the distinctive nature of public historical processes—in contrast to either formal academic work or conventional antiquarian local history—offers, in itself, the resources for responding to this crisis. Clearly, broad humanistic perspective, reflection, and interpretation must be central to the process. But closer attention to the nature of public history also suggests the importance of humanists relinquishing what, in many cases, has been a kind of interpretive monopoly and to find better ways of sharing this authority with the relevant publics. This is not without its risks, but they are worth taking, for it is only in this way that we can move from the static celebration of the past toward what must—to have any value—be a mutual and active exploration of values.

Chapter 9

Town into City:
A Reconsideration on the Occasion of
Springfield's 350th Anniversary, 1636-1986

Springfield Present and Past

I first came to Springfield in 1965, as a history graduate student begin-
ning the research that would eventually become my 1972 book, *Town into
City: Springfield, Massachusetts and the Meaning of Community, 1840-1880.*[1]
Shortly before I left a year and one-half later, I recall that a reporter named
Peg Schumacher wrote a very gracious newspaper feature describing my
research and my interest in the city. She concluded by predicting that my
book would be a success, and that I would go on to "write other books about
Springfield's history."

While it is not for me to evaluate the first prediction, I must confess that
I never lived up to the second; although I have gone on to specialize in the
history of city development generally, my Springfield research did not extend
beyond that dissertation project. I have retained a great fondness for the city
and still have some close friends that I made during my research year here.
Most of what I know about Springfield history, however, is contained in the
book, and it would serve little purpose to repeat it here.

What I offer, instead, are some comments designed to help put that story
in a wider context, one appropriate both to the reflective mood of Springfield's
anniversary celebration and to the general framework of urban-historical scholarship in which I have been working since I finished my book some fifteen
years ago. In reviewing again Springfield's growth between 1840 and 1880,
roughly the period in which it changed from a modest town to a major inland
city, my main purpose is to extract whatever lessons that history may hold for
cities and their people today, both here in Springfield and more broadly
as well.

To seek the lessons of history is a deceptively treacherous endeavor, of course. It is one thing to march bravely forth under the banner of George Santayana's over-quoted maxim, "Those who forget the past are condemned to repeat it." But Santayana was a philosopher, not an historian. His remark describes an attitude best applied to past mistakes one seeks to avoid in the future, and even then one has to avoid taking him too literally: bad generals are always prepared to re-fight the last battle rather than to anticipate the inevitably different next one.

In fact, I have long had the feeling that as far as urban history is concerned, the maxim might be reversed to read: "Those who remember the past are condemned to repeat it." And if this sounds like a good thing, considering the seeming success of the city-building celebrated in a 350th-year anniversary, remember the droll observation of Karl Marx, a man not usually noted for his sense of humor, to the effect that history always repeats itself—the first time as drama, the second time as farce.

Among other things, this means that history provides no pat formulas one can simply repeat; Springfield's nineteenth-century expansion offers few recipes that would produce the same results in today's urban-planning kitchens. What history does offer is a chance to learn about the *process* of change: how choices are conditioned by circumstance; how vast social and economic structures interact with chance, will, and imagination; how the pressure for change arises, and how the direction, definition, resources, and opportunities for change become the object of struggle and contention in the urban community. And as we come to appreciate these complex dynamics in the past, we are, I hope, empowered to work with them more effectively in the present—where we must make our own choices to meet our own unique conditions. This being said, let me consider the relationship between nineteenth-century Springfield and the city today, in the 350th year of its history.

Springfield Present and Past

My return visit to Springfield, after an absence of some years, provides two very different impressions; perhaps it is best to use both of them as a starting point for our historical excursion.

The first allows me to correct a happily outdated judgment in my book. In my chapter on the surge of civic architecture in the 1860's and 1870's, mostly downtown, I described what was then considered "the finest public building in Western Massachusetts," the Springfield Institution for Savings (SIS) on the northeast corner of State and Main Streets. And I noted, somewhat patronizingly, that "today it seems a thoroughly modest and ordinary structure, the survival of which is not a very flattering comment on the progress of Springfield's central business district (CBD), in the present century."[2] The last ten years have certainly proved that I should have stuck to strictly historical judgments, for the transformation of the CBD has been truly spectacular—the civic center to which the SIS building finally gave way, the towering hotels and Bay State West project, the high-rise apartments and the street changes, the major new commercial buildings on and around Court Square, and the completion of the interstate highway net through downtown. The change is dramatic and inescapable; clearly, much has happened in Springfield.

Or has it? I visited my former neighborhood, which is near Winchester Square on the Hill. The only visible changes here have been for the worse—the commercial center, on the verge of disaster fifteen years ago, has toppled over the edge since, and presents a picture of near-total disintegration; the seeming business prosperity downtown has evidently not trickled uphill in Springfield. Meanwhile, the surrounding streets and homes appear comparatively stable—a modest, struggling district showing signs of involvement and household commitment, evidence of community continuity, survival, and determination in the face of deep, unrelenting economic distress.

Together, these contrasting observations raise larger questions: when we say Springfield, who and what do we mean? Which is more central, the picture of Winchester Square or the famous "imitation Time Magazine" booster publication that trumpeted the arrival of the new Springfield—and included many pictures, but few of the top of the Hill? How do we define and measure progress, and what do we take as its best indicators? It is not simply a matter of attitudes, values, or politics, but rather of how one defines the problem at hand. When impatient disciples demanded to know, "What is the Answer?", a wise woman once responded, "Well, what is the Question?"

The importance of defining broad questions is especially acute for historians of the middle and end of the nineteenth century. This was an era of enormous complexity in every dimension—tremendous innovation, growth, and change in the structures of business, industry, and work; sustained social and political conflict over the direction and meaning of these changes; and a churning volatility in the population itself: its structure and location and the basic patterns of individual, family, and group life.

In Springfield and similar communities, then as now, it is easy to miss some of this complexity when focusing attention on the front pages and the more dramatic changes or events. To the media, the business community, the civic leaders, and perhaps many of the on-looking citizens, the city meant growth, economic progress, building, and institutional development; these were what mattered and provided the standards by which Springfield would be measured. And yet, listen to this very different image of American society, written at a point of confident growth and expansion a century or so ago, and for reasons that will become apparent, worth quoting at length:

I cannot do better than to compare society as it was then to a prodigious coach which the masses of humanity were harnessed to and dragged toilsomely along a very hilly and sandy road. The driver was hunger, and permitted no lagging, though the pace was necessarily slow. Despite the difficulty of drawing the coach at all along so hard a road, the top was covered with passengers who never got down, even at the steepest ascents. These seats on top were very breezy and comfortable. Well up out of the dust, their occupants could enjoy the scenery at their leisure, or critically discuss the merits of the straining team. Naturally such places were in great demand and the competition for them was keen, every one seeking as the first end in life to secure a seat on the coach for himself, and to leave it to his child after him. By the rule of the coach a man could leave his seat to whom he wished, but on the other hand there were many accidents by which it might at any time be wholly lost. For all that they were so easy, the seats were very insecure, and at every sudden jolt of the coach persons were slipping out of them and falling to the ground, where they were instantly compelled to take hold of the rope and help to drag the coach on which they had before ridden so pleasantly. It was naturally regarded as a terrible misfortune to lose one's seat, and the apprehension that this might happen to them or their friends was a constant cloud upon the happiness of those who rode.

But did they think only of themselves? you ask. Was not their very luxury rendered intolerable to them by comparison with the lot of their brothers and sisters in the harness, and the knowledge that their own weight added to their toil? Had they no compassion for fellow beings from whom fortune only distinguished them? Oh, yes; commiseration was frequently expressed by those who rode for those who had to pull the coach, especially when the vehicle came to a bad place in the road, as it was constantly doing, or to a particularly steep hill. At such times, the desperate straining of the team, their agonized leaping and plunging under the pitiless lashing of hunger, the many who fainted at the rope and were trampled in the mire, made a very distressing spectacle, which often called forth highly creditable displays of feeling on the top of the coach. At such times the passengers would call down encouragingly to the toilers of the rope, exhorting them to patience, and holding out hopes of possible compensation in another world for the hardness of their lot, while others contributed to buy salves and liniments for the crippled and injured. It was agreed that it was a great pity that the coach should be so hard to pull, and there was a sense of general relief when the specially bad piece of road was gotten over. This relief was not, indeed, wholly on account of the team, for there was always some danger at these bad places of a general overturn in which all would lose their seats.

It must in truth be admitted that the main effect of the spectacle of the misery of the toilers at the rope was to enhance the passengers' sense of the value of their seats upon the coach, and to cause them to hold on to them more desperately than before. If the passengers could only have felt assured that neither they nor their friends would ever fall from the top, it is probable that, beyond contributing to the funds for liniments and bandages, they would have troubled themselves extremely little about those who dragged the coach.[3]

This is from the world-famous 1887 novel *Looking Backward*, written by Edward Bellamy, a novel with an important Springfield connection: Bellamy grew up in Chicopee during the period my book discusses, and during its latter years he observed Springfield from his desk as a writer for the Springfield *Union*; surely, what he saw in the swiftly changing city and region helped form the broad social vision unfolded in his novel. Just as today's view from Winchester Square helps us keep the downtown "renaissance" in perspective, it will help to keep Bellamy's critique in mind as we turn our historical focus to the major city-building developments that are the concern of my book, and my remarks here.

The City-building Process and its Lessons

Legally, Springfield changed from town to city in 1852, but the process of becoming a city in more than name and form took much longer. It involved a rapid tripling of the population from some 11,000 in 1850 to 33,000 in 1880. It involved the evolution of a sophisticated economy based on diversified manufacturing centered on, but hardly limited to, armory-related production and on the city's evolving role as the major regional railroad, commercial, and business center. It involved tremendous physical and architectural change downtown and in swiftly expanding neighborhoods. It produced a definitively urban infrastructure with paved streets, domestic water service, and trunk sewers. It involved the development of recognizably modern urban institutions—a professionalized public school system, a reformed pubic welfare structure, the beginnings of public hospital care. It saw the emergence of a sophisticated urban culture, and social conflicts equally characteristic of Gilded Age urban life. Springfield even had its own mini-version of "Tweedism"—allegations of municipal corruption that, however disturbing, seemed a kind of token of the city's having ascended into the "big leagues" in terms of political machines and troubled urban administration.

All these developments are detailed in the book. As I reread them after some years, I am struck by a theme that supports so much of the narrative that I never quite opened it up for fuller discussion as such. This is the simple observation that city-building does not just "happen" as part of an independent process of "growth"; it is not a matter of obvious, necessary, inevitable, or even natural responses to stages or levels of urbanization. Rather, it represents something far more complex and interesting: a community's varied understandings, usually imperfect, of what was happening in and around it, and the even more complex process by which diverse people defined a range of options and how choices among these were made—choices that, in sum, add up to what can seem a century later a deceptively smooth process of institutional growth.

Consider, for instance, what at first might seem to be the unlikely proposition that Springfield's expansion in the late 1860s and early 1870s—the most substantial, definitive period of institutional growth—traces largely to the city's agonizing responsibility, during the Civil War, for raising troops and caring for wounded veterans returning home through the city's railroad terminals.

I found, in my study, that many otherwise necessary and justifiable changes in the city, before the war, were simply not considered because the expense would require borrowing and taxes, and because the notion of extensive municipal spending for public purposes was literally unimaginable, given the tradition of most New England communities during that period. But the Civil War obligations, largely imposed from outside by extraordinary circumstance, changed all that: the city government saw spending soar from $70,000 to $235,000, more than doubling per capita. Debt tripled, forcing the city to develop mechanisms for managing such an obligation responsibly. The emergency passed, but the mechanisms and a new attitude towards public spending remained, with the result that the postwar years saw Springfield bring to environmental and institutional proposals a new, distinctly municipal approach, with the finances to match: after an 1866 tax rate that would not be surpassed until the 1920s, the burden of spending shifted steadily onto a structure of long-term municipal bonds and notes. The change was not simply a response to urban pressures, but a more complex evolution in community politics, values, and relationships.

Similarly, one might think that the development of municipal water and sewer systems would be a relatively simple matter: the population density grows; adequate private wells and cesspools become mutually exclusive; public responsibility for bringing in pure water and removing waste is assumed. Here, too, I found a much more complex story with some intriguing twists: in addition to the implicit "threshold of spending" barriers just mentioned, which for so long inhibited what might seem necessary and obvious responses to the needs of a rising population, a more particular conceptual reorientation concerning water had to be found.

In the long history of towns such as Springfield, municipal water had been intended for only one purpose, protection of property against fire; sewer drains, similarly, were for the purpose of draining and hence improving property. In both cases, the cost was appropriately shared with adjacent property holders deemed protected or "bettered" by the improvement. The move toward general municipal systems for drinking water provision and waste-water removal had to follow a gradually altered perspective from property to public health, and one with dramatic administrative implications, because far from there being a direct link to taxable property holders, those most in need (and hence likely to threaten the health of others) were those without property to protect, poor workers living in the most densely settled areas of the industrial city—Bellamy's coach pullers. All of this, I found, made for a fascinating and rich story on every level from technology and administration to politics and even art—if you will believe that the then-novel notion of an entire city linked organically by a trunk sewer system could inspire eloquent poetry both for and against!

Such comments make the Springfield of 100 years ago seem quaint, provincial, and very far away. Indeed it was, and distant in some deeper structural ways as well. Then it was an expanding city in an expanding region of a dramatically expanding national economy; today it is in a struggling section of a troubled national economy whose industrial base is at best "mature" in a world perspective, which really means in decline. The nineteenth-century growth I chronicle was directed by a consolidated political and economic elite grounded in and deeply committed to the community; today, few aspects of Springfield's economy are locally owned and controlled, raising the question of what local community can mean when there is no longer much of a genuinely local economy.

Finally, it is obvious that the social structure and dynamics of today's city have little in common with that of a century ago. Not only is the population arrayed much differently, in class, racial, and ethnic terms, but the relation of people to the community institutions, on which so much of my analysis turned, is close to inverted. Then, in Springfield and similar cities, the "business classes" and established families were understood to be elites securely rooted in time and place; rather, the working people and the poor were taken (often inaccurately, in fact) to be rootless, drifting from place to place in search of subsistence, without a visible "stake" in the local community's fortunes and hence indifferent to most local decisions. Now, of course, it is those very working-class communities that we understand to be grounded in place, at the heart of our older cities, while capital flees to the sunbelt or the Third World, and business leaders scale the corporate ladder by moving from one branch city or office or firm to another, with commitment to a specific place no more interrupting their ascent than it characterizes the interchangeable suburbs they so often inhabit.

Nevertheless, I think there is still considerable, even surprising relevance for today's Springfield in the story of its first emergence into urban form and stature. Let me then draw together some themes, running all through the city-building process I trace in my book, that begin to suggest how powerfully this history can speak to us in the present.

The first lesson of this story is the central role of the urban political process in the broadest sense, meaning not just government institutions, but the community opinion, leadership, and pressure that all contribute to defining the issues, identifying the options, bringing whatever passes for expertise to bear, setting the limits for what seems imaginable and realistic, and, finally, making actual decisions and exercising power. In late nineteenth-century Springfield, this process was dominated by the business community and those property owners and civic leaders considered to have the greatest "stake" in Springfield's growth and development; shortly thereafter, as I discuss presently, it came to mean something considerably more inclusive and contentious. But the point in common is that the defining process of city-building is more broadly political and even cultural than it is mechanical, technical, or administrative in nature.

A second major theme is that understanding a city's history requires remaining aware of what is happening outside the local context and understanding how that frame of reference becomes central to local self-definition. Cities such as Springfield were subject to what has to be called a kind of frantic peer pressure in the competition for survival and growth in industrializing America. Keeping up with the Worcesters and the Hartfords (and pulling far ahead of the Northamptons and the Westfields) was not just a matter of status—it seemed a matter of survival. And as the city grew, so did its frame of reference: a piping system that might have seemed appropriate in one year suddenly came to appear provincial and pedestrian the next, whether the demand for water had perceptibly intensified in the interval. Another example, in the years after the Civil War, was the tremendous rush to erect imposing churches and commercial buildings on a scale unknown in Springfield, but more broadly recognizable as the epitome of the urbanity to which the city now aspired. A similar point could be made about the regular circuit of major cities ridden by city school committeemen, as they studied what kind of professionalized school administration setup they ought to be devising.

These two themes come together in a third, which I trace with some care in the book: the emergence of the overarching, abstract notion of "public interest"—of Springfield being more than just the sum of its private constituencies, powerful or not, but rather having a collective, interdependent community identity beyond, which could serve as a touchstone, or yardstick, for assessing policy and community issues. This, I argue, was central to what began to make political life and decisionmaking so different in the urban setting, permitting the community to begin to take on roles and chose directions unreachable given the understandings and relationships of the informal world of the older town.

Not that this necessarily made things easier or simpler—quite the opposite, in fact. Increasingly, the implied tension between private gain and the broader public interest became a point of division in the political process, especially as the broader climate around Springfield changed. The 1870s saw a major depression that was widely taken as a kind of moral judgment on an era of overrapid expansion and business adventurism; it was matched by a political crisis centering on municipal corruption, epitomized by New York City's Boss Tweed. Together, these produced in Springfield a major trauma—the city halted in its tracks, and not only because of economic constraint. More deeply, an agonizing reappraisal of the whole rationale and direction of growth and the processes that had been fueling it emerged, a sustained debate over the purpose of public spending and public life. Among other things, an older leadership that had helped turn government and business into an engine of growth now feared that they were losing control of the political process and that this powerful engine now could be turned against them as different hands reached for the throttle: once the notion of public interest became general, abstract, and open—as opposed to self-evidently identical with the traditional interests—it might be up for grabs.

The crisis passed: the economy recovered, confidence in the community's ability to risk and manage growth resumed, the political and social challenge never quite materialized. But Springfield moved into its next decade, the 1880s, as a very different place for its several decades of change, and my book closes by noting a number of the harbingers that would give the next period enough complexity to make me glad I was stopping when I did—the preaching of Washington Gladden, later one of the founders of the Social Gospel, something akin to today's social-justice-focused Liberation Theology; the founding of a working-class oriented penny paper, the Springfield *News*, by Edward Bellamy (just a few years from *Looking Backward*) and his brother Charles; the emergence of a vital local labor movement and, later than in other cities, an effective Irish-American political presence at last.

Springfield thus moved toward the twentieth century under a new and definitively urban kind of umbrella, a framework for conflict that would allow the divisions and strains in a complex community to find the kind of political expression impossible in the closed society of the New England town. Those towns are commonly revered as the wellspring of American democracy, but I argue that this newer, urban conception of community politics has perhaps more to do with the kind of democracy needed in a complex, multicultural society such as ours, even if it sometimes complicates the process of formulating urban policy. To test this claim, let me illustrate, in a concluding section, how my general approach might be applied to the situation of cities such as Springfield today.

Translating Past Into Present

My first theme, above, concerned the centrality of a broadly defined political process—the role of organization and leadership and participation in focusing on choices, framing options, and choosing among them. This is especially important today, on all sides of our vastly expanded political community. It is crucial to realize that we are not in the grip of totally unmanageable forces; there is no "invisible hand" directing either growth or decline, with obvious consequences and implications to which we can only adjust. Rather, we still have choices to make and they increasingly turn on recognition of the interdependence of all elements in a complex urban community. In this sense, my hunch is that determining the "public interest" involves more than just a struggle between Bay State West and Winchester Square, to cite the two symbols of downtown and neighborhood I used earlier. Instead, it involves more complex choices and balances that will test Springfield as a community.

In framing and making these, the late-twentieth-century city is even more in the grip of trans-local forces—my second theme—than a century ago; understanding and responding to these as they effect localities becomes even more important. It has become stunningly manifest, in the last few years, that the once industrial-based cities of the Northeast, including industrial-commercial centers such as Springfield, face the challenge of a seismic realteration of the national and international economic landscape, a shift that seemingly offers these older cities only decline and obsolescence. At the same time, new technologies such as computerization have initiated changes almost certain to outstrip the nineteenth-century's Industrial Revolution in depth, force, and unpredictability of consequences. The current moment, then, offers both threat and promise. Cities are not so much in competition with each other for scarce resources as they are (to switch the metaphor from the destructive seismic to the threatening but hopeful hydroelectric) in a contest to figure out how to tame successfully these awesome tidal waves of change and turn their power in a positive direction.

In this sense, my third theme—the discovery of dramatic new forms, meaning, and opportunities in the public life of the urban community—takes on special importance. Our brief excursion into Springfield's past leads to some specific illustration of what this may mean. In the nitty-gritty of clean and dirty urban water, we saw how Springfield made great strides forward only when it came to abandon long-entrenched, traditional understandings of what a sewer or hydrant was actually for, much less how to build, pay for, and manage such a utility; progress required a leap to new definitions, conceptions, and mechanisms that could meet a public interest increasingly dependent on a very different kind of service.

Today, what might we identify as a rough parallel? Where may "obvious" traditional understandings, supported by a full range of political, legal, financial, and administrative mechanisms, be in the process of becoming as inadequate as the once unquestioned notion that water supply means fire protection, and sewers mean property drains? Living in the shadow of the

Love Canal as I do, I can point first to questions involving toxic waste man-agement, disposal, storage, and movement, where traditional notions of responsibility and accountability are clearly inadequate to the relationship between cities and the giant corporations. More broad, although also a local concern in Buffalo as I gather it is in Springfield, is the matter of plant clos-ings, corporate removal, and capital flight: all across the country, efforts are underway to redefine the obligations that corporations have to their workers and the communities that surround them and to limit their ability to destroy or severely disrupt those communities, despite decades of mutual depend-ence, just because the profit line sags or, even worse, an international conglo-merate takeover drains profits from a viable facility and then seeks to toss away the husk.

Other, different examples can be imagined, with perhaps different politi-cal implications. My point is less the specific case than it is the general lesson: we need to understand that living in history, now as in the 1860s, 1870s, and 1880s, means being alive to changing needs and situations, and realizing our capacity to alter definitions, priorities, and procedures accordingly. And this, in turn, requires a broadly participatory politics that forces alternatives to the surface, where choices can be made in the light of a hopefully vital demo-cratic process.

This is how we can begin to learn from history. The general lessons of the past must be remembered, as Santayana said. But other inheritances must, in effect, be actively forgotten, if we are not to be held back by what has been called the dead hand of the past, and trapped in visions inadequate to present circumstances. The study of history, I believe, is not so much the study of "what happened" as it is the study of "how things change." And as such, the point of excursions into the past, even on the inspiring occasion of a city's 350th birthday, is not to revere or imitate the past; rather, it is to understand the responsibility and freedom we have to shape the course of history in our own time and place, as our ancestors did in theirs.

Chapter 10

"Get the Picture?":
A Review Essay

Syracuse, From Salt to Satellite: A Pictorial History. Henry W. Schramm and William F. Rosebloom. (Published under the sponsorship of the Greater Syracuse Chamber of Commerce, 1979, 244 pp.)

A Panoramic History of Rochester and Monroe County New York. Blake McKelvey. *Partners in Progress, Profiles of Rochester's Leading Businesses* by Howard C. Hosmer. (Sponsored by Rochester Area Chamber of Commerce, Inc., 1979, 264 pp.)

Albany, Capital City on the Hudson: An Illustrated History. John J. McEneny. Picture research by Dennis Holzman, special material by Robert W. Arnold III, editorial coordination by Margaret Colvin Tropp. (Sponsored by the Albany Institute of History and Art, 1981, 248 pp.)

Buffalo, Lake City in Niagara Land: An Illustrated History. Richard C. Brown and Bob Watson. Picture research by Clyde Eller Helfter and editorial coordination by Margaret Colvin Tropp. (Produced in cooperation with the Buffalo and Erie Country Historical Society, 1981, 336 pp.)

The Upper Mohawk Country; An Illustrated History of Greater Utica. David Maldwyn Ellis. Picture research by Douglas M. Preston. *Partners in Progress* by Anne P. (Happy) Marsh and Gwynn V. Jones. (Sponsored by the Oneida Historical Society, 1982, 224 pp.)

All published by Windsor Publications, Inc., Woodland Hills, California.

The books reviewed in this essay are popular, illustrated histories of upstate New York cities, written by well-known community historians to fit a mold produced and shaped by Windsor Publications in cooperation with local agencies and supported by the business communities of each of the portraitized cities. Intended for general readers, or at least their coffee tables, such picture books are not usually taken very seriously by those more deeply involved in the study and writing of local history, much less in historical scholarship more broadly defined.

This neglect may be a real error. Popular form need not preclude historical insight, and rich illustrations offer the interpretive possibilities of any good documentation. Even more, to ignore such works is to forfeit valuable opportunities for reflecting on the relation between historical scholarship and the public's general interest in history, especially local history. It is this interest that historical societies and museums, in recent years, have been striving with considerable energy to develop, in part through popular or commercial projects such as those under review here. And the broader relationship between formal scholarship and our culture's general historical sensibility has itself been a recent subject of unusually intense debate. Indeed, perhaps the most striking characteristic of the current moment is the resonance between professional controversies about the direction of scholarly writing over the last ten or fifteen years, and more general discussion about the state of historical awareness, or lack of it, in our schools, communities, culture, and public discourse generally.

The latter has been the focus of two surprising best-sellers, one introducing the notion of cultural illiteracy and terming it a modern epidemic, the other more or less faulting higher education for making it possible, if not actually causing it. Another analysis has concluded, on the basis of extensive surveys of eleventh graders, that historically amnesiac generations are issuing forth from our high schools, having been poorly served by what, if anything, may have passed for historical studies in the secondary schools. Widely publicized reports by the Department of Education and the NEH have announced an even more general crisis of historical and cultural memory, requiring a major reorientation of formal and informal education so that the basic facts and stories of a supposedly shared heritage may be restored to what is held to be their rightful place in public consciousness. All of these works tend to fault the historical profession for leaving the public stranded on the other side of an immense gap, cut off from a coherent grasp of history because scholars have allegedly preferred to talk only with each other in increasingly arcane terms.[1]

Academic discussions have been arriving at a point at least superficially similar, from points of origin whose enormous diversity is itself suggestive. Critics have held up as evidence of a deeper cul-de-sac both the barely comprehensible incantations of social-scientific quantification and the left-leaning critique of much of the bottom-up New Social History. Older jeremiads have taken on a new Thermidorian energy, as critics have proclaimed the passing of the new history and the rediscovery of the old, calling for a reinvigorated focus on political history, traditional narrative, and straightforward synthesis.[2]

The thunder has not only been on the right. Many of those in the vanguard of the social-historical revolution have themselves been struggling to resist the isolation of the academy; their efforts to construct new bridges between scholarship and political discourse, over which traffic might pass in both directions, have been a major component of the current interest in public history. Other critics on the left have seen in the academic institutionalization of a generation of younger historians, however progressive their approach, a darker and more fundamental contradiction, and a less remediable cause of the deracination of public discourse.[3]

There is a sense in which these contrastive complaints tend to cancel out, leaving a kind of common-sense middle ground: however one assesses the scholarship of recent decades, many evidently feel that perhaps it is time for a redirection of energy toward synthesis rather than analysis, wholes rather than parts, narrative that can tell a coherent story, and history that, in sum, is more sharable in public discussion.[4] And to the extent that this is true, it becomes important to reexamine our assumptions about the value of what has often been dismissed as popular local history. One need not assume that once-overlooked genres necessarily have riches buried in their prosaic pages, although real surprises might emerge along this line. More to the point, we simply need more critical respect for the demands of the form, if we are serious about forging better syntheses of scholarly insight and publicly accessible narrative.

Thus it is that the recent vitality of what has come to be called public history and the shifting sands of both cultural and historiographical criticism have together shaped a vantage from which it may be especially useful to cast a retrospective glance at this grouping of urban picture biographies—works written at the beginning of the present decade and otherwise obscure, then and now, to the view of any save the citizens of each locality.

The Picture Book Genre

An appreciation of what the genre has to offer, actually or potentially, must begin with a frank acknowledgement of its severe limitations: these books are what they are, and cannot be what they are not. They are commercial productions dependent on a collaboration between local authors and the financial sponsorship of each city's business community, mediated through the agency of the publisher and a local institution, usually either the Chamber of Commerce or a historical society. Each concludes with a throwback to nineteenth-century written-on-subscription municipal and county histories: a section called "Partners in Progress" consisting of profiles of individual companies, evidently included in exchange for substantial contributions toward the costs of publication, which is how Windsor Publications can produce such handsomely printed volumes at costs, in 1980, averaging around $21.[5]

The volumes are uniform in their coffee-table style appearance: each is a hardbound 9" x 11" book, with a dramatic color dustcover. The illustrations are lavish throughout—all the volumes have a major section of color plates, and virtually every page of each 150-200-page text is individually designed, intricately interweaving columns of print with sidebar features and black-and-white documentary illustrations. This makes it almost impossible to read in a linear way, which is just as well—the well-captioned illustrations are usually quite worth the detours they demand, suggesting that the volumes are intended more to be thumbed-through than read from cover to cover.

This is not to say that the texts are not seriously written; most of the authors seem, indeed, to have given considerable attention to making their narrative work in this context and for its intended audiences. Some of the authors are well-known amateur historians very much at home in this genre, while others are accomplished scholars (particularly Rochester's Blake McKelvey and Utica's David M. Ellis), who have already written widely about their region, and here take on what they evidently understand to be a very particular challenge. In this respect, because many professional and academic readers assume that commercial auspices and popular intent provide only obstacles, it may be useful to consider the form as also possessing dimensions that expand rather than limit the possibilities of effective historical narrative. Two such advantages seem particularly relevant to the works being considered here.

On a most general level, to write popular local urban history is to address readers who can be assumed to have at least a general familiarity with the present-day community, its physical features, streets, parks, major public buildings and landmarks, social groups and institutions, major businesses and economic circumstances, and so forth. The narrator can play off this knowledge to make history come alive for readers, creating interest in the origins and the evolution of the familiar—the "future of the past"—as well as curiosity about the "paths not taken." Familiarity also permits a greater narrative flexibility that is especially helpful when a text is juxtaposed to diverse illustrations whose main interest is their particularity: what might seem fragmentary and jumbled to an outsider may actually be quite coherent and digestible to the local reader, who is able to organize the diverse images and pieces in a frame shaped by contemporary experience in the given city.

Thus, in a sense surprisingly analogous to that encountered in the writing and reading of professional history, the local reader can be understood as bringing to the reading of the text a valuable experience and authority. The author's success depends, to a considerable degree, on how well he or she intuitively understands the nature of this authority and can help the reader invoke it as a resource, making reading an experience simultaneously confirming and challenging. This combination is arguably essential if readers already familiar with the contemporary community are to find its history real, and if they are to be led to examine with new eyes conventional assumptions about the local past, how this matters to the present, and how community history might bear on possible futures leading out of the current moment.

A related opportunity of the genre is the chance to explicate the broader transformations of American life in concrete terms and on a human scale. Urban history involves connections between the local environment and forces, institutions, and developments, some of them quite complex, that are regional, national, and even international in scope. Curiosity about the local can open such broader worlds and issues to view; even more, the wider context can help those tracing local history to chart a course between an overgeneralized picture of regional systemic rise or decline, and a boosterism that vastly overemphasizes the ability of a community, or the business and social groups within it, to act as independent variables in determining their own historical course. A successful popular history has a distinctive capacity to help readers appreciate the play of both contingency and agency in local experience.

This may sound abstruse, but it is actually quite common-sensical when concretely explored, especially through the lens of the business and industrial enterprises that are almost inevitably at the center of books like these. And the cities of upstate New York are particularly appropriate for opening a broader economic and social history to view, given their location, population characteristics, and the factors bearing on the curve of their nineteenth-century rise, early-midtwentieth century height, subsequent decline, and variously real or hypothesized revitalization in the not-quite-postindustrial metropolitan present.

These considerations—the linking of present and past through engaging the experience of readers presumed to be local residents, and the linking of local and translocal dimensions of history through a grounded narrative of economic-centered change—provide something of a framework for assessing how well, within the possibilities and the resources of the form, these several volumes tend to meet the challenges, transcend the limits, and realize the distinct potential of this type of historical narrative.

Five Cities

All of the books start strong, in large part because of their subjects' particular setting in time and geography: the early history of upstate New York cities exerts a compelling narrative pull in that the circumstances virtually require the authors to begin with dramatic episodes grounded in a broader

national history, and then encourage them to show how this history is interwoven with the fabric of local development. This is fortuitous, because if
readers have usually approached community history in overly homey and parochial terms, images of American history generally have been the converse—
based on the near-mythic events and personalities at the center of a shared
early American heritage focused on the colonists and Indians, the political
and military struggles of the American Revolution and its aftermath, and the
frontier and the westward expansion. Enshrined in an often static and symbolic patriotic space, such material is what many people see as the real stuff
of history, which has a lot to do with why it is usually so hard to make the
historicality of social and economic change seem real, much less interesting
or memorable, to broad audiences.[6]

But in early upstate New York, the two dimensions are complementary in
the most instructive sense. A local narrative can barely begin without giving
readers a reasonably broad grasp of the imperial struggles among the English, French, and Americans, and the relation of all to the Native Americans,
over the great crescent from northern New England across upstate New York
to the lakes and the Ohio Valley, a rich and exciting story given a powerful
explanatory focus when brought to bear on the origins of particular regions
or communities shaped by it. A popular history of these communities thus
has a chance to generate considerable momentum at the start, by establishing
a voice and tone that bridges the anecdotal and the analytic, and that sets the
local within a complex and sophisticated general framework.

By and large, the books do take advantage of this opportunity, illustrating the story with a wealth of fascinating documents and illustrations. They
are very good at showing the local implications of the pivotal role of the Indians
and the impact of the imperial rivalries diplomatically and militarily; they
illustrate, even more usefully, the particular ways in which this complex history shaped the economic character and role of local business on the frontier,
with results extending well into the nineteenth-century. *Utica* is especially
strong in this regard, although all are distinctive in one respect or another.
Albany, for instance, is quite good at linking the spaces and landmarks of the
colonial city to the present environment, in ways that make this seem less a
curiosity than an historical relationship that reveals the shaping of the city
over time—a good example of how the reader's own knowledge of the area
becomes a resource for interpretation.

The momentum helps carry each narrative through the Erie Canal era,
itself a landmark of national history and hence a legitimizing support for
the local focus. After this point, however, the authors are on their own in
framing local narrative—the Civil War has a major local impact in each city,
but not in ways that fundamentally shape the history, hence introducing
the narrative difficulty, relative to the early period, of a diminished reso-

nance between the dramatic frame of national history and the structures of local experience.

Understandably, the authors seem almost reluctant to leave the early periods behind—four of the five books devote nearly one-half of their text to the seemingly more "historical" years prior to the end of the Civil War; the one that doesn't, *Syracuse*, is the rule-proving exception—its narrative quickly becomes the most fragmented and least satisfying of all. In general, however, all the works have to face the problem of how to maintain a coherent narrative once the heroic structures of a locally specific frontier expansion are exchanged for an industrial growth in which the region is only more generally representative, much less when this in turn gives way to a twentieth century that requires description of conflict, stasis, decline, and an increasingly limited capacity for moving against powerful currents of change centered far outside the local community.

Sustained narrative requires consistent actors and a consistent voice, and the task of narrative urban biography has traditionally pulled authors, especially of popular treatments like these, toward evocation of an anthropomorphized fictive community that can be said to act, will, think, and feel. In the past, this was usually effected by making the overall community virtually synonymous with its leading citizens and businessmen, whose personalities, activities, perspectives, and interests could be described concretely, giving focus and direction to the broader personalization of "the city." Given the commercial auspices of these Windsor books, and the boosterish "Partners in Progress" business galleries that form the coda to each volume, it could easily be predicted that this would remain the central narrative mechanism for holding the centrifugal vectors of urban history together.

In fact, however, we encounter something rather different. The authors are all sufficiently sensitive to the pluralism of their respective cities today, and to the conflict and complexity at every stage of community history, to avoid offering business leadership as emblematic of the city itself. But abandoning this pretense cannot itself meet the need for what seems to remain a presumed necessity, a consistent narrative personality located within the circle of community enclosing both past history and present readers. Rather, the authors continue to attempt to speak in the fictive community's voice; it is their several ways of doing this that differentiate them from traditional civic popular history, and from each other.

The *Syracuse* volume represents one instructive extreme. The implicit strategy here is perhaps closest to that associated with television news or with newspapers such as *USA Today* where community seems grounded simply in shared experience and where the experiences chosen for attention are therefore those presumed to be most broadly and uncomplicatedly shared. Hence, far more than the other books, *Syracuse* tends to pivot around evocation of significant landmarks in national history linked superficially to local events or developments. Beyond this, local coverage ricochets from topic to topic, although the analogy of contemporary media is helpful in making this seem less than random: the text is quite resonant with the depressingly universal modern formula by which fires, accidents, crimes, weather, sports, and the heartwarming human-interest anecdote become the organizing pillars of an only superficially dynamic and actually more deeply static image of community life. In this, a pointed irony surfaces: of all the volumes reviewed here, *Syracuse* is the most distant from academic history, from the analytic temperament critics have decried in social history; as such, it seems most attentive to the general reader's presumed hunger for an engaging, coherent alternative. Yet, it is the most fragmented and unreadable of the books. Lacking a convincing synthetic voice or stance, it becomes a jumble of minutiae that, even for local residents, can convey the story of urban history no more satisfyingly than local television formats capture the reality of contemporary community news and experience.

Blake McKelvey's *Rochester* is far more successful, mainly because it approaches the problem of narrative on a deeper level, anticipating the advice of recent critics that political history has an underappreciated capacity for generating coherent narrative motion through time. A genuinely political narrative, of course, is precisely what contemporary media journalism somewhat compulsively resists, because the notion of meaningful political conflict seems so inconsistent with the harmonious fictive community it is driven to project. McKelvey, however, grounded in the older Progressive tradition and a lifetime of scholarship involving not only Rochester history but also the broader synthesis of American urban history, pushes past such hesitations, offering a story organized, especially in its latter chapters, around public affairs, broadly defined. Here, the community is real, not fictive, and is best-expressed through government, sometimes aligned with business, sometimes in opposition. Although there are costs, this approach produces a satisfying and comprehensible sense of Rochester's development over time. The political and governmental focus is less able to deal with many aspects of social and cultural development, but McKelvey's is the most successful of all the volumes in providing, for example, a framework that permits extensive discussion of the planning and renewal issues, and the evolving local-federal relationship, which is so central to modern urban history.

Albany and the first half of *Buffalo* stand closer to the traditional model, in that the business-centered notion of growth and development is the organizing theme. But a more comprehensive perspective, and in the latter case even a somewhat ironic distance, permit the authors to use this to broader historical advantage. *Buffalo* makes especially good use of illustrative entrepreneurial stories both to explicate the dynamics of developmental change and to reveal perhaps unsuspected complexity in the history of now familiar institutions and names. (Interestingly, this technique characterizes those few parts of *Syracuse* that really seem to work, such as the discussion of how the Carrier company, now organically associated with the image of the city by virtue of the famous Carrier Dome, was itself a late arrival, lured to town to fill the plant vacated by Syracuse's own failed Franklin Motor Company—in part because Willis Carrier was a fan of the elegant Franklin automobile.)

The Buffalo volume is unique in the group for having the most synthetic title —in nearly twenty years in the city, I have never heard its region referred to as Niagara Land, as it is here. The book's two authors are not really collaborators; rather, Bob Watson authored the major section on the nineteenth century, and Richard C. Brown authored the section on the twentieth. The contrast between the sections helps reveal some of the choices such authors face. Watson's narrative moves smoothly and engagingly in the traditional mode noted above. When Brown continues, however, the text shifts to a focus on the city's structure, basic changes in transportation and their implications, and other topics that help give a more logical and recognizable sense of the city as a real environment; the contrast reminds the reader how much was missing from the seemingly comprehensive early chapters. Unfortunately, Brown then falls back on just that transcended mode—the anecdotal entrepreneurial focus—for dealing with the complex story of Buffalo's mid-century decline, which resolves down into a series of dramatic but cumulatively unhelpful vignettes.

To this reader, at least, David Ellis's study of Utica, *The Upper Mohawk Country*, most satisfactorily solves the challenge of constructing a coherent synthesis grounded in a broader history and capable of trenchant structural insights into the processes of urban growth and decline, while still holding to the form of an accessible, detail-and-anecdote-rich local narrative. Here, it is the best insights of a well-digested social history that provide the not-so-fictive community at the center of the exposition, especially in the nineteenth-century chapters that generate the book's momentum. Ellis's attention to work and occupational structure, ethnicity, family, and gender, effortlessly synthesizing the rich work of scholars such as Mary Ryan, is at once helpful and unobtrusive. More deeply and instructively, this focus provides grounds for a smoother pivot than in the other studies for dealing with the city's declining fortunes in the twentieth century, where narrative can hardly be heroic, yet cannot afford to be numbingly depressive, either.

Looking back to the broad current debates noted at the start of this essay, there is a wider lesson in Ellis's demonstration that social history can itself make for coherent narrative. Actually, this should not be all that surprising: however much the city and its leadership changes, people still work, go to church, join clubs and unions, form families, raise children, seek housing and build neighborhoods, and use transportation. In skillful hands, it proves possible to use historical coverage of such phenomena to strike the balance described earlier—to permit people to identify their own experience with parallels in the past, using the present as a vantage for broader understanding while simultaneously using the past to develop a deeper sense of the historical flow in which today's familiar world is but a moment in transition.

The Potential of Popular History

Such observations return us to our starting point and permit some informal reflections on the broader problems posed there. These five volumes suggest that little utility or even meaning is found in the posited donnybrook between an alienating modern social-historical consciousness and a satisfyingly old-fashioned style of straightforward narrative to which we should return. In these popular histories, informal narrative can be as fragmented, disjointed, and nearly unreadable as anyone's image of overly academic analysis, and maybe more so. And among these authors the most academically grounded and oriented prove the most capable of constructing clear, engaging narrative capable of dealing with the complexity of change over time. These results are not coincidental or even paradoxical, if the challenge is properly understood.

The issue, then, would seem to return to the substantive question of how best to project an accessible version of local history adequate to the realities of urban complexity, especially in all its twentieth-century contradictions. Clearly, the limits of all of these works in this respect indicate how much more we need to synthesize and translate the best insights of modern historical studies and make these available to general audiences. Unless this is done, the grave social, economic, and policy dilemmas of the contemporary city will remain disconnected from and uninstructed by a history that actually has much to say to the present. And popular narrative, in turn, will remain in the grip of the civic pieties and putative shared assumptions of a genuinely and even perniciously fictitious fictive community.

At the same time, these books also suggest how much popular history has to contribute, especially if it can mobilize even more powerfully than it does here its inherent capacity for engaging the knowledge, insight, and authority of its readers, who generally know and care about their own communities. In this respect, there are instructive lessons about not-fully-realized opportunities if we consider, by way of a conclusion aimed at constructive suggestion, how as a group the volumes handle the illustrations themselves—a dimension so central to the conception of the overall Windsor project, yet so definitively particular in interest and attraction, as to resist general discussion.

As noted earlier, the illustrations are lavish, individually fascinating, and beautifully laid out; each book amounts to a treasure trove of locally meaningful documents, some familiar and some unknown, of portraits, manuscripts, and remarkable prints and photos documenting many aspects of urban life over the past two centuries. But there is something cumulatively disquieting about the parade of documentation: illustrations are presented as if their broader historical meaning is reasonably self-evident, or, if not, is sufficiently explained by full captions annotating the content or explaining its background. The reader is asked to do little but look, and the illustrations are not generally approached instrumentally, as ways to enhance the reach or depth of the narrative itself. Much is included to see and appreciate, but this is a limited way of conceiving of what the illustrations and documents have to contribute to the readers' involvement in historical exploration.

Perhaps the point is best made by noting exceptions, such as a streetscape of the heart of downtown Syracuse whose caption prods readers to notice a sign announcing Socialist party headquarters right next door to the City Bank. With this modest nudge, the photo, which would otherwise seem routine, helps readers to new curiosity about the meaning and context of politics at that time, and to contrast the 1890s to the present in this respect. Or the page from a city directory printed in *Utica*, whose information on postal rates and fire company members is noted and commented on in ways that link directly to the text's subtle discussion of commerce and community in the early stagecoach era.

It is surprising how infrequently this kind of energy is generated in the books as a whole. Little use is made of illustrations to surprise readers, or force them to look more closely; readers are offered little help, or encouragement, in turning whatever curiosity or interest the documents stimulate back into the text and the historical themes discussed there. And there are very few instances of what might be called active intervention to make the illustrations even more organic to the narrative—through juxtaposition of unusually linked illustrations, for example, or views of the same spot at different times, much less superimposing annotation such as boundary or neighborhood lines on an aerial photo, for instance.

More generally still, the concept of illustration that virtually defines the look and feel of the books becomes, in a curious and ironic way, the feature most subversive of their broader public purpose. By this I refer to a notion of historical exclusivity that silently controls the project: only "genuine" historical "documents" are qualified for inclusion as illustration. The books offer no independently generated maps, charts, diagrams, or annotated graphics for exploring and presenting such things as the changing spatial patterns of the community over time, comparisons of economic land use, comparative distributions of different population groups at different times, or any of myriad topics familiar to anyone who has read at all seriously about cities and urban history. And this in spite of the fact, as such readers also know, that tremendous advances in graphic design and imagination now make possible creatively drawn maps and inventive new types of multidimensional representation that can make very complex issues and relationships accessible—especially when employed with such forms as familiar city shapes, boundaries, and reference points.

It is worth reflecting on how the exclusive privilege accorded actual historical documents may inadvertently be related to the tendency the illustrations have to encourage in readers a kind of passive consumption, turning pages and glancing at photos the way one eats popcorn in a movie or thumbs through magazines in a waiting room. For all the respect of the approach, it suggests that history is a straightforward thing to be seen, rather than a relationship to be puzzled through or actively reexamined. The reluctance of the historians and book designers to move beyond this themselves in their use of illustrations undercuts a major way in which the readers could be most easily activated in books like this; using knowledge of the familiar to provide a base of competence and authority for measuring the distance, and reflecting on the relationship, between past and present. Such involvement could only be enhanced by a wider use of open-ended illustrative forms, including but moving well beyond archivally retrieved documents set in the book equivalent of museum display cases, to be seen but not touched or used.

From both perspectives, then, the limit of these generally solid books is not that they are too academic or too popular, but rather that they are not serious enough about either of these qualities and do not fully take advantage of the opportunity of the municipal picture biography for combining them creatively. If these are failings, they are certainly understandable, especially considering both the auspices of the Windsor project and the state of discussion when it was conceived, in the mid to late 1970s; even if the volumes considered here are imperfect examples, they have played an underappreciated role in advancing this important dialogue.

Today, one senses that such projects confront a more particular dilemma, given the richer research awaiting popular synthesis on the one hand, and invocations to avoid such academic approaches and to embrace old-fashioned narrative, on the other; it will be interesting to see what the next generation of picture books are like.[7] For, if the Windsor volumes are any indication, the challenge of synthesis remains before us, the challenge of involving any city's readers in a popular history that provides a legacy of form and process touching all who live in the complex communities of modern America.

Chapter 11

Audience Expectations as Resource and Challenge: Ellis Island as a Case Study*

The audience, ironically enough, is perhaps the most consistently overlooked and most poorly understood element in contemporary discussions of public history and interpretive strategy.

It has become common for such discussions to invoke images of audiences—the different audiences we hope to attract; the different needs audiences bring; the different experiences we intend to provide for audiences; and the enhanced historical insight, understanding, and sensitivity we hope audiences will derive from our work. In all this, however, the focus is on *statement*—usually little examination is made of the *process* by which audiences actually approach, engage, and digest historical interpretations, certainly not among those coming at the problem from a primary concern with historical content. To the extent this dimension has attracted attention, it has been among graphic and exhibit designers focused on the experience of the exhibition visit, rather than on the relationship between audience and historical content and interpretation. The program at the Past Meets Present Conference reflected this emphasis: the only presentation directly addressing the nature of audience response was by a design consultant; for the most part, the historians concerned themselves with the content and implications of the statements presentations make to audiences.

This chapter is a modest contribution toward righting the balance—toward developing a critical vocabulary by which the relationship of audience to presentation can be understood as a complex element central to the historical interpretive process. It grows out of one of the "expeditions" that were a distinguishing feature of the Past Meets Present Conference—in our case, a visit to Ellis Island—and discussions among participants con-

---

*This chapter has been co-authored with Dwight Pitcaithley.

ducted on the boat to and from this remarkable National Park Service (NPS) historic site.

Ellis Island, a stone's throw from the Statue of Liberty, was the nation's primary immigration processing center from 1892 until 1954. In 1965, Congress declared it a historic site as part of the Statue of Liberty National Monument. The complex of forty-one structures includes a hospital, dormitories, kitchens, laundry rooms, contagious diseases ward, and the processing facility in the main building.

The past history of this site's status and interpretation, much less the story of the present and continuing restoration and development being charted by the Statue of Liberty/Ellis Island Foundation, is worth book-length treatment in and of itself. Rather than attempting to cover all of this, our intent here is to see what can be learned more generally from our experience as visitors and audience in late 1984, before the contemplated restoration and reinterpretation had even been given shape. We wish to discuss how a sensitivity to audience figures in assessing the interpretive choices presented by any site generally and by the particular kind of site Ellis Island may be taken to represent: the highly visible and famous landmark/shrine whose history, in the broadest terms, already has meaning and familiarity to most of those visiting it.

This familiarity, we suggest, represents both a resource and a problem that together make the major landmark/shrine a very special public-historical interpretive challenge. Audiences may bring to the site a host of general but very firmly fixed images, derived from family and personal history, popular culture and tradition, primary and secondary basic education, modern media treatments, and so on. Unlike an exhibit on a more specialized topic, or the presentation of a less well-known historic site connected to broader events, or a display of not-usually-seen artifacts and documents, or a reconstruction of everyday experience in another time and place—unlike all of these, audiences may be presumed to bring to the visiting of a major site at least a general image and story, and a framework suggesting the place of that story in a wider history.

How to work with and yet against these groundwork images is a formidable challenge: to ignore them and "start from scratch" is to risk boring or patronizing the audience, while to accept them as the ground of interpretation is to risk imprisonment in precisely the conventional assumptions it is the purpose of interpretation to broaden, challenge, and transcend. This suggests an interpretive tension in which both audience and presenters are complicit. Rather than being distinguished from each other as active/passive, provider/receiver, both audience and presenters bring active interpretive processes to their on-site meeting. As we will suggest below, appreciating and working out from the base of this shared interpretive ground to the visiting experience can help in developing the special potential of the major site.

But the problem is more complex than even this would suggest because audiences bring more than just a particular set of stories or images to such landmarks—they may have, however implicitly, general expectations as to the way major historical significance is signified, a sense of what is appropriate to the dignity and stature of major commemorations. This suggests another level of the tension between audience expectations and presenter "designs," another sense in which successful interpretation may arise out of a kind of implicit negotiation between what audiences bring in, and that which they experience on-site. Each of these dimensions—the stylistic expectations audiences bring to the major site generally and the particular interpretive expectations they bring to the shrine whose story is already familiar—deserves brief comment before turning to the example of recent Ellis Island presentation in more detail.

Visitors' ideas as to what is appropriate to the major site have their own powerful roots in culture and tradition, yet these ideas are not unchanging: they evolve, in both a stylistic and a deeper sense, and need not be considered as immutable by those of us concerned about broadening the range of the possible in historical presentation. In fact, these formal or stylistic ideas develop out of an ongoing dialogue between interpretive programmers and their publics.

The historical significance of an old building or set of buildings is relative in a special sense, defined by each generation for purposes unique to that period. As understandings of the relation of past to present change, we reassess the value of those tangible fragments set aside as official or unofficial historic sites. Just as the Vietnam generation is finding solace and regeneration in the black granite Vietnam Veterans' Memorial (to the surprise of many who disparaged the controversial design), the Civil War generation celebrated its memories by raising enormous amounts of money to erect a monument in 1897 to Ulysses S. Grant. Indeed, by all accounts, the emotions triggered by the granite wall in Washington are similar in kind and degree to those raised at the turn of the century for Civil War veterans visiting the General Ulysses S. Grant National Memorial—Grant's Tomb to us—a once-revered site that has become merely a curiosity today, a place for graffiti and (Groucho) Marxist jokes.

Similarly, nineteenth-century America recognized the historical value of the battlefield at Gettysburg, erecting monuments in all shapes and sizes to the men who fought and died there. These memorials evoked powerful memories and deep emotions for visitors. The veterans who commissioned the monuments strove to create a contemplative site, a place encouraging reflection on the meaning of those three awful days in the summer of 1863, and to a large extent they succeeded. Yet for today's tastes and needs, those same monuments are disparaged as intrusions, obstacles to a clear understanding of the actual battle and the larger history: the park-like setting is criticized for not evoking the historical reality of the time.

Thus, the "monumentative" and contemplative approach to historic preservation before, say, the advent of Colonial Williamsburg, is no longer appreciated as an appropriate way of commemorating the past; the public has come to expect the visual, requiring restored, reconstructed, and refurnished sites and costumed replication. This "new" form of historic site management is not inherently better or worse, in that any interpretive approach can be ludicrous or moving—or both, at different times. The important thing is to understand that current modes of commemoration/interpretation are neither inevitable nor eternal. At any time, the development of alternative forms of interpretive presentation requires both imaginative new techniques and a respectful comprehension of the way past approaches may have worked with and for changing audiences. The enduring question for historic site managers seems to be: how can we evoke a sense of the past in a manner that stimulates curiosity and provokes understanding?

The particular expectations the public brings to a given major site may involve little more than an implicit set of symbols or images—such as Washington at Valley Forge—but these, too, have had different, changing meanings over time. Today, few are unaware of the national fundraising campaign on the part of the Statue of Liberty/Ellis Island Foundation; it is the largest restoration project in our history. A best-selling novel and a television mini-series read and viewed by millions further reinforce Ellis Island's particular recognition and clear symbolism. Yet fewer than thirty years ago, the little island was on the auction block. Abandoned by the Immigration and Naturalization Service in 1954 and unwanted by other federal agencies, it became a surplus government property that the General Services Administration (GSA) proved unable to sell. The NPS declared the island to have little historical significance. The former immigration center's sudden change of fortune, its opening as a historic site by the Park Service in 1976 and the success it subsequently has had as an attraction thus stand as a fine example of America's changing sense of what we should historically commemorate and how; its prospective major restoration is presenting crucial choices that make it all the more important to understand this process clearly.

As a general matter, both the opportunities and the dilemmas of presenting such symbolic sites to general audiences vary in direct proportion to the strength and vividness of the images people bring, in at least two senses with special meaning for Ellis Island and similar sites. The first involves the question of who feels a direct stake and connection to the site's story, in what terms, and why. The more there is a preexisting personal and personal/ emotional connection to the story for a substantial share of the audience, the more interpreters are provided with a powerful base of identification from which a dramatic and meaningful program can be presented. More than twelve million immigrants entered the United States through Ellis Island, many of whom are still alive, and most of whose children, grandchildren, and great-grandchildren have powerful connections to the story of immigration; it is hard to conceive of an approach to site interpretation that would not seek to invoke this connection as a resource.

Yet the opportunity is not without its costs. Too great a reliance on visitors' preconceived notions and emotions may constrict their interest in or openness to new historical interpretations and the presentation of contextual information. Moreover, excessive evocation of the familiar may exclude those visitors outside the bounds of that immediate connection, preventing them from exploring and appreciating the historical experience from other vantages—from which the story may look very different. Thus the dilemma of how to make Ellis Island meaningful to black Americans whose enslaved immigration had of course nothing do with Emma Lazarus, or how to address other visiting Americans, even immigrants and their descendants from other periods and circumstances (Hispanics, for example, or Vietnamese and Chinese, or even the Irish of the mid-nineteenth century), who may have a quite complex and less predictable response to the implicit paradigm of the Golden Door, the Statue of Liberty, and all the images of late nineteenth and early twentieth century immigration.

Such considerations blend into a second general concern—the dilemma of the implied story itself, the tension that frequently may exist between the audience's interest in having a particular version of the story told, with all the opportunities this opens for powerful interpretation, and the responsibility presenters have to offer the truest, most correctly framed history they can.

In some cases, this will involve rather profound questions of value and perspective, such as those that make the evolving interpretations of the Custer Battlefield National Monument in southeastern Montana a fascinating case in point. Administered by the United States War Department until 1940, the early interpretation of this site reflected both general public images and orthodox historiography, thereby presenting the life and death of George Armstrong Custer in heroic terms while minimizing the real plight of the Sioux and Northern Cheyenne. The rising sensitivity and appreciation for the historical perspective of Native Americans, nurtured in part by writers such as Vine Deloria, gradually led the NPS to revise its interpretive presentation toward a more balanced and comprehensive treatment of the battle and the wider context surrounding it.

Characteristically, though, the tension may be far more subtle, presenting itself, somewhat disguised, as a choice between the more conventional story that can be presented easily, and the more complex historical version that does not as readily suggest a workable programmatic approach. This problem is further complicated by what J.B. Jackson has discussed as our "need for ruins," the American tendency to require buildings or sites to go through phases of growth and decline before they seem eligible for saving, at which time historical significance is attached to a "Golden Age" whose restoration is then attempted.[1] The result is not a reflection of the past, but a sanitized, present-day conception of one portion of that past. The very restoration can disrupt the "sedimentation of culture" that has accumulated at the site; it demands that visitors suspend credulity by receiving the site not as a genuine remnant of history, but as a disjointed piece of the past that somehow has returned to pay us a visit in the present. And in sites such as Ellis Island, to which visitors bring strong symbolic expectations, such an approach can seem mandated by audience needs and hence even harder to modify in more historically accurate and meaningful ways.

Ellis Island was many things to many people, as suggested in the visitors brochure we were given on our visit, entitled "Island of Hope, Island of Tears." Although built as an immigration center, the role in which it has captured the nation's attention, the island also served as our primary detention and deportation center during the early 1920s, the Depression, World War II, and the second Red Scare in the 1950s. Between 1892 and 1954, almost one-half million aliens were expelled from the United States, many through Ellis Island. As the immigrant processing waned and detention and deportation increased, the site was modified: bars covered windows, chain-link fences and barbed wire appeared, interior partitions were introduced, and the Island gradually came to look like the medium security prison it had, in fact, become.

These changes are certainly part of the site's place in the story of immigration, for the rise of nativism, the quota acts, and the Red Scares say as much about us as a nation of immigrants as does the drama of the Golden Door and the steerage immigrants with their bundled belongings. Can both sides be told at once, especially to audiences expecting the symbols of the latter? Do we choose to represent with greater verisimilitude the island seen by earlier immigrants? Or should we deliberately violate that vision so as to avoid presenting a history from which has been stripped the traces of a nation's bias against immigrants and its recurrent political intolerance, evidence that immigration was frightening and traumatic not only for the immigrants trembling at the Gate, but for the United States as well? The tension comes to earth in highly tangible form: which buildings are restored and to what period? Is the chain-link fence removed? What features are commented on by guides or texts and in what manner?

Such concerns figure centrally in current debates about the approach that should be taken by the current restoration. The current political and developmental issues, turning on private versus public roles, and history versus the merchandising of "McEllis Island, Twenty Million Served" have been widely discussed elsewhere.[2] But more concrete design and restoration issues have also surfaced directly related to the issues of audience expectation of concern here. Several of the early plans developed by the National Park Service, for instance, envisioned demolition of some of the less important buildings on the island, in order to open up space for passive park land, interpretive markers, and metal-plate photographs that might have imparted a sense of the island's changing appearance over time. Retention of foundation stones to outline former buildings would evoke the past without the enormous expense of preserving every structure. Such techniques were intended to draw on visitor imagination for the more personal recreation of the past as fact and process; the approach has a long and successful tradition in the NPS, particularly in southwestern archaeological parks. But public review of those early planning documents was negative: no matter how difficult or expensive, buildings should not be destroyed; the island should be restored "as it was."

Against this background, legislation in 1980 that permitted the leasing of federally owned historic buildings, coupled with the creation in 1983 of the Statue of Liberty/Ellis Island Foundation both solved the problem and begged the question. It would now be possible to lease major portions of the island, to preserve all buildings to NPS standards and to interpret the whole of the island. With that very opportunity, however, the complex interpretive issues and historical choices discussed above become inescapable. If we can do almost anything with the site, what should be done, and why?

With these considerations in mind, let us see what can be learned from a closer look at the interpretive approach we encountered at Ellis Island in 1984, on the eve of major restoration and reinterpretation planning, an approach generally similar to those offered from the opening of the island to visitors in 1976. Echoing the point above that constraints and opportunities can be sides of the same coin, the condition of the unrestored island sharply limited what could be presented to visitors and how, virtually compelling an interpretive approach that, as it happened, opened up imaginative interpretive possibilities quite nicely suited to the site's historical content.

Essentially, Ellis Island in this 1976-1984 period has been an unrestored ruin, encountered in a virtually abandoned state, with rubble on all sides, weeds growing through the floors, sunlight or rain pouring in the roof in places, abandoned equipment and random pieces of furniture strewn about. There are no exhibits, labels, text, or other indications of the history-viewing present; the sense is that one is looking at a site which has not much been touched since occupants departed and operations ceased many years ago, leaving a sort of institutional ghost town through which visitors are permitted to wander in silence. But because the physical condition of stairs and floors is so uncertain, visitors cannot move at will and must be conducted in groups on a carefully protected path. And because it has not yet been possible to develop any documentation, exhibitions, or special interpretation materials, the burden of presenting the site falls entirely on the guides, whose carefully prepared narration is, in counterpoint with the ghostly spaces through which visitors are led, the sole source of historical content and comment in the visit.

The narrator's "spiel," as we heard it, has ample historical content, both specific and general, but is essentially dramatistic in construction: the intent is to have visitors re-create the feelings and experience of the immigrants in their own minds, by following, step-by-step, the path new arrivals might have followed in moving through the immigration process in the buildings of Ellis Island. Thus, tour groups are met near the dock, where the guide sets the context historically and emotionally, trying to evoke the trembling fear and apprehension of the new arrivals—"Strangers, in a Strange Land," our guide intoned at regular intervals, with affecting sincerity and drama.

From there, the group is led through the baggage area, where the arrival process is discussed, and into the famous great hall where visitors are seated on the very benches used by actual Ellis Island immigrants. Here, great care is taken to evoke the dramatic detail of the complex clearance procedures— the summoning to the official table; the clustering of interpreters; the checking of documents and the interrogation as to education, jobs, and relatives; the initial health screenings, with the fateful chalk marks that separated so many for examination, detention, and possible deportation; and so on. In all this, our guide worked hard to make the ghosts visible, to make the process imaginable, to have visitors sense Ellis as the immigrants must have—as an imposing, alien structure that represented both the last barrier to America as well as its welcoming embrace.

The tour continues through derelict hallways, passing by and looking into detention areas, an abandoned dispensary, and the dining hall. A very modest arranging of a few left-behind artifacts suggests the abandoned functions of particular rooms, but generally the central counterpoint remains that between the narrator's description of anecdotal experience, the ghostly image of the now-empty spaces, and the audience's imagination. Finally, the group is asked to experience the thrill and anxiety of the actual entry into America, as it passes through the area where banks, immigrant aid offices, ticket windows, and other dubious lodging, employment, and transportation services greeted the newcomers. Lest the warm embrace of *landsmen* seem too romantic a coda to the cold intimidation of the great hall's bureaucracy, the guide takes special pains to depict the confusion, corruption, and cynical exploitation that were frequently the immigrant's fate at this point, and the tangled history of efforts to reform this sordid aspect of the immigration service. And then, as for the immigrants themselves one-half century earlier, it is out into the suddenly bright daylight, and the boats.

In sum, this site interpretation is necessarily constrained within an extra-ordinarily limited range of choices that are conventional, controlling, and anything but sophisticated in modern terms. And yet it works, so much so that many visitors, our group included, express regret that their ghost-town experience will not be possible once the impending restoration and interpretive development of the site is complete. This feeling does not reduce solely to the power of the silent ruin, but traces as well to the approach taken in the guide's narration: both, in turn, have much to do with the dimension of audience expectations, that mutuality of interpretive process discussed above.

What makes the interpretation work, it seemed to our group on discussion, was the effort taken to invoke the experience, knowledge, and images brought in by the audience as active, largely silent, elements in the interpretation, and then to broaden and deepen these through evocative description. The tour is thus experienced, by most visitors, as an active process of imaginative recreation. Rather than presenting immigration and Ellis Island in a sophisticated historical narrative, the script takes the basic content and meaning of the larger history almost for granted and works hardest at developing, expanding, and clarifying this, partly in terms of detail, but more centrally in terms of emotional and imaginative depth. Thus, the success of the tour traces in large part to a success in understanding the audience as much as the site—to working both with and against the expectations, images, perceptions, and human curiosities brought by visitors presumed to have some initial sense of the general story and its meaning.

But these advantages carry some of the price discussed earlier, as illustrated by tensions and omissions our group detected at those points where the script—clearly crafted by historically informed and conscientious hands—sought to include points not comfortably fit within the framework of personal dramatistic evocation and recreation around which the tour is organized. For one thing, the historicity of the island and its procedures—the different entry forms and practices at different times, for different groups, under different circumstances—proves hard to communicate when so much work is being put into evoking a clear, dramatic image of a singular process, which itself turns out to be something of an ahistorical composite. Then, too, given the central choices there was little opportunity for meaningful connection offered those who do not as personally identify with the European turn-of-the-century immigrants at the heart of the Ellis Island drama. Beyond this, the other-than-port-of-entry history of Ellis Island could not be comprehensibly explored within the framework of our tour, either. The references were there—wire-screened enclosures in the baggage area, for instance, were identified as a relic of the island's later detention/deportation function—but somehow the continuum of this development was never made very clear, perhaps because there was no opportunity to set Ellis Island within a broader, far more complex story of population movement, both voluntary and forced and both to and from the entire Western hemisphere, a story in which immigration to the United States is only a small part. To engage such audiences and concerns, a less dramatic and less exclusively site-specific interpretation would be necessary.

Finally, audience expectations, images, and assumptions seem to have exerted their most inhibiting force in constraining the interpretation politically within a celebratory framework. Only in part a consequence of the dramatistic evocation, this is perhaps more a gesture to the reverence it is assumed the public expects in its formal national historic shrines. Judgments inconsistent with this celebration thus find little place in the story and do not "take" when mentioned. Thus, the depiction of corruption and exploitation was accompanied by a heroic narrative of top-down reform, a problem solved; the political deportation of radicals, such a substantial and disgraceful feature of Ellis Island history during and after World War I, was barely mentioned. After the tour we asked our guide about this omission. Interestingly, he turned out to know a great deal about the history, mentioning that each guide was required to do a research project as part of their training, and that his had been on deportation of radicals. But all that, he went on, was just "too complicated" to work into his narration.

Thus the history of Ellis Island, as presented in what will soon come to seem the restored site's interpretive prehistory, 1976-1984. It would be a shame, however, if either the limits or the very formidable strength of this ghost-town period were forgotten in the process of restoration and full interpretive development. For visitors will still disembark from their ferries with expectations, images, and perceptions about the island, its story, and its shrine-like status. The constraints and opportunities we have discussed will thus remain central issues that should inform whatever plans are developed.

In a broader sense, the way these questions are resolved will be a measure of the degree to which audience expectations, needs, and interests are coming to be understood as central features, both as opportunity and problem, in the design of public-historical interpretation. The constriction of cliched images and narrow symbols, the dilemma of one part of a story so easily illuminated and recognized that other themes equally important yet less symbolically accessible are obscured or repressed, intentionally or inadvertently—these traps will always be there. But so will the potentially active historical imagination and consciousness of visitors. Invoking and empowering this imagination and consciousness can make the interpretation of sites such as Ellis Island a powerfully shared experience. Public perceptions, expectations, curiosities, and even misconceptions can provide the ground for an interpretive dialogue capable of evolving into a genuinely deeper and more relevant understanding of history and historical process.

Chapter 12

Urban Public History in Celebratory Contexts: The Example of the "Philadelphia's Moving Past" Project[1]

Although substantial interest in urban public history has surfaced in recent years, work and discussion have rarely had much to do with one particular and substantial vein of the research making the most dramatic impact on formal academic scholarship in the field. When interpreting urban history, presentation theory and practice have generally turned to oral history and popular documentary approaches to social and family history, often with a community or bottom-up orientation, rather than to the much-debated and presumably abstruse questions, methods, data, and sources central to the social-scientific "new urban history" of the past fifteen years.[2]

This tendency has been no less pronounced in interpretive programs based on themes—work and occupational mobility, for instance—that have been the subject of extensive social-scientific research. And when the interpretive context is one that presumes a wide and diffuse public audience as opposed to one at least partially self-selected by the content or focus of the program or museum, it would seem that social-scientific history is the last thing we can expect to find, much less advocate as useful.

This chapter describes an experiment in public history that used just such data and ideas from the "new urban history" in just such a context: Philadelphia's year-long tercentenary "birthday party" in 1982. This illustrates more broadly the general programming challenge of what I will call "the celebratory context," a common genre of which the recent Statue of Liberty extravaganza is only the most extreme and problematic example.

Social-scientific historical research can be successfully translated and presented in such settings, I will argue, but the real lesson of the Philadelphia experiment is broader. Beyond demonstrating merely the legitimacy and effectiveness of such approaches, it suggests how social science materials can address real needs in the new and somewhat problematic field of public history. Far from being marginal or peripheral, such approaches may actually help to clarify, engage, and resolve dilemmas that have frustrated precisely that reordering of the relationship between general public and academic scholarship that public history claims to effect.

Before turning to a case-study discussion of the Philadelphia project, of which I was one of the principal designers while serving as a research associate at Theodore Hershberg's Philadelphia Social History Project (PSHP) at the University of Pennsylvania, it might be helpful to say a few words about these dilemmas; they not only inform my assessment of the project retrospectively, but were in one form or another central to our work from original conception to ultimate enactment.

My understanding of public history has been shaped by much work in and on oral history. I have argued that this material is not a short-cut to interpretation, dramatically by-passing intellectual intervention by going to the sources for history in the Cronkite/Von Rankean sense, to link public and academic authority right at the start.[3] Nor is it simply new raw material for historians to process and incorporate in traditional ways. Rather, both source and subject are involved in generating and on a variety of levels interpreting the data, creating unique documents in the process of the interview. In public presentation, the challenge is to have such materials express and advance this uniqueness: in the same sense that both interviewer and interviewee are the "authors" of an oral historical document, public-historical presentation has the challenge of finding ways of sharing the "author-ity" of interpretation with the public.

This has not frequently happened, however, in part because the tendency has too often been to treat the content of the data—whether emotional or informational in nature—as something to be literally "presented" *to* the public, rather than explored *with* them, however implicitly. We are, it seems to me, only beginning to develop ways of thinking and talking about the complex choices, strategies, and decisions involved in using such material in public—to see the public-historical context as alive in ways that have immediate consequences for the nature of historical presentation, rather than as a medium through which we translate scholarship for a wider audience.

Such observations have a broad relevance to current historical programming. In 1986, I served on an NEH history panel in the museums division, examining some thirty-five proposals, most of them extraordinarily well prepared. They were a reasonably good sample of state-of-the-art approaches to historical interpretation and presentation in public settings—hardly limited to formal museum chambers as such. What struck me with particular force was that scarcely any of them spoke at all, much less in depth or precision, to what might be called strategic challenges: how the program would work with and for the kind of audience expected, how an understanding of the context or setting informed what could be communicated about the subject matter and themes of concern, what sort of responses and reactions were hoped for, and to what effect—in short, what the designers understood to be, historically and intellectually, the design challenge and the proposed solution or approach in a public historical sense. Rather, we found in the applications' elaborate justification of the historical themes to be presented per se, their intellectual and scholarly pedigree and provenance, and an argument as to the importance of bringing them to a wider public. Only rarely was this process itself imagined to be complex or demanding in any intellectual sense; that seemed something to be subcontracted to designers, rather than of primary importance in its own right.

I hope these observations are recognizable to those who have had the experience of trying to design, to "sell"—whether to grant agencies, community groups, or private sponsors—and to implement a public history project. For those who have not, I hope the vantage will be accepted for the moment as one from which to examine our attempt in Philadelphia to raise such an interpretive challenge to a conscious level and to design a response, one to which a social-scientific data base proved central.

A Complex Challenge

From the start of citywide planning for what was to be called the *Century IV* celebration of Philadelphia's tercentenary (1682-1982), a number of us at the PSHP thought about participating. Century IV was clearly going to say a lot about history, and we decided that if the efforts of the PSHP and the new urban history by extension were to make a broader difference, it was important that the scholarship find a public voice in such a celebration. Accordingly, representatives of the PSHP, the Philadelphia Area Cultural Consortium (which had developed pioneering historical tours focused on ethnicity and urban industrial history), and some key members of the Century IV planning staff together developed a preliminary plan that won an NEH Chairman's Planning Grant to design a full-fledged proposal.

The resulting project design flowed from challenges made explicit at the start. First, we set out to show that a citywide year-long birthday celebration could contain, at least in small part, something other than self-promotion, trivial entertainments, and commercial exploitation. More particularly, we proposed that historical programming could turn these into resources—taking advantage of the huge audiences and the generalized historical curiosity inherent in the tercentenary celebration to devise an alternative to parochial urban boosterism, self-congratulatory biography, and Philadelphia's especially irrelevant self-image still centered on Independence Hall, Benjamin Franklin, and the Betsy Ross House. Historical programming could help people understand the Philadelphia of the present, and could stimulate discussion of policy choices and community issues, promoting deeper community awareness and intergroup understanding in a troubled and divided city. The first challenge, then, was to see how the attributes of the citywide celebratory context—its massiveness, inclusiveness, superficiality, and frenetic energy—could help support and stimulate meaningful historical dialogue and discussion.

A related challenge was to prevent the citywide and regionwide nature of the celebration from overshadowing all sense of group and neighborhood identity—especially given how important community and neighborhood issues had become in modern Philadelphia. This was the challenge of making history meaningful on the human scale and in the neighborhood settings in which most people actually experience the city. It also involved the challenge of participation: beyond the usual genuflections to bottom-up involvement, we felt the celebratory context mandated a special effort to find ways in which history and the city could be explored by Philadelphia's people in their own terms and from their diverse vantages, to the end of generating a very different picture of what was important and why than might predictably be projected by an official birthday celebration.

Finally, we set out to show that the findings of the new social history could make for successful public programming—and quite naturally. One of the central paradoxes of recent scholarship is that the very means by which we have been able to explore and understand the lives of ordinary people—in social history the data banks and statistical analyses of projects such as the PSHP—have tended to produce scholarship seemingly inaccessible to general academic readers, much less a broader reading public, much less the people of the neighborhoods and groups such histories study. Our hypothesis was that this did not have to hold for public history—that the data-based view from the bottom up could actually make for a more engaging kind of historical exhibition than the view from William Penn's famous hat atop City Hall. In numerous public lectures and presentations, Ted Hershberg was discovering how meaningfully PSHP research, especially on the historical structure of black Philadelphia, could be presented to diverse audiences—discoveries that helped refine the "Tale of Three Cities" essay that is to most readers the most meaningful and accessible of the papers in the important volume of papers summing up the project's work. Hershberg's assistant, Henry Williams, had run some spectacularly successful and popular workshops at public libraries with what he called "The History Booth"—using manuscript census printouts to help visitors look up who lived in their street a century ago.[4]

These perspectives led us to propose a solution to the programming challenge of the citywide celebratory context that was paradoxical and controversial in three senses: the route to success in such a setting, we argued, required not less academic and intellectual content but rather more; not a broad generalized perspective on the City and its Spirit and History over three centuries, but a highly particular one grounded in neighborhood and group complexity, and focusing on the history of industrial and now postindustrial Philadelphia; not a more controlled and formulaic presentation but one open to genuine interaction, playful spontaneity, and substantive shaping by the people of Philadelphia themselves. All these rested on the even more paradoxical notion that social-scientific materials and the products of the new social history would provide the improbable glue, the intellectual coherence that would tie it all together, and the experiential base that might make it actually work for the diverse audiences and purposes of a celebratory context.

An Ambitious Response

Here as in a grant proposal, everything looks clearer and works better than ever could be the case in practice. And in our experience the eventual reality bore even less resemblance to the projections: our efforts were limited and flawed in many respects, the major NEH grant proposal we prepared was rejected, and consequently, the project was mounted on a vastly truncated and in some respects fatally compromised scale. These considerations will help to underscore some of the broader lessons to be drawn, although first it will be useful to have a sense of the overall design constructed in the fantasyland of a grant proposal. Let me therefore sketch very briefly how we thought our ambitious complex of aims might be realized.

Relatively speaking, for us the themes came into focus first, emerging as a sort of grid we used to test and refine the design concepts. Whatever the forms of our project, we determined, certainly in sum and hopefully in each aspect three clear thematic dimensions would have to be present. First, the project would have to help people see and explore the larger historical patterns and systems within which Philadelphia's history was set—to see group, community, neighborhood, and city as elements subject to historical forces, opportunities and constraints understandable only on a map far broader in time and space than the focus of the Century IV celebration. Second, our programs and materials would represent social units—neighborhoods as well as the city itself—as a complex set of systems, rather than as an anthropomorphized personality with a biography, or as a simple expression of place or ethnicity. The imprint of the PSHP was especially strong here (Hershberg's stress on "city as process") in our desire to help people understand and work with (and play with) the "building blocks" of urban change, as seen tangibly on a neighborhood basis: housing stock, jobs and "opportunity structures," changing ethnic, racial, and general demographic characteristics, cultural patterns and institutions, and so on. Finally, we determined to explore, as both an intellectual requirement and as a route to public programming, the historicality and contingency of everyday life experience: patterns in individual and family life, work and social relations, gender roles and age patterns, and the like, the very dimensions so commonly discussed with little sense of how such things change or evolve, or even that they do, as opposed to being fixed in human nature or character.

Our central belief was that all these dimensions or levels had to be almost constantly present, if an adequate re-vision of what we mean by a city's history was to be possible as a product of the programming; for any of the three to be missing would be to invite one or more of a series of highly problematic fallacies—neighborhoods as communities indistinguishable from romanticized villages or towns; historical trends as removed from individual experience; and so on. And we believed, with equal strength, that each and all of these themes could illuminate the present as well as the past, and hence could function as pivots for moving from one to the other, exploring the relation between historical and contemporary urban life. Thus, we tried to inform our design with a set of complex thematic requirements that had intellectual importance in their own right and could also serve as functional guides to strategic programming choices that might work on the street.

The project that evolved in response to these considerations was no less complex, and involved three distinct components that could be both self-standing and functionally interwoven. The major component was to be what we called the "Historymobile"—a travelling history exhibit/workshop/event housed in a refitted city bus that would transport modular exhibits, interactive workshop materials, and a fold-down stage to various locales where a program could be mounted and presented in the street. Rather than presenting history "to" the public, the idea was to provide a portable bank of skills, exhibits, documents, and hands-on materials through which people could help discover and build that history for themselves and set it in a wider context.

The Historymobile program was designed to work for a spectrum of events. On the exhibit level, it could be an engaging ancillary attraction at the expected massive public events that would be the highlight of Century IV programming. It could be available "on demand" at community events of all kinds throughout the year, bringing more interactive programming to a community organization street festival, a church supper, or a school or library event. Its fullest potential, however, was to be developed in sustained interaction with people in six carefully selected target neighborhoods, through which community people and project personnel could, over the course of the year, together create from historical source material their own program of neighborhood documentation and public events, and a specific community history exhibit that would remain a permanent contribution of the project.

The second component was to be a summer Institute in Urban Public History, for teams of teacher or community members from the six target neighborhoods. The idea here was to go beyond the NEH Institute-style introduction to new historical ideas, concepts, and literature, although this would be the focus of morning sessions, by adding afternoon workshops exploring ways to develop and present such approaches in public programs. Institute students would link this component and the Historymobile, taking a leadership role in the neighborhood specific projects that would be developed through a summer-long series of events in the target areas.

Finally, to serve residents of the entire metropolitan region and tourists visiting the city, we planned a unique program of "Urban Issue Tours." Building on the proven and practical format of historical bus and walking tours, these would be topical, oriented around contemporary problems or issues placed in historical perspective—we designed tours around ethnic succession, gentrification, uses of green space, creative re-use of industrial structures, and so on. Where the Historymobile program was to be neighborhood-specific and cross-thematic, the tours would be theme-specific and cross-neighborhood in nature. Indeed, many were to be not so much tours as movable discussion groups: at major stops, residents, officials, and activists would meet with visitors to discuss general themes and specific neighborhood perspectives.

We felt this combination of elements began to address the rather diverse challenges of the celebratory context. But to assess the overall approach, it is important to have some sense of the more detailed design ideas and strategies we hoped to employ. Space permits me to illustrate these only in reference to the Historymobile, in any event the only component to be realized in something approaching the intended form. Our big breakthrough in designing the Historymobile was to shift from thinking of a movable exhibit used in a bus—the original notion—to a movable exhibit/workshop that could be set up in the street on a far grander scale. We were helped in this direction by what turned out to be a fortuitous decision to hire Jim Hamilton—a design consultant with a background not in exhibitions and museum work, but in theater and public event planning. Working with him, we came up with a plan calling for a basic exhibit that could be displayed on up to twelve rectangular collapsible kiosks with large umbrella canopies. The kiosks would display text, graphics, and other materials introducing the three major thematic foci, as noted above. In the fuller programs, the kiosks would form a pavilion leading to or surrounding a workshop plaza: banners and signage would then direct viewers to theme-specific activities.

We projected three very general types of activities as examples of how the themes might be embodied in popular and instructive activities, in addition to the more academically grounded documentary exhibits on the kiosk panels. The first theme involved setting neighborhood life in a "Big Picture"; we thought it might be possible to involve people in building a giant map through which individual and family histories could be displayed by inviting visitors to stretch strings or lines from the focal point to points of family origin or destination. As patterns emerged on such a map—intended to be some forty feet long and fifteen feet high—interpretive materials could be found and displayed illustrating the social, economic, and cultural meaning of relationships thus given spatial expression for all to see.

The second theme mentioned earlier involved the building blocks and processes of neighborhoods. To involve people in exploring this, we envisioned a vast expansion of the History Booth idea. Neighborhood residents would look up in census print-outs information about who lived in their house a century ago, and then would display this information through attaching color-coded markers of various kinds about age, sex, occupation, ethnicity, family structure, and so forth on a mammoth billboard-sized lot plan of the neighborhood, displayed near the research area. Over the course of a day, and in several successive visits in target neighborhoods, a portrait of the social history of the neighborhood would begin to appear as the map became filled in: supportive materials could then be retrieved and displayed (artifacts of crafts and work, of family life, and so on) to respond to the patterns discernible themselves through group discussion and interpretation.

The final theme, dealing with the historicality of personal and family experience, we thought might be embodied through a free-form "People Wall and Neighborhood Family Album," on which contributed items, mementos, photos, or copies or representations, might be displayed, in conjunction with such things as "accession booth" where family documents or artifacts might be brought in for examination for possible value and historical discussion, and an "oral history room" inside the bus, for on-site interviews and documentation. We hoped to coordinate these various activities through a presentation stage folding down from the bus, which would provide a focus for a program of activities interspersing history-related presentation, discussion, and interpretation (involving both outside interpreters and neighborhood figures in the process) and a range of neighborhood-generated music, storytelling, or other community-determined events. All this, we thought, would support an afternoon or day-long event of considerable substance as well as entertainment interest, one in which local people would themselves be directly involved in generating, discussing, and interpreting their own neighborhood's history.

This sketch begins to suggest how we hoped the challenge of a not very serious entertainment and street-festival context might yet be made to support activities that were attractive, fun, engaging, and substantive—and which might provide a meaningful kind of community self-exploration. By focusing on historical process rather than on the substance of historical events, and by providing both tools and guidance in something approaching historical research as an activity rather than simply exhibiting a specific texted version of history, we hoped to complement the games, entertainment, and fast-food atmosphere of a street festival, inviting elaborations limited only by the curiosity and ingenuity of those involved in a specific neighborhood project.

The Real World

So much for the theory. We never had the opportunity to test this vision in practice, nor even to begin to enact the other two components, because we failed to receive the major NEH grant that would have made the entire project possible. But the NEH response itself, if viewed as an indication of how such challenges were understood, provides a kind of inverse confirmation by embodying quite precisely the sort of attitudes we had sought to challenge. Although we regretted being unsuccessful in our assault, the confrontation at least left us feeling we had identified some of the right targets.

Much in the NEH response was disappointing and vexatious, but rather than succumb to the disappointed grant-seeker's temptation to rebut this or that criticism, some on-target, some based on misreading, and some completely off-the-wall, let me observe that the negative level of panelist response varied inversely with evident respect for and understanding of the special challenge at hand—the celebratory context and its capacity for supporting meaningful public history. It also varied inversely with the degree to which panelists recognized our argument that social-science approaches to urban history offered a new way for people to engage, interact, and understand historical process. Our several positive reviews from the panel explicitly discussed just these dimensions, but the dominant negative views tended to state the obvious as an argument: that a public street festival was not a serious locale for historical presentation, in contrast presumably to a museum, and that no recognizable "content" (that is, historical narrative or conventional story line) existed for our projected exhibit material or program.

The most pervasive fear seemed to be that the approach would be what one panelist called. "a circus," an uncontrolled public arena devoted to fun rather than to sober reflection. Indeed, our artist's conception of the planned environment had tried to evoke a large, diverse crowd in public space. Our NEH officer told us afterward that this had "fortunately" arrived too late, because it would have guaranteed an even more strongly negative vote from the panel—it looked too much like people having fun, he said. We took this as a kind of backhanded confirmation, however painful: our plans had been rejected not for their particulars, but almost by definition. The challenges upon which we had based our entire approach were not accepted as legitimate; indeed, they were not really even recognized as such.

Because we still felt the challenges were estimable and worth the effort of response, we persisted in efforts to finance the project through other sources, public and private, and did scrape together enough to get the Historymobile outfitted, with a truncated exhibit and neighborhood program. This experience provided further evidence of how deeply rooted, beyond NEH academics, was the resistance to some of what we thought worth testing in our approach. The obstacles were encountered, predictably, in the implementation stage, and fought out over the specific content and design of kiosk exhibits—organization, text, and illustration. Our proposal boldly announced that we would risk choosing more content over less, more text over sparse labels, and analytic content, as in the building-block approach, over conventional topics. In practice, it proved hard for the academics, the design people, and media consultants to agree, and in the final enactment the latter two generally prevailed: the kiosk texts abandoned much, although not all, of our conceptual framework, pared the content to almost nothing, and favored large photo-blowups rather than more creative constructions, diagrams, and maps. The unkindest cut of all was a decision to have the title kiosk consist of a photo of the City Hall statue of William Penn—precisely the image we had most hoped to avoid.

Exhibit Set-Up: Tubing for kiosks being assembled for a program in a neighborhood setting. All materials had been transported to the site in the Historymobile Bus, seen in the background. The bus has also been used to block the street, creating a plaza and providing a backdrop for stage presentations.

Umbrella canopies being stretched over kiosk frames, which have been weighted with garbage cans filled with water from a nearby hydrant.

Exhibition graphics and text printed on nylon have been stretched around the kiosk frames. Removable photographic document panels, secured by velcro strips, are here being placed on the kiosk.

The completed installation, this time in a downtown plaza.

The "History Booth"; interpreters use Sanborn maps, manuscript census xeroxes, and computer printouts to identify the residents of city neighborhoods a century ago and to discuss their history with visitors.

And yet, we discovered when the bus started rolling and the exhibit and program actually hit the streets that none of this turned out to matter very much. The events proved extraordinarily successful in just the ways we had hoped they might be, and in ways that confirmed the insights on which we had designed the program. The dramatic canopied kiosks were very popular with the public. They created a sense of a festive yet serious event, attracting and holding substantial crowd attention. My own observation, on the several days I was able to watch the show in operation, was especially confirming: people showed more interest in those kiosk exhibit panels that had more content and complexity, whether graphic or textual, rather than more of the bold "illustrations" or simplistic labels on which the designers had been so insistent. In fact, the single most attractive panel, in terms both of people drawn to it and the amount of time spent there, was a prosaic Housing Authority map of Philadelphia's officially designated neighborhoods, each with a number keyed to a long list of names on the adjacent panel. And it was clear that what made this attractive was the quality of the experience it offered beyond the content as such: I could see people examine the map, then look to the names, back and forth, testing their neighborhood knowledge and expectations against the answers revealed by linking numbered space to the map's legend.

This implied interactivity was explicit in the most consistently successful element of the program—the PSHP data-based History Booth, the idea from which we started and the residue of our more elaborate plans. To each destination, the bus would carry large area Sanborn maps, photocopies of the 1880 manuscript census for the neighborhood, and other PSHP data printouts and manuscripts. Enthusiastic crowds of people lined up, each taking a turn looking up his or her address and discussing with the interpreters what was found. This went far beyond just curiosity: in the afternoon I spent on the desk, virtually every search led to a discussion about social history—the nature of occupations, the mix of types in an area then as opposed to now, the relation of ethnicity to class, the meaning of boarders, extended families, whether "no children" meant children who might have already left the home at an early age, and on and on. We had prepared, almost tongue-in-cheek, a certificate to be filled out after each search—attesting in stilted formal language to the presence 100 years ago of the following individuals with such and such characteristics at the said address. It seemed to us an important and chastening indicator that people did not take these as jokes—indeed, very frequently they asked for additional copies or blank forms on which they might have the information inscribed in impressive calligraphy, suitable for framing.

Although never able to move from the individual to the collective neighborhood level of exploration we had hoped to produce, these exchanges demonstrated everything we might have hoped to see: that people found these data interesting; that discovering them led to broader and personally meaningful insights into urban social space and change; that interpretation could be an active and shared process, and that the very "author-ity" of historical understanding could in this way be a self-discovered and self-generated public resource in an urban community. While our NEH panel had found the challenge of the celebratory context beneath their dignity, our field experience leads me to conclude that it is, indeed, really the opposite—not only a possible venue for creative interpretation, but one that could encourage and support imaginative approaches to a new kind of historical interpretation. People do not bring to such settings a self-conscious intention to be educated or to engage in a serious confrontation with history; but they do bring great good will and a kind of open-ended, diffuse curiosity, and they come in huge numbers that are anything but self-selected in terms of historical themes.

All this means that the possibilities of historical interpretation become similarly open-ended. And it also means that dramatic new approaches to historical information and meaning, such as found in social-science history, offer as yet untapped possibilities: however abstruse and demanding in the academy, such questions, methods, and results may well prove to be enormously fertile as grounds for new kinds of historical presentation in public space. Social science historians used to feeling that their academic colleagues neither understand nor really respect them may find in the general public, strolling casually through the fluff of a celebratory extravaganza, more suitable partners for historical discussion.

Chapter 13

The Presentation of Urban History
in Big City Museums

A growing number of major American cities now have museums, whether public, private, or somewhere in between, that offer to citizens, visitors, and schoolchildren a formal version of the city's history—a civic "presentation of self." This chapter considers some of the problems and opportunities of this very particular dimension of public-historical practice. Its aims can also be more general, however, because the urban history museum stands at the precise intersection of a complex of distinct concerns that, taken together, define the current moment in the evolution of public-historical presentation. These concerns include meeting the obligations of a museum to its diverse and often conflicting public constituencies, fixing the role of modern historical scholarship and scholars (often but not exclusively academic), and resolving the tension between the need to develop and display collections and the need to focus on broader didactic or thematic historical conceptions. Every history museum confronts one or more of these issues to a certain degree, but for the urban history museum, for reasons explored here, they are all central and interconnected.

The usefulness of the big city museum as a context for engaging broader issues is coming to be widely recognized. At the 1984 Past Meets Present conference—organized by the New York Council for the Humanities as a first attempt at bringing historians, designers, and museum professionals together to crystallize an emerging discourse about common concerns—the most productive discussions focused on conference field trips to urban and community history exhibits, ranging from the Chinatown History Project and the Museo del Barrio in New York to the Silk City project that linked several museums in Paterson, New Jersey. At the same time, urban museums need to draw on a wider perspective; at the next major meeting to engage such issues, the 1987 Common Agenda conference, an influential working paper argued that city museums were "only beginning to explore urbanization and urban-

ism as explanatory paradigms, the potential of the urban museums as possibly a unique history museum type, or the responsibilities of such an institution
in documenting and collecting contemporary city life." In consequence, one
of the few specific implementation steps proposed in the final report of Common Agenda was that "a coalition of urban-based North American museums
should interpret the story of how we became an urban-suburban civilization
on a scale unprecedented in the twentieth century."[1]

Such a task force has now been formed with imaginative and knowledgeable museum professionals from institutions already providing fine examples
of innovative approaches to urban historical exhibition. Over the next few
years, the results of this collaboration should be evident, a testament to how
much of the energy for the reimagining of history museums is being generated from within the profession. Given that such concentrated effort and
expertise is being brought to bear on the challenge of the urban history exhibit
and collection by informed museum professionals, there may be some complementary value in offering here a view not only from the outside, but from
the bottom up, which in museum terms means from the vantage of the visitor
strolling through the galleries in more or less casual curiosity.

In such a spirit, this essay considers some major city history museums
with special attention to the formal urban-biography core exhibits. Resources
precluded anything approaching a representative sample of city or exhibit
types, but in any event my aim is neither to survey and typologize the many
nor to select an exemplary few. Rather, I want to explore a vocabulary for
discussing what is going on in the standing major-city biography exhibit,
based on visits made without prior discussion with museum personnel or
investigation of the collections or institutional background of any exhibit. My
approach sought to approximate the perspective of visitors who encounter
these exhibits with little preparation—an audience that can be presumed to
be interested in the history *in* the museum, but is probably not aware of or
concerned with the exhibition history *of* the museum. These examples lead
us to consider a few more intentionally chosen exhibits representing what I
identify as some important directions in current interpretation. Discussion of
these directions, I hope, may help close the circle, linking this outsider's perspective to the insights of the Common Agenda group and other professionals currently so active on this very lively interpretational frontier in cities
across the country.

Our tour begins with the permanent exhibits, in 1987, at the Museum of
the City of New York, the Atwater Kent Museum in Philadelphia, and both the
Missouri Historical Society and the Old Courthouse in St. Louis. And like a
tour guide struggling to hold visitors in the orientation center or on the bus
before releasing them to the exhibition itself, let me suggest that our survey
will prove more useful if we first consider a number of themes central to the

challenge of the municipal history exhibit at this specific moment of public-historical museum development.

Challenges in Three Dimensions

Each of the three general concerns noted above has a particular meaning for the official or semiofficial city history exhibit, making its challenge both especially problematic and especially interesting. First is the form and content implied by the commitment to municipal self-portraiture. In the American context in which city identities have long been commonly projected in terms of economic growth and progress, the frame for urban biography has been almost necessarily deductive, a linear, heroic form into which a city's growth and development must fit. This process has tended to harness the narrative of the past to an optimistic assessment of a city's present and future.

This tendency is reinforced by the official or semiofficial sponsorship of many such museums, because it comes to seem natural that a core exhibit should offer a municipal history with meaning and direction, constructively leading to the collective future for which the city sponsors are in some sense responsible. Such an instrumental approach to collective mytho-biography is reinforced as well by the complex audiences such museum exhibits characteristically are expected to address: a regular procession of local schoolchildren presumed to need a simplified, graspable story line; visiting tourists, dignitaries, and businessmen for whom it seems appropriate to put a best municipal foot forward; and a diverse general population that many museums have sought to gather under a unifying historical umbrella, building and reinforcing community through the act of celebrating it historically. In practice if not in theoretical necessity, the narrative form, the self-promotional purpose, and the evocation of a presumptive community have long been almost impossible to distinguish in conventional municipal exhibits.

The celebratory impulse is an obvious obstacle to good historical interpretation, as is the all-embracing fictive community. But the narrative form is different in that, less obviously, it may be a real resource, as much part of the solution as part of the problem. Much recent social history has been held vulnerable to the charge that its findings have fragmented even academic understanding by failing to generate coherent narrative, the story-structures that ultimately should be built from the products of all the toil in the forests and quarries of historical research. Whatever the academic validity of this criticism (it often has masked a rear-guard assault on the political implications of recent scholarship) it does represent a pressing concern for museum presentation, where the public's right to a graspable, engaging, and coherent exhibit should be axiomatic. In this sense, the inherited story-line structure of the municipal portrait offers a solid, audience-supportive foundation, if only its dimensions can be stretched to support the kind of edifice implied by modern urban-historical scholarship.

More particularly still, the urban-biographical narrative perspective inevitably involves some mix of broad economic and political forces; of regional, national, and even international relationships; and of a complex of social groups and relations across the racial-ethnic and class spectrum, however prosaically approached. Even proponents concede that the new social history has focused on neglected groups and particular subcultural experiences at the frequent expense of precisely these broader systemic perspectives. Thus the conventional frame of the municipal biography may offer a useful structure for realizing that elusive presentational synthesis of particular social experiences with broader political and economic analysis.

In informing this structure with contemporary scholarship, we encounter a second dimension requiring attention: the particular content, form, and meaning of urban-historical scholarship as a subcategory of the new social history, and its implications for museum interpretation and presentation. Urban history was arguably the first evolving new speciality to climb from the hothouse swamp of intellectual ferment in the late 1960s onto broadly recognized historiographical ground. Responding both to the social-political urban crisis of that period and to the new historical awareness of social-scientific methods and approaches, the so-called new urban history had an enormous impact, especially in its focus on social and geographic mobility through analytically retracing the lives of the actual inhabitants of the nineteenth-century city.

The enterprise has foundered somewhat of late, however; much of its energy has been drawn into the broader concerns of the new social history, and critics have recurrently noted that the promise of a coherent analysis of urban structure and processes has not been realized. And even the milestones of intellectual progress mark a road that would seem to lead away from the museum, a road paved with a formidable macadam of statistics, quantification, historical data banks, and complex economic and planning models. As with the narrative tradition, then, modern urban scholarship would not seem to offer an encouraging base for innovation in public-historical scholarship. But here, too, the liability may offer some surprising advantages in that, however ironically, these forbidding methods have produced some of the most concrete insights and vivid detail about the lives of actual, identifiable common people, those usually invisible and certainly silent in the artifact collections and documentation drawn on for conventional exhibits.[2]

Finally, we need to reflect on the relation between collection and interpretation, between displayed artifact and didactic design, as this defines the terrain within which effective urban-historical museum exhibits, as distinct from illustrated academic lectures, can be mounted. Recent commentary has tended to see modern scholarship as a kind of populist knight riding to rescue history from tradition-bound, elite-serving museums. Often quite correctly, critics have faulted the museums for having confused cart and horse—for permitting an obligation to display their "things" to overwhelm interpretation, imprisoning it within airless display cases. Accordingly, fever-ish imagination has been devoted to opening the museum so that new ideas, values, and subject matter might ventilate the intellectual space of the exhibit. In the process, however, historians have often undervalued the artifactual base of most museums' collections and what these artifacts contribute to the museum experience. Indeed, scholars have often proven quite insensitive to the whole notion of how and why a museum exhibit is interesting to its visitors.

This is not simply a matter of academics casting the exhibit process in their own intellectual image. The problems are real enough, and the critique intimidating enough, that the academic approach has been largely internal-ized by many museum professionals seeking to modernize their exhibit approaches. Relatively less attention is being paid to the collections and how the interest they hold for visitors may serve as a resource for new approaches to historical interpretation. Instead, inordinate emphasis is often placed on the "script" content and the conceptualization behind it, as if the point were to present the "right" message "to the public, its points "illustrated" by arti-facts, rather than to offer an environment within which historical materials and ideas were discussed "with" visitors, however implicitly.

This is a subtle but important distinction, which is just beginning to be recognized more widely. In Edward Alexander's classic overview, *Museums in Motion*, for instance, virtually no attention is given to how history museums and their audiences interact, aside from a rule-proving exception: a discus-sion of communications theory, feedback loops, and behavioral objectives that has no particular relation to historical communication as such. And at the vanguard Past Meets Present Conference, for all the exciting dialogue among historians and museum professionals, there was almost no discussion linking the two on questions of presentational choices involved in effectively reaching an audience with a given historical thematic exhibit. Those talking about space, display, and design issues tended to be the professional designers who, quite naturally, approached these questions in terms of flow, imagery, and audience psychology, not as matters with implications for historical con-tent and interpretation.[3]

Recent experience on a National Endowment for the Humanities (NEH) museum panel suggests that there is something more general in this indiffer-ence. The panel I served on examined some thirty-five proposals, most of them professional, sophisticated, and well-prepared. Yet scarcely *any* spoke at all, much less in depth or precision, to what I would term the strategic challenge of the proposed exhibit: how it intended to work with and for the kind of audience anticipated; how this context informed what could and could not be displayed or communicated; how content and design were related to hoped-for responses and reactions, and to what effect. Almost totally missing was any consideration of the collections approach and the design challenge of the particular theme or content, and the proposed solution offered by the exhibit interpretation and plan. Rather, the grant writers were relentlessly drawn to elaborate demonstrations of the intellectual pedigree and scholarly provenance of exhibit concepts, and affirmations of the importance of bringing them to a varied public. But the process of actually doing this was rarely discussed as complex or demanding in any serious intellectual sense—this was implied to be something the design consultants and collection people would address later.

Some of this may trace to the fact that these were applications to NEH, after all, and that such an intellectual focus is what applicants thought they were expected to advance. But NEH's Museum Division panels are generally composed equally of museum professionals and academics, and even if correct, the guess as to what was expected of applicants only underscores the point that academic historical discourse and the museums' traditional concern with the uses of collections and the power of artifacts remain on separate tracks. The two dimensions ultimately need to be joined in and for the visitor, of course, and in doing so I think that the degree of attention to the audience role in how an exhibit actually works may be a crucial variable.

In the area of formal municipal history exhibits, the problem of audience extends across the conventional academic/museum divide, yet each side has real resources that can be mobilized to address it. Much in the new social and urban history can generate innovative ways for helping visitors see their own lives and experiences reflected in the narrative flow of city history. And because the conventional municipal exhibit is usually not "about" a focused collection, but must use a wide range of objects to tell a broader story far from explicit in the artifacts themselves, it rests to a real extent on precisely the inquiry-driven approach to the use and development of collections that the Common Agenda group, for instance, sees as one of the most promising bridges for linking museums and historical scholarship.[4] Indeed, as we shall see presently, important clues to how artifacts can figure in presentation and interpretation can be rescued from even the most parochial, pedestrian, and pompous exercises in historical puffery.

Thus alerted to some of the barriers to and opportunities for innovative public-historical presentation in the large-city urban history exhibit, we can move out of the interpretation center into some of the museums themselves.

A Visit to Some Current Exhibits

Founded in 1923, the Museum of the City of New York claims to be the first museum in the nation explicitly dedicated to the history of a major city. Housed in an imposing Georgian building at Fifth Avenue and 103rd Street, it is somewhat off the visitor's beaten path in Manhattan, and it gives the impression of a sleepy, old-fashioned facility with rich, traditional collections, just beginning to show some vitality and to struggle for broader relevance, vitality, and scope in its offerings and programs. The featured exhibit on my 1987 visit was "Bellevue Hospital: 250 Years in Service to New York," and it was smartly designed and quite professional, mixing artifacts, well-chosen photographs, and a sophisticated text. While it contains little that might disturb the Bellevue alumni whose grant supported it, this exhibit does offer historical insight into the complexity of defining and providing institutional welfare, medical, and psychiatric services in a growing metropolis.

The formal, permanent city history exhibits, however, are very dated. They stem from an era in which history largely meant the Colonial and Revolutionary Periods, and in which maps, a few tools and artifacts, and a great deal of furniture were arranged to evoke a long-departed urban milieu. The two major galleries focus on Dutch New Amsterdam and British/Revolutionary New York City. The latter consists mostly of furniture, costumes, and Gilbert Stuart *Washington*s. The Dutch gallery is an imposing example of an old-fashioned form: there is a replica of a fort whose steps and balustrades one can walk. And there is a marvelous diorama surrounding an elaborate model of lower Manhattan with corresponding maps. But there is nothing that really suggests the nature or process of urban growth, nor is there any clear interpretation of why this city, in this place, at this time, had this particular form or history.

Beyond that, the museum's exhibits are explicitly collection-focused rather than historically interpretive: there are a number of period rooms from actual elite homes, an Alexander Hamilton room, silver displays, a map and print collection, and two small galleries focused on the Stock Exchange and the port, both concerned more with display of memorabilia, models, and so on rather than extensive historical interpretation. These exhibits (as well as the famous dollhouse, toy, and costume collections on the third floor) are interesting in the different ways that such artifacts can engage one's historical curiosity—but they do not pretend to a coherent urban-historical statement.

For this purpose, the museum relies on a relatively new centerpiece: a splashy multimedia, audiovisual show entitled "The Big Apple" (the museum's new logo is based on the same) sponsored, quite prominently, by ITT and evidently directed at schoolchildren. In an object-bordered gallery room stands a huge red apple; as the show starts, it opens to reveal multiple slide screens. The show that follows is in constant visual motion, accompanied by narration spiced with music, sound effects, and periodic snippets of dialogue by actors.

The script is embarrassing as advertising, much less as history. It races from landmark to landmark—Verrazano, the Dutch, the Revolution, Robert Fulton, the clipper ships, Central Park, the Statue of Liberty, and so on—stitching the whole together with predictable homilies: New York City illustrates the American trinity of vigorous commercial development, technological growth, and individual opportunity; success rewards "energetic, hard-working people, creative, ingenious, and inventive people from all over the world"; New York is a melting pot for groups such as the Irish (who, "after a difficult period of adjustment due to shortages of jobs and housing and religious discrimination . . . are assimilated and become another important part of New York"). For the twentieth century, the pacing becomes incoherently frenetic ("By 1930, the time of the great economic depression, the population reaches nearly seven million. And as New York's population rises to enormous heights, so do its buildings . . ."), punctuated by a mention of Puerto Ricans and a hollow tribute to Harlem, where "the entire scope of black America's unique culture survives and flourishes." This permits the conclusion that "New York City is a city of all nations. A city of all peoples and for all peoples . . . . A city for the young and a city for the old. A city for the rich and a city for the not-so-rich . . . ."[5]

The show is more instructive as a display of presentational techniques. Interestingly, the jazziest are the least effective: much of the visual material is impressive, but gains little from the rapid-fire split/multiple screen projection. To imagine even young schoolchildren finding the theatrical moments anything but ludicrous is difficult: "There's talk our new Director-General, Peter Minuit, will offer, in the name of our Dutch West India Company, to buy legally the Island from the Indians!", and then "Governor! Governor! The English ships are entering the harbor!", giving us New York, where a man exclaims, "Life is harder here than in England, but this is a place to grow, a place for the future!" The dialogue doesn't get much better under American auspices.

Where it is grounded more in the traditional strengths of the museum, however, the Big Apple show is surprisingly effective. Its greatest contribution is housing the show not in a theater, but in a museum gallery, for just as one is getting used to the barrage of slides and music, a new dimension opens up: "In 1613, Block moors his ship, the *Tiger*, near the southern tip of the small island the natives call *Manhattan*. Unfortunately, the ship catches fire, burns, and sinks in the harbor. High on the wall, to your left, are some of the actual charred timbers of the *Tiger*, discovered fifty years ago." As heads turn, the timbers are picked out by the beam of a spotlight. The technique is used repeatedly:

Behind you, back here on your right, this fourteen-passenger horsecar and others like it help to meet the internal transportation needs of the growing community . . . .

This is the era of the great clipper ships. Look to your left: that's a carved figurehead from a British East Indian ship. Sailing the Seven Seas from China, Africa, Europe, and the Spice Islands, these ships bring their cargoes to South Street, on the East River.

Even when the text is corny, there is something powerful about the way the spotlight stills the breathless motion of the slideshow. It provides a moment for silent concentration on a real artifact, and does so far more effectively than would the pointing finger of an actual tour guide. This reminds us of the most traditional virtue of museums: the unconstrained imaginative power of objects from the past, if we can be encouraged to pause and look at them closely.

The Museum of the City of New York, then, seems a representative embodiment of the strengths and weaknesses of very conventional approaches to city history. Its attempt to make a Great Leap Forward via technology indicates how unpromising is this effort in the absence of an accompanying effort to rethink the history itself. But it also suggests, more usefully, that the strengths of traditional collections need not be jettisoned and may actually provide substantial support for more innovative techniques, approaches, and interpretation.

The Atwater Kent Museum in Philadelphia, occupying an imposing Greek Revival building that was once the Franklin Institute, dates from 1939, which makes it the second oldest formal city museum in the country. It is trimmer and more focused than its Manhattan predecessor, and is currently undergoing substantial revitalization and redevelopment from an ambitious staff. The major exhibit, "Philadelphia, 1680-1880," was designed in the late 1970s, when the Atwater Kent attempted to interpret far more systematically than the Museum of the City of New York the process of historical development in a major city. This core installation captures well the intellectual and presentational content of a serious museum approach on the eve of the current wave of innovation and reflection.

The exhibit is traditional in style and tone: it occupies a large terraced room through which the visitor walks past a chronological/thematic sequence of artifact displays, most in cases, supplemented by a few larger graphics and hangings. The most unusual interpretive display technique, in fact, dates from the 1938-1940 WPA project out of which the museum itself evolved— this is a large scale model of Elfreth's Alley, Philadelphia's most famous eighteenth-century street, oriented around a view from the complex of back alley and yards; a cleverly placed mirror permits good view of the neat brick frontage of the rowhouses as well, suggesting through its refraction the contrast between the serene neat image and the more complex social reality of eighteenth-century neighborhood life. More generally, while organized around the displayed collection, the exhibit is not quite artifact driven: it follows a logical sequence of topics grounded in a reasonably clear if conventional narrative conception.

A panel at the start sets the tone: Philadelphia "germinated from a seed" planted by Penn and the Quakers, "flowered" into a commercial and cultural center, and (the botanical metaphor gives out at that point) "became a dynamic industrial metropolis" by the late nineteenth century. The displays, we are told, intend to depict what "shaped the city, guided its development, and made it unique."

The first displays deal well with the geographic setting and overall growth patterns, displaying a series of population distribution charts for the entire time period and maps illustrating the role of rivers and land in shaping Philadelphia's development. They represent a rather aggressive frame-setting start. The exhibit then settles to a more conventional movement relying on dramatic artifacts and familiar topics—a number of cases on William Penn, the 1682 city plan, and the Quaker way of life, both domestic and commercial, followed by a sequence focused in eighteenth-century life—taverns, homelife, and particularly artisan crafts and culture, discussed as central to understanding, both as cause and effect, Philadelphia's increasingly cosmopolitan economic role in the colonies and in Atlantic commerce. But the momentum generated here is not seized to help explain the evolution of a city or its role in broader changes. A series of cases on the Revolutionary War loses a sense of Philadelphia almost entirely, choosing instead to highlight evocative curiosities (Liberty Chairs, carved eagles, the requisite grapeshot and river chains) not connected to any urban narrative.

The remainder of the exhibit is organized around promising thematic headings—"Maritime Philadelphia" and "By Industry We Thrive"—that suggest the evolution from a mature commercial economy to an industrial city. The artifacts, a number of them reclaimed through urban archaeology, are especially good at illustrating a range of industries identified with Philadelphia, from engines to lace and cigars and pharmaceuticals. But the limited stock of interpretive energy, it seems, is expended entirely on a number of well-taken points about the processes of growth. Nothing else gives the visitor much sense of the structure, population, space, or feel of either a commercial or industrial city, much less how one shifted into the other. Strong on some of the things that happened in the city, the exhibit makes little attempt to describe, much less interpret, the processes of city growth and life as these change over time. The exhibit seems to have lost its focus and energy near the end, presenting some topics (such as transportation) out of any helpful sequence and closing with a surprisingly thin evocation of the 1876 Centennial.

In sum, the exhibit is reasonably coherent and substantive, avoiding the heroic mode and approaching the process of growth with some sense of its complexity. Ultimately, however, it remains caught in the paradox announced at the start, trying at once to show Philadelphia as unique while also more analytically interpreting it as an example of more general dynamics and processes of urban growth in the context of American history. It avoids too much of a plunge in either direction, which leaves it solidly balanced on the strength of its artifactual display—a straightforward and engaging exhibit, but not particularly inspired on either the design or conceptual level.

Other standing exhibits at the Atwater Kent focus on particular aspects of municipal institutional history—gas and water, fire, and police; a similar approach is more productive here, because the artifacts are particularly interesting in human terms (leaves from police mug-books, for instance) and because the way services link people, environment, and institutions makes even a brief treatment a base for interesting reflection on the workings of an actual city. These rooms provide something of a bridge between the traditional cast of the major exhibit and newer special projects just taking shape, to be discussed below.

Two museums in St. Louis offer permanent exhibits on the history of the city. As a complement to its elaborate Museum of Western Expansion underneath the mammoth waterside Gateway Arch, the National Park Service has opened the magnificent Old Courthouse nearby as an exhibit and interpretive center devoted to St. Louis's more particular role in the process and the way this in turn shaped the city and its people. Several miles away, a similarly conceived permanent display entitled "Where Rivers Meet" is found in the Missouri Historical Society's Jefferson Memorial Building in Forest Park. While still essentially traditional in historical conception, both exhibits suggest some of the new currents beginning to shape presentation in the last ten years.

The Old Courthouse presents urban history in four rooms each representing a distinct era: "St. Louis: The Early Years, 1764-1850"; "St. Louis: Becoming a City, 1850-1900; and "St. Louis Entering the Twentieth Century, 1900-1930" are explicitly historical, while "St. Louis Revisited: 1930-Present" is a pastiche of evocative current and retrospective materials, dealing mostly with architectural history.

Perhaps because the Old Courthouse is more interpretive center than museum, and hence weaker on artifacts, the exhibit is heavy on design and graphics. There are dramatic photo-blowups and document extracts on several of the surrounding walls, time-line charts, and kiosks featuring period-specific portraits of St. Louis people, ordinary as well as famous. These are added cumulatively so that each period kiosk is more full and varied in every sense, a quiet way of making the usually heavy-handed point about an American city's pluralistic composition. But many artifacts are displayed, with considerable imagination, to evoke larger environments: each room features a large, impressive triangular platform in the center, arranged so that it displays an exterior environment from two sides and a corresponding interior as one circles around.

The logic of historical explanation is clear, if schematic: early St. Louis is a matter of the fur trade, river traffic, and the French-American transfer. Within this frame, the exhibit works hard to evoke the role and character of the Mississippi waterfront town, an evocation made more necessary because, ironically, the Gateway Arch and the Expansion Park of which this museum is a part have obliterated that historical environment almost entirely. If frontier urbanization derives from larger economic settlement patterns, the maturing city is presented in terms of the shift from commerce to industry and a consequent reorganization of the nation's economic space and urban network, here aptly symbolized by the 1874 Eads Bridge that at once suggested the triumph of steel, the triumph of rails over the river and its steamboats, and the necessity of St. Louis's finding another role in the emerging modern industrial era. The twentieth century is handled less coherently: it is a tougher problem, and the lure of the 1904 World's Fair, Charles Lindbergh, and nostalgic domestic artifacts proves irresistible.

An accompanying orientation film, *Gateway to the West*, mirrors the strengths and weaknesses of the exhibit. More an illustrated lecture than a narrated film, it features a professor as a "walking head" posed before a sequence of attractive backdrops, telling St. Louis's story. Among his better moments are a description of how early prosperity owed less to frontiersmen than to the European "accident of fashion" that raised the price of beaver pelts so high, and a discussion of the steamboat era focused on the city's role as an outfitting and transfer point for westward movement. But the gateway theme proves exhausted once the railroad ends this era; the film leaps to a formulaic tribute to resurgent St. Louis in the late twentieth century.

The Missouri Historical Society's exhibit, "Where Rivers Meet," is conceptually quite similar and follows a parallel rhythm although it is more conventional in layout and more solidly grounded in a rich artifactual collection. The early section is excellent geographically, featuring some helpful schematic maps that clarify St. Louis's centrality in an elaborate river system extending through the Midwest and West—something not very obvious to modern audiences. But it is less sophisticated than the Old Courthouse on the dynamics of trade in the fur and steamboat eras, relying instead on boat models and an elaborate wheelhouse platform-cum-diorama, and it is equally unhelpful in dealing with railroading, beyond the Eads Bridge—neither exhibit mentions the struggle of St. Louis and Chicago interests for railroad control of the West, for instance. The end has a modest attempt to link social history to municipal history: the effects of turn-of-the-century immigration are treated more extensively, with attention to the process by which some stayed on rather than passing through, and their patterns of settlement in the city.

An accompanying audiovisual slide presentation retraces the story and carries it through the twentieth century in predictably heroic terms: the community spirit of 1904, later fanned by Lindbergh, flickers through the era of slums and skyscrapers, in which St. Louis was left behind by progress, "gasping its last breath" until a "newly ignited fire of pride" revives the city and makes it once again "a meeting place for all." Within this frame, however, the presentation underscores the point that urban development involves the complex intersection of "people, buildings, and history," a model not inconsistent with more sophisticated interpretation than it receives here, and a good one with which to arm visitors heading into a conventional narrative exhibit.

Finally, at the Missouri Historical Society as at the Atwater Kent, the most exciting urban history presentations are in ancillary exhibits focused on aspects of municipal life: a magnificent room on firefighters is as rich in curious artifacts as one might wish while also managing to present the process of firefighting, the relation of firehouses and water systems to the social geography of the city, and the long struggle between the volunteer system and professionalization. Equally interesting if idiosyncratic is a permanent tribute to a St. Louis curiosity—the "Veiled Prophet," a pseudo-mythic Mardi-Gras-like masked ball created by Victorian boosters and soon crystallizing as an elite ritual, with a prominent debutante as queen each year. Many costumes are displayed, and the gallery is ringed by pictures of each queen from 1878 on, the implicit effect of which is cumulatively fascinating: although all are portraits of rich young women of debutante age, there is enormous variation in the social statements implicit in their dress, expression, and posture. There is also description of the form's more recent experimentation with various street and civic festival incarnations, especially after heavy political criticism; that blacks could not participate until 1979 tells us perhaps more than St. Louis boosters might wish the exhibit to reveal.

To the extent that the St. Louis, Philadelphia, and New York exhibits can be taken as defining something of a point of departure for contemporary efforts to reimagine urban-historical museum presentation, what can be said more generally about this established interpretive approach? Perhaps it can best be summarized in the thematic concerns discussed at the start of this chapter.

The narrative approach to framing the life-story of a city in anthropomorphic terms, a city whose birth, growth, troubles, dreams, and triumphs can be set in the context of the national history within which it acts—this construct has manifest deficiencies as a way of understanding historical change. But it also has some less obvious virtues. In addition to providing a ready framework for organizing exhibits with focus and narrative flow, the device has, in the exhibits we have seen, proven reasonably effective at handling some kinds of systemic change—such as the sequence of economic bases through which a city can move, in conjunction with technological, structural, and political changes in the world around it, matters quite relevant to a public that needs to understand similar changes in urban America today. The construct has seemed able to deflect the fatal temptations of both a heroically individualized "city father-ism" on the one hand, and technologically deterministic forces of change on the other, conceptions which in so many other contexts exert an irresistible pull on exhibit designers. The anthropomorphized urban biography thus stands as something of a countervailing force to approaches even further removed from historical reality.

Our examples suggest, however, that this approach is less frequently or comfortably applied to modern history, including most of the twentieth century. In part, this is because only recently have traditional museums felt pressured to extend the realm of the historical toward the present; more deeply, it is tempting to speculate that the kinds of statements that seem acceptable when applied to distant periods would beg too many questions, would be too transparently inadequate as descriptions of a world viewers know at closer hand.

Together, these considerations suggest that rather than casting the narrative biographical story line aside as obsolete by definition, seeking ways to modernize it might be worthwhile—to rethink how it might still be used as a framing element that would help us discuss in broad terms how urban communities have functioned in the context of equally generalized historical constructs, forces, and systemic structural changes.

As for the second concern, neither social-scientific urbanological insights nor the new social history, by the evidence of our survey, have made much of a dent on interpretive content or design, unless one counts very modest efforts to suggest that the city population and the chamber of commerce are not exactly the same. The occasional references to blacks, immigrants, laborers, women, and ordinary people in general are just that—not much more serious than the frantic compensatory acknowledgments toward the end of the "Big Apple" media show. Perhaps the reason for this neglect is not that more analytic or social-historical approaches are that unacceptable in their own terms, but rather that it has proven so hard to imagine them within the heroic narrative—hence, the greater ease with which we found a refreshing variety of perspectives animating the special exhibits on urban services and institutions, exhibits that do not labor under this narrative burden and thereby seem to find accessible the materials from which very different notions of urban structure and life can begin to be imagined and evoked.

Finally, few clear patterns exist by which this or that approach to exhibit content and design imply consistent understandings about what will generate audience involvement and reflection. The more aggressive and conceptual modern exhibit designs seem engaging in concept, but are often curiously patronizing; the older ones are the opposite, in that tired concepts never quite suffocate the fascination of the richly varied things on display, sometimes quite imaginatively set forth. By and large, however, the exhibits we have examined, including the ancillary films and media materials, rely on the classic combination of a relatively unmediated display of artifacts, to which the response can be open-ended and unpredictable, and an authoritative historical voice intoning the seamless narrative of a city's biographically coherent movement through time.

It remains to be seen whether newer approaches to urban historical analysis, to social history, and to the very purposes and structure of museum exhibits can combine to reach audiences in deeper and different ways— whether innovative programming can both generate and arise from a less didactic approach to interpretation, whether it can reach genuinely diverse audiences with complex relationships to the embrace of the presumptive community of the city, and whether, more generally, it is possible to be more sensitive to the needs, responses, and contributions viewers make, if only in the imagination with which they receive and digest historical exhibits.

To this end, let us turn to brief consideration of a number of current developments, both planned and realized: new approaches at the Atwater Kent; recent developments in Baltimore, both at the city history Peale Museum and the ambitious young Museum of Industry; and in New York City, where South Street Seaport is designing an ambitious new central museum space and permanent exhibition to anchor its interpretation of the site and artifacts of the Port of New York. Again, my own recent visits represent only slightly-more-than-random samples, but little in what follows suggests that these are unrepresentative or anomalous.

The Emerging Shape of Presentation and Interpretation

At today's Atwater Kent, welcoming text in the entry vestibule suggests a significant reorientation: the museum formally announces its dedication to preserving, collecting, and interpreting the history of the city, but defines this as explicitly including Philadelphia's complex social history and popular culture. It also moves away from the heroic stress on uniqueness and urban pride, declaring that "although the Museum's interpretive focus is on the Philadelphia experience, it depicts the city's history within the context of the broad patterns and trends of American life . . . . [It] seeks to reach a large general audience by presenting Philadelphia's history as representative of our nation's development."

The clearest departure from tradition is the way the museum, in this same vestibule, invites visitors to approach and experience historical collections using their own authority as interpreters. Rather than assuming, as conventionally, that visitors are *tabula rasa* on which history is to be inscribed, the Atwater Kent asks them to think about how artifacts can reflect their own experience and knowledge of the city and to critique the exhibits from this vantage. Moreover, as the details of daily life and culture have historical meaning and as the present is soon to be history itself, visitors are asked to help the museum decide what artifacts of contemporary Philadelphia life ought to be collected now, and why. Alongside a modest display of once ordinary but now historical artifacts from the recent past (a Flexible Flyer sled, Stetson hatbox, and Philco radio, all important local products), the museum provides notebooks in which visitors can contribute suggestions, comments, and critiques.

Perhaps more in tone than in substance, this welcome touches on all of the themes noted above: it announces an intention to move the narrative mode away from the narrowly urban-biographical, to refashion historical content through exploring the social history of urban life and processes, and to make the relation between the museum and its audience reciprocal, open-ended, and alive, a central element in both collection development and exhibition design.

It is too early to determine how these ambitions will work out in practice, as redesigning a museum is a slow process involving much more than the articulation of a new policy direction. Current steps, however, are encouraging: a staid gallery of Philadelphia paintings and prints has now been transformed into a room titled "The City Beneath Us," whose changing exhibits will relate the process and findings of urban archaeology in Philadelphia to the contemporary city; another exhibit will aim at helping audiences understand "the way in which the Museum develops, cares for, and uses its collections"; and the core urban history installation is slated for total reconception and redesign.[6]

The major new exhibit at the time of my 1987 visit, "Made in Philadelphia, 1830-1930," is also an improvement. Its attention to the evolution of industrial Philadelphia omits none of the major foci that would have dominated such an exhibit in the past—from Baldwin Engine, Disston Saw, Stetson Hat, and Cramps Shipyard of the nineteenth century to General Electric and Rohm-Haas of the twentieth century. But the text is far more sophisticated in discussing the process of industrial development, providing an anchor for discussion and documentation of wider patterns of economic change, of the relation of production to complex commercial and consumption patterns, and of the links between industrial work and workers—their backgrounds, skills, families, and neighborhoods.

The exhibit draws on recent scholarship, particularly Philip Scranton and Walter Licht's *WorkSights*; both authors were involved in the developing the exhibit text, and excellent use is made of some of the most dramatic illustrations from their volume: photographic enlargements complement specific artifacts, often picturing the context of operation by workers.[7] While in form it attempts few dramatic presentational innovations, the exhibit's linking of economic development and daily life does suggest how socially-grounded economic history can recast the story of urban growth in ways open to innovative development. And some final panels hint at how a different conception of the audience's role can energize the gallery experience: the exhibit closes by recalling that entry-vestibule request in helpfully specific terms, asking visitors to think about their own family history of work, tools, neighborhoods, businesses, and industry and to think of things the exhibit might have missed—things that might actually be in their own attic. The point is only superficially to invite donations; the effect is rather to stress that if today's personal can be historical, then urban history, process as well as artifact, can be understood as alive and real in the present, a point nicely implicit throughout the exhibit.

In Baltimore, the relation between history and the present has been seized upon as an instrument and expression of the city's current rebirth. This renaissance has been an inspiring process somewhat uncomfortably propelled by the enormously successful HarborPlace waterfront mall/boutique complex and associated gentrification. In this context, the turn to history implies a certain search for legitimation. Whatever its sources and the uses to which it is put, however, the impulse has taken on a life of its own, with generally impressive results. A constellation of City Life Museums offers a comprehensive perspective on Baltimore history and material culture. Much of this is in one complex of buildings: the Carroll Mansion, memorializing in conventional ways the longest-surviving signer of the Declaration of Independence; the 1840 House, in whose hands-on, nonartifacted interiors living history performances attempt to evoke the mid-nineteenth century; the Center for Urban Archaeology, featuring actual workshops and an exhibit explaining the process of such work; and the new Courtyard Exhibition Center.

The main burden of formal urban-historical display and interpretation has been assumed by the Peale Museum a short distance away, which in 1978 began to shift dramatically from its largely artistic orientation (housed in painter Rembrandt Peale's 1814 mansion, it based its early collection on the Peale family's work and related Baltimore prints and maps). Its rebirth has involved major rebuilding, reorganizing and a new approach to collecting, display, and audience development. All this surfaced in 1981 in its dramatic permanent exhibit, "Rowhouse: A Baltimore Style of Living," which has deservedly attracted national attention and praise.[8]

The "Rowhouse" installation is remarkable in that although nominally about a specialized topic, it offers a strikingly inclusive social, economic, and institutional profile of Baltimore's overall history, one grounded in the most prosaic details of ordinary life and in the very buildings that still house a large proportion of Baltimore's residents (and of the museum's visitors.) That a museum whose role is to be the formal expression of Baltimore history presents this refreshing vantage as its major, defining exhibit is an extraordinarily powerful statement, even before the specific content is considered.

That content is not disappointing. The show sets chronological narrative, organized in several major phases, against a sequence of dramatic period settings that display and analyze both exterior detail and interior rowhouse life. Without any sense of breathless rushing or clutter, the frame somehow permits intensive examination of architectural history, broad urban economic development patterns, complex legal financial mechanisms, the links between real-estate developers and their clients, and the relation of all these to neighborhood, work, family life, ethnicity, and class.

At every point, such themes are reflected in a fascinating variety of graphics, documents, and illustrative artifacts. Indeed, much of the remarkable vitality of the installation seems grounded in this resonance between themes and things, and I was not surprised to learn that this relationship had been perhaps the central concern of a staff intent on revitalizing an institution. Resisting the temptation to see imported academic concepts and dazzling design techniques as ends in their own right, as the redemptive knights saving the museum from its stodgy self, the curators consciously used them for resuscitation: as one commented later, they had deliberately sought a topic that would require them to collect new artifacts, intending to show how "exhibit-driven collecting" could be used as a way "to refocus and reenergize the collecting process."

By thus expanding the symbiosis between modern interpretation and the traditional collecting and display functions of museums, the exhibit has succeeded at being at once enormously popular and deeply instructive: it leaves visitors with new tools, ideas, and understandings (of everything from style to the complex social and developmental influence of Baltimore's unusual ground-rent tradition) with which to examine the city they encounter upon emerging from the museum. "Rowhouse" is hardly beyond criticism in its decisions and emphases, but as an approach to urban biography, to exploring social and urban complexity, to interpreting collections so as to help visitors to reflect on the relation of history to their own world, it is far in advance of anything discussed so far in this chapter.[9]

Other developments in Baltimore suggest some additionally salient directions. The remarkable new Baltimore Museum of Industry, for example, is gathering in an abandoned factory a spectacular collection of industrial tools and machines, assembled into recreated work environments that support not only demonstration by skilled workers, but more ambitious programming about their lives and environments. The museum thus provides a powerful counter to the gentrifying impulse that would render the industrial environment antiseptically and nostalgically distant, something appropriate only to a boutique design or a condominium-marketing strategy—an interpretive danger all too real in today's Baltimore.[10]

Warning signs are also evident in Baltimore, for history as a tool of civic revitalization is not history in necessarily reliable hands. Some of these dangers are evident in the City Life Museum's Courtyard Exhibition Center, whose premier exhibit, "Rebuilding an American City: Baltimore Today" traces the historical roots and processes of the current municipal vitality over some thirty or forty years. This exhibit bravely takes on some complex topics, from the intricacies of urban renewal legislation, to the workings of city, state, and federal politics, to the role of neighborhood activists and organizations and the issue of race in modern America. This is ground rarely engaged by public presentation, yet central to understanding modern American cities. The exhibit approaches its topics with state-of-the-art techniques: oral history tape loops accompany a slide show featuring a diversity of political actors and community activists; we see shocking video footage of a major racial disturbance within a civic event in 1970: also provided are dramatic graphics, carefully drawn maps, a place for visitor suggestions, and an elaborate electronic display titled "It's Your Choice!" offering policy options on a number of issues, with the display dependent on which choice the visitor selects.

Unfortunately, in this heady atmosphere the air of municipal self-congratulation can be suffocating. For all the attention to complex policy issues and interactive display design, the narrative seems driven to tell a story scarcely translated from its inherited nineteenth-century form, a story of civic will triumphant, of virtuous leadership, of community consensus arising out of conflict, and so on. The video of the 1970 racial disturbance, for example, is bracketed with another video of a successful civic celebration in 1972, featuring happy, strolling, racially mixed crowds: evidently Baltimore's racial problems had been handled with brisk dispatch. And the "It's Your Choice!" board works in the following manner: if the question is whether urban renewal should focus on neighborhoods or downtown, visitors choosing the latter are told that Baltimore understood the importance of downtown and acted decisively to revitalize it; visitors choosing the former learn that Baltimore did not sacrifice its communities in favor of downtown, but rather acted decisively to combat neighborhood decay.

In Baltimore, then, a somewhat hyperactive but genuine and broadly grounded municipal revitalization is providing the major impetus to a broad range of museum and public-historical activities, which in turn are conceived as playing a major role in sustaining this civic momentum. The moment is one of enormous potential for the urban-historical museum, with both the opportunity for and the access to exciting new ideas and techniques opening up considerably. That this carries with it some reasonably obvious problems and dangers does not make the opportunity less interesting, but rather more—the struggle to turn this energy in new directions seems very much worth engaging.

This image describes well the mood at the relatively new South Street Seaport Museum in New York City, where I focus not on an existing exhibit, but rather on the planning process that confronts a situation exaggerating enormously the risks and opportunities of the present interpretive juncture, thereby helping to clarify the challenge faced less dramatically elsewhere. The challenge in this setting is not so much latter-day boosterism as new-model commercialism, in the form of the mammoth South Street Seaport project developed by James Rouse, which is well on its way to becoming New York City's biggest tourist complex, with an estimated fifteen million visitors yearly. The museum itself originated as something of a tiny, underfinanced dog wagged by the enormous commercial tail of this development, for which it helped provide a legitimizing historical pedigree. This Rouse enterprise is different from his own Baltimore HarborPlace project not only in scale, but in that history is far more explicit in the overall commercial conception—evoked in the signs and boutiques, invoked by strolling costumed hawkers and a variety of ersatz community events, and provoked by a spectacularly overdone commercial multimedia extravaganza, "The Seaport Experience," where "a surprise-filled theater" transports the visitor to the time "when ships were tall, men were bold, and even a kid in Nebraska could hear the call of the sea." Notwithstanding some attempts at lashing down the script with historically responsible lines, the show sails out on the romantic seas which lap the seaport as well: this is history as commercial concept, history in the hands of "interpreneurs."

The young museum set amidst all this faces a Faustian dilemma: it is temptingly provided with millions of curious visitors strolling nearby, alerted to and attracted by at least the aura of history; it sits on a genuinely important site whose fascinating story is central to one of the world's most important cities and to the entire development of modern society over the past several centuries, and it has a growing collection that ranges from maps and artifacts to spectacular dockside ships to historical buildings just revealing their treasures under restoration—an upper-floor door was recently opened to reveal a virtually intact nineteenth-century Seaman's Hotel, for instance. But the very forces creating the opportunity seem likely to overwhelm it entirely. Even if it cannot pretend ever to wag the tail, can this pup of a museum find a way to stand on its own and offer something of genuine historical value to those who are drawn to notice it—a huge number, in museum terms, if only a minuscule proportion of the millions eating, drinking, networking, and buying their way through the Rouse arcades?

The approach to date has been the "Museum Without Walls," described as "an accumulation of encounters and events" involving ships, guided tours, self-guided walking tours, lectures, small exhibits, and so on—beyond this essay's focus on major installations. Interestingly, however, the institution's recently approved Master Plan recognizes that the site and context require a "Museum *With* Walls," a "highly visible, very tangible response to the visitor's inquiry, 'Where is the Museum?'" Accordingly, it proposes, and is currently designing, a major 25,000 square feet exhibit and support space to occupy three floors of a landmark building at the very center of the district—"a presence strong enough to compete with the surrounding activity."[11]

The 1985 Master Plan outlined an initial conceptualization for the proposed major permanent exhibit, and the museum is moving slowly and deliberately to develop it, aware that its margin of error is very small: the situation requires a precise combination of historical insight and imagination with great sensitivity to the interpretive requirements of the setting. To this end, the museum recently convened a day-long conference involving some twenty historians. This conference can provide the stopping point for our tour, as it brings the academic-museum dialogue to the surface in an appropriately unfinished form well capturing the open-endedness of the current moment.

It would be easy, but unfair, to see the six hours of discussion as a kind of caricature, with academics and museum people running true to stereotype and proving predictably frustrating to each other. Certainly, talk careened back and forth across the same set of topics, with no discernible resolution in sight at day's end. Nevertheless, the discussion did develop a certain focus, hopefully useful to museum planners; its contours, in any event, are quite relevant to the themes we have been following.

In the first place, the scholars—quite diverse in terms of intellectual orientation and standing at a variety of points in relation to the politics of the new social history—were close to unanimous in seeking to steer the museum's ship away from the route charted in the Master Plan. This had organized prospective exhibits around five chronological/thematic phases drawn initially from Robert Albion's 1939 classic, *The Rise of New York Port, 1815-1860* and from a sequel volume being completed now under museum auspices. The segments were to be "Predestination, 1640-1815"; "Entrepreneurship, 1815-1860"; "Revolution, 1860-1914"; "Institutionalization, 1914-1965"; and "The Modern Port, 1965-Present." To this didactic strategy was wedded a proposed interpretive one: each period would be "personified" through concentration on an "appropriate exemplar or series of witnesses."

In this scheme, the historians sensed the hold of precisely the traditional conceptions the museum has a *tabula rasa* opportunity to transcend. The periodization seemed the most dated and misleading, obscuring any number of important historical themes and relationships behind a progression that in the early periods was fundamentally wrong in several respects, and in the later periods so generalized as to provide little interpretive guidance. In the impulse to "personalize," almost everyone sensed an approach that would be counterproductive in the extreme, one reinforcing the heroic implications of the narrative structure rather than counterbalancing the academic reach of the text, and one that would be interpretively retrograde by assuming audiences require human detail that could best be provided through exemplary personalities, mainly individual, powerful history makers and a few more ordinary "witnesses" thrown in for new-social-history balance.

As a result of this critique, most of the day was spent brainstorming alternate approaches. Many agreed that bottom-up historical perspectives represented a major responsibility and opportunity not yet developed in the museum's plan, implying interpretation focused more on the lives of seamen and port people, and on economic growth and change as both made by and experienced from their vantage. But it was more widely felt that such a reorientation would not itself suffice—that social history alone could tend to obscure the larger currents of change, the way the Port of New York represented a complex historical ecology, a city-building force, and an element in the complex web of world economic and political relationships, all of which were in important and distinct historical motion.

To this extent, most of the group sensed that the proper target of interpretation would be found at the intersection of two axes: one involves the way in which individual experience and local structures can be related to broad-scale systemic changes and the other involves the way in which the past's relation to the present can be understood and expressed, that paradox by which people need to find the past recognizable, as textured and as human as the present, in order to appreciate its complexity and reality, yet at the same time need to appreciate that history means differences as well—in the way things worked, the way people lived and thought and what they valued. If the cross hair of these axes could be trained just right, an exhibit strategy would have a chance to present a very different conception of what and who was relevant to the history of New York Port, and what that had to contribute to an understanding of the present.

This approach presumes an implicit dialogue with the audience, and not surprisingly this was the least developed aspect of the discussion. There was relatively little discussion of how to define, much less make, particular choices about precisely what to exhibit and how in order to reach and involve the audience. Both museum staff and historians seemed to assume that clarifying their historical message *to* the public was a necessary first step; it was harder, in this context, to discuss how thinking of that audience in more active terms, as people coming with implicit questions to be answered, assumptions to be challenged, experience to be drawn on, and ideas to be engaged might itself provide some important direction in locating the best target for our cross-hair sights.

Towards a Fourth Dimension

In several senses, the South Street Seaport seminar can be taken as a good summary of this chapter's examination of current urban-historical museum exhibition, poised as the field is on the edge of an exciting new period of development and experiment. The narrative structure of a city's "story," we have seen, is a warhorse that needs less to be retired than to be reshod, so that its thematic strength can be used to pull very different wagons. Our visits suggest as well that the lessons of social, economic, and political history, all the newer ways scholars have been exploring for expressing what and who a city is, and how its structure, processes, and culture evolve historically for all its people—these need not be inconsistent with such stories, and, in fact, must be turned to if we are to imagine newer forms of narrative that are effective. And finally, we have detected a perhaps underappreciated power in that most fundamental and venerable of museum functions, the collection and display of meaningful artifacts.

This constellation suggests how requisite it has become to join such notions and bring them to bear on the problem of historical interpretation. Urban and social historians have developed a wealth of exciting new insights, but they have not yet been able to present these consistently in publicly engaging ways. Historical museums have always known something about drawing and even satisfying audiences, but these audiences have traditionally been somewhat narrow, and it is not clear how meaningful and interesting their museum experiences have been. As the Common Agenda and Past Meets Present conferences suggest, an increasing interest is evidenced in discovering how academic historians and museum professionals can help each other shape a new kind of historical dialogue with the public precisely at a time when there is a broader appreciation of how imperative it has become to deepen public awareness of our place in history, and history's place in the dynamics of our lives and communities today.

But this dialogue promises more than merely another response to this recently discovered crisis in cultural and historical literacy. The urban-historical museum perspective suggests more deeply a recasting of the problem. Larry E. Tise, the former director of the American Association for State and Local History, has observed that whatever the supposed indifference to history in schools and however great the collapse of historical memory revealed by tests, there has been "an almost unbelievable explosion of interest in history" in museums, tourist sites, popular literature, and even the media—in "the vast arena . . . where Americans of their own free choice make decisions about what they will see, do, and read." The issue for museums and historians who care about them would seem to be less a matter of generating interest than of learning more about what drives an existing interest, and thereby finding ways of meeting it with historical interpretation on mutually meaningful common ground.[12] And this suggests, finally, the broader importance of the fourth dimension we have been able to track in the above examples, beyond the roles of narrative, scholarship, and artifact: the underappreciated capacity of the audience itself to help resolve dilemmas of presentation or interpretation of urban historical complexity.

We are just beginning to explore what this might mean for a broad interpretive strategy. In the Common Agenda report, for instance, L. Thomas Frye calls for a broadened conception of how informants and sources, not excluding the actual visitor standing before an exhibit, can contribute to interpretation a special "historical specificity through direct knowledge and experience," while the museum retains responsibility for "interpreting the objects within the context of a broader shared cultural experience."[13] Such a model is promising, but it does not really involve a very different distribution of interpretive authority as Frye reveals in his well-intentioned but somewhat imperious advice that museums become more involved in "collecting the people along with their objects." Perhaps closer to what I have in mind is the observation by Barbara Melosh and Christina Simmons that "exhibits necessarily embody assumptions about what audiences already know; like other social texts, they carry on an implicit dialogue with an imagined audience."[14] In this essay's selective tour, we have seen the importance of this dimension for understanding precisely how the surveyed exhibits do or do not work as intended for the diverse audiences that come to big city urban history museums; our examples suggest the importance of making the dialogue more explicit than implicit, for audiences that are more tangible and particular than imaginary.

Perhaps one final example will help make the implications of such an approach even clearer. Planners at the Brooklyn Historical Society are using an audience-sensitive approach to resolve otherwise immobilizing problems in capturing a complex social history within an attractive exhibit narrative, especially given a very small available space: after much struggle, they decided to abandon an overall chronological approach and to build the exhibit around a series of popular symbols at the center of the visitors' initial image of Brooklyn and its history—the Brooklyn Bridge, Coney Island, the Navy Yard, the Dodgers, and the Brooklynites themselves as colorful characters. These were chosen quite deliberately so that concise interpretation of each could develop a different dimension of a broader history, from social and cultural to economic to political, and link past and present. The exhibit will be enterable at any point, literally and figuratively, and the visitors' interest in these symbols of Brooklyn (and the artifact-rich displays that illustrate and interpret them) will provide a comfortable base of competence and involvement from which new historical materials and understandings can be engaged.

This is only one way in which respect for the audience's own experience might become a force supporting and propelling complex interpretation. The more general point is that involving the audience as a strategic element must mean something well beyond the already familiar tokenism in exhibit content or the shallow gimmicks that offer the illusion of active participation and involvement. Rather, our survey has suggested that we need to broaden not only techniques and historical concepts but the very way we understand audiences to be engaged in the communicative process itself, and to make this understanding a more active resource in historical exhibits. In this regard, the urban-historical setting provides special and substantial opportunities for sophisticated dialogue if we can become better at respecting our visitors' very real knowledge and experience and learn how to turn both presumed certainties and areas of ignorance into the energy of activated curiosity. In the final analysis, this is the only force capable of permitting an exhibit, however sophisticated its concept, design, or artifacts, to come alive for the people who happen to visit it and to stay with them after they have left.

Notes

Chapter 2

1. This essay originated in a talk delivered in October 1979 at the SUNY-Buffalo Law School, as part of an unusual symposium. Marcel Ophuls had joined the law school's faculty and students as a Mitchell Lecturer for a week focused on his documentary films, a body of work that explores the meeting ground of law, ethics, politics, and morality as found in some of the focal points of modern history—the Holocaust and the Nuremberg trials, the Nazi occupation of France, and the conflict in Northern Ireland. At the end of several days of screening and informal discussion, a public symposium featuring M. Ophuls was held. The discussion focused in particular on *The Memory of Justice*, the film most relevant to its American law school audience.

Because readers may not have a viewing of Ophuls's long, complex movie fresh in mind, and many may not have seen it at all, what I have done in this essay is to recast my remarks in more general terms. Toward the end, however, I return to a brief discussion of *The Memory of Justice*, in part as a way of repaying a considerable intellectual debt, because so much of my own thinking about documentary and oral history has been crystallized, well before the Mitchell lectures, by Ophuls's films and the human spirit animating them.

2. The 1972 presidential campaign is the rule-proving exception. With the stage set for a major ideological confrontation, somehow the play was cancelled: McGovern came to seem a simpleton or a fool or worse, partly (but hardly entirely) because of his own errors. All efforts to produce a referendum on the war issue foundered on the hardly coincidental emergence of McGovern's credibility and image problems. Accordingly, to most Americans there seemed to be no "real" or "serious" alternative to Nixon, and therefore no deeper choices to be made, about the war or, in fact, anything else.

3. New York: Oxford University Press, 1978.

4. These remarks were made in a conversation. For a fuller elaboration of their author's perspective, readers are referred to Chinweizu, *The West and the Rest of Us: White Predators, Black Slavers, and the African Elite* (New York: Random House, 1975). This is a remarkable book—a comprehensive synthesis of colonial African history, a

devastating critique of the neocolonial corruption of most postindependence African institutions, and a world history from an African vantage—a furiously yet also relentlessly incisive "victims's-eye view" of the inexorable expansion of the West and its usual historical rationalizations.

5. I discuss some of these points in "The New York State Labor History Association's Fourth Annual Meeting: A Participant's Critique," *International Labor and Working-Class History*, 16 (Fall 1979) 51-55.

6. See Chapter Seven, below, "Oral History, Documentary, and the Mystification of Power: A Critique of *Vietnam: A Television History.*"

7. Studs Terkel, *Hard Times: An Oral History of the Great Depression*, (New York: Pantheon, 1970); *All God's Dangers, The Life of Nate Shaw*, Compiled by Theodore Rosengarten (New York: Knopf, 1971); and Jeremy Brecher, *Brass Valley* (Philadelphia: Temple University Press, 1982).

8. See Chapter One, above, "Oral History and *Hard Times.*

9. See Rosenberg's review essay, "The Shadow of the Furies," *New York Review of Books* 23 (January 20, 1977) 47-49, and Ophuls's extensive, eloquent reply, *New York Review of Books* 24 (March 17, 1977) 43-45. Also, see Dorothy Rabinowitz's review, "Ophuls: Justice Misremembered," in *Commentary* (December 1976), 65-67.

Chapter 3

1. The best sellers, of course, are E.D. Hirsch, Jr., *Cultural Literacy: What Every American Needs to Know* (New York: Houghton Mifflin, 1987) and Allan Bloom, *The Closing of the American Mind: How Higher Education Has Failed Democracy and Impoverished the Souls of Today's Students* (New York: Simon and Shuster, 1987). The 1987 NEH study by the chairman of the National Endowment for the Humanities is Lynne V. Cheney, *American Memory: A Report on the Humanities in the Nation's Public Schools* (Washington: Government Printing Office, 1987), which follows the 1983 report of the National Commission on Excellence in Education, *A Nation at Risk: The Imperative for Educational Reform* (Washington: Government Printing Office, 1983). The new study is Diane Ravitch and Chester E. Finn, Jr., *What Do Our Seventeen-Year-Olds Know? A Report on the First National Assessment of History and Literature* (New York: Harper and Row, 1987). For a representative example of the mass-mediated digestion of this debate, see the cover story, "What Americans Should Know," *U.S. News and World Report*, Sept. 28, 1987, 86-94.

2. See two useful reviews of Ravitch and Finn, *What Do Our Seventeen-Year-Olds Know?* that develop this point: Deborah Meier and Florence Miller, "The Book of Lists," *Nation*, Jan. 9, 1988, 25-27; and Etta Moser, "What They Do Know," *ibid.*, 27-28.

3. The best single discussion, as well as the best case study application, is Catherine L. Albanese, *Sons of the Fathers: The Civil Religion of the American Revolution*

(Philadelphia: Temple University Press, 1976) See also Hirsch, *Cultural Literacy*, 98-103, for a discussion especially relevant to the context of this essay.

4. I much appreciate Professor Zelinsky's interest in the problem, and his sending me the data from his March 1, 1984 survey of a Geography 1 class of 115 students. This material is discussed and presented with his kind permission, Wilbur Zelinsky to Michael Frisch, March 5, 1984 (in Michael Frisch's possession).

5. Albanese, *Sons of the Fathers*, 9, 28.

6. *Ibid.*, 261-62 n 51.

7. *Ibid.*, 158-159.

8. *Ibid.*, 172, 170.

9. See the full and interesting account in Joseph Jackson, *Encyclopedia of Philadelphia*, (Harrisburg: n.p., 1931), 1054-1055.

10. My personal favorite is Professor Manning Marable's report of the black student in a black studies class who came up to ask, "Now, who is this Malcolm the Tenth, and what was he king of, anyway?" (Professor Marable confirmed this anecdote in a conversation in Buffalo in February 1987.) This is instructive in indicating that the problem of cultural loss, whatever else it may mean, is a shared one, not simply a matter, as usually presented, of the dominant culture's heritage being insufficiently respected by those held to be in need of its ministrations.

11. Diane Ravitch, "Decline and Fall of Teaching History," *New York Times Magazine*, Nov. 17, 1985, 50 ff.

12. Walter Goodman, "Conservatives' Theme: The West is Different," *New York Times*, May 5, 1985, Section 1, 21, a report on an anticommunism conference, the first event sponsored by the State Department's new and controversial Office for Public Diplomacy.

13. Sidney Hook, "Education in Defense of a Free Society," *Commentary*, 78 (July 1984), 17-22, esp. 21, 22. Hook delivered the speech on receiving the Jefferson Award for "intellectual achievement in the humanities," bestowed as its highest honor by the National Endowment for the Humanities.

14. The reference is to a witty review of Bloom's *Closing of the American Mind*: William Greider, "Bloom and Doom," *Rolling Stone*, Oct. 8, 1987, 39-40. For other relevant critiques, see Martha Nussbaum, "Undemocratic Vistas," *New York Review of Books*, Nov. 5, 1987, 20-26, and Robert Pattison, "On the Finn Syndrome and the Shakespeare Paradox," *Nation*, May 30, 1987, 710-720.

Chapter 6

1. *One Village in China: All Under Heaven, To Taste a Hundred Herbs, Small Happiness.* 58 minutes each, color, 16mm film. Also available in video cassette (VHS/

Beta/¾"). Directed by Carma Hinton and Richard Gordon; edited by David Carnochan; produced by Richard Gordon, Carma Hinton, Kathy Kline, and Dan Sipe. Distributor: New Day Films, 22 Riverview Drive, Wayne, N. J. 07470-3191.

See, also, Jo Blatti, Ann Waltner, Marilyn Young, Lary May, and Michael Frisch, "*One Village in China*: A Review Symposium," *Oral History Review*, 15/2 (Fall 1987) 115-35.

Chapter 7

1. Quoted in R. C. Raack, "Caveat Spectator," *Organization of American Historians Newsletter*, 12/1 (February, 1984), 25.

2. *Vietnam: A Television History* (hereafter, *VATH*), Program Four, "LBJ Goes To War," transcript, 31. All quotes are from a set of transcripts provided by the producers to Professor William Graebner, in connection with his preparation of the *Instructor's Guide to* Vietnam (New York: Knopf, 1985). My appreciation to Professor Graebner for permitting me access to these documents, which I have checked against the documentaries as broadcast.

3. *VATH*, Program Three, "America's Mandarin," transcript, 15.

4. *VATH*, Program One, "Roots of a War," Doung Van Khang, transcript, 38.

5. *VATH*, Program Three, "America's Mandarin," Thich Ti Hanh, transcript, 33.

6. *VATH*, Program Four, "LBJ Goes to War," Nguyen Thanh Xuan, transcript, 19.

7. *VATH*, Program Five, "America Takes Charge," William Earhart, transcript, 17.

8. *VATH*, Program Five, "America Takes Charge," Charles Sabatier, transcript, 45.

9. *VATH*, Program Six, "America's Enemy," Dr. Tung, transcript, 40.

10. *VATH*, Program Nine, "Cambodia and Laos," Peng Thuon, transcript, 42.

11. *VATH*, Program Five, "America Takes Charge," transcript, 26-37. Schell's book has recently been republished in a broader collection of his journalism, including a recent retrospective essay: Jonathan Schell, *The Real War: The Classic Reporting on the Vietnam War* (New York: Pantheon Books, 1987).

12. *VATH*, Program Three, "America's Mandarin," transcript, 34.

13. *VATH*, Program Ten, "Peace is at Hand," transcript, 51.

14. *VATH*, Program Ten, "Peace is at Hand," transcript, 26.

15. *VATH*, Program Ten, "Peace is at Hand," transcript, 55.

16. *VATH*, Program Ten, "Peace is at Hand," transcript, 36.

17. *VATH*, Program One, "Roots of a War," transcript, 46.

18. *VATH*, Program One, "Roots of a War," transcript, 48.

19. *VATH*, Program Eight, "Vietnamizing the War," transcript, 42.

20. *VATH*, Program Eight, "Vietnamizing the War," transcript, 16.

21. *VATH*, Program Eight, "Vietnamizing the War," transcript, 16.

22. *VATH*, Program Eight, "Vietnamizing the War," transcript, 4.

23. *VATH*, Program Six, "America's Enemy," transcript, 16.

24. *VATH*, Program Six, "America's Enemy," transcript, 17.

25. *VATH*, Program Six, "America's Enemy," transcript, 36.

26. *VATH*, Program Six, "America's Enemy," transcript, 36.

27. *VATH*, Program Six, "America's Enemy," transcript, 40.

28. *VATH*, Program Six, "America's Enemy," transcript, 36.

29. *VATH*, Program Six, "America's Enemy," transcript, 42.

30. *VATH*, Program Five, "America Takes Charge," transcript, 47.

31. *VATH*, Program Six, "America's Enemy," transcript, 22.

32. *VATH*, Program Four, "LBJ Goes to War," transcript, 33.

Chapter 9

1. Michael H. Frisch, *Town Into City: Springfield, Massachusetts and the Meaning of Community, 1840-1880* (Cambridge: Harvard University Press, 1972).

2. Frisch, *Town Into City*, 151.

3. Edward Bellamy, *Looking Backward* (New York: Random House, Modern Library Edition, 1951) 3-5.

Chapter 10

1. The best-sellers, of course, are E.D. Hirsch, Jr., *Cultural Literacy: What Every American Needs to Know* (New York: Houghton Mifflin, 1987) and Allan Bloom, *The Closing of the American Mind: How Higher Education has Failed Democracy and Impoverished the Souls of Today's Students* (New York: Simon and Shuster, 1987). In the general as distinct from academic press, some trenchant recent reviews and critiques of these works include Robert Pattison, "On the Finn Syndrome and the Shakespeare Paradox," *Nation* (May 30, 1987), and, particularly on Bloom's polemic, the desperate tone of which is aptly captured in its mannered title, William Greider, "Bloom

and Doom," *Rolling Stone* (October 8, 1987), and Martha Nussbaum, "Undemocratic Vistas," *New York Review of Books* (November 5, 1987).

See also Diane Ravitch and Chester E. Finn, Jr., *What Do Our Seventeen-Year-Olds Know?* (New York: Harper & Row, 1987), and two excellent linked reviews, Deborah Meier and Florence Miller, "The Book of Lists," and Etta Moser, "What They *Do* Know," in *Nation* (January 9, 1988). The 1987 NEH study by Chairman Lynne V. Cheney is *American Memory: A Report on the Humanities in the Nation's Public Schools*, which follows the 1983 report of the National Commission on Excellence in Education, *A Nation at Risk: The Imperative for Educational Reform*; both are available from the Government Printing Office. For a representative example of the way all of these discussions have been digested in mass mediated public discourse, see the cover story, "What Americans Should Know," in *U.S. News and World Report*, September 28, 1987.

2. See, for example, Gertrude Himmelfarb, *The New History and the Old* (Cambridge: Harvard University Press, 1987), and a balanced assessment by Lawrence Stone, "Resisting the New," *New York Review of Books* (December 17, 1987). For a less polemical critique of recent historiography than Himmelfarb, see William E. Leuchtenberg's Organization of American Historians Presidential Address, "The Pertinence of Political History: Reflections on the Significance of the State in America," *Journal of American History* 73 (December 1986) 585-600.

3. See especially Susan Porter Benson, Stephen Brier, and Roy Rosenzweig, eds., *Presenting the Past: Essays on History and the Public* (Philadelphia: Temple University Press, 1986), and two excellent review essays on the broader implications of this collection, much of which originally appeared in Radical History Review: W. Andrew Achenbaum, "Public History's Past, Present, and Prospects," *American Historical Review* 92 (1987) 1162-74, and Warren Leon, "So, You Want to Be a Public Historian!", *Journal of Social History* 21 (1987), 327-35. For the recent Left critique, see Russell Jacoby, *The Last Intellectuals: American Culture in the Age of Academe* (New York: Basic Books, 1987).

4. Perhaps the best crystallization of this position is in Thomas Bender, "Wholes and Parts: The Need for Synthesis in American History," *Journal of American History* 73 (1986), 120-36, and a special *Journal of American History Roundtable* in response to this essay, with contributions by Nell Irvin Painter, Richard Wightman Fox, Roy Rosenzweig, and a reply by Bender: "Roundtable: Synthesis in American History," *Journal of American History* 74 (1987), 107-30.

5. Because these sections border on advertisements and are not written by those primarily responsible for the basic text and the illustrations, I have not considered them to be included in the material formally under review in this chapter. But readers should not conclude that the *Partners in Progress* compilations are therefore without interest or significance. True, some of the company profiles are predictably parochial in their puffery: "Who would imagine," one begins breathlessly, "that two brothers, both recent arrivals in the Utica area from Scotland, could establish an industrial laundry service serving not only New York, but also Massachusetts, Vermont, and more recently Connecticut, Pennsylvania, New Jersey, and Maryland?" (*Utica*, 205). In gen-

eral, however, they offer useful capsule business histories, rich with detail on entrepreneurship, the rise and fall of particular trades and products, business and financial relationships, and the social and cultural background of individual business-men and their families. And because it is generally easier for readers and researchers to control for bias so explicit, the "Partners in Progress" sections may actually prove more useful than the general text in providing focused, business-specific historical information on a city's commercial and economic community.

6. I discuss this problem in "American History and the Structures of Collective Memory: A Modest Exercise in Empirical Iconography," Chapter Three, above.

7. One such volume has just been published, arriving too late for inclusion here even had the assignment not been limited to the Windsor volumes as a project-specific group: See Scott Eberle and Joseph A. Grande, *Second Looks: A Pictorial History of Buffalo and Erie County* (Norfolk and Virginia Beach: The Donning Company, 1987). This volume is jointly sponsored by the Buffalo and Erie County Historical Society, and the Key Bank of North America, N.A. It is outwardly similar in format to the Windsor volumes, and its illustrations are as exclusively historical. An initial reading, however, suggests that it is written with substantially more historical sophistication than most of the Windsor volumes and that the authors have approached the selection and annota-tion of illustrations with a great deal more imagination as to how their historical mean-ing can be unfolded for and with readers.

Chapter 11

1. See John Brinckerhoff Jackson, *The Necessity for Ruins and Other Topics* (Amherst: University of Massachusetts Press, 1980).

2. See, for instance, Lynn Johnson, "Ellis Island: Preservation from the Supply Side," *Radical History Review*, 28-30, 1984, 157-68, and the more recent articles in *Nation* by Roberta Brandes Gratz and Eric Fettmann, "The Selling of Miss Liberty," vol. 241, no. 18 (November 9, 1985), 465-76, and "The Battle for Ellis Island," vol. 241, no. 18, (November 30, 1985), 579-89.

Chapter 12

1. The project this chapter discusses was a collaborative work involving many indi-viduals, but especially the following colleagues: Cynthia Little, now of the Historical Society of Pennsylvania; Nancy Moses, now a private consultant; and Henry Williams of the University of Pennsylvania. Together, we organized the efforts that developed a plan, wrote the grant proposal, and helped implement the public program exhibit discussed here. For all of this we are jointly responsible, but Little, Moses, and Williams are not implicated in the arguments of this paper, for which I take sole responsibility.

2. I have discussed the academic development of this field in "Urban History as an Example of Recent Historiography," *History and Theory*, 18/3 (1979) 350-77.

3. I refer here to an intriguing resonance surrounding the appealing goal of an unmediated representation of the past. Every history graduate student identifies Leopold von Ranke, the founder of scientific history, with the maxim that the goal of scholarship should be to tell history *wie es eigentlich gewesen*—as it actually was. And every viewer over thirty recalls that Walter Cronkite, the founder of modern television anchor journalism, closed every newscast with a similar invocation, saying, "And that's the way it was, Friday, May 4, 1979..."

4. See Theodore Hershberg, ed., *Philadelphia: Work, Space, Family, and Group Experience in the Nineteenth Century—Essays Toward an Interdisciplinary History of the City* (New York: Oxford University Press, 1981), especially Hershberg, et al., "Tale of Three Cities: Blacks, Immigrants, and Opportunity in Philadelphia, 1850-1880, 1930, 1970," 461-91.

Chapter 13

1. See the book resulting from the New York conference, Jo Blatti, ed., *Past Meets Present: Essays About Historic Interpretation and Public Audiences* (Washington: Smithsonian Institution Press, 1987), especially the introduction summarizing the conference format, issues, and "expeditions": Jo Blatti, "Past Meets Present: Field Notes on Historical Sites, Programs, Professionalism, and Visitors," 1-20. See also Thomas J. Schlereth, "Defining Collecting Missions: National and Regional Models," and the conference's recommended "Specific Actions," in Lonn W. Taylor, ed., *A Common Agenda for History Museums: Conference Proceedings, February 19-20, 1987* (Nashville: American Association for State and Local History and Smithsonian Institution, 1987) 24, 13.

2. I discuss these general intellectual developments in "American Urban History as an Example of Recent Historiography," *History and Theory* 18/3 (1979), 350-77, and I consider some of the public-historical implications of the "new urban history" in Chapter Twelve, above, "Urban Public History in Celebratory Contexts: The Example of the 'Philadelphia's Moving Past' Project."

3. Edward P. Alexander, *Museums in Motion: An Introduction to the History and Functions of Museums* (Nashville: American Association for State and Local History, 1979), 169-71; Blatti, *Past Meets Present*, includes conference papers and post-conference reflections on these issues in Section II: "Design and Technique in the Realization of Interpretive Programs," 95-130.

4. "Collections Working Group," and Schlereth, "Defining Collecting Missions," in Taylor, *Common Agenda*, 9, 26-27.

5. Quoted from the full text of the script, available at the museum on request as "Classroom Study Guide For the Big Apple, a multimedia presentation of the history of

New York in the Museum of the City of New York, funded by the International Telephone and Telegraph Corporation."

6. My thanks to Atwater Kent Museum Executive Director John V. Alviti for discussing these plans with me after my unannounced 1987 visit. The museum has subsequently initiated a lively newsletter discussing its ongoing development in detail. See, for example, Atwater Kent Museum *News and Notes*, I/1 (April, 1988).

7. Walter Licht and Philip Scranton, *Work Sights: Industrial Philadelphia, 1890-1950* (Philadelphia: Temple University Press, 1987).

8. See, for instance, the extensive and thoughtful review/critique by Roger B. White, "Whither the Urban History Exhibit? The Peale Museum's 'Rowhouse,'" *Technology and Culture* 24 (January 1983) 76-90.

9. Visitors receive an elaborate souvenir handout in the form of a tabloid newspaper, *The Rowhouse Times*, which summarizes the exhibit, reproduces some of its text and graphics, and offers additional background information on rowhouses in history and as a contemporary urban concern. This is available on request from The Peale, Baltimore's Historic Museum, 235 Holliday Street, Baltimore, Md. 21202.

10. This museum regularly publishes a newsletter, *Nuts and Bolts*, describing its collections, exhibits, programs, and plans. Copies are available from the Baltimore Museum of Industry, 1415 Key Highway, Baltimore, Md. 21230.

11. Peter Neill, "Report From the President: The Master Plan, 1985-1990," *Seaport: The Magazine of the South Street Seaport Museum*, 19/3 (Fall 1985), 4-9.

12. Larry E. Tise, "Organizing America's History Business: A New Ethic and Plan of Action," Special Report, Technical Information Service, American Association for State and Local History, n.d., but 1987. I discuss some of the broader issues implied by the current "cultural literacy" debate, in Chapter Three, above, "American History and the Structures of Collective Memory."

13. L. Thomas Frye, "Museum Collecting for the Twenty-First Century," *Common Agenda*, 35-36.

14. Frye, "Museum Collecting," 36; Barbara Melosh and Christina Simmons, "Exhibiting Women's History," in Susan Porter Benson, Stephen Brier, and Roy Rosenzweig, eds., *Presenting the Past: Essays on History and the Public* (Philadelphia: Temple University Press, 1986), 203.